WORTHY to ESCAPE

Why All Believers Will Not be Raptured
Before the Tribulation

ADRIAN ZENZ, PhD
&
MARLON L. SIAS

WESTBOW
PRESS
A DIVISION OF THOMAS NELSON

Unless otherwise indicated, all Scripture quotations are taken from the New American Standard Bible®, Copyright © 1960, 1962, 1963, 1968, 1971, 1972, 1973, 1975, 1977, 1995 by The Lockman Foundation Used by permission. (www.Lockman.org)

Scripture quotations marked ESV are taken from The Holy Bible, English Standard Version® (ESV®), copyright © 2001 by Crossway, a publishing ministry of Good News Publishers. Used by permission. All rights reserved.

Scripture quotations marked NLT are taken from the Holy Bible, New Living Translation, copyright © 1996, 2004, 2007 by Tyndale House Foundation. Used by permission of Tyndale House Publishers, Inc., Carol Stream, Illinois 60188. All rights reserved.

Scripture quotations marked NKJV are taken from the New King James Version®. Copyright © 1982 by Thomas Nelson, Inc. Used by permission. All rights reserved.

Scripture quotations marked (NIV) are taken from the Holy Bible, New International Version®, NIV®. Copyright © 1973, 1978, 1984, 2011 by Biblica, Inc.™ Used by permission of Zondervan. All rights reserved worldwide. www.zondervan.com The "NIV" and "New International Version" are trademarks registered in the United States Patent and Trademark Office by Biblica, Inc.™

WestBow Press books may be ordered through booksellers or by contacting:

WestBow Press
A Division of Thomas Nelson
1663 Liberty Drive
Bloomington, IN 47403
www.westbowpress.com
1-(866) 928-1240

Because of the dynamic nature of the Internet, any web addresses or links contained in this book may have changed since publication and may no longer be valid. The views expressed in this work are solely those of the author and do not necessarily reflect the views of the publisher, and the publisher hereby disclaims any responsibility for them.

Any people depicted in stock imagery provided by Shutterstock are models, and such images are being used for illustrative purposes only.

Certain stock imagery © Shutterstock.

ISBN: 978-1-4497-6908-6 (hc)
ISBN: 978-1-4497-6906-2 (sc)
ISBN: 978-1-4497-6907-9 (e)

Library of Congress Control Number: 2012918093

Printed in the United States of America

WestBow Press rev. date: 12/4/2012

Contents

Acknowledgements

I want to thank my lovely wife Debbie of 37 years for putting up with me and raising our five wonderful children. My appreciation also extends to all of my children and their husbands for bearing with my passionate teaching on the end times. I am grateful to the late brother Robert Ewing for teaching me the outline of the two raptures in God's Word when he visited St. Paul Bible College in 1972. Likewise, sincere thanks go to my former pastor Tom Porta for his encouragement when I was in the hospital after a heart attack in March 2009. Tom asked me, "Do you think you will have time to write your book on Christ's coming?" I told him that was a confirmation from God that I needed to get started on the book.

I also am very thankful to God for calling my son-in-law Adrian to join me in this book project. With his help, it has become more readable, understandable, and accurate. Finally, I want to humbly thank my God for providentially orchestrating a fire at my neighbor's, which landed me in the emergency room before my heart stopped from a heart attack I hadn't even known had begun. This gave me second chance at life and motivated me to fulfill a 30–year calling to write this book. Praise be to God for His miraculous work.

Marlon Sias, 2012

God called me in the spring of 2011 to join Marlon in writing this book, and it has been an amazing time of learning and growth. In the process of writing, I have learned so many new truths from God's awesome Word, and I am extremely thankful for having received this special opportunity.

My profound gratitude extends to my wonderful wife Rachel, whose sacrificial and loving support enabled me to spend so much time on making this book happen, and whose encouragement kept me focused on the task. I am also grateful to my employer and Christian brother Sören Steinmann, who supported me throughout this process and permitted me to flexibly arrange my time so that I was able to complete the writing.

Dr. Adrian Zenz, 2012

Both authors want to thank John Johnson, Marlon's friend since college days, and Pastor David Turnidge, for reviewing this book and providing many useful comments. Our gratitude also extends to Bethany Sias for her extensive help with the cover design. Finally, we are very grateful for the comprehensive, detailed, and professional editing done by Tia Hasanova from Global English Express. Her dedicated work greatly contributed to this book.

This book was professionally edited by

Tia Hasanova, Global English Express

www.globalenglishexpress.com

Our Hermeneutical Principles

It is vital that our readers are aware of our hermeneutical approach to Scripture. Hermeneutics is the art and science of interpretation, and we use the following hermeneutical principles in this book.

The first principle we follow is Cooper's well-known rule of literal interpretation, or what Martin Luther referred to as *sensus literalis*:

> When the plain sense of Scripture makes common sense, seek no other sense; therefore, take every word at its primary, ordinary, usual, literal meaning unless the facts of the immediate context, studied in the light of related passages and axiomatic and fundamental truths, indicate clearly otherwise.[1]

The problem is that throughout the history of the church, end times prophecy in particular has not been taken in its literal sense where a literal interpretation is called for. This has diluted its impact on our understanding of the future. At the same time, however, end times scriptures have many metaphors and symbolisms, and one can therefore also err by taking them literally when they are clearly meant to be taken symbolically. For example, in Revelation 17 Babylon is symbolically depicted as a "whore" who "rides" on the beast. These are symbolic, non-literal depictions (there won't be a literal "woman" riding on a literal "beast"). Scripture often uses symbolism to convey deep spiritual truths. It is therefore essential to distinguish between passages that are meant to be taken literally and those that are purposefully described in a symbolic manner. Rightly dividing between literal and allegorical means of interpretation requires reliance on the Holy Spirit.

Since end times prophecy is by far the most difficult theme in all of Scripture, one should be cautious about teaching it unless one has received a clear and specific calling to do so. We, the authors, would have never dreamed of embarking on this work without such a calling, and we are greatly humbled by our total inability to convey truth without the Truth Himself being at the very center of this effort. As we are nearing the time of Christ's return, God is calling individuals across His church to correctly interpret the often encrypted meanings of end times scriptures. God made this promise to Daniel, who struggled to understand what he had been told because he had not received the ability to interpret it:

> As for me [Daniel], I heard but could not understand; so I said, "My lord, what will be the outcome of these events?" He said, "Go your way, Daniel, for these words are concealed and sealed up until the end time. Many will be purged, purified and refined, but the wicked will act wickedly; and none of the wicked will understand, *but those who have insight will understand.*"
>
> (Daniel 12:8–10, emphasis added)

God has promised to reveal His Word to us in His own time. We should therefore not be surprised if we, who live at the end of the age, hear of prophecies and teachings that add new meanings and details regarding God's will for the end times. However, especially since deceptions have been prophesied to multiply, all of them must in the Berean manner be tested by the revealed Word of God and be found to agree with the entirety of Scripture: "Do not quench the Spirit; do not despise prophetic utterances [God still speaks prophecy through His people in our day!]. But examine everything [both prophecies and Bible interpretations] carefully; hold fast to that which is good" (1 Thessalonians 5:19–21).

Secondly, an important interpretative principle for understanding the book of Revelation is to affirm that it only talks about the future and not about past events. The implication of this is that every aspect of John's prophecy is yet to be fulfilled. The very first verse of the book teaches this fact: "The Revelation of Jesus Christ, which God gave Him to show to His bond-servants, the *things which must soon take place*" (Revelation 1:1, emphasis added; compare Revelation 4:1, which talks about "things which must take place after this").

Thirdly, scriptural interpretation requires viewing a passage in its context. Here, we must distinguish two types of context: the immediate context, which are the parts of Scripture that immediately surround the passage in question; and the wider context, which identifies the type of book (Gospel, Epistle, Psalm, Old Testament prophecy, etc.) in which a text is located. Additionally, there is the important principle of comparing Scripture with Scripture. This means that a word, phrase or concept should first be studied in light of its use in other passages in order to interpret how it should be understood in a particular context.

Ultimately, Scripture is "always its own best interpreter."[2] Understanding God's Word requires us to go deeper, meaning that we need to closely examine the origins of words and their usage in the cultural context of the time in which a text was written. For such an endeavor, theological dictionaries, which are far more comprehensive than Strong's Exhaustive Concordance entries, are essential exegetical tools.

In order to dig deeper into the meanings of the scriptures, we employed the following resources: our standard Bible translation is the 1995 New American Standard Version (NASB) with Strong's references. We also consulted other translations that reflect a predominantly literal approach to Scripture, especially the New King James Version (NKJV) and the English Standard Version (ESV). In selected instances, we determined that a more paraphrased translation best communicated the core message of a text and employed the New Living Translation (NLT). For our study of Hebrew and Greek words, we employed the Enhanced Strong's Dictionary, Thayer's Lexicon, Vine's Expository Dictionary, and the Baker-Zodhiates Complete Word Study Bible, besides the Strong's Exhaustive Concordance. Additionally, more in-depth Hebrew study was complemented by the Theological Wordbook of the Old Testament (TWOT).

For Greek word study, the resource of choice was the New International Dictionary of New Testament Theology (NIDNTT), an enlargement and translation of the famous German reference work *Theologisches Begriffslexikon zum Neuen Testament*. Our Greek text was the Nestle Aland 27th edition of the *Novum Testamentum Graece*, with Mounce-Koivisto morphology. For cultural background information and additional theological expositions, we occasionally drew upon the Intervarsity Press (IVP) Bible Background Commentary, the Expositor's Commentary (abridged), and the John MacArthur New Testament Commentary. However, commentaries never determined our major theological interpretations.

We encourage all our readers to be Bereans and verify everything we say. For this end, we have added the Strong's numbers for each Greek and Hebrew word that we examine in this book, so that our readers can easily look them up. For those who do not have a Strong's Concordance available, there are excellent internet resources online that enable a free look-up of words by Strong's numbers, including the Thayer's Lexicon. One of them is the Blue Letter Bible website at www.blueletterbible. org. This resource also features a KJV and an NASB Bible with Strong's numbers displayed behind each word.

Fourthly, we consider it important that the teaching contained in this book must be upheld by all of Scripture, including both Old and New Testaments, as well as the Gospels and Epistles, and particularly by God's most special revelation of the end times, the book of Revelation itself. In many ways, the book of Revelation is the most complete and detailed revelation of end times events and should therefore be treated as such. At the same time, its main teachings are confirmed by Old

Testament prophets and align with the words of Jesus in key passages such as Matthew 24 or Luke 21. Throughout this book, we will demonstrate the reality of this principle, showing how wonderfully the Word of God confirms and complements itself.

1. David L. Cooper, *The World's Greatest Library: Graphically Illustrated* (Los Angeles: Biblical Research Society, 1970), 11.
2. Robert van Kampen, *The Sign* (Wheaton, IL: Crossway, 2000), 29.

Chapter 1

Introduction

Nevertheless, when the Son of Man comes,
will He really find faith on the earth?
Luke 18:8 NKJV

Jesus Is Coming!

We all know it: Jesus will come back soon, perhaps sooner than we think. The Bible tells us that He is coming for a pure and spotless bride, a bride ready for a glorious union with her heavenly Husband at the celestial marriage supper. In Ephesians, Paul writes the following:

> Husbands, love your wives, just as Christ also loved the church and gave Himself up for her, so that He might sanctify her, having cleansed her by the washing of water with the word, *that He might present to Himself the church in all her glory, having no spot or wrinkle or any such thing; but that she would be holy and blameless.*
>
> (Ephesians 5:25–27, emphasis added)

This reunion of us, the bride, and Jesus, our Bridegroom, is meant to be an incredibly joyous event. But it will also be a stunning revelation. For the first time, we will see the risen Christ—King of kings, Lord of lords—in His full splendor and glory. The book of Revelation, God's guide for us concerning the end times, begins with just such a vision:

> I saw one like a son of man, clothed in a robe reaching to the feet, and girded across His chest with a golden sash. His head and His hair were white like white wool, like snow; and

His eyes were like a flame of fire. His feet were like burnished bronze, when it has been made to glow in a furnace, and His voice was like the sound of many waters. In His right hand He held seven stars, and out of His mouth came a sharp two-edged sword; and His face was like the sun shining in its strength.

When I saw Him, I fell at His feet like a dead man. And He placed His right hand on me, saying, "Do not be afraid."

(Revelation 1:13–17)

The moment of Jesus' return will not only be a revelation of Himself to us, but it will also be a revelation of how ready or unready we are to meet Him, our heavenly Groom.

Many books have been written and many talks have been given on the subject of Jesus' return. Debates rage over the details of when and how He will come. However, in the midst of these at times rather unloving discussions, we lose sight of the need to prepare and be ready for Christ's return. After all, Jesus is not coming to rescue lukewarm groups of halfhearted followers. He won't be gathering people steeped in the mores of the world yet eager to escape the coming wrath of God. Rather, the parable of the ten virgins shows clearly that our coming King is expecting a bride who has been actively anticipating and preparing herself for His arrival.

For I am jealous for you with a godly jealousy; for *I betrothed you to one husband*, so that to Christ I might *present you as a pure virgin*.

(2 Corinthians 11:2, emphases added)

Our marriage to Jesus is yet to come—it will happen when He returns. Right now, our job is to prepare ourselves for the wedding day. We are in a preparation period that the Jews call "betrothal." Betrothal is similar to our concept of engagement, except that at betrothal, the couple is already legally married, although they do not yet live together. We, God's people, are the bride whom the groom is waiting to take to himself when the time has come.

Now, the question is what kind of bride will the groom find? Will she be excited to see him? Will she be ready and prepared for this most significant moment of her entire life? Can you imagine a bride who views the groom's arrival as an unwelcome interruption of her licentious and carefree lifestyle? Can you picture the groom's horror if she has been having secret affairs with other lovers—if the groom's appearance turns out to be a shameful revelation of her compromised life? What if she was so preoccupied with other pursuits that his coming would put her in a state of a shock, and she would have to ask him to just wait another moment so she could quickly get ready for the wedding night? Imagine not only the embarrassment of the bride but also the profound disappointment of the groom. Having spared no effort, time, nor expenses on preparing a lavish wedding feast and readying a wonderful new home for their married life, he is now faced with the stark reality that his beloved bride is woefully unprepared for the great day of their reunion. His heart is broken by her disregard for him, her hidden betrayal of his trust, and her preoccupation with secondary things.

The sad reality is that much of today's church represents a bride that is so influenced by the world and preoccupied with other things that she is either indifferent to her Groom's coming or indifferent to His standard of purity and personal holiness—or both. This lack of urgency is caused by our tendency to view the coming of Christ as something that has little significance in our daily Christian walk and even less relevance to our pressing everyday worries and struggles. We consider end times prophecy discussions complicated and contested, best left to the theologically-trained or to "end times nerds." Juggling jobs, family, friends, and church commitments, we prefer to focus on those parts of Scripture that promise comfort and ease for the here and now.

Many of us argue that it does not matter when or how Christ comes. After all, we have enough on today's plate. Besides, aren't all our church activities more important than apparently irrelevant debates about the end times—a seemingly distant phase in the future? Wouldn't it even be better to completely avoid the whole topic because it can be so divisive?

On the other hand, there are many of us who do actively anticipate the return of Christ to rescue us before the onset of the Great Tribulation, the moment in history when Satan's Antichrist will oversee the world's greatest-ever persecution of the faithful church. Still, does the often–lukewarm Western church truly view the rapture as the long-anticipated moment of the resplendent reunion of a pure and spotless bride with her eternal Lover? Or is the rapture merely a timely solution to our personal problems and wavering spiritual commitment? If we are honest, we realize that our "blessed hope" of Christ's return is often not more than an easy way out of having to face the real issues. Yet what is so glorious about the coming of Jesus when His arrival is greeted more with carnal sighs of relief than godly shouts of joy? We proudly boast that Jesus will deliver us from the fierce judgment that the God-rejecting world will surely face. Yet while He has not yet come, how often are we busily engaged in the very same spiritually unproductive or even outright ungodly activities as the world, at times thinly concealed beneath a Christian veneer? How often do we seek preachers and churches that offer us quick "fix-me" solutions to our self-created troubles, and then we project this very same expectation onto the glorious appearance of the Lord? All these are signs that we have yet to fully grasp what it means to become a spotless bride for Jesus.

When end times prophecy appears in popular Christian culture, it is often treated like a real science fiction thriller, a grand epic spectacle that trumps the magnitude of *Lord of the Rings*. But amidst all the makeshift frenzy, many of us lack a clear and coherent understanding of what the

Bible actually says about these times or how biblical teachings should be accurately understood and interpreted. When we are primarily stimulated by the anticipation of sensational elements, we can end up being more passionate about special effects spectacles and expectations of global catastrophes than about the personal sanctification that Jesus is longing to work out in us. After all, He is not merely appearing to bring just punishment on those who reject Him, but He will first come to judge us, His bride, according to our deeds.

Some advocate stockpiling canned foods and preparing armed bunker systems. However, this may actually be quite contrary to God's plan for believers in those days, since He not only commands us to be salt and light in a fallen world but also wants to get all the glory for Himself by supernaturally protecting and providing for His people—especially in the most trying times. After all, there are many accounts of missionaries being supernaturally protected by angels whom they could not see but who put their attackers to flight. However, it takes significantly more faith to trust in God's angelic (or other) protection than to rely on the shotgun in one's hand. Shouldn't the opposite be true? This is perhaps what Jesus meant when he spoke these words of His return:

> Now, will not God bring about justice for His elect who cry to Him day and night, and will He delay long over them? I tell you that He will bring about justice for them quickly. However, when the Son of Man comes, *will He find faith on the earth?*
>
> (Luke 18:7–8, emphasis added)

No matter where you are at in your walk with Jesus or where you stand on the topic of the end times, we desire to take you on a journey in this book. It will be a journey deep into God's Word, venturing into parts of Scripture that you may have never read before or that may have seemed like an undecipherable secret message. We will explore unfulfilled prophecies and connect truths throughout the pages of the Bible that may have seemed disconnected, hard to understand, and unrelated to our daily lives. As you enter into the revelation of God's will for these final days of church history, we pray that you will discover a greater meaning and purpose about these times that we live in. Above all, our great hope is to inspire you to become a devoted bride of the heavenly Bridegroom, a bride who understands the great urgency of the task ahead and whose life focus is to ready herself for that great day. This urgency is what Paul so aptly expressed when he wrote:

> This is what I mean, brothers: the appointed time has grown very short. From now on, let those who have wives live as though they had none, and those who mourn as though they were not mourning, and those who rejoice as though they were not rejoicing, and those who buy as though they had no goods, and those who deal with the world as though they had no dealings with it. For the present form of this world is passing away.
>
> (1 Corinthians 7:29-31 ESV)

Not All Will Be Ready: A Tale of Ten Virgins

The picture painted in the book of Revelation about the final reunion between Jesus and His bride, the church, stands in stark contrast to many of the views and attitudes that prevail in today's church. God's revelation of the end times powerfully exhorts us not to waste our time and just passively await Christ's return. His Word beckons us to let the anticipation of the upcoming grand finale of human existence profoundly change the way *we ourselves* walk along Calvary Road—the road of personal sanctification and holiness in the power of the cross. Note the bride's state upon the Lamb's coming:

6

Then I heard what seemed to be the voice of a great multitude, like the roar of many waters and like the sound of mighty peals of thunder, crying out, "Hallelujah! For the Lord our God the Almighty reigns. Let us rejoice and exult and give Him the glory, for the marriage of the Lamb has come, and *His bride has made herself ready.*"

(Revelation 19:6–7, emphasis added)

The passage reveals that "His bride has *made herself* ready." Of course, we the bride cannot get ready without complete reliance on Christ and His finished work on the cross. However, it is clear that we also have a pivotal role to play in the preparation process and that failing to prepare will have severe consequences. The fact that we are saved by grace—and grace alone—must not be used as a pretext for minimizing the spiritual responsibilities that God has clearly assigned to us, especially in regard to getting ourselves ready for the coming of His Son! This process of getting ready—of sanctification—must take place before Jesus returns. Ephesians 5:26–27 does not say that Jesus will sanctify His bride after He comes, but that He is right now desiring to "sanctify and cleanse her," so that she will be "holy and without blemish" at His arrival! This does not imply that we can achieve sinless perfection in this age. Such perfection will indeed only come once we are raptured or resurrected and receive our glorified eternal bodies. Even so, Christ is expecting a sanctified bride, set apart and prepared to receive her heavenly Bridegroom.

One of the most significant teachings of Christ concerning preparation for His return is the well-known parable of the ten virgins:

Then the kingdom of heaven will be comparable to ten virgins, who took their lamps and went out to meet the bridegroom. Five of them were foolish, and five were prudent. For when the foolish took their lamps, they took no oil with them, but the prudent took oil in flasks along with their lamps. Now

while the bridegroom was delaying, they all got drowsy and
began to sleep.

But at midnight there was a shout, "Behold, the
bridegroom! Come out to meet him." Then all those virgins
rose and trimmed their lamps. The foolish said to the prudent,
"Give us some of your oil, for our lamps are going out." But
the prudent answered, "No, there will not be enough for
us and you too; go instead to the dealers and buy some for
yourselves."

And while they were going away to make the purchase,
the bridegroom came, and *those who were ready went in with
him to the wedding feast*; and the door was shut. Later the other
virgins also came, saying, "Lord, lord, open up for us." But he
answered, "Truly I say to you, I do not know you." *Be on the
alert then*, for you do not know the day nor the hour."

(Matthew 25:1–13, emphases added)

In this parable, the ten virgins symbolize the whole church (the
number ten in Scripture represents totality or entirety). Five of the
group were wise, but five were foolish. Five prepared themselves, while
five were unprepared. Five were ready when their Lord came and were
consequently let in through the door, while five were not ready and
were left outside a shut door. This parable sends a powerful message
that not all Christians will be equally ready when Christ finally comes,
and as a result, they will face very different fates during the end times.
All of the virgins were saved, and all of them had oil, which symbolizes
the sanctifying power of the Holy Spirit.[1] But only the wise ones had
brought flasks of extra oil in anticipation of the long wait. Only they
had devoted themselves to personal sanctification and spiritual growth,
setting their minds on "things above, not on things that are on the earth"
(Colossians 3:2). Therefore, only they were ready to meet Jesus, their
Bridegroom.

The parable of the ten virgins points to other Scripture passages that shed additional light on the practical applications of what the open and closed doors represent for believers in the end times. Take for example the preservation promise to the faithful, overcoming church of Philadelphia in the Book of Revelation:

> Because you have kept the word of My perseverance, I also will keep you from the hour of testing, that hour which is about to come upon the whole world, to test those who dwell on the earth.
>
> (Revelation 3:10)

These words of Jesus signify that the church will be kept from the "hour of testing" that will befall "the whole world," meaning the Great Tribulation of the Antichrist. There is a second passage where Jesus gives this promise, and this time it is even more directly linked to the Great Tribulation. In the end times account recorded in Luke 21, Jesus describes all the events that must take place during the final years. Then, at the very end of his description, he adds this very significant preservation promise:

> Watch therefore, and pray always *that you may be counted worthy to escape all these things* that will come to pass, and to stand before the Son of Man.
>
> (Luke 21:36 NKJV, emphasis added)

With the phrase "all these things," Jesus refers to the birth pangs, wars, and persecutions that precede the Great Tribulation. He is also referencing the "days of vengeance," "great distress upon the earth," and finally the "desolation" of Jerusalem (vv. 20, 22, 23), which refers to the Great Tribulation itself. These two passages teach that the church should not have to go through the Great Tribulation or even some of the preceding events (this whole period is often referred to as the "Tribulation Period"). These passages inform the pretribulation view of the end times, a view which states that the church is raptured before (*pre-*) the tribulation.

The Rapture Is a *Conditional* Promise

However, the pretribulationist perspective makes the crucial assumption that Scripture's preservation promises apply unconditionally to *all* believers, and therefore to the *entire* church. But this is not the case! Both of the promises in Luke and Revelation are clearly conditional. Jesus' statement in Luke 21:36 is dependent on being "watchful all the time," and only those who are indeed continually watchful will be "counted worthy to escape all these things." Similarly, it is "because you have kept the word of My perseverance" that Christ pledges to keep the Philadelphians from trial. He affirms that despite intense pressure, they "have kept My word, and have not denied My name" (Revelation 3:8).

It is important to realize that the seven churches of Revelation represent not only seven literal historic church communities. Taken together, they also symbolize different groups of the global end times church. Consequently, the Philadelphian church represents only one section within God's church, depicting the most true and faithful disciples of Christ, those who have "overcome" and stayed faithful in trials. Of the seven churches that Jesus sends letters to, five receive severe warnings and exhortations to "repent." Only Philadelphia and Smyrna, less than one-third of the total, receive only praises and no criticism. In contrast, the letters to the five non-overcoming churches demonstrate the compromised and distracted spiritual state that the church will be in just before Jesus' coming.

So then, what will happen to those who are like the lukewarm Laodiceans, the spiritually dead Sardians, the Ephesians who left their first love, or the churches in Pergamum and Thyatira who practiced and tolerated spiritual compromise and carnal, sinful lifestyles? What will it be like for those who, like the five foolish virgins, are literally shut out and "left behind" because they are not (yet) ready to meet their Lord? Their situation is symbolized by the closed door that the foolish virgins face. Their consequences are shown more specifically in Christ's threat to the followers of the false prophetess Jezebel in Thyatira. He declares that unless they repent of their doctrinal error and immoral practices, He will "throw her [Jezebel] on a bed of sickness, and those who commit adultery with her into *great tribulation*, unless they repent of her deeds." (Revelation 2:22, emphasis added). This is one of only three times that the phrase "great tribulation" (Gr. *megas thlipsis*) is mentioned in the entire Bible. As we will see in more detail later, this statement is not just specific to the historic Thyatiran church but a reference to the final, greatest-ever persecution of the believers.

In Luke 21:34, two verses before His preservation promise, Jesus exhorted his followers with this sobering warning: "Be on guard, so that your hearts will not be weighted down with dissipation[2] and drunkenness and the worries of life, and that day will not come on you suddenly like a trap." Similarly, the Sardian church is warned: "Therefore if you do not wake up [from spiritual drunkenness], I will come like a thief, and you will not know at what hour I will come to you." (Revelation 3:3b). Christ's preservation promises to the faithful, overcoming groups of the church are therefore complemented by clear warnings of the very opposite to his spiritually unprepared followers: they are in danger of having to endure "great tribulation."

For the carnal groups of Christianity who live in complete ignorance of the need to prepare spiritually for the return of their Bridegroom, the Great Tribulation will prove to be exactly that which Christ described: an "hour of testing." It will be the "refining fire" the Laodicean church is warned against. The Laodicean's spiritual lukewarmness prompted Jesus to warn them of "discipline," advising them, "buy from Me gold refined by fire" (Revelation 3:18). Those who failed to prepare themselves for

Christ's coming while they had the chance will then be given a second opportunity to present themselves before Him as "holy and blameless." It is not by their own strength that they reach such a place of spiritual readiness, but through active and willing participation in that which Christ has prepared for them as they finally follow Him along the Calvary Road.

There will therefore be *two* raptures: a *first fruits rapture* for those who have, by grace, walked faithfully and wisely, preparing themselves and putting on an attitude of active watchfulness towards the Lord's coming, and a *late harvest rapture* for those who are steeped in carnality and woefully unready to face their Master. The aim of this book is to bring all of Scripture together for developing a biblical teaching of two raptures based on spiritual readiness and to explore how we can get ready for Christ's coming.

Refined in the Fire of Testing

Many Christians are not familiar with the biblical teaching of spiritual refinement through trials and sufferings. This refinement process should not be confused with the unbiblical doctrine of purgatory, a Catholic teaching based on works as a self-righteous, self-accomplished effort. The concept of purgatory entails receiving punishment for earthly sins after one has died in order to enable the sinner to still somehow make it into heaven. It represents a vain attempt to add something to the finished work of Christ on the cross. This teaching is based on the false assumption that the deserved punishment for our sins can be anything less than eternal separation from God. Purgatory is only punitive and not redemptive. It ignores the fact that punishment by itself cannot bring about any spiritual growth and neither can it justify us before God.

In contrast, the sanctifying effect of tribulation for believers while we are still here on earth is an essential biblical teaching. In Acts 14:22, Paul encourages the believers in Lystra, Iconium and Antioch by emphasizing,

"Through many tribulations we must enter the kingdom of God." In Romans 5:3 he teaches that "we also exult in our tribulations, knowing that tribulation brings about perseverance; and perseverance, proven character; and proven character, hope." James similarly reminds the disciples that "the testing of your faith produces endurance ... so that you may be perfect and complete, lacking in nothing" (James 1:3–4). Peter explains to the scattered and persecuted early Christian groups that through "various trials" their faith must be "tested by fire" in order to reveal it as being true and genuine and consequently "result in praise and glory and honor at the revelation of Jesus Christ" (1 Peter 1:6, 7, 8). Finally, Hebrews 12 teaches that God disciplines his children, because even though discipline is painful, "it yields the peaceful fruit of righteousness" (v. 11).

In all of these passages, our Father working in us through the Holy Spirit is the one producing these spiritual results. But we His children have to actively make the choice of either cooperating or rebelling by evading the essential training in godliness that our heavenly Dad has in store for us. Even Jesus Himself had to go through this discipleship school of suffering:

> Although He was a Son, He learned obedience from the things which He suffered. And having been made perfect, He became to all those who obey Him the source of eternal salvation.
>
> (Hebrews 5:8–9)

These verses reflect a universal spiritual principle that even Christ had to submit to: spiritual maturity and obedience are the result of suffering. This does not refer to the suffering brought upon us by our own foolishness and disobedience, but God-planned, God-permitted trials, specifically designed by our loving Father to bring out the best in us. Rather than representing punishment, such trials for believers are intended to prune us, as the vinedresser prunes the branches so that they "may bear more fruit" (John 15:2). This does not mean that the "wise virgin" believers only represent a tiny elite of "spiritual superheroes." Rather, they symbolize those humble men and women of God who put Jesus first in their lives. Their foolish counterparts do trust in Jesus for their salvation, but they are living their lives according to the values and preoccupations of the world.

It is this fruit-producing suffering that the faithful churches of Smyrna and Philadelphia had willingly submitted to. Of these two, the Philadelphians had completed the path of trial that their Lord had set before them and consequently received the promise that they would be spared the greatest of all trials. It will be just the same for the "Philadelphians" of the end times church: unlike the "foolish virgin" believers of the rest of God's church, they will get the "open door" (Revelation 3:8) through which to escape the tribulations. In contrast, those in lukewarm Laodicea were being exhorted, "Behold, I stand at the door and knock; if anyone hears My voice and opens the door, I will come in to him and will dine with him, and he with Me" (v. 3:20). This teaches us two things. Firstly, it is *up to us* to hear and open the door. Secondly, if we do not hear and fail to open the door, we will be like the foolish virgins who faced a closed door at Jesus' return, and we will only be raptured after the end times tribulation of the church. Ultimately, those who avoid suffering in the present by compromising in relationship with the world (as Jezebel's followers did) will have to suffer even more in the future, while those who, like the Philadelphians, submit to God's training routine now will be spared further suffering and testing in the times ahead.

But God is faithful toward all who believe in Him. After this intense period of refinement, Christ will also come in time for these "foolish" children to escape the fiery wrath of God that will be poured out on the unbelieving world. As Scripture has clearly promised, "For God has not destined us for wrath, but for obtaining salvation through our Lord Jesus Christ" (1 Thessalonians 5:9). Ultimately, all of God's children will be with him in eternity where "every tear" will be wiped away.

Fruit-Bearing and Eternal Rewards

Viewing the Great Tribulation as a spiritual refinement process for carnal Christians and the first fruits rapture of the wise virgin believers as a reward for spiritual preparedness could be dismissed as a works-oriented or legalistic way of thinking. However, such criticism overlooks the important biblical teaching that not every believer will receive the same rewards. We emphatically affirm that salvation is not by anything but faith in Christ alone. Likewise, our sanctification, the process of becoming increasingly Christlike, is entirely dependent on God's gracious, undeserved enabling. If we consider anything we do as adding to our justification, as making us "more acceptable" before God, then we have become legalistic like the Pharisees. Legalism is when we consider the good works we do as our own achievement that we have done *for* God rather than *in* Him and consequently feel that we can make ourselves righteous through self-effort. The reality is that we cannot do anything that adds to that which God has done for us. Paul clearly describes righteousness as a "free gift" that we receive because Christ died for us (Romans 5:15–17).

However, it is equally vital to affirm that once we have received the free gift of salvation and become children of God, the powerful work of God in us cannot be without demonstrable results! As John Piper aptly put it, "not only does the New Testament say we must 'believe,' but also that this faith must be so real that it produces the fruit of obedience."[3] True, genuine saving faith *cannot* leave a person unchanged; no, *it must bear fruit.* Jesus himself taught this fruit-bearing principle on numerous occasions, especially in the parable of the fruit tree:

Grapes are not gathered from thorn bushes nor figs from thistles, are they? So every good tree bears good fruit, but the bad tree bears bad fruit. A good tree cannot produce bad fruit, nor can a bad tree produce good fruit. Every tree that does not bear good fruit is cut down and thrown into the fire.

(Matthew 7:16b–19)

True, faith *must* result in "good fruit," meaning that faith and the works that come from faith are inseparable. This is affirmed by the fact that once we are in heaven and seated at the glorious wedding banquet, our wedding garments will represent the spiritual fruit resulting from our faith: "It was given to her [the bride] to clothe herself in fine linen, bright and clean; *for the fine linen is the righteous acts of the saints.*" (Revelation 19:6–8, emphasis added).

An equally important aspect of the principle of fruit-bearing is the Bible's teaching on rewards for believers. Not every believer will enjoy the same degree of eternal rewards and spiritual authority once they arrive in heaven. For example, in the parable of the minas (or pounds) in Luke 19, Jesus represents himself as "a nobleman [who] went to a distant country to receive a kingdom for himself, and then return" (v. 12). The story continues as follows:

And he called ten of his slaves, and gave them ten minas [or pounds, a unit of money equivalent to about four months wages] and said to them, "Do business with this until I come back"....

When he returned, after receiving the kingdom, he ordered that these slaves, to whom he had given the money, be called to him so that he might know what business they had done. The first appeared, saying, "Master, your mina has made ten minas more." And he said to him, "Well done, good slave, because you have been faithful in a very little thing, you are to be in authority over ten cities." The second came, saying, "Your mina, master, has made five minas." And he said to him also, "And you are to be over five cities."

(Luke 19:13, 15–19)

Clearly, the slaves (or servants, symbolizing believers) are rewarded directly according to the amount of fruit they have produced for their Lord. All servants initially received one mina each, which represents the resources, talents and skills that God has endowed us with. The first servant in the parable generated a stunning increase of 1,000 percent, which earns him a "well done" from the master, as well as "authority over ten cities."[4] Similarly, the second servant increases his master's resources by 500 percent, and in exact proportion to this achievement receives authority over five cities.

The parable of the minas shows that Jesus will give *eternal rewards* based on our *present faithfulness*. Similarly, Paul wrote about the fact that our present actions will have lasting eternal consequences:

> For we must all appear before the judgment seat of Christ, so that *each one may receive what is due for what he has done in the body, whether good or evil.*
>
> (2 Corinthians 5:10 ESV, emphasis added)

In his description of the judgment seat of Christ in his first letter to the Corinthians, Paul further elaborated on what the eternal consequences of our actions will look like:

> For no man can lay a foundation other than the one which is laid, which is Jesus Christ. Now if any man builds on the foundation with gold, silver, precious stones, wood, hay, straw, each man's work will become evident; for the day will show it because it is to be revealed with fire, and the fire itself will

test the quality of each man's work. *If any man's work which he has built on it remains, he will receive a reward. If any man's work is burned up, he will suffer loss; but he himself will be saved, yet so as through fire.*

(1 Corinthians 3:11–15, emphasis added)

The "loss" that Paul talks about here is not related to salvation, which cannot be lost (John 10:28), but a loss of rewards for a "man's work." At the judgment seat of Christ, which is only for born-again believers, each person's work will be tested by "fire." Only that which survives the fire test will result in a "reward." But the wood, hay and straw are the works done without God's approval, without His provision, and without giving Him all the glory. Regardless of how well-intended or "spiritual" they may have appeared, these works will fail the fire test and result in a loss of eternal rewards. Rewards and loss of rewards are therefore contrasted and described as direct consequences of our works performed while we are still on the earth.

Jesus Himself clearly affirmed this truth in the last chapter of Revelation, at the very end of His eternal Word: "Behold, I am coming quickly, and My reward is with Me, *to render to every man according to what he has done*" (Revelation 22:12, emphasis added). In this verse, Jesus tells us plainly that there will be eternal consequences for our present deeds, whether good or bad. Likewise, Paul wrote to the Colossians:

Whatever you do, do your work heartily, as for the Lord rather than for men, knowing that from the Lord you will receive the reward of the inheritance.... For he who does wrong will receive the consequences of the wrong which he has done, and that without partiality.

(Colossians 3:24–25)

All these scriptures and parables are intended to prepare us for Christ's return by giving us insights into what our Master will expect from us, His servants, when He returns. Jesus rightly expects to find fruit in our lives when He comes, since He has given us everything ("talents" and "minas") we need for fruit-bearing! Well-known author Randy Alcorn summarizes biblical teachings on rewards in his book *Money, Possessions and Eternity*, and contrasts them with the characteristics of salvation:[5]

Table 1. Comparing salvation and eternal rewards

Salvation	Rewards
Past (1 John 3:2)	Future (Revelation 22:12)
Free (Ephesians 2:8–9)	Earned (1 Corinthians 3:8, Revelation 22:12)
Can't be lost (John 10:28–29)	Can be lost (2 John 8, Revelation 3:11)
Same for all Christians (Romans 3:22)	Differ between Christians (1 Corinthians 3:12–15, Revelation 22:12)
For those who believe (John 3:16)	For those who work/bear fruit in Christ (Matthew 6:4–6; Mark 4:20; John 15:1–6; Revelation 22:12)

Alcorn writes:

> This is an unpopular subject, but Scripture is clear. Not all Christians will hear the master say: "Well done, good and faithful servant" (Matthew 25:23). Not all of us will have treasure in heaven (Matthew 6:19–21). Not all of us will have the same position of authority in heaven (Luke 19:17, 19, 26). We will have differing degrees of reward in heaven (1 Corinthians 3:12–15). There is no hint that, once given or withheld, rewards are anything other than eternal and irrevocable.[6]

The Unity and Diversity of God's Church

Another argument against two separate raptures is the unfounded assumption that such a view is incompatible with the unity of the church. But the key problem of this statement lies in its very essence. How do you define "the church" in an age of deception, lukewarmness, and immorality? "The church" as it presently exists is so diverse that it defies any coherent definition or description. Are those who assume it to be unified referencing the lukewarm Western churches or the often-persecuted churches in other nations? Where does the true bride of Christ start, and where does it end? The differences in levels of spiritual maturity and readiness for the return of Christ within "the church," even amongst those who are truly born-again, are staggering!

A division of the body of Christ into faithful and less faithful (but still saved) believers is not only implied in the parable of the ten virgins, which splits the church into two distinct groups. Even in the first century AD, the letters to the seven churches of Revelation reveal drastic differences within the early church. All seven were located in Asia Minor, faced an extremely similar cultural context (Greek paganism), and were a more-or-less direct result of Paul's missionary work. Still, less than a century later, these fellowships had already become extremely diverse in terms of their walk with their Lord. As a consequence, Jesus' evaluations of them could hardly be more different. While the Philadelphians are promised to be kept from the "hour of testing," the followers of Jezebel are clearly warned of the very opposite—that they will be thrown "into great tribulation." The implication of this is evident: just as not all believers will receive the same rewards and authority in heaven, not all believers will fare the same when Christ returns to receive his bride. There were wise and foolish virgins back then, and there will be the same when Jesus comes.

North American Christians especially like to use the Bible to teach economic capitalism. But ironically, we Western believers are easily tempted to propagate a false spiritual communism. In spiritual communism's heaven, all believers' eternal rewards and spiritual authority are exactly the same, meaning that their level of commitment and fruit-bearing while on earth have no eternal implications at all. This could not be further from what Scripture teaches us! Following the biblical principle of reaping rewards for bearing fruit, being taken at the first fruits rapture, which pretribulationists take so easily for granted, is simply a reward for one's spiritual readiness. If Jesus would merely come to rescue a spiritually-asleep bride from the mire of her lukewarm spirituality, His repeated exhortations to be "watchful" and ready for His return would be pointless. Therefore, the primary purpose of this book is to make the church aware of the need to prepare itself for this epic moment. Our prayer is that God will use our work to illuminate the final moments of history before Jesus' return.

> The Spirit and the bride say, "Come." And let the one who hears say, "Come."…
>
> … He who testifies to these things says, "Yes, I am coming quickly." Amen. Come, Lord Jesus.
>
> (Revelation 22:17a, 20)

Chapter 1 Notes

1. See Zechariah 4. This will be explained in further detail in chapter 3.
2. Dissipation (Gr. *kraipale, Strong's Concordance,* G2897) is the headache or dizziness caused by excessive drinking.
3. John Piper, *Desiring God* (Sisters, Oregon: Multnomah, 2003), 68.
4. This authority most likely refers to the millennial reign of Christ on earth, since the eternal state that follows afterward has just one city, the New Jerusalem (see Revelation 21–22).
5. Randy Alcorn, *Money, Possessions and Eternity* (Wheaton, IL: Tyndale House, 2003), 127. The authors modified the table by adding Scripture references.
6. Ibid., 125.

Chapter 2

The End Times World Order and How We Got There

When I, Daniel, had seen the vision, I sought to understand it....

... he said to me, "Son of man, understand that the vision pertains

to the time of the end."

Daniel 8:15, 17

Preparing the Stage for the Antichrist: How Close Are We Now?

Many pretribulationist Christians believe that the "second coming" of Jesus could have literally occurred "anytime" since the days of the early church. This belief is called "imminence." When the return of Jesus is said to be "imminent," it means that He could appear right now at this very moment, and could have appeared at any moment since His ascent into heaven. But fact is that Christ's coming has in no way been imminent since those early days. Multiple scriptural conditions first had to be met. Daniel 9:27 teaches us that the Antichrist will establish a treacherous peace covenant with Israel, a fact that we will examine in more detail in subsequent chapters. In order for this to become possible, the Jews had to first again establish their own nation. This did not occur until 1948, when British Palestine became Israel. Then in 1967 the Israelites took control of Jerusalem. Taking back their own city was again a key requirement to fulfill the prophetic words given by the angel Gabriel to Daniel regarding the events of the last days—events that concern "your [Daniel's] people and your holy city" (Daniel 9:24).

But now and for the first time, all biblical conditions for Christ's first end times appearance—the first fruits rapture—have been met. The only event that we believe is yet to come before this appearance is a severe global economic crisis, much worse than that of 2008–2009, which will pave the way for the Antichrist's rise into power. For the first time in history, the coming of Jesus is indeed becoming imminent.

How close are we now? Both Daniel and Jesus prophesied that the Antichrist would defile the temple by setting up a so-called "abomination of desolation." This requires that the Jews gain control of the temple mount in Jerusalem, which is currently the site of the Al-Aqsa mosque and the Muslim Dome of the Rock shrine, and construct a third temple (after the second temple[1] was destroyed by Titus in 70 AD). Daniel 9:27 says that "he [Antichrist] will make a firm covenant with the many for one week, but in the middle of the week he will put a stop to [the temple-based] sacrifice and grain offering." This makes it virtually certain that part of Israel's peace treaty brokered by the Antichrist will include a deal that enables it to establish this end times temple, perhaps right next to the Muslim sites. Moreover, the Jews will need to install a new order of Levites before temple worship can be initiated. Preparations for this are underway, as actual descendants from the tribe of Levi have been confirmed through genetic testing.[2]

Therefore, watching political events related to this process may give us an idea of how close we are to the first fruits rapture. There will be signs of a war in the Middle East and signs of an economic crisis. Both events will help to bring the Antichrist into a position of world domination (his rise to some degree of power will happen before that). But the first fruits rapture will occur before the first seal of Revelation 6 and therefore prior to the Antichrist-brokered peace treaty. Therefore, God's first fruits will never get to witness these things. Likewise, the sequence of events in Matthew 24 suggests that the preaching of the gospel to the ends of the earth may not actually conclude until the mid-point of the final 7-year period. All of this indicates that the rise of the Antichrist is now indeed only a matter of a short time.

How Close Are We Now? Understanding Daniel's Empire Visions

Aside from the developments in Israel, how can we know when the stage is set for the Antichrist to step on the scene? When and how will he be able to achieve world domination and initiate the unprecedented persecution of God's people?

Thousands of years ago, God provided his faithful servant Daniel, who served under king Nebuchadnezzar in exile, with a master blueprint of key aspects of world history. God showed Daniel not only some of the actual events of the end times, such as the Antichrist brokering a covenant with Israel, but He also revealed to him two sets of world empires that would arise and set the stage for the time of the end.

In Daniel 2, Nebuchadnezzar, king of Babylon, had a strange dream. Nobody could know or interpret this dream, but God gave insight and interpretation to Daniel. The king's dream was about a figure with a golden head, a breast of silver, a brass belly, legs of iron, and feet and toes that were partly iron and partly clay. Daniel interpreted this dream for the king, stating that the head of gold symbolized Nebuchadnezzar's glorious Babylonian Empire and implying that the breast of silver stood for the Medo-Persian Empire that followed, the belly of bronze for the Greek Empire of Alexander the Great, and the iron legs for the Roman Empire, whose armies were distinguished by iron-made leg and body armor. The feet and toes, which were made of a mix of iron and clay, represented a number of different nations and peoples that would come out of the Roman Empire but never form a true and lasting union. Daniel 2:43 states, "they will not adhere to one another, even as iron does not combine with pottery."

Indeed, ever since the Roman Empire, Europe has not been truly united. Theoretically, the European Union (EU) could eventually lead to such a unity. Whether this will be the case or not remains to be seen, but so far, Daniel's vision still holds true. The European Union is still far from the unity that it aspires to be. Instead, it is frequently characterized by considerable divisions, such as, for example, Britain and Denmark refusing to accept the Euro currency or Germany disagreeing with France and Britain over NATO's intervention in Libya. Generally, power relations within the EU are uneasy, often dependent on the changing moods between Germany and France, who consider themselves the union's core nations, with Britain playing the role of the suspicious onlooker who often blocks the will of the two core nations.[3]

Interestingly, in Daniel's vision, he then saw a huge rock which struck the statue at its feet. The rock symbolizes Christ and His Kingdom that will supersede all other worldly kingdoms. The fact that it strikes the statue at its feet indicates that the feet and toes, the nations that try to mix but never form a true unity, will still be existing at Christ's future coming and will be the ones that He conquers before setting up His millennial reign. This will certainly be true of at least most EU nations.

A little later, Daniel then received another vision, again about four empires but this time symbolized through animal-like beasts: a lion, a bear, a leopard, and a terrifying beast with iron teeth (ch. 7). Traditionally, these empires have been interpreted to be the same as those in the first vision. But several facts would contradict such an assumption. Firstly, Daniel's vision here is clearly about "four kings who *will* arise [*in the future*]" (v. 17, emphasis added). Because he receives this vision in the "first year of Belshazzar" (v. 1), Babylon's last ruler shortly before the Medo-Persian takeover, it would seem contradictory that the first beast-empire should again be Babylon. After all, this empire already exists. Moreover, as Gerhard Maier, author of the Daniel section of Germany's famous conservative commentary *Wuppertaler Studienbibel* notes, the lion with wings does not necessarily stand for Babylon; it can equally represent Medo-Persia or Egypt, whereas there is no clear link between Medo-Persia and the second beast (the bear).[4]

Secondly, between these visions, Daniel received yet another vision (ch. 8) about two of the four empires from the first vision: Medo-Persia, symbolized by a ram, and Alexander the Great's Greece, depicted by a goat with a large horn. The goat overpowers the ram, just as Alexander defeated the Persian Empire but then immediately splits into four horns (kingdoms). This was fulfilled when Alexander died right after his rapid conquests, and his empire was divided between four of his generals. Because Medo–Persia and Greece are therefore already associated with two animals (ram and goat), it is unlikely that they should be represented among the four beast-like animals of chapter 7 by different animals! Rather than giving Daniel the same vision repeated again, God honored Daniel by providing him with a new revelation that extends even further into humanity's future.

Table 2. The four empires of Daniel 2 compared with the four empires of Daniel 7

	Four empires in Daniel 2	Four empires in Daniel 7
1	Golden head (Babylon)	1st beast (lion with eagle's wings)
2	Silver chest (Medo-Persia) [a ram in Daniel 8]	2nd beast (bear)
3	Bronze belly/thighs (Greece) [a goat in Daniel 8]	3rd beast (leopard with four wings and heads)
4	Iron legs (Rome)	4th beast (different and terrible, with iron teeth)
Final result	Feet and ten toes of iron and clay (European nations that emerge from the Roman Empire)	Ten horns and a little horn (the Antichrist) that emerge from the fourth beast

The third argument against the two visions being the same is that this would mean that the fourth beast of chapter 7 must be the Roman Empire. Many follow this logic because in both visions, the fourth empire is described as having iron-like qualities. However, in chapter 2 it talks about *legs* of iron, whereas in chapter 7 the beast is depicted as having *teeth* of iron. In chapter 2's vision of the statue, the iron functions like a body armor, an apt description of the Roman armies. But in the fourth beast, the iron is the means of attack. An even greater discrepancy is the fact that the fourth beast is described as "different from all the beasts that were before it," as "terrifying and dreadful and exceedingly strong" (v. 7). The legs of iron in the statue, however, were not so markedly different from its preceding empires.

Moreover, the description of the fourth beast says that it "devoured and broke in pieces and stamped what was left with its feet" (v. 7). This was not a characteristic of the Romans, who sought to peacefully integrate the populations they conquered. Certainly, they brutally suppressed those who rebelled against them, but in general, the Roman era was characterized by a peacefulness known as the *Pax Romana* ("Roman peace"). Because no one was powerful enough to challenge Rome for about 200 years—from 27 BC to 180 AD—the period was an unprecedented time of peace. Rather than ravaging the regions they conquered, the Romans actually developed them by improving their infrastructure (especially roads) and implementing effective administrations. If anything, it was the Assyrians who were notorious for their unsurpassed cruelty towards their captives.[5]

Table 3. The 4ᵗʰ empire of Daniel 2 compared with the 4ᵗʰ empire of Daniel 7

The 4ᵗʰ Empire of Daniel 2	The 4ᵗʰ Empire of Daniel 7
Legs of iron (defense)	Teeth of iron and claws of bronze (attack)
Not said to be different from the preceding empires. Roman rule typically characterized by peace and prosperity.	Said to be markedly "different from all the beasts [empires] that were before it" (7:7): terrifying and dreadful, it will "devour the whole earth and tread it down and crush it" (7:23)

The Fourth Beast Empire

Consequently, it would seem more logical that the four empires of Daniel 7 are different from those in Daniel 2. In fact, it makes much more sense that they belong to the modern era rather than to ancient times, pointing towards nations that are much more relevant for the history of God's people closer to the end times than these ancient empires could be. Just like in the first vision, these four modern nations do not intend to represent all human empires around the world and throughout history but only those with a direct relationship to God's people and those that made a key contribution towards setting up the end times stage.

From this perspective, we suggest that the dreadful fourth beast with teeth of iron represents Hitler's Germany or perhaps all three Axis powers of World War II (Germany, Italy and Japan). Hitler's Germany was the first nation in world history to pioneer the strategic deployment of tank armies and mechanized army units. Previously, tanks were utilized alongside regular armed forces in a support role, meaning they were typically scattered between them. Hitler, however, recognized the potential of employing large groups of tanks in order to deeply penetrate enemy territory, and the resulting *Panzer* (tank) armies and mechanized army divisions formed the backbone of his lightning-like *Blitzkrieg* approach. As a result, he crushed the Polish army, which was still riding on horseback, within weeks. This directly correlates with the iron teeth and bronze claws of the fourth beast.

The Japanese were the first nation to use massive air strikes in naval battles (most notably in the surprise attack on Hawaii), thereby turning modern fighter planes into a key element of their lighting-like naval warfare. Likewise, Hitler's invasions involved an unprecedented strategic use of aerial warfare, such as the precision bombing capabilities of the *Stuka* (Junker 87) dive bombers, the massed use of bombers to cripple Soviet ground forces at the onset of the German invasion, and the invention of self-guided medium-range rockets (V1/V2) and of supersonic jet engine aircraft (Messerschmidt 262).[6] If ever there was a global empire that brutally used its "iron teeth" to ravage the world, these Axis powers certainly fit the description.

Both Germany and Japan were "different" from previous empires in that they subjected their conquered populations not only to brutal suppression but also to unprecedented levels of mass slaughter. The Japanese committed extensive and systematic genocide amongst the Chinese, resulting in a death toll of 3-4 million Chinese soldiers and 7-16 million civilians.[7] In the Nanjing massacre alone, Japanese soldiers slaughtered hundreds of thousands of unarmed civilians and raped tens of thousands of women. Throughout its conquered territories, the Japanese army used rape as a means of terrorizing and subduing local populations. On the German side, the systematic extermination of an estimated 5-6 million Jews was a historically unprecedented act of brutality that directly targeted God's people. Additionally, up to 12 million Soviet civilians died as the result of Nazi ethnic cleansing or armed clashes, prompting Russian historians to refer to Hitler's invasion as an act of unsurpassed genocide.

In total, World War II was the by far most devastating and also the most global war that humanity ever witnessed, turning vast areas of Europe, northern Africa, Southeast and East Asia, and the Pacific into vicious battlefields and prompting the development and only-ever deployment of nuclear bombs. The estimates of military and civilian deaths resulting from this global catastrophe range from 62 to 79 million, dwarfing the human impact of any previous man-made disaster. This certainly explains why the fourth Axis beast-empire is described as so "dreadful," "terrifying," and "different" from the other beast-empires.

The Consequences of the Fall of the Axis Beast-Empire

But there is one significant similarity between the Roman Empire from Daniel 2 and this Axis nations beast from Daniel 7. In both cases, the demise of these empires profoundly changed the global political scene and gave rise to a new world order. In Daniel 2, this is symbolized by ten "toes" and in Daniel 7 by "ten horns" (kingdoms).

The collapse of the Roman Empire paved the way for the birth of today's European nation states. Likewise, the global struggle of the allies against the Axis powers, which ended with the Axis's surrender in 1945, was the main impetus behind the formation of the United Nations (UN) and the European Union. The UN was founded in 1945, the same year that the war ended, with the specific purpose of fostering international cooperation and promoting world peace by preventing future global conflicts. Similarly, the EU arose from an initial union between Western Germany, France, and the Benelux nations,[8] after Britain's Winston Churchill had already called for the establishment of a "United States of Europe" in 1946. Both the UN and the EU were therefore created out of a desire to achieve lasting peace and global unity. The Antichrist will appear to achieve exactly these two goals and unite the world under his rule by making promises of global peace and prosperity.

Apart from changing the world's political scene, World War II was also instrumental for the development of postmodern philosophy. Because of the vast destruction caused by the war, people began to doubt concepts of absolute truth and the continual progress of the world's development. This skepticism about human progress and the promises of established religions led to the rise of postmodern relativism, which holds that no religion or ideology can have the absolute truth (except of course, postmodernism itself!). As a consequence, postmodernism has championed the concept of tolerance, which says that every view or belief is equally valid and true. In this context, Christianity, which asserts that God revealed His absolute and eternal truths to us, that other belief systems are ultimately inspired by Satan, and that those who reject faith in Jesus will be sentenced to eternal punishment, is branded as intolerant fundamentalism.

It is very likely that the global persecution of true believers will center on the charge that they promote "intolerant views," especially related to preaching against homosexuality. In fact, the anti-Christian "tolerance" campaign is already beginning to gain momentum. In England, a street preacher was arrested in May 2010 for proclaiming that homosexuality is sin. The Telegraph newspaper wrote that "Dale McAlpine was charged with causing 'harassment, alarm or distress' after a homosexual police community support officer (PCSO) overheard him reciting a number of 'sins' referred to in the Bible, including blasphemy, drunkenness and same sex relationships."[9] He was locked up in a police van for several hours. As early as 2004, a Swedish pastor had been sentenced to one month in prison for "inciting hatred against homosexuals" after he preached on this topic.[10] By speaking out against homosexuality, the pastor had violated a "hate crimes" law that forbids such criticism.

Such "hate crime" laws are also being drafted and put in place in other Western nations. Other significant legal developments are equal opportunity or anti-discrimination laws put in place throughout the European Union that forbid employers to discriminate based on gender or sexual orientation. That way, it becomes illegal for churches or Christian organizations to refuse to hire homosexuals into important positions. Hate crime and anti-discrimination laws will likely play a major role in the suppression of biblical Christianity. As early as a few years or a decade from now, it may be illegal to publicly profess key tenets of the Christian faith. Even now, such views have become social taboos, causing many churches to gradually move towards compromise in these areas.

The Antichrist and the "Ten" Nations

Another interesting congruity between Daniel's visions of Roman and Axis empires is that the succeeding nations that emerge after their collapse will still be present when Jesus returns. Like the ten toes that emerge from the legs of iron (Roman Empire) in Daniel 2, the fourth beast in Daniel 7 is depicted as having "ten horns," which represent "ten kings" that will arise "out of this kingdom" (v. 24). Which nations are they? Scholars have in vain attempted to determine exactly ten European nations or peoples that emerged out of the Roman Empire or the fourth beast. Such identification is simply not possible. The rise and fall of European nations has been extremely complex. For example, Germany and Italy consisted of many little sovereign dominions for centuries and did not become unified nation-states until the late 19th century. Not all of the many peoples that existed after the fall of the Roman Empire have become modern nation-states, and some have been completely assimilated into other groups. Likewise, even though the European Union once had ten members, by the end of 2011 it had grown to 27 nations.

Therefore, it is better to interpret the "ten" kingdoms as a symbolic number. Throughout Scripture, the number ten symbolizes completeness or fullness. God gave the Israelites Ten Commandments, which were to reflect the essence of His law. Egypt was struck by ten plagues, which is analogous to the fullness of God's judgment and wrath on sinful humanity—to be repeated at the end of the age. The Israelites tested God ten times during their wanderings in the wilderness (Numbers 14:22), representing both the fullness of God's testing and refining process and the full extent of their disobedience and rebellion against Him. One tenth (the tithe) was the fullness of that which belonged to God from one's income. The ten silver coins in the parable of the lost coin (Luke 15) represent the fullness of sinners, which Jesus came to find and save;[11] the ten lepers he cured reflect the fullness of His healing power for all humanity; the entirety of God's people on earth is expressed in the ten virgins. The fullness of the security of the saints in Christ is expressed in a list of ten things that cannot separate us from God (Romans 8:38–39). The fullness of time for the tribulation of the church at Smyrna, designed to complete their process of overcoming discipleship, was "ten days" (Revelation 2:10). Finally, the Antichrist will arise from "ten" kings, and he will reign together with "ten" kings under him, representing the fullness of the powers of evil in the end of the age (Revelation 17:12–13).

It is therefore unnecessary to try to conjure up ten post-beast nations, either for the Roman Empire of Daniel 2 or of the Axis beast empire of Daniel 7. In both cases, the demise of these empires gave rise to a complete or full number of nations according to God's sovereign will. These nations, in turn, will dominate the global political setting in which the Antichrist will rise to power. It seems reasonable to suggest that they are not just European nations. For example, the United States is also an offshoot of the Roman Empire, because it was established by European peoples. Moreover, the Axis beast spanned most of the globe. Its fall facilitated not only the rise of the United States and Russia but also of China to global power. Additionally, World War II played a key role in the end of colonialism, paving the way for developing nations such as India, Indonesia, or South Korea to rise to positions of significance. All of these countries are now members of the G-20, a forum of the world's most economically important developed and developing nations. In this context, it is entirely possible that the G-20 or similar forums of global dominance and power are what is meant by the "ten" nations of Daniel 2 and 7.

Daniel's Empire Visions Point Directly to the Antichrist

In Daniel 7, God expands on the beast-empire vision. Daniel sees ten horns (kings or kingdoms) arising from the fourth beast and after them "another horn, a little one, [which] came up among them, and three of the first horns were pulled out by the roots before it; and behold, this horn possessed eyes like the eyes of a man and a mouth uttering great boasts" (v. 8). Later on, this little horn is clearly identified as the Antichrist himself:

> He will speak out against the Most High and wear down
> the saints of the Highest One, and he will intend to make

alterations in times and in [God's] law; and they will be given
into his hand for a time, times, and half a time [3.5 years].

(Daniel 7:25)

This directly corresponds to the description of the Antichrist in
Revelation 13:

Then I saw a beast coming up out of the sea, having ten horns
and seven heads, and on his horns were ten diadems, and on
his heads were blasphemous names. And the beast which I
saw was like a leopard, and his feet were like those of a bear,
and his mouth like the mouth of a lion. And the dragon gave
him his power and his throne and great authority. I saw one
of his heads as if it had been slain, and his fatal wound was
healed. And the whole earth was amazed and followed after
the beast....

... There was given to him a mouth speaking arrogant
words and blasphemies, and authority to act for forty-two
months [3.5 years] was given to him.... It was also given to
him to make war with the saints and to overcome them, and
authority over every tribe and people and tongue and nation
was given to him.

(Revelation 13:1–3, 5, 7)

Both sections confirm that the Antichrist will reign over the whole
earth and overpower the saints for a period of 3.5 years and that he
will be characterized by a boastful mouth. Interestingly, Revelation 13
describes him as having the characteristics of the first three beasts from
Daniel 7 but not of the dreadful fourth beast. This is consistent with
the fact that he will rise to power through haughty and arrogant—but
probably also extremely eloquent and charismatic—speaking skills,
causing the "whole earth" to be "amazed" and to follow and worship

him (Revelation 13:3). The Antichrist will not be a terrorizing tyrant like Hitler, which would be extremely unpopular in our current day and age. Quite the contrary, the present generation will much rather be wooed by a smooth talker, a peace broker, a seemingly virtuous and tolerant person who epitomizes the postmodern spirit of the age (freedom and tolerance). At the end, Satan will truly come to dominate the world as an "angel of light" (2 Corinthians 11:14) when he poses as a benevolent man of peace.

The Nature of the Antichrist: Identifying the Other Three Beast-Empires

The characteristics of the Antichrist and his rule become clearer when we understand the three beast empires whose features he will share. Their precise identification is of course speculative. Scripture does not give us enough information to be absolutely certain, but it does provide us with hints and metaphors that will, with God's guidance, point us in the right direction. Whereas the four empires from the vision of the statue in Daniel 2 were successive, meaning they did not overlap in time but followed one another (usually with the successor conquering the preceding empire), the four beast-empires in Daniel 7 also arise one after the other, but here there is no indication that they cease to exist because of the rise of the next. Quite to the contrary, in 7:11–12 it says that they or their successors' "dominion [is] taken away" but they receive "an extension of life." This indicates that they not only continue to exist until the return of Christ but also into the millennium.

The Judgment of the Four Beasts in Daniel 7:9–12

In Daniel 7, we get an explanation of how the four beasts are judged.

> I kept looking
> Until thrones were set up,
> And the Ancient of Days took *His* seat;
> His vesture *was* like white snow
> And the hair of His head like pure wool.
> His throne *was* ablaze with flames,
> Its wheels *were* a burning fire.
> A river of fire was flowing
> And coming out from before Him;
> Thousands upon thousands were attending Him,
> And myriads upon myriads were standing before Him;
> The court sat,
> And the books were opened.
>
> Then I kept looking because of the sound of the boastful words which the horn was speaking; I kept looking until the beast was slain, and its body was destroyed and given to the burning fire. As for the rest of the beasts, their dominion was taken away, but an extension of life was granted to them for an appointed period of time.
>
> (Daniel 7:9–12)

The common interpretation here is that the destruction of the beast in the "burning fire" is the same as the judgment of the Antichrist ("beast") at Armageddon (Revelation 19:20). However, even though the Antichrist is called "beast" in Revelation, in all of Daniel, the Antichrist is never identified as a "beast" but rather as a "little horn."

Verse 11 mentions both the "horn" and the (fourth) "beast" as separate entities. Consequently, this verse cannot be describing the Antichrist's judgment in Revelation 19. Secondly, Revelation 19:20 clearly states that the Antichrist is thrown into the lake of fire "alive," whereas in Daniel 7:11 the beast is both "slain" and "destroyed" before being "given to the burning fire." Thirdly, the sequence of chapter 7 positions the glorious coming of the "son of man" (Christ) at Armageddon to receive His millennial kingdom *after* the judgment of the beasts (vv. 13–14). But if Daniel 7:11 and Revelation 19:20 refer to the same event, then this appearance of Christ to obtain His kingdom would have to come *before* this judgment. This means that Daniel 7:11–12 must take place *before* Armageddon.[12]

The better interpretation is therefore to understand 7:11 as the judgment of the Axis beast. Eyewitnesses stated that Hitler first took a cyanide tablet, then shot himself in the head, and finally his body was burned by his guards using nearly 200 liters of petrol in order to prevent it from falling into Russian hands.[13] He was first "slain" and "destroyed" and then subjected to "burning fire." Therefore, he was literally killed in three ways as prophesied by Daniel.

Regarding the other three beasts, their judgment, which is in the future, will consist of having their "dominion" stripped away from them before Jesus comes in glory to receive "dominion, glory and a kingdom" (vv. 13–14). However, they will receive "an extension of life," meaning that they will continue to exist in the millennium but under Christ's dominion (see chapter 14 for more details). Based on the text, the judgment of the fourth beast and that of the other three beasts does not have to occur at the same time; it is entirely plausible that there is a time gap between both judgments, because the judgments are qualitatively different.

The four beast-empires from Daniel 2 therefore span the period between the ancient world and the first coming of Jesus, while the four beast-empires from Daniel 7 bridge the time from Christ's death until the advent of the modern world and the end times appearances of Jesus. Specifically, Daniel's vision only includes empires that still played a significant political and spiritual role during the rise of the final Axis beast empire, which culminated in the creation of a new (post-World War II) world order. Just as with the four empires of the statue vision in Daniel 7, which did not include all great empires of antiquity but only those 600 years prior to Christ's birth, the four beast-empires of his latter vision only pertain to a period of several centuries before the great historical convergence of World War II. Consequently, medieval or post-medieval empires such as the Islamic Caliphates, the Holy Roman Empire, the Eastern Roman (Byzantine) Empire, the Ottoman Empire (Turkish), the Austro-Hungarian Empire, or the Portuguese and Spanish empires are not featured amongst the four beasts.[14]

Likewise, just as the statue of Daniel 2 only included empires that pertained to the fate of God's people, the Jews, and therefore did not

Figure 1. The arms of Richard Lionheart (left) and of Queen Victoria and all subsequent British monarchs until today (right). The three lions are known as the "three lions passant guardian." Source: Wikimedia Commons.

mention other empires (such as, for example, Qing China or the Persian Sassanid Empire), the four beast-empires only represent those that had a direct and important relationship to God's church. Therefore, non-European empires are not part of the prophetic sequence.

If we limit our selection to empires that fit all of the above criteria, we end up with the following shortlist of major modern European empires that, apart from the Axis powers, played crucial roles during both World War II and the subsequent creation of a New World Order: the British Empire, the French (colonial) Empire, the Russian Empire (later the Communist

USSR), and perhaps indirectly the United States as an offshoot of the British Empire.[15] As it turns out, precisely these empires are represented by the first three beasts.

First Beast Empire: The British Lion and the American Eagle

In Daniel 7, the first beast, a lion with eagle's wings, is said to have its "wings … plucked, and it was lifted up from the ground and made to stand on two feet like a man; a human mind [*or: heart*] also was given to it" (v. 4). This description can be said to fit the British Empire. Traditionally, England has been symbolized by a lion as early as its coats of arms can be traced back in history—all the way to king Richard "The Lionheart" in 1198. It continues to feature prominently on the arms of Britain's current Queen Elizabeth. The lion, being the supreme creature in the animal kingdom, also symbolizes majesty and power, and the British Empire was indeed the largest and most impressive empire in all of human history. It was founded in the late 16th century just after the Reformation (all four beasts in Daniel 7 represent post-reformation empires). In 1783, its eagle's wings—representing the United States, whose national symbol is the eagle—were "plucked off" when the United States won its revolutionary war and Britain conceded its independence.

As prophesied, the nature of the empire soon received a new "mind" after this loss. Under Queen Victoria, Britain was the most powerful nation in the world, and this unchallenged status led to the era of the *Pax Britannica* ("British peace"), a time of relative global peace, during which the empire reached its greatest territorial extent and became the world's largest-ever empire.[16] The empire entered the Victorian period, which was characterized by prosperity, refined sensibilities, and national self-confidence. Rather than just being preoccupied with military prowess, the nation's focus shifted to cultural tastes, scientific advances, architectural achievements, political statesmanship, and the industrial revolution. During this era, Britain pioneered key inventions such as the steam engine, the telegraph, and the railway, and the natural sciences emerged as the major academic disciplines that they have been up to this day. The "lion" spearheaded humanity's transition into modernity.

A perhaps more significant "mind" or rather "heart" change occurred in the spiritual realm. After losing it's "eagle's wings," the British Empire experienced major spiritual changes—often inspired by awakenings in its former colony, the United States. William Wilberforce's anti-slavery campaign began in 1823 and achieved its purpose, the complete abolition of slavery, in 1834. Around the same time, the rise of the Plymouth Brethren under Darby changed Britain's spiritual landscape. Even though the work of George Whitfield and John Wesley, two extremely influential figures in the nation's Christian history, took place in the 18th century, the full impact of their spiritual work arguably came to fruition in the 19th century. Methodist church membership multiplied from 76,000 at the time of Wesley's death in 1791 to 412,000 in 1901, and by that time many other evangelical denominations had also experienced stellar growth across British society.[17] This new openness for God's full gospel and the true salvation message may lie behind Daniel's observation that the lion received a human heart or mind (Aramaic: *lebab*[18]), a reference to the "heart of flesh" mentioned in Ezekiel 36:26 that is receptive for the "new spirit" that born-again believers receive upon salvation. Britain's openness towards the full and true gospel certainly surpassed that of the other European nations, and evangelicalism there remains far stronger than on the European continent.

After American independence, the empire also became a major hub for Protestant missions, beginning with William Carey's journey to India in 1793 and reaching its peak with the founding of Hudson Taylor's China Inland Mission and the Cambridge Seven[19] in the late 19th century. Likewise, the Keswick conventions, which proved pivotal for spiritual renewal and the promotion of missions in Britain, started in 1875. In 1917, British troops took Jerusalem and set up the British Mandate of

Palestine, thereby playing a key role in the eventual restoration of the Jewish nation.

However, as time went on, Britain became increasingly preoccupied with its own greatness and wealth, and its spirituality declined. God used the global transformations caused by World War II to remove the empire from its position of supremacy over the whole earth. Around the time of its withdrawal from Palestine in 1948, which gave the Jews the opportunity to form their own nation, the empire began to rapidly disintegrate.[20]

Ironically, this decline paved the way for the rise of the lion's former wings, the United States of America. Even though the United States had already begun to rise to the status of a world empire (or superpower) since its 1898 war against Spain,[21] it achieved its greatest world supremacy in the aftermath of World War II. During the Cold War, the "eagle" was the primary guarantor of freedom and peace in Europe and around the globe, because it was the only nation that could effectively stop the advance of Communism.

Figure 2. The rise of the "eagle": the rise of the U.S. as a global superpower effectively began in 1898 with the war against Spain. Soon, the American Empire extended across the Pacific, spanning a distance of over 10,000 miles. Source: Wikimedia Commons.

Just as the lion is the most majestic and powerful of all land animals, the eagle is equally associated with majesty and reigns supremely in the realm of the air. Following this symbolism, the British Empire achieved the greatest territorial extent of all empires in human history (nearly a quarter of the earth's land area at its peak), while much of the global power of the United States has literally come from "wings": possessing the world's largest and most technologically-advanced air force, owning by far the most aircraft carriers, and pioneering related technologies such as stealth aircraft, the Space Shuttle, and more recently unmanned drones, which are of increasing strategic importance.[22] The United States has also been an "eagle" in a spiritual sense in that it has been the largest sending nation of missionaries. But after the expensive wars sparked by the 9/11 attacks on the Twin Towers and the 2008 economic crises, the American "Empire" is now also in decline, with its economic and military hegemony being challenged especially by China. Likewise, its spiritual zeal has been greatly weakened through the lures of material wealth, the temptations of the sexual revolution, and doctrinal compromise with the spirit of the age.

Revelation 13:2 describes the Antichrist as having the mouth of a lion. This means that he will be mighty and powerful in speech. It also implies that, like the British Empire, his dominion will be over the entire globe. Just as the lion reigns supreme over all other animals, the Antichrist will be the preeminent and unchallenged ruler of all humanity. But unlike the British Empire, the Antichrist will not need to achieve this through military force. Rather, Revelation 13 indicates that his global dominion will be brought about through spiritual, political, and economic power, reinforced by the demonic supernatural workings of his false prophet.

Second Beast Empire: The Bear

The second beast of Daniel 7 is a bear, which "had three ribs in its mouth between its teeth; and it was told, 'Arise, devour much meat'" (v. 5). Just as England's national animal is the lion, the bear is widely recognized as the national symbol of Russia, beginning with a legend involving Czar Yaroslaw the Wise who reigned in the 11th century. The significance of the bear for Russia's national identity continues as the animal has been chosen as the mascot of the 2014 Olympic winter games in the nation's city of Sochi. In the Bible, bears are depicted as deadly predators that suddenly devour their unsuspecting prey, attacking with blind fury and rage when being provoked (Lamentations 3:10; 2 Kings 2:24; Proverbs 17:12).

For many centuries, Russia was mostly preoccupied with itself and its expansion into the vast territories of the Asian East. Under czars Peter the Great and Catherine the Great, the nation developed into a gigantic global empire that extended its influence from Alaska to central Asia to the borders of Prussia and Austria.[23] Just like the polar bear is the largest land carnivore on earth, Russia became (and still remains) the nation with the largest land area. Because of its size, Russia was never conquered, but rather devoured its enemies as they entered. This happened

Figure 3. Cartoon depicting the Russian bear sitting on the tail of the Persian cat, while the British lion looks on. This is a satirical way to describe the two empire's competition for hegemony in central Asia. Source: Wikimedia Commons.

to Napoleon's army in 1812, whose invasion attempt eventually ended in utter defeat. Similarly, Hitler's *Blitzkrieg* attack in 1942 managed to overtake much of the nation's Western regions but then stalled at the onset of winter. Worn down by the vast distances, overstretched supply lines and the harshness of the weather, the German army was gradually forced to shift into reverse gear.

This became the moment for the Russian bear to arise. Defensive was turned into offensive, and the Soviet army "devoured" all of Eastern Europe, turning its nations into Communist dictatorships, and persecuting its religious groups—Christians and Jews alike. The bear had been aroused and provoked to fury. Through World War II, the Soviet Union became a global superpower and dominated world history for much of the 20th century. But in a sense, the Russian bear had already risen and devoured the flesh of its own people when Joseph Stalin came into power in the

1920s. Back then, Stalin quickly abolished private property ownership and implemented forced collectivization. When the inefficiency and disorganization of such huge social and economic transformation was compounded by a large famine, an estimated 6-8 million Russians died of starvation. Another 6-7 million perished in Stalin's Gulag labor camps or as a result of forced deportations into remote regions. Altogether, up to 15-17 million lives were lost under his rule, and many more thousands died at the hands of the brutal Communist governments that he put in place throughout Eastern Europe, Korea, Cuba, and Africa. Additionally, Stalin began to systematically persecute Jews and suppress Jewish culture after the new state of Israel aligned with the United States.[24]

Communist Russia under Stalin epitomized the Biblical picture of the bear as a merciless and deadly ravager, irrational and untamable in its fury, who ruthlessly and relentlessly devours whatever it can get its claws on. The description of the Antichrist as having "feet [*paws*] … like those of a bear" therefore implies that he will be ferocious and cruel, with little regard for human life, showing no mercy to his prey. When provoked, he will respond with fury and rage, tearing apart his opponents until they are utterly crushed. Like a bear standing on its feet, he will be exceedingly strong, unmovable and unconquerable, able to overcome anything in his way and prevailing in all his purposes. Just as bears have essentially no other animal predators as they themselves are the largest land predator, none of his enemies will be able to stand against him.

Third Beast-Empire: The Leopard and the Nature of the Antichrist

The third beast in Daniel 7 is "like a leopard, which had on its back four wings of a bird; the beast also had four heads, and dominion was given to it" (v. 6). Many commentators believe that the four heads symbolize the four kingdoms into which Alexander the Great's Greek

Empire split after his death. However, in the book of Daniel, the division of an empire into smaller kingdoms is always represented by horns, and the break-up of Greece is specifically depicted as four horns arising from the great horn of the Greek "goat" (Daniel 8:8).[25] No major Western or other nation can unambiguously be identified with a leopard. This challenges us to find appropriate associations elsewhere.

Multiple heads or faces and wings were typical characteristics of ancient near Eastern mythological beings. Babylon's national god Marduk, for example, is depicted with two heads and two wings, and some Babylonian gods had four faces. The description of a leopard with four heads and four wings would certainly have evoked the impression of a supernatural spirit being within the contemporary reader, but not one that could readily be associated with an actual ancient god figure. The identification of this third beast may therefore instead lay in the characteristics of the leopard itself and the spiritual attributes that these characteristics point to.

The leopard is the smallest of the *panthera* animals (leopard, lion, tiger, jaguar), weighing on average less than a third of a lion. Nevertheless, they are just as dangerous as lions. Leopards rely on stealth and agility to make up for their smaller size. Their more petite bodies are complemented by a massive skull with powerful jaw muscles, enabling them to take on prey that is much larger than them. Leopards are cunning and opportunistic hunters, meaning they will only go after their prey when their chances of success are high. They attack under cover of the night, stalking their prey silently, then pouncing on it at the last minute, and strangling its throat with a quick bite. Whereas the other two beasts only make up part of the Antichrist's description (the lion his mouth and the bear his feet), the leopard reflects the Antichrist's entire being. The Antichrist beast is said to be "like a leopard" in his nature and appearance. This matches his depiction in Daniel 7, where he is said to be smaller than the ten preceding horns, yet ends up subduing them all and achieving world domination. Likewise, in Daniel 11 the prince of the covenant

(Antichrist) is said to "practice deception" and "gain power with a small force of people" (v. 23).

The deceptive, leopard-like power behind the Antichrist is the prevailing spirit of the age, the world's dominant philosophy, and it is already becoming quite obvious what that will be: postmodern relativism and tolerance thinking. Postmodernism has its roots, as the name implies, in modernism: the belief that modern (non-traditional) ways of thinking, together with modern science and technology, can change the world for the better so that humans will become progressively more developed. Postmodernism challenges this view, considering it naïve to think that the world is on a path that will only lead from progress to progress. But its own approach is of course greatly shaped by the modernist worldview that it critiques. Ultimately, both modernism and postmodernism are the brainchild of the so-called "age of reason" or enlightenment.

The enlightenment was an intellectual movement that started in 17th century Europe, involving many famous thinkers such as Kant, Voltaire, and Locke, and influencing fathers of the American Revolution such as Benjamin Franklin, Thomas Jefferson, and Thomas Paine. According to Kant, the enlightenment was "mankind's final coming of age," the liberation of humanity from an "immature state of ignorance and error." The aims of the enlightenment movement were in many ways valid and good. It sought to challenge oppressive monarchs, overcome the bondage of superstition, base human progress on the powers of reason and scientific advancement, and promote equality and religious and political freedom. The ultimate outcomes of the enlightenment worldview were modern science, democracy, liberalism, and humanism. Our present world would be entirely unimaginable without the enlightenment movement.

But on the downside, the enlightenment also gave rise to the current arrogance and rebellion against God that increasingly pervades humanity. The essence of humanism is, as the word implies, that everything should center on human beings. As Smith put it, "humanist philosophy displaced God at the centre of all things in favour of the human."[26] The outcome of this process is open rebellion against both God and God-given human authority structures.

This development is now being brought to its logical conclusion with the new generation that is being raised around the world in preparation for the rise of the Antichrist. Children are increasingly being brought up according to an anti-authoritarian worldview that undermines the authority of parents and other authority figures. Rising numbers of countries are banning all forms of physical punishment of children, the primary scriptural method for instilling respect for authority in the young generation and protecting them from rebellious tendencies (Proverbs 13:24; 23:13–14; Hebrews 12:4–11; compare Ephesians 6:1). This is all done with the best of intentions and under the guise of preventing "violence" in the home. But true scriptural spanking is loving discipline and not violence, and neglecting the wisdom of God makes the church increasingly vulnerable to the schemes of the enemy. Another important God-given authority structure that Satan is attacking through the postmodern spirit is that of gender authority structures. God calls men in positions of servant leadership of His spiritual body (the church) and as humble spiritual leaders of their homes. Through notions of gender equality and the unfortunate fact that men have often abused positions of power over women, the enemy is undermining God's unique but different role assignments for men and women. The resulting confusion of gender roles contributes to the breakdown of the family and to a lack of spiritual leadership in Christian homes.

Additionally, the scientific advancements that followed from enlightenment principles enabled the breakthroughs of the industrial revolution. Widespread industrialization facilitated the mass production of goods. However, rather than using these resources for God's glory, humans were now pursuing utilitarianism, the doctrine proposed by enlightenment philosophers John Stuart Mill and Jeremy Bentham, which says that we should do whatever gives us greatest happiness. Utilitarianism provided the foundation for modern theories of economics, which assume that people are utilitarian beings that exist in order to maximize their own pleasures.[27] This utilitarian mindset means that the wealth created by the industrial revolution only fuels the rampant materialism that controls our society.

The ultimate impact of the enlightenment on the culture, society, economy, and technology on the current end times era is aptly summarized in 2 Timothy:

> But realize this, that in the last days difficult times will come. For men will be lovers of self, lovers of money, boastful, arrogant, revilers, disobedient to parents, ungrateful, unholy, unloving, irreconcilable, malicious gossips, without self-control, brutal, haters of good, treacherous, reckless, conceited, lovers of pleasure rather than lovers of God, holding to a form of godliness, although they have denied its power…
>
> (2 Timothy 3:1–5)

All of these predictions are now being fulfilled before our very eyes, as the egotistic utilitarianism, materialism, relativism, and sexual licentiousness of our generation is about to reach its climax.

The Spread and Spiritual Impact of the Third Beast-Empire

One of the most important historic events for the spread of humanist enlightenment was the French Revolution, during which the monarchy was overthrown, the hold of the Catholic Church over society was broken, and liberal values started to permeate all classes of society. The revolution had a profound impact on social and cultural development throughout Europe, also for example influencing Karl Marx and subsequent Marxist and Communist thinkers. The spread of Revolutionist ideals was greatly helped by the rise of Napoleon Bonaparte, a French general who played an active role in the revolutionaries' battle against the king. Within a decade, his armies had overrun almost the entire European continent.

Wherever he went, Napoleon implemented the humanist and secularist values of the French Revolution, closing down churches and monasteries and using them as horse stables or ammunition depots. In many ways, Napoleon spearheaded the secularization of Europe, all in the name of the "religious freedom" that he ostensibly promoted. His policies towards the Jews were especially revealing in this regard: in the name of championing minority religious rights, Napoleon lifted societal restrictions on the Jews, who had been marginalized because of their faith. However, his reason for doing so was not to preserve their culture or faith, but to assimilate them into a secularizing mainstream society:

> [It is necessary to] reduce, if not destroy, the tendency of Jewish people to practice a very great number of activities that are harmful to civilisation and to public order in society in all the countries of the world. It is necessary to stop the harm by preventing it; to prevent it, it is necessary to change the Jews. [...] Once part of their youth will take its place in our armies, they will cease to have Jewish interests and sentiments; their interests and sentiments will be French.[28]

It is amazing how close Napoleon's strategy came to the workings of postmodern tolerance thinking. Postmodern tolerance says that all belief systems are equally valid and right, but in actual practice it fiercely opposes belief systems such as Christianity (or Judaism) that insist on possessing a revelation of God's absolute truth. Today's tolerance will tolerate you if you are also "tolerant"—in the sense of believing that all views are equally true and none is absolutely true. But if you are not, then you will not be "tolerated" either. In theory, you have religious and other "freedom." But in reality, you are expected to assimilate into the postmodern relativistic tolerance worldview.

The modern humanist thinking that arose from the enlightenment served to promote atheism, evolutionism, and naturalism (which denies God's involvement in nature, especially in supernatural ways such as healing); in short, a complete worldview that did away with God in every aspect of human life. But postmodernism, the worldview that arose in reaction to modernism, is a much more sophisticated tool of Satan, and will be just what the Antichrist needs. Arguing against it is like being one who "grasps oil with his … hand" (Proverbs 27:16), because there is almost nothing that it directly denies or confirms. This makes postmodernism so deceptive and so difficult to attack.

Most importantly, the postmodern approach is not only intellectually sophisticated and therefore appealing to the world's elites, but it also has an appearance of virtue and humility. Because postmodern relativism seems to be absolutely "true" (even though it ironically denies the existence of any absolute truth), it is catching on in all strata of society. Postmodernism's core message is that our perception is colored by our worldview, and therefore we can only know truth relative to who we are—but not absolutely. This is of course true from a purely human standpoint, but God is still able to communicate absolute truth to us, because He does not suffer from human limitations. The postmodern worldview therefore portrays any belief system, such as Christianity, that claims to know absolute truth as arrogant and ultimately as dangerous to society. In contrast, its own relativism is deemed to reflect humility, making it essential for human progress and world peace.

Because of these unique characteristics, postmodern relativistic tolerance thinking is the primary way in which "Satan disguises himself as an angel of light" (2 Corinthians 11:14). Rather than being a resurrected Hitler or Stalin, the Antichrist will impress the world with his seemingly humble, peaceful, and tolerant appearance. Already, the belief systems of many theological institutions and church groups have been undermined by postmodern relativism and tolerance demands.

Once the Antichrist has led major numbers of Christians into scriptural and behavioral compromise, he can then portray the persecution of the remaining minority of Bible-believing, "fundamentalist" Christians as an unfortunate "necessity." In reality, however, postmodernism is not virtuous at all. Rather, it is the epitome of lawlessness—the satanic principle that whatever seems right to you is right, implying that one can essentially do what one wants. It is no coincidence that the Antichrist is described as the "man of lawlessness" in 2 Thessalonians 2:3. Postmodernism is therefore the perfect environment in which he can rise to power and unleash his "mystery of lawlessness [that] is already at work" (2 Thessalonians 2:7).

Overall, the four-headed, four-winged leopard perfectly depicts the third postmodernist beast-empire, a global spirit-being that will represent the very nature of the Antichrist. Its four heads symbolize the relativistic, multi-faced nature of the postmodern worldview. The four wings represent not only its spiritual nature, but also its rapid spread and global penetration. And the leopard stands for the agile, cunning, stealthy, and lethal nature of this worldview that will overcome its prey in an unsuspected moment.

The cunning leopard approach—the Antichrist's strategy with which is already now deceiving both the world and much of the church—will be executed with the overpowering, merciless tenacity of a bear and the powerful, impressive roar of a lion. Daniel 7 tells us that he will initially appear to be "small" but will then ultimately be "larger" than all the other kings. He is also said to have "eyes like the eyes of a man" (v. 8), a clear indication that the Antichrist will be a person—a human individual—and not an abstract force, power, entity, or organization (contradicting those who believe that the Internet, "www," will be the Antichrist). His rise to power will be like the attack of the leopard: quiet and stealthy, with people not thinking much of him but then suddenly overpowering the world, and even God's people, when the moment is right.

The Historic Convergence: How all Four Beast-Empires Converged at the Rise of the New World Order

In total, the four beast-empires of Daniel 7 represent successively arising modern European empires (Britain, Russia/USSR, France, and Germany) and their allies (for example, Japan) as well as former and present colonies (U.S., Canada, Australia, India, and much of Africa and Asia). At their peak, these empires controlled almost every nation and people group on the globe. Even China, the only other significant non-European empire since the 17th century (apart from the declining Ottoman Empire, now modern Turkey), was largely under British-European dominion until after World War II.[29] Even though the first French Empire ended with Napoleon's defeat at Waterloo in 1815, France soon expanded its colonial empire (most of which lasted until the 1950s) and continued to be a key player in European and global politics. Together with Germany and Britain, it is a primary influential nation of the European Union, and French is the second official language of the United Nations besides English.

Moreover, all four beast-empires have played a key role in shaping today's political, economic, intellectual and spiritual landscape. We have already outlined Britain's spiritual-intellectual contribution. Germany contributed major thinkers such as Immanuel Kant, Hegel (who influenced Marxism and later postmodern thought), Karl Marx (who inspired the rise of Communism), and many liberal theologians of the 19th century liberalist movement. Perhaps more than any other nation, French philosophers and thinkers have played a pivotal role in the formation of postmodern thought. Especially noteworthy is the social theorist Michel Foucault, who also was a professed homosexual and whose writings had a profound impact on the societal acceptance and recognition of homosexuality.[30]

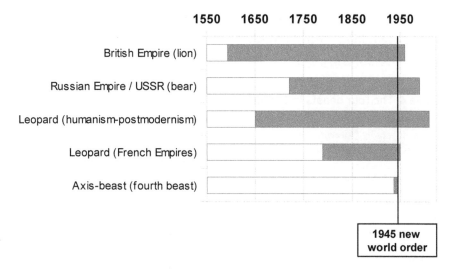

Figure 4. The beast empires of the New World Order

The reason that God revealed exactly these four beast-empires to Daniel is that they all had a crucial part in the great convergence of the 20th century in what was probably the most important global historic event since the fall of the Roman Empire: World War II. Britain (along with the U.S.), Russia, France, and Germany were the key players in this war. But World War II was not just a political but also an ideological and spiritual watershed. Its aftermath created the following:

1. The conditions for the establishment of the current New World Order (UN, EU, IMF, World Bank, G-20)
2. The conditions for the rise of the Antichrist's end times philosophy (postmodernism)
3. The conditions for the return of the Israelites to their own land, culminating in the establishment of Israel in 1948 and therefore the gradual phasing out of the times of the Gentiles. The times of the Gentiles will be fully completed when Jesus returns to rapture all remaining Christians at the late harvest rapture. When

"the fullness of the Gentiles has come in," then God will also fulfill His eternal promise that "all Israel will be saved" (Romans 11:25, 26).

Table 4. The four beasts in Daniel 7 and the empires they represent

Four beasts in Daniel 7	Interpretation as empires	Historic timing (the four empires arose in succession)	Related characteristics of the Antichrist
1st **beast**: lion with eagle's wings that are plucked out	British Empire, which loses the U.S. and then changes its nature during the Victorian era	late 16th century to 1950s[31] (U.S. independence in 1783)	Mouth like a lion: powerful, mighty and charismatic in speech
2nd **beast**: bear that arises to devour much flesh	Soviet Russia under Stalin	Russian Empire: from 1721 (Peter the Great) Stalin's Soviet Union: 1922–1952 (the Soviet Union dissolved in 1991)	Feet like a bear: tenacious, relentless, brutal, merciless, unconquerable, irrational and uncontrollable in his hate and rage
3rd **beast**: leopard with four wings and four heads	Enlightenment movement, giving rise to liberalism and humanism, boosted by the French Revolution and propagated by Napoleon. It culminated in the postmodern movement, including the sexual revolution, which promoted the normalization of homosexuality[32].	*Politically*: French Revolution: 1789–1799 Napoleon's French Empire: 1804–1815 (followed by the French Colonial Empire, which declined after World War II) *Spiritually*: Enlightenment era: from late 17th century *Postmodernism*: beginnings in the 1930s but rose to prominence from the 1950s–1970s and spread into popular culture through the flower power movement and the sexual revolution of the 1960/70s.	He "is like" a leopard: agile, cunning, deceptive, surprises his prey, able to devour powers that are much larger than him. Uses the postmodern worldview to take control and justify the persecution of God's people.
4th **beast**: different and terrible, with iron teeth	The World War II axis powers (especially Hitler's Germany; also Italy and Japan)	German Empire: from 1871 Japanese Empire: from 1868, with Hirohito's aggressive Japanese Empire from 1926 to 1945 Hitler's Germany: 1933–1945	---

Ten horns and a little horn (the Antichrist) that emerge from the 4th beast	"Ten" (a complete or full number) of nations that emerged from the New World Order created by World War II. The Antichrist will subdue three of them (Daniel 7:8, 24).	Since 1945	---

Presently, all four beast-empires still exist. However, their peak has passed, with the last of them, Russia, losing its world empire status in 1991 with the fall of the USSR. The current world is dominated by global superpowers and alliances that either arose as a direct consequence of the fall of the fourth beast-empire or rose to a position of power and influence in the wake of the New World Order that ensued: the United States, the European Union, Russia, China, and emerging developing nations such as India or Brazil.

All of these global players are now members of the G-20 group of nations, which represent the world's politically and economically most powerful countries.[33] Together, the G-20 nations make up more than 80 percent of the world's GDP, 80 percent of world trade, and two thirds of the world's population. This group was founded in 2008 and can truthfully be said to represent post-World War II's New World Order.

But this is not all. The historically-unprecedented event of World War II proved to be a crucial watershed for the rise of the Antichrist in a wide range of aspects, not only politically and economically, but also technologically and culturally. The post-war world became increasingly globalized and interconnected, driven by major advances in technology, production, and infrastructure. The war sparked massive research into computer and space technology. In many ways, the widespread penetration of personal computers, mobile devices, rockets, and satellites all have their roots in research and development efforts that began during the war and continued as a result of the cold war that followed.

Modern communication technologies such as mobile phones, the Internet, and social media platforms such as YouTube and Facebook have enabled the penetration of relativistic postmodern thinking into the farthest corners of the world—even those that formerly used to be so remote that they remained disconnected from the rest of the planet. For example, Tibetan nomads living on the Himalayan plateau now commonly own sophisticated mobile devices that can play music and video clips or access the Internet. Likewise, once-isolated peoples are now equally integrated into the global economy and financial system that has spread around the globe, powered by governments and influential multinational corporations. As a result, the heritage of the convergence of the four beast empires at World War II is a new, globally-interconnected world that is ready and waiting for their "savior," the Antichrist, to take control.

It is our conviction that the advent of the Antichrist is now not a matter of centuries but a matter of a few decades or less. Many generations before us got this one wrong, but now God is clearly speaking to His people and telling them to get ready. The beast sequences of Daniel are pointing to our very day and age. It is unquestionable that we are the "generation" of end times believers that Jesus spoke about: the "generation" that will literally see "these things take place" (Matthew 24:34). Here, we understand "generation"[34] in the broadest sense as those living in the era after World War II and 1948–1967, the age when the times of the Gentiles are drawing to a close. [35]

Jesus told us that "that day and hour no one knows," but He did say that we can know the general season: "Now learn the parable from the fig tree: when its branch has already become tender and puts forth its leaves, you know that summer is near" (v. 32). This spiritual analogy is understood to refer to the national re-establishment of Israel in 1948 (symbolized by the putting forth of leaves), which tells us that its spiritual regeneration is near.[36] Daniel's beast-empire sequences give us a second and perhaps even stronger indication that we are indeed the generation who will "see all these things." Now, time truly is short. We must prepare ourselves to meet Jesus, our heavenly Bridegroom. If we don't prepare now, we risk the fate of the foolish virgins—being excluded from the first rapture. But if we are serious about becoming the true bride of Christ, then we will be like the wise virgins and exuberantly rejoice over our long-anticipated reunion with our Groom.

Chapter 2 Notes

1. The first temple, constructed by Solomon, was destroyed by the Babylonian king Nebuchadnezzar in 587 BC.
2. Research has identified a particular genetic marker that is only present in such descendants. See Randall Price, Jerusalem in Prophecy (Eugene, Oregon: Harvest House Publishers, 1998), 270.
3. As of late 2011, many EU nations are increasingly negatively disposed towards Germany, because Germany's chancellor Angela Merkel has continually rejected the idea of a common Euro-bond debt strategy in order to prop up the financial situation of the EU's financially struggling nations.
4. Gerhard Maier, *Wuppertaler Studienbibel* (Wuppertal: R. Brockhaus, 1993).
5. This will be discussed in more detail in chapter 10.
6. Germany's level of technological development was years ahead of the allies. It is acknowledged that captured German rocket technology enabled the U.S. to significantly speed up its development of the Apollo spacecraft, being a key factor for its ultimate victory in the space race against the Soviet Union.
7. All figures in this paragraph are from the Wikipedia article "World War II casualties," http://en.wikipedia.org/wiki/World_War_II_casualties.
8. "Benelux" stands for *Be*lgium, the *Ne*therlands and *Lux*embourg.
9. Heidi Blake, "Christian preacher arrested for saying homosexuality is a sin," *The Telegraph,* http://www.telegraph.co.uk/news/religion/7668448/Christian-preacher-arrested-for-saying-homosexuality-is-a-sin.html.
10. "Swedish Pastor Sentenced to Month in Prison for Preaching Against Homosexuality," *LifeSiteNews,* http://www.lifesitenews.com/news/archive/ldn/2004/jul/04070505.
11. Just one coin is said to be "lost" in the parable for the sake of the story. Jesus expressed it that way in order to make His point, that if you loose something you will search hard for it. But of course, like in the story of the lost sheep, every single human being is spiritually lost. Those "coins" that are no longer "lost" were therefore "lost" (unsaved) before Christ took hold of them and saved them.

12. This also implies that Daniel 7:9–11 is not the same as the Great White Throne judgment, which occurs in Revelation *after* the millennial kingdom. Rather, it is a special judgment of the beast-empires.

13. John Borneman, *Death of the Father: An Anthropology of the End in Political Authority* (Oxford, New York: Berghahn Books, 2002), 212. Compare the comprehensive Wikipedia entry "Death of Adolf Hitler," http:// en.wikipedia.org/wiki/Death_of_Adolf_Hitler.

14. The Spanish Empire was most likely omitted from the four beast-empires, because by the 1830s, most of its territories had either been seized by another nation or become independent. From the 1650s, its influence in Europe was being eclipsed by France and Britain and later by Prussia/ Germany and Russia. Its last act of global spiritual significance was its participation in the Thirty Years War, where Catholic nations sought to defeat the German protestant states that had arisen from the reformation. This occurred in the mid-17th century. During this war, Spain lost important territories (the Netherlands) and much of its influence in Europe. By the time of World War II, Spain only owned a few overseas territories, and its political, economic, and spiritual influence, even in Europe, was relatively small. Likewise, the former Ottoman Empire had declined significantly since the late 19th century (in fact starting from its defeat by the Russian Empire in 1768–74) and was abolished in 1922 shortly before the establishment of the modern Turkish Republic. The Austro-Hungarian Empire (with Austria and Hungary and core regions) also ended with its defeat in World War I. During World War II, both Spain and Turkey remained neutral and played no significant role in the war or in the New World Order that arose after it, while Austria had been taken over by Hitler. The other empires listed above had already dissolved many centuries before.

15. The Japanese Empire is also indirectly included through the Axis beast even though it did not have as much of a spiritual bearing on God's people.

16. The *Pax Britannica* lasted from 1815–1914.

17. See "Wesleyan Methodists," Spartacus Educational, http://www.spartacus. schoolnet.co.uk/REmethodism.htm.

18. *Strong's Concordance*, H3825.

19. The Cambridge Seven were a group of seven Cambridge university graduates, all from well-known families, who forsook their earthly career opportunities and instead opted to become missionaries to China through Hudson Taylor's CIM (this took place in 1885). The best-known member of this group was C.T. Studd, who gave up his cricket career in order to follow God's call to China.

20. Almost all of its colonies had achieved independence by 1965; most significant was probably India's independence from British rule in 1947.

21. This date marked the beginning of American Imperialism, during which the U.S. acquired substantial numbers of overseas territories (Guam, Puerto Rico, the Philippines, Hawaii, and many other Pacific Islands).

22. The U.S. is far more advanced in the technology of military drones than any other nation.

23. The three ribs that the lying bear devours might indicate the three main directions (east, west, and south) in which the empire expanded.

24. He had initially favored the rise of Israel as an independent nation.

25. The association of heads with kings in Revelation 17:8–10 is about successive kings and not related to an empire splitting up into smaller kingdoms.

26. Warren Smith, ed., *Science Fiction and Organization* (London: Routledge, 2001), 144.

27. In economics, this is referred to as the maximization of an individual's utility.

28. From a letter written on November 29, 1806, to Champagny, Minister of the Interior. Quoted in "Napoleon and the Jews," Wikipedia, http://en.wikipedia.org/wiki/Napoleon_and_the_Jews.

29. China was subdued by Britain during the opium wars starting in the 1840s, with other European empires taking control of major Chinese seaports, and then by the Japanese Empire from 1937 until 1945.

30. Other important French postmodern philosophers include Jacques Derrida, Jean Baudrillard, and Jean-François Lyotard.

31. By the 1950s, most British colonies (notably India) had gained independence, and the empire effectively ceased to exist.

32. Postmodernism is critical of the enlightenment, but that does not change the fact that without the enlightenment movement, postmodernism would not exist. Moreover, core ideals of the enlightenment such as humanism and liberalism are key features of postmodern thinking.

33. The G-20 represents the entire EU even though only four EU nations belong to it. Therefore it effectively includes 43 countries.

34. We do not wish to speculate about the precise length of a generation in Jesus' statement. Jesus explicitly said that we can know the general season but not the hour or day. This excludes us from being able to guess the exact year in which Christ will return. Many who have attempted to predict the year have been utterly shamed by such unscriptural predictions. However, Jesus most certainly wants us to know the season we are in. Therefore, we can discern that we are now in the general "season" of the end times, meaning that the first fruits rapture could occur within a few decades or even within a few years. From Jesus' words, it seems possible that the generation who witnessed the events of 1948 or 1967 will not completely have died out before the first fruits rapture.

35. The end of the Times of the Gentiles will be discussed in more detail in chapter 10.

36. The symbolism of Israel as a fig tree is evident from Jesus cursing the fig tree just before He enters Jerusalem (Matthew 21:18–22). The tree has leaves but is without fruit, which is a picture of Israel being a nation (leaves) but failing to have spiritual fruit (figs). Old Testament references to Israel as a fig tree include Jeremiah 24 and Hosea 9:10.

Chapter 3

We Are the Bride:
What It Means to Be Engaged to Jesus

Then one of the seven angels … came and spoke with me, saying,
"Come here, I will show you the bride, the wife of the Lamb."
Revelation 21:9

God's "Marriage" to His People

The title of this chapter may startle you somewhat. Me, engaged? The fact is, regardless of whether you are single or married, engaged or widowed—if you are a born-again follower of Jesus, you are engaged to Him. More precisely, you are in a phase that the Jews call "betrothal." What does that mean?

From Old Testament times, God chose the image of marriage to describe His unique relationship with His people. In the writings of the prophets, God referred to Himself as a husband, with Israel as His spouse:

> For *your husband is your Maker, whose name is the* LORD *of hosts*; and your Redeemer is the Holy One of Israel, who is called the God of all the earth. "For *the* LORD *has called you, like a wife* forsaken and grieved in spirit, even like a wife of one's youth when she is rejected," says your God.
>
> (Isaiah 54:5–6, emphases added)

Through Jeremiah, God lamented that Israel had become unfaithful like a married woman whoring after other men, and thereby broke their covenant with Him "although I was a husband to them" (Jeremiah 31:32):

I remember concerning you the *devotion of your youth*, the *love of your betrothals*....

... Can a *virgin* forget her ornaments, or a *bride* her attire? Yet My people have forgotten Me days without number....

... And I saw that for all the *adulteries* of faithless Israel, I had sent her away and given her a *writ of divorce* ... she polluted the land and committed *adultery* with stones and trees.

(Jeremiah 2:2, 32; 3:8–9, emphases added)

Because Israel is like a betrothed "virgin" to Him, God compares Israel's idolatry to marital unfaithfulness. In Jewish culture, betrothal was the time between engagement and wedding. In contrast to most Western cultures, during the betrothal period the couple was already legally married and could only be separated by an act of divorce. Even though they could not yet live together nor have sexual relations, they were required to behave toward others as someone who was already married. Consequently, when Israel left the "devotion of [her] youth" and the "love of [her] betrothals" to whore after other gods instead of remaining a faithful virgin, it was an act of adultery, which would invariably result in a "writ of divorce." It was for this very reason that Joseph intended to quietly dissolve his betrothal with Mary, because he wrongly believed that she had committed adultery during their betrothal period (Matthew 1:19). Had this been true, then he would have had every right to put her away. This is what God symbolically did with the nation of Israel when He sent her into exile. But then He later promised through the prophet Hosea:

I will betroth you to Me forever, yes, I will betroth you to Me in righteousness and in justice, in loving kindness and in compassion, and I will betroth you to Me in faithfulness. Then you will know the LORD.

(Hosea 2:19–20, emphasis added)

In the New Testament, we, the church, are also symbolized as a bride, betrothed to Christ. The actual start of our married life with Christ will not occur until the marriage supper of the lamb (Revelation 19) after Christ's return. Meanwhile, we are in the betrothal period and therefore must keep ourselves pure before the Lord. Paul put it this way:

> For I am jealous for you with a godly jealousy; for *I betrothed you to one husband*, so that to Christ I might *present you as a pure virgin*.
>
> (2 Corinthians 11:2, emphases added)

Marriage Covenant and the Betrothal Period

When we look at the Bible, we quickly see that our *entire* relationship with God is closely modeled after the Jewish marriage process. At the very beginning of this process, the father of the groom would select a prospective bride for his son. This is what God does when He sovereignly chooses and calls us, the "elect," to Himself, as Paul wrote: "God has *chosen* you from the beginning for salvation.... It was for this He called you through our gospel" (2 Thessalonians 2:13–14). Once a suitable bride had been identified, the two fathers of the prospective couple would then negotiate the bride price (Hebrew: *mohar*). The bride price compensated the bride's family for the 'loss' of their daughter, who would now belong to the groom and his family. In the same way, Jesus told the people that we used to belong to "our father the devil," and we would only "want to do the desires of your father" (John 8:44).[1] Therefore, Christ had to die on the cross to pay the terrible bride price necessary for redeeming us from Satan's hands (although this price was not actually "paid" to Satan).[2] Consequently, Paul tells the saints that "you are not your own [f]or you have been *bought with a price*" (1 Corinthians 6:19–20). It is only because Christ paid this price that we have been set free from bondage to the devil and now literally belong to Jesus, not to ourselves!

Before the betrothal period (*erusin*) came the engagement ceremony (*shiddukhin*), where the groom would offer the bride a cup of wine, called *kiddush* (lit. meaning "sanctification"). The bride would then, as a symbol of her acceptance of the groom's offer of marriage, drink the cup, and the marriage covenant was thus sealed. This is exactly what we do when we take communion: by drinking the cup of wine, we seal and then continually commemorate the New Covenant (betrothal) with Christ, because His blood is the "blood of the covenant" (Matthew 26:28). Then, it was common for the bride to take a full immersion bath (*mikvah*) as a symbol of spiritual cleansing.[3] Equally, we Christians enter into and confirm our discipleship through the act of baptism by full immersion into water, which symbolizes the death of our old nature and the spiritual birth of the new nature that God gives us: "Therefore we have been buried with Him through baptism into death..." (Romans 6:4). It is in baptism that we are symbolically "born [again] of water and the Spirit" (John 3:5).

After these symbolic acts, both parties would sign the marriage covenant (*ketubah*). The presence of two male witnesses was required to make the covenant legally valid. This is why Moses and Elijah appeared at the Mount of Transfiguration, together with Jesus (the "groom") and three of His most intimate disciples (who represented the bride, the future church). God Himself, the father of the groom, also showed His presence through the voice out of the cloud (Matthew 17:5), meaning that all required parties for the establishment of the marriage covenant were present. In Revelation 11, it is prophesied that two witnesses will again appear to testify to the world about the New Covenant between Jesus and His bride. It is likely that these will again be Moses (as giver of the law) and Elijah, who is considered to be the greatest prophet and also predicted to come again before the Day of the Lord in Malachi 4:5.[4]

The end of the engagement ceremony marked the formal beginning of the betrothal period. Now, the groom would return to his home to prepare a wedding chamber (*chuppah*) for the bride. This chamber would typically be in his father's house. Jesus made this very promise to the disciples when He said:

> In My Father's house are many dwelling places ... I go to prepare a place for you. If I go and prepare a place for you, I will come again and receive you to Myself.
>
> (John 14:2–3)

Before the groom's departure, he would offer the bride a bridal gift (*matan*) as a pledge of his love and commitment to her. Christ's bridal present to His church is the Holy Spirit in our hearts, "who is given as a pledge of our inheritance" (Ephesians 1:14; see also 2 Corinthians 1:22).

The bride would use the time before the groom's return to prepare herself for married life. This would include sewing the wedding dress and sharpening her homemaking skills. Significantly, one of the terms used by the Jews for the betrothal period is *kiddushin*, which means "sanctification" or "set apart." In the same way, our present task is to allow God to prepare us spiritually for reigning with Christ in His Kingdom, where we will humbly submit to our Lord, just like the Jewish bride would humbly submit to and serve her husband.[5] But instead of making our own wedding garments, God has already "clothed [us] with garments of salvation" (Isaiah 61:10), garments which we are unable to provide for ourselves. Our responsibility is to abide in Christ in order to keep them pure and spotless, "without stain or reproach until the appearing of our Lord Jesus Christ" (1 Timothy 6:14), just like the overcoming saints in Sardis who "have not soiled their garments." Thankfully, each time we stumble, we can come to the cross to let the blood of Jesus wash them white again. But it is up to us to humble ourselves and come to the cross and receive continual renewal:

[B]ut if we walk in the Light as He Himself is in the Light, we
have fellowship with one another, and the blood of Jesus His
Son cleanses us from all sin.

(1 John 1:7)

Coming for Marriage: The Return of the Groom

After about one year, the groom would then return to take his bride
to the wedding ceremony (*nissuin*). First, however, his father would have
to approve of his wedding preparations, examining whether the living
arrangements for the new couple were complete. Only then could
the groom embark on the trip to fetch his bride. Likewise, Jesus said
about the time of His coming that "no one knows, not even the angels
of heaven, nor the Son, but the Father alone." (Matthew 24:36). The
groom's arrival at the home of the bride would usually take place at
nighttime. The groom, his friends and two male witnesses would leave
the groom's father's house and conduct a torch light procession to the
home of the bride. In theory, the groom was expected to snatch away his
bride, secretly 'stealing' her as an act of surprise. Because of this, the bride
was traditionally obligated to have a lamp full of oil ready by her bed
throughout the night. In reality, however, the bride and her bridesmaids
were alerted to the coming of the groom by the shout of the groom's
best man, who would run ahead of the procession, and by the blowing of
ram's horns (*shofar*). This would give her and her attendants the chance
to quickly get ready.

In contrast, Jesus' gathering of the first fruits will be a quieter affair.
In Matthew 24:43, he likens it to a thief breaking into a house. Rather
than a shout that will rouse the whole world as at the late harvest rapture
when "every eye will see," the first fruits gathering of the Lord will be
more like a "thief in the night" (Luke 12:39; 1 Thessalonians 5:2) or a
subtle knock on the door: "Behold, I stand at the door and knock. If
anyone hears My voice and opens the door, I will come in to him and

dine with him, and he with Me." (Revelation 3:20). The dining that Jesus talks about here is the heavenly marriage supper, a prophetic promise that those who hear His subtle call and open the door will in turn get an open door that leads them straight to the heavenly wedding banquet.

A similar picture is found in Luke 12:35–37. Here, Jesus calls us to be like servants who are waiting for their master's return, keeping our "lamps lit" (like the ten virgins!), and ready to "immediately open the door to him when he comes and knocks." If the servants faithfully open when the master knocks, He makes the astonishing promise that the master will then "gird himself to serve, and have them recline at the table, and will come up and wait on them." Again, we have a picture of the wedding banquet, but this time it will be Jesus serving and honoring us, His servants! Like in Matthew 24, Jesus then compares His coming to a thief breaking into a house, again suggesting that the rapture of those who are ready and prepared will be like a quiet stealing away. In contrast, His coming for the late harvest will be a public spectacle, witnessed by "all tribes of the earth" (Matthew 24:30).

But what about the shout in the parable of the ten virgins? Is that not the shout depicted in 1 Thessalonians 4:16? The contexts show that this cannot be the case. In the 1 Thessalonians passage, it says that Christ will "descend with a shout [Gr. *keleusma*[6]]." The Greek term here signifies a shout of command, as that of a commander to his army, and only occurs this one time in the New Testament. In the Septuagint, the Greek version of the Old Testament, this word is found in Proverbs 30:27, where it says that the "locusts … advance [*keleusma*] in ranks." The results of Christ's *keleusma* shout of command and the attendant trumpet call are seen in Matthew 24:31, where it says that he "will send forth His angels … to gather together His elect." This shout will initiate a complex global operation that is carried out by sovereign force. Here, it is not a matter of choice, because all those who are saved—all the "elect" who are left—will be gathered to escape the wrath, regardless of their state of alertness or readiness.

In contrast, the word for "shout" in the parable of the ten virgins is the Greek term *krauge*[7], which refers to an outcry, either in anger, or in distress or grief. In the Septuagint, *krauge* is widely used to describe the cries of those in tribulations and sufferings—for example, those of the Israelites or other nations as a result of God's judgment on them (see Jeremiah 14:2; 18:22; 30:15; 48:5). Elisabeth also employs this shout when she bursts forth into blessings as she sees Mary, who is pregnant with her Savior (Luke 1:42). The *krauge* shout is therefore an emotional outcry, expressing intense feelings or communicating urgent messages. In a Jewish wedding such as the one depicted in Matthew 25, this shout would not be issued by the groom himself, but by his best man, who would run ahead of the groom's procession. The shout that alerts the ten virgins to the groom's coming will therefore *not come from Jesus*, and consequently cannot be the shout of command described in 1 Thessalonians 4:16. Instead, it will come from His forerunners.

Who will Jesus "best men" be? His first coming gives us some clear indications. John the Baptist, who announced Jesus' coming to the Jews, said about himself, "I am a voice of one crying in the wilderness, 'Make straight the way of the Lord'" (John 1:23). He was the voice, the "shout" that alerted the people of God to the impending arrival of their Savior and challenged them to prepare themselves. In the same way, the "best men" that announce Christ's future coming are chosen men and women of God, prophets and teachers, who give the bride of Christ a final warning, announcing the last opportunity to consecrate themselves for Jesus' return. Their "shouting" has already started, and the time for us to get ready to meet our Lord is gradually running out!

After arriving at the bride's home, the groom and his friends would then lead her and the bridesmaids back to his father's house. During this joyful procession, the bride would be treated like royalty, being carried in a litter and wearing a diadem on her head. When the bridegroom approached the wedding ceremony site, the cantor would chant "Blessed is he who comes!" In the same way, when Jesus wept over Jerusalem, he prophesied that they would not see Him again until they would say, "Blessed is he who comes in the name of the LORD" (Luke 13:35). With these words He therefore indicated that one day His people would welcome Him as their eternal bridegroom.

Before the onset of the festivities, the groom and bride would retreat to the wedding chamber and consummate the marriage, while the guests waited outside. Soon after, the groom would emerge from the chamber with evidence of the virginity of the bride, and the celebrations would begin. The bride would remain in seclusion in the chamber and only be brought out toward the end of the festivities, which would usually last for seven full days. In the same way, Christ, our husband-to-be, will return to receive His virgin bride, the church, and take them to His father's "house." There, the "marriage supper of the Lamb" will be fully prepared, and the hosts of heaven will anticipate our glorious arrival. Our marriage with Jesus will be "consummated" as we enjoy unprecedented and unhindered intimacy with our Savior. Following the Jews wedding traditions, we, the bride, will not come out for the marriage supper described in Revelation 19 until the ending of the 7 years of the 70th week, just before we ride with our Groom to the battle of Armageddon.

During the seven-day festivities, food, wine, music and dance were freely offered to the guests. This is why it was such an embarrassment for the groom when the wine ran out at the wedding in Cana and so significant that Jesus turned the water to wine. This first miracle of His ensured that the wedding festivities could continue and the reputation of the groom and his family would not be tarnished (John 2:1–11).[8] If Jewish wedding banquets are the just a "shadow of heavenly things" (Hebrews 8:5), then the heavenly marriage banquet will be a joyous feast beyond our wildest imaginations! As it is written:

Eye has not seen, nor ear heard,

nor have entered into the heart of man,

the things which God has prepared for those who love Him.

(1 Corinthians 2:9 NKJV)

In heaven, our new life as the married bride will come to full fruition as we live with Jesus, and He with us in our midst, for all eternity:

And I saw the holy city, new Jerusalem, coming down out of heaven from God, made ready as a bride adorned for her husband. And I heard a loud voice from the throne, saying, "Behold, the tabernacle of God is among men, and He will dwell among them, and they shall be His people, and God Himself will be among them."

(Revelation 21:2–3)

The traditional Jewish marriage process consisted of three main parts, which are directly equivalent to elements in our Christian walk, as shown in Table 5.

Table 5. Jewish wedding customs compared with our Christian life

	Jewish Wedding Custom	Our Christian Life
1st	Engagement ceremony	Spiritual rebirth when we accept Jesus as Lord and Savior (salvation)
2nd	Betrothal period ("sanctification")	Our current Christian walk on earth (sanctification)
3rd	Wedding ceremony	Our glorious reunion with Christ at the heavenly banquet (glorification)

Our present relationship with Jesus is that of a bride to her husband-to-be. Our present responsibility is to keep ourselves sanctified and pure throughout our betrothal period, until our heavenly Groom comes to take us to His house.

Interpreting the Parable of the Ten Virgins

With this background, we can now begin to fully appreciate the deep meanings that Jesus expressed through the parable of the ten virgins. We know that the parable speaks of the return of the groom at the end of the betrothal period. He is coming to lead his bride to the wedding banquet. At first, the parable seems strangely incomplete—it features all the aspects of a traditional Jewish wedding, except for the bride! The parable only mentions "virgins" who function as bridesmaids. But we must remember that this is about Christ coming for His church. There is therefore not one single bride, but ten "virgins" (Gr. *parthenos*[9]). The number ten is often used in the Bible to express fullness or completeness. Here, it symbolizes the entire church, and a virgin represents someone who is about to reach a marriageable age and should therefore be preparing for marriage. The absence of the bride in the parable therefore simply highlights the fact that it is the ten virgins who are, symbolically, getting married to the coming groom.

The overarching theme of the parable is that of preparing for the moment when the groom comes. From the Jewish marriage analogy discussed above, it is also evident that all ten virgins are born-again believers: all are betrothed to the groom, meaning they drank the wine of the New Covenant, entering into it by faith alone, and all carry oil lamps, which in the Old Testament tabernacle symbolized the continual presence of God by His Spirit (Exodus 27:20–21; also Zechariah 4). Because the Holy Spirit only dwells in those who have accepted Christ as their Savior, and those who once had saving faith are eternally secure in Christ, all ten virgins are headed toward eternity with God. Not only does Jesus say in John 3:36 that "He who believes in the Son has [present tense] eternal life," but in John 10:28 He affirms regarding His "sheep" that "I give eternal life to them, and they will never perish; and no one will snatch them out of My hand" (strong double negative in the Greek). The eternal security of believers also comes from the eternal, indestructible character of the newborn spirit nature that believers receive, which is discussed in chapter 8.

Just like in a real wedding in those times, the groom in the parable is delayed, and the ten virgins become tired and weary from waiting. It says that they all "slumbered and slept" (NKJV). This expression carries a deeper meaning, for even though this whole phrase might apply to all ten virgins, it is equally possible that the five wise "slumbered" (Gr. *nystazo*,[10] to nod, become drowsy, drop off to sleep), while the foolish ones "slept" (Gr. *katheudo*,[11] to sleep or have died). *Katheudo* is also used to describe the unbelievers in the last days, who "do their sleeping [*katheudo*] at night, and those who get drunk get drunk at night." (1 Thessalonians 5:7). Likewise, it is the word that Jesus employed when he found the disciples "sleeping [*katheudo*], for their eyes were very heavy" in the garden of Gethsemane on the night of His betrayal (Mark 14:40). In contrast, the Greek term for "slumbered" only occurs twice in the New Testament, and only in the parable of the ten virgins is it used to describe nodding off into slumber (the NASB translates it as "got drowsy").

This scriptural comparison therefore indicates that these two expressions may potentially denote two very different states of resting. The wise virgins become drowsy and rest but are still spiritually alert, while the foolish virgins are more like the immature disciples the day before they would fearfully desert their captured Lord: engaged in a deep spiritual state of sleep that comes from a lack of maturity and compromise with an ungodly world. Paul even uses the very word *katheudo* to warn the saints against drifting off into spiritual sleepiness through involvement in "unfruitful deeds":

> Do not participate in the unfruitful deeds of darkness, but instead even expose them; for it is disgraceful even to speak of the things which are done by them in secret. But all things become visible when they are exposed by the light, for everything that becomes visible is light. For this reason it says,

"Awake, sleeper [*katheudo*],

And arise from the dead,

And Christ will shine on you."

Therefore be careful how you walk, not as unwise men but as wise, making the most of your time, because the days are evil.

(Ephesians 5:11–16)

Next, the coming of the groom is announced with a shout, and the bridal party knows that the great moment they have so anxiously anticipated has come. After all this waiting, it is suddenly time to get up and greet the groom and his party! But alas, this is also the dreadful moment when the differences between the virgins come to the light. Now, it becomes so evidently clear who has been wisely preparing and who has been preoccupied foolishly with other things. The mistake made by the foolish virgins is in failing to bring extra vessels of oil. The lamps the virgins would carry outside the home were sticks with strips of cloth that had been dipped in oil wrapped around them. It was common knowledge that these oily wraps could only burn for a short while and therefore needed frequent replacement. The oversight of the foolish virgins was therefore in failing to do the blatantly obvious. Bringing extra oil was a known necessity, something that a responsible bridesmaid would certainly not forget to do! Moreover, the parable implies that oil could be purchased easily, meaning that the fault of not procuring some was entirely with the foolish virgins.

But instead of taking responsibility for their actions and hurriedly going out to obtain extra oil, the reaction of these imprudent attendants is to try to persuade their wise companions to share their oil supplies. But the prudent virgins wisely refuse this brazen request. Because the way to the groom's house is long, the shared oil reserves would not last, and the procession would soon be enveloped in darkness when all of the ten virgins' lamps went out. This would be disastrous, because bridal processions were an extremely important aspect of Jewish culture.[12] The foolish virgin's appeal is effectively an invitation to follow them into spiritual compromise. If the wise virgins conceded, the groom's joyful wedding procession would be enveloped in utter darkness, which we can take as symbolic for spiritual darkness. If all believers dilute their "oil," Jesus would effectively be left with a spiritually "dark" church where no one is ready to meet Him. Rather than acting selfishly, the wise virgins therefore rightly tell their foolish companions to go and "buy some for yourselves" instead of sharing that which cannot and should not be shared (v. 9). Their refusal is an act of great wisdom.

In order to understand the severity of the mistake made by the foolish virgins, its spiritual consequences, and why and how the "oil" for our spiritual "lamps" must be bought, we need to examine the various ways that oil was symbolic in the Old Testament. Under the Old Testament law, oil played two different roles. Firstly, the Israelites were to keep a lampstand in the Holy Place, upon which olive oil lamps were to "burn continually" (Exodus 27:20–21) without interruption. This was a symbol of the perpetual presence of God. It was essential to keep the lamps burning at all times. Secondly, they were to mix together a special "anointing oil," to be used to consecrate the "tabernacle and all that is in it" so that it would be holy (Exodus 40:9; also 30:22–33). Similarly, the priests were anointed with oil (Exodus 29:7). Later on, Israel's kings were anointed in the same way, such as when Samuel anointed David to be king (1 Samuel 16:12–14). The anointing with oil signified that someone was especially chosen, set apart and empowered by God to serve Him in a particular and important role.

Likewise, we believers "have an anointing from the Holy One," and we are told that "His anointing teaches you about all things, and is true and is not a lie" (1 John 2:27). This anointing in us that teaches us the truth about God is none other than the Holy Spirit, about whom Jesus said:

But when He, the Spirit of truth, comes, He will guide you
into all the truth; for He will not speak on His own initiative,
but whatever He hears, He will speak; and He will disclose to
you what is to come.

(John 16:13)

The psalmist knew this truth when he wrote, "Your word is a lamp
to my feet and a light to my path." (Psalm 119:105). His words also link
the work of the Spirit back to the lampstand, whose light symbolizes the
work of the Spirit in us when He illuminates the Word of God to us.

Apart from revealing truth, the Spirit also empowers us in our
Christian walk. Jesus described the Holy Spirit as a "helper" (John 16:7)
and a source of "power" (Acts 1:8). Even a cursory look at the book of
Acts and the Epistles shows the central role of God's Spirit in our ability
to follow Christ and bear fruit for Him. Here again, the Spirit is linked
with oil, as James exhorts the elders of the church to anoint sick persons
with oil as they pray for them (James 5:14), with the oil being figurative
for the healing power of the Holy Spirit.

As with the symbolic act of anointing priests and kings in the Old
Testament with oil, the "oil" of the Spirit represents firstly, our ability to
carry out God's will in God's strength, and secondly, to be sanctified and
holy, set apart and ready to do God's work in God's time. Because "His
commandments are not burdensome" (1 John 5:3), we know that we can
pursue our daily walk in the "joy of the Lord [which] is your strength"
(Nehemiah 8:10). And what is our source of joy? The Psalmist exclaims
that "God has anointed you with the oil of gladness" (Psalm 45:7),
thereby saying that the Spirit ("oil") is where our "gladness" comes from.
It is only when we gladly carry the "yoke [that] is easy and [the] burden
[that] is light" (Matthew 11:30) that our lives are a living testimony to
the abundant blessings which we have received. Running out of oil is
therefore not just a picture of a lack of works, but of a lack of works
done for God and in God, enabled by Him alone, works that bring glory

to Him and not to men. Human works that are done without the Spirit quickly run dry and come to a grinding halt. Even when they seem to bear fruit, they only lead to pride and self–righteousness.

Consequently, when the foolish virgins are said to run out of oil as their "lamps are going out" (v. 8), there is no doubt that they are running out of the power and anointing of the Holy Spirit, which is the only source that can continually quicken their own newborn spirits. Therefore, their works not only diminish greatly, they also become legalistic and self-glorifying, giving the foolish virgins a source of identity and reputation that should only be rooted in Christ. Here, we should not press the analogies given by the parable too far. Rather than saying that the foolish virgins ran out of Holy Spirit power right when Jesus returned, the emphasis of the parable lies on their lack of preparation over the course of their entire Christian life. Maybe they failed to focus on their spiritual growth early on, or maybe they once ran strong in the "race" and were headed for the "prize" but then failed to "run with endurance" (Hebrews 12:1), no longer running in "such a way that you may win" (1 Corinthians 9:24). Maybe they were once passionate but then grew weary and distracted, gradually losing sight of the reason, the motivation, and the goal that we are all called to pursue. This is why God exhorts us to run the race all the way until the finish line:

> Therefore, since we have so great a cloud of witnesses surrounding us, let us also lay aside every encumbrance and the sin which so easily entangles us, and let us run with endurance the race that is set before us, fixing our eyes on Jesus, the author and perfecter of faith.... For consider Him who has endured such hostility by sinners against Himself, *so that you will not grow weary and lose heart.*
>
> (Hebrews 12:1–3, emphasis added)

Here, it is significant that the Greek word for wise, *phronimos*,[13] comes from the verb *phroneo*, to think or to set one's mind on something. In Romans 8:5, Paul writes: "For those who are according to the flesh set their minds [*phroneo*] on the things of the flesh, but those who are according to the Spirit, [set their minds on] the things of the Spirit." Likewise, in Colossians 3:2, he exhorts us to "set your mind [*phroneo*] on the things above, not on the things that are on earth." The wisdom of the wise therefore lies in their correct focus, in setting their minds on "things above," whereas the foolish (Gr. *moros*,[14] foolish, stupid, senseless, or dull) lack both knowledge and the discernment of what is truly important. They are like the seed "which fell among the thorns," like those who "have heard" but whose spiritual life is "choked with worries and riches and pleasures of this life." As a consequence, they "bring no fruit to maturity" (Luke 8:14–15).

What It Means to "Buy Oil"

In the parable, the wise tell the foolish to "buy" more oil. Can the Holy Spirit be bought for money, as Simon foolishly assumed and received a sharp rebuke from Paul for such a carnal suggestion (Acts 8:18–24)? Certainly not! But in Isaiah, God calls out to His people to buy from Him:

> Every one who thirsts, come to the waters; And you who have no money come, buy and eat. Come, buy wine and milk without money and without cost. Why do you spend money for what is not bread, and your wages for what does not satisfy? Listen carefully to Me, and eat what is good, and delight yourself in abundance.
>
> (Isaiah 55:1–2)

Here, God is not actually thinking of a regular monetary transaction. His invitation is to those "without money" and the purchasing is done "without cost." The "money" that the Israelites have can only buy them that "what does not satisfy." In contrast, the "abundance" that His people should delight in, the fullness of God's blessings and grace, is not something that we can obtain by giving something to a God who already owns everything. Before God, the richest of us are like those "who have no money," because riches cannot buy that which God freely gives. Yet Proverbs 23:23 exhorts us to "buy truth, and ... get wisdom," and to lukewarm Laodicea, Jesus says:

> I advise you to buy from Me gold refined by fire so that you may become rich, and white garments so that you may clothe yourself, and that the shame of your nakedness will not be revealed; and eye salve to anoint your eyes so that you may see.
>
> (Revelation 3:18)

Even though Laodicea was materially-speaking a very wealthy church, Jesus calls them "poor and blind and naked" (v. 17). The city of Laodicea was actually extremely rich due to its garment manufacturing and its well-known medicines – especially its eye salve! So Jesus' words are full of irony: even though the believers there were well-off, well-dressed, and well-treated, they lacked spiritual riches. The "gold refined by fire" is a reference to the fiery trials by which we must be tested and refined. This is a picture of the sanctification of the believer, of dying to our old self so that the life of Christ may grow in us. Eye salve refers to having a spiritual, rather than worldly or carnal, outlook on life: "for we walk by faith, not by sight" (2 Corinthians 5:7).

All scriptural references to "buying" from God are therefore a picture of sanctification: He invites us to buy spiritual riches, spiritual values, and a spiritual mindset to replace our worldly worldviews. But this "buying" is addressed to those "without money," and the goods we are called to "buy" carry no price tags! This signifies that, just like the free gift of salvation, sanctification is also something that we cannot achieve except by the grace of God. Jesus said, "I am the vine, you are the branches; he who abides in Me and I in him, he bears much fruit, for apart from Me you can do nothing" (John 15:5). But spiritual fruit is something that we must want and actively pursue. Even that which is free cannot be obtained without us getting up and leaving our comfort zones in order to go and receive it. Christ's invitation to "buy" from Him therefore means to pursue a spiritually fruitful and righteous walk with Him. Only in Jesus can we be fruitful and grow in sanctification, but if we do not follow His invitation and "take up [our] cross daily" (Luke 9:23), then we will miss out on the spiritual riches and eternal rewards that He has in store for us. This is why the wise virgins refused to share their oil: the daily anointing and filling of the Spirit is not something that can be shared. Each one of us must come to Christ daily and personally obtain it from Him, freely and "without cost." This is precisely what the foolish virgins failed to do, and it was the main reason why they were so woefully unfit to meet their heavenly Groom.

We are Betrothed: What Jesus Rightly Expects from Us When He Returns

The Jewish marriage process and the parable of the ten virgins therefore give us a picture of the expectations that Christ has towards us when He returns to lead us to the marriage supper. Just like the ten virgins, we, the bride of Christ, are in the *kiddushin*, the betrothal period of sanctification:

> For I am *jealous* for you with a *godly jealousy*; for *I betrothed you to one husband*, so that to Christ I might *present you as a pure virgin*.
>
> (2 Corinthians 11:2, emphases added)

The primary focus of our betrothal period is two-fold: firstly, to prepare for married life, and secondly, to remain pure and set apart for our husband-to-be. Both of these are intimately linked: we can only prepare for life with Christ in eternity by staying pure and single-minded, and we will only remain in such a sanctified state when we are continually focused on getting ready for life in eternity. Just imagine in what condition a groom would like to find his bride when he comes for her. What would he think if he would find her being intimate with other men? What if she was so preoccupied with other tasks, hobbies, or interests that she was totally unprepared to meet him? What if she did not even look forward to his coming and greeted him with an air of indifference? What if she felt that his coming presented an unwelcome interruption of her carefree, single lifestyle that she had been enjoying so much? The groom would have spent an entire year exerting all his energies to prepare a most beautiful wedding chamber and save up for a lavish banquet. Realizing how little affection his bride has for him and how little effort she had put into her wedding preparations would break his heart and cause him profound sadness. This is why God is a jealous God, desiring all our affections and wanting to be our one and only focus—not for His sake, but for ours! A bride who does not have her whole heart set on being joined to her husband-to-be is the greatest disappointment a groom can imagine.

Returning to our parable, what therefore happens to the foolish virgins? They hurry away to "buy" some last-minute sanctification. But in reality, shops would have been long closed by then. We all know that our walk with Christ is a marathon and not a dash and that it is too late to get "oil" when Christ is already knocking at the door. The intention to "buy oil" at midnight is nothing but a futile act of desperation. While the foolish virgins are gone, the bridegroom comes, and the wedding starts. Significantly, it says that the "door was shut" (v. 10). This is where the imagery of the parable now entirely departs from customary wedding traditions. The closed door carries a solely spiritual meaning: it carries the meaning of being "too late" as the consequence of unreadiness.

We have all gone through a door before, the *door of salvation*: "I am the door; if anyone enters through Me, he will be saved, and will go in and out and find pasture." (John 10:9). But this door is different. It is the *door of readiness*, of overcoming, which, unlike salvation and eternity in heaven, is not guaranteed to all believers. Only the first fruits from Revelation 14, who by God's enabling keep themselves pure and undefiled for their coming Groom, will get in. This overcomer door actually opens both ways, because it also depends on us hearing the voice of the Master and opening. In Luke 12, we believers are exhorted to be "like men who are waiting for their master when he returns from the wedding feast, so that they may immediately open the door to him when he comes and knocks." (v. 36). Similarly, to Laodicea the Lord says: "Behold, I stand at the door and knock; if anyone hears My voice and opens the door, I will come in to him and will dine with him, and he with Me" (Revelation 3:20). The picture of the door therefore symbolizes the fact that our wedding with Christ is a *mutual act*: He returns for us, but we must also be willing to come with Him. He comes and knocks, but we must hear and open the door. When this opportunity has passed we cannot run after Him and expect to be let in. Likewise, the foolish virgins end up in front of a closed door. What does this closed door signify?

The argument of this book is that there will be two raptures, symbolized by the harvest of the first fruits and the late harvest (more details on this in subsequent chapters). The first act of a Jewish wedding ceremony was the entrance of groom and bride into the wedding chamber, where they would consummate the marriage. The bride was required to be a true virgin who had never defiled herself with sexual relations (unless of course she was a widow), and this virginity had to be proven to the waiting parents and wedding guests immediately afterward. But Jesus will do it differently. He will spare His unready virgins (who did not remain pure "virgins") the shame of being exposed as impure.

Rather, only true virgins will be raptured at this point, and only they get to consummate the marriage right at the beginning of the seven "days" (the seven years of the 70th week).

The closed door in the parable means that the "foolish virgin" believers are initially shut out and have to spend the cold, dark night on the streets, where dogs and all kinds of unruly people roam freely. A picture of this, although in a different context, is given in Revelation 22:15: "Outside are the dogs and the sorcerers and the immoral persons and the murderers and the idolaters...." The chilling, gloomy night outside represents the hard times in the tribulations of the 70th week of Daniel, along with the unbelieving world.

But unlike the sorcerers and the immoral, who are depicted as being shut out of heaven, the foolish virgins are still saved. Their betrothal to their Lord remains eternally secure, and He will be closer to them than ever throughout all their trials. Before the cold night is over, they will be let in at the "second or third" watch of the night (Luke 12:38), at late harvest rapture (in the traditional Jewish division of a night into three watches, the coming of the groom in the parable of the ten virgins would have been toward the end of the first watch). As dawn breaks, "every tear" is wiped away. Then, as refined and spotless virgins, they will also have that special time of intimacy with their groom as their marriages are consummated. The foolish virgins are finally reunited with the wise, "marry" their Lord, and also get to share in the joys of the heavenly banquet.

Are we the first to propose the first fruits rapture perspective? Is there more scriptural evidence for the first fruits rapture than the parable of the ten virgins? What did the early church believe? How did the church's views on the end times develop and change throughout history? When we dig deeper, we see how God is progressively restoring His end times truth—a truth that the enemy sought to cover up during the darker times of church history—but that is now being brought into the light.

Will "Foolish Virgin" Believers Completely Miss the Heavenly Banquet?

Advocates of a partial or conditional rapture (first fruits rapture) often argue that foolish virgin believers are completely shut out of the heavenly marriage banquet and will only enter the eternal state after the millennial reign of Christ.[15] But there are two strong arguments against such a view. Firstly, the marriage banquet is one of the most significant moments in a believer's life. It is the act that finalizes the betrothal process and marks the beginning of our actual "marriage" to Jesus. As we have seen, our relationship with Christ is closely modeled after the Jewish marriage process. To think that a believer would miss out on the second most important event in the entire process (the most crucial one being the moment we were born-again) is inconceivable—it would mean that part of the bride of Christ won't actually get married to her groom!

Secondly, Revelation 20:4 talks about those "who had not worshiped the beast or his image, and had not received the mark on their forehead and on their hand; and they came to life and reigned with Christ for a thousand years." Now, Revelation 14 clearly states that those who will worship the beast or his image will face the full wrath of God, as well as eternal torment in hell. Therefore, it follows that those who are saved and will enter heaven must not have engaged in such worship, including all foolish virgin believers who had to go through the tribulations of the 70th week. Because those who refused such worship are promised to reign with Christ, the foolish virgins will also participate in His rule. Because Revelation 2:26–27 says that only overcomers will reign with Christ, it follows that the foolish virgins will, through the refining fires of tribulation, finally have become overcomers. This is confirmed by Revelation 21:7: "He who overcomes will inherit these things [eternity with God], and I will be his God and he will be My son." The implication of this verse is that only those who have overcome will inherit eternity and be with God forever. Ultimately, therefore, all those who are saved will be overcomers, meaning they will have performed "righteous acts" that will constitute their wedding garment at the heavenly marriage banquet.

Further confirmation comes from the Jewish harvest feast cycle: the Feast of Ingathering is followed by seven days of rejoicing before the Lord (Leviticus 23:40). This is a picture of the joyous heavenly wedding banquet, at which both first fruits and late harvest grains will together delight themselves in the glorious splendor of their divine groom. However, based on Luke 12:37 and 14:8, it would appear that those who have walked more closely with their Lord may receive special honors and occupy more distinguished seats at this banquet.

Chapter 3 Notes

1. Here, Jesus does not refer to people who are destined to hell. We all were once slaves to sin and therefore were effectively children of the devil. This is made clear by the fact that Jesus' words in John 8:44 were addressed to "those Jews who had believed Him" (v. 31). Likewise, Paul wrote, "For He rescued us from the domain of darkness, and transferred us to the kingdom of His beloved Son..." (1 Colossians 1:13). "And you were dead in your trespasses and sins, in which you formerly walked according to the course of this world, according to the prince of the power of the air, of the spirit that is now working in the sons of disobedience" (Ephesians 2:1–2).
2. The comparison here with the Jewish betrothal agreement does have limits, because Jesus' atonement for us was not a mutual agreement between God and Satan. Rather, God sovereignly redeemed us, and Jesus paid the price of redemption to God. By doing so, He abolished Satan's rightful claim on us that he had had since the original sin of Adam. Through the act of redemption, Satan lost this right by being "compensated" with the blood of Christ. This ransom price of course did not benefit him. Quite the contrary, it destroys his works and his power.
3. In some Jewish communities this bath was also taken by the groom.

4. "Remember the law of *Moses* My servant, even the statutes and ordinances which I commanded him in Horeb for all Israel. Behold, I am going to send you *Elijah* the prophet before the coming of the great and terrible day of the LORD" (Malachi 4:4-5, emphases added). Interestingly, Moses and Elijah are both mentioned in this passage!

5. Compare 1 Peter 3:6, where it is written, "Sarah obeyed Abraham, calling him lord."

6. *Strong's Concordance,* G2752.

7. Ibid., G2906.

8. Compare Craig S. Keener, *IVP Bible Background Commentary, New Testament* (Downer's Grove, IL: IVP Academic, 1993), 268.

9. *Strong's Concordance,* G3933.

10. Ibid., G3573.

11. Ibid., G2518.

12. See also Keener, 597–598.

13. *Strong's Concordance,* G5429.

14. Ibid., G3474.

15. See for example James Harman, *The Kingdom* (Maitlad, FL: Prophecy Countdown Publications, 2009) or Lyn Mize's First Fruits website, www.ffruits.org.

Chapter 4

Recovering End Times Truth Throughout History

As for me, I heard but could not understand; so I said, "My lord,
what will be the outcome of these events?"
He said, "Go your way, Daniel, for these words are concealed and
sealed up until the end time."
Daniel 12:8–9

About the time of the end, a body of men will be raised up who will
turn their attention to the prophecies, and
insist upon their literal interpretation, in the midst of much clamour
and opposition.
Sir Isaac Newton, 17th century physicist

Early and Middle Age Church Beliefs About the End Times

The early church never developed a systematic theology of the end
times, and their beliefs about the exact timing of the rapture remained
quite vague. However, the early church fathers did believe in a literal
fulfillment of end times prophecy, including the book of Revelation,
which was accepted early on as part of the inspired Word of God. They
had a clear expectation of a personal Antichrist who would appear before
the end, a literal return of Christ for His church, and that believers would
reign with Christ on earth in His millennial (1,000-year) kingdom as
foretold in Revelation 20.

Generally, we can discern two early church views on the timing of
the rapture. Most church fathers such as Justin Martyr, Irenaeus, Cyprian,
and Tertullian believed that the church would have to go through the
Great Tribulation brought on by the Antichrist and that the rise of the

Antichrist was the last remaining sign before the rapture would take place.[1] To give just three of many examples, we cite the writings of Tertullian and Justin Martyr, two of the most famous early fathers, as well as the *Didache*, the authoritative church manual written in 110 AD:

> ... that the city of fornication [Babylon] may receive from the ten kings its deserved doom, and that *the beast Antichrist with his false prophet may wage war on the church of God* ...[2]

> The man of apostasy [Antichrist] ... shall venture to do unlawful deeds on the earth *against us the Christians.*[3]

> For as lawlessness increases, they will hate one another and will persecute and betray. And then the world-deceiver will appear as a son of God; and will work signs and wonders, and the earth will be delivered into his hands.... *Then all created mankind will come to the fire of testing*, and many will be offended and perish; *but they that endure in their faith will be saved by the Curse Himself* [Jesus who was cursed for us]. *And then will the signs of the truth appear;* first a sign of a rift in the heaven, then a sign of a voice of a trumpet, and thirdly, a resurrection of the dead.... Then will the world *see the Lord coming on the clouds of heaven.*[4]

Note that it says that the Antichrist will war against the "church of God," meaning not just a group of "tribulation saints"—a term whose equivalent cannot be found in Scripture.

In contrast, the Shepherd of Hermas argued, based on visions that he received, that Christians can escape the Great Tribulation by holy and blameless conduct.[5] Therefore, pretribulational scholars often cite his writings. But contrary to pretribulationism, the Shepherd of Hermas *never* taught an unconditional, all-inclusive rapture. Rather, he believed in a *conditional* pretribulation (first fruits) rapture that depends on personal preparation and "serving the Lord blamelessly":[6]

> Go, therefore, and tell the elect of the Lord His mighty deeds, and say to them that this beast is a type of the great tribulation that is coming. *If then ye prepare yourselves*, and repent with all your heart, and turn to the Lord, it will be possible for you to escape it, *if your heart be pure and spotless*, and ye spend the rest of the days of your life in *serving the Lord blamelessly*.[7]

Scholars disagree over the Shepherd of Hermas' work, because other sections seem to indicate that the author is describing the church as being refined but yet preserved through the tribulation.[8] However, this seeming contradiction is solved if we understand that there will be two raptures: first, a conditional first fruits rapture before the tribulation and then an all-inclusive late harvest rapture during the second half of the 7-year period. Therefore, the overall combined teachings of the early church point us not just toward *one*, but toward a total of *two* distinct raptures. This perspective was subsequently lost, and not recovered until the 19th century.

From the third and fourth century on, the early church's literal belief in end times events came under attack. Certain groups developed extreme views of the last days and used them to justify excessive indulgences. Such distorted teachings discredited literal end times beliefs, and tarnished the credibility of the book of Revelation within the church. Also, Origen, an early Christian theologian from Alexandria, was profoundly influenced by Greek philosophy (especially neo-Platonism) and sought to combine this worldview with biblical teachings. Greek philosophy emphasized the importance of the spiritual over the physical. Consequently, Origen and the Alexandrian scholars began to favor spiritualizing over literally understanding of the book of Revelation and other end times prophecies, arguing amongst other things against the scriptural teaching that believers will literally reign with Christ on earth.[9] This approach became known as the allegorical method of interpretation, which continues to be the most popular way to interpret end times scriptures to this day.[10] During his lifetime, however, Origen was essentially the only major Christian intellectual who adopted such a non-literal approach.

The most important historical figure to systematically challenge a literal belief in end times teachings was Augustine of Hippo, one of the famous theologians of the early church who profoundly influenced Christian theology. Augustine initially believed in a literal fulfillment of end times scriptures such as the earthly reign of Christ but soon changed his mind. He developed the theological perspective of amillennialism: the belief that there is no literal future reign of the believers with Christ on earth from Jerusalem. Instead, Augustine specifically proposed that this "reign" was already taking place through the contemporary rule of the church from Rome and that Satan was supposedly bound following his defeat through Christ's death on the cross. During Augustine's lifetime, the Roman emperor Theodosius I had elevated Christianity to the official state religion in 380 AD, paving the way for the creation of the Roman Catholic Church. This made it easy to believe that because worldly and religious powers were united, the rule of the popes was already the fulfillment of the millennial reign of Christ.[11]

Augustine's doctrines were quickly adopted as the official view of the Catholic Church, and it became even heretical to apply prophetic texts about the earthly reign of Christ to the future![12] The Catholic interpretation of Revelation was soon used to legitimize the use of force against non-Christian populations, since the popes as the earthly representatives of Christ viewed themselves as having the right to "rule the nations with a rod of iron." By applying future-oriented prophecies about the future reign of Christ to the present church age, religious wars such as the Crusades could easily be justified. Additionally, such understandings of end times scriptures sanctioned the Catholic Church's increasing political and economic influence in the world. However, Catholicism did retain a futuristic interpretation of a literal, future reign of the Antichrist as an individual, who would come to dominate the world during the end.[13]

End Times Beliefs of the Reformers

The reformers such as Martin Luther and John Calvin unfortunately adopted the amillenialism of the Catholic Church. A major reason behind this was that they, like Catholics, were fairly anti-Semitic, viewing the Jews as the killers of Jesus and therefore having been cut off from salvation. Both reformers and Catholics did not believe that God had a future plan to redeem the Jews, nor did they maintain that the Jews or their land had a role to play in the end times. A future reign of Christ from Jerusalem certainly did not fit into this view. Luther dismissed a belief in an earthly rule of Christ as something that only "the Jews dream."[14] Moreover, he regarded the book of Revelation as being hard or even impossible to understand and for a while doubted that it should be given full status as an inspired book of the Bible:

> Everyone may form his own judgment of this book [Revelation]; as for myself, I feel an aversion to it, and to me this is sufficient reason for rejecting it.[15]

To make matters worse, the reformers developed the so-called "historicist interpretation" of Daniel's end times prophecies and of all scriptures related to the rule of Antichrist. Whereas futurism views end times prophecy as being all about the future (meaning the Antichrist is yet to come), historicism interprets these prophecies as having already been fulfilled in the past or as currently unfolding in the present. Rather than believing in a future personal Antichrist, the reformers therefore viewed the Antichrist has having already appeared in the form of the popes and their rule of terror against the true believers. They modified the day-year principle of Old Testament prophecy, claiming that one week represented not seven years but 7 x 360, which equals 2,520 years (one "day" in Daniel's vision not referring to 360 days, but to 360 years!). Daniel's 70th week was therefore interpreted to refer not to 7 years, but to 2,520 years, spanning not a brief period at the very end of the age but a vast amount of time throughout church history. Half of this period, which according to the book of Revelation marks the duration of the Great Tribulation of the Antichrist, therefore amounts to 1,260 years.

To this day, some hold to the historicist view that the Great Tribulation occurred during the time when the Catholic Church held supreme power rather than being an event that we must still anticipate. Many date ranges are given for this supposition, with one of the most popular being the 1,260 years from 538 AD, when the last of the three opposing Arian kingdoms was uprooted, until 1798 when Napoleon's general Berthier took Pope Pius VI captive (however, the earthly rule of the popes was probably most affected by the founding of modern Italy in 1871, when Rome became the capital of a secular Italian government and the pope's temporal authority was essentially restricted to the Vatican area in the city).

For several centuries, historicism was the dominant Protestant view of end times scriptures. From the 19th century onward, however, this perspective began to lose favor. Firstly, the earthy powers of the popes had been greatly curbed in 1871 (and before by Napoleon). At the same time, conservative Protestants began to view the rapid rise of social and theological liberalism in the 19th century as a more significant threat than the weakening Catholicism. Secondly, historicism literally "ran out of time": the supposed 2,520 year period from Daniel's time (677 BC) ended in 1844![16] Historicism caused the Great Disappointment of the Millerites, who firmly expected Jesus to return in 1844. This was based on William Miller's calculation of 2,300 years[17] from the first decree of

Artaxerxes to Ezra in 457 BC (457 BC plus 2,300 years, plus 1 year for BC/AD conversion results in 1844 AD).

Figure 5. William Miller's calculation of the return of Christ being in 1844 AD. Source: Wikimedia Commons.

Christ of course did not return on that date, but the event caused much disillusionment, which shows the dangers of historicist calculations (a recent example is Harold Camping's doomsday prediction for May 2011, which led many unbelieving Americans to mock the whole idea of a rapture). Unfortunately, the very idea of historicism tends to promote attempts to predict the time of the return of Christ, even though Jesus himself has clearly said, "But of that day and hour no one knows, not even the angels of heaven, nor the Son, but the Father alone" (Matthew 24:36).

Since Jesus' comings are intimately connected with the advent of the Antichrist at the beginning of the tribulation and his defeat at Armageddon, we must not only refrain from speculating about the timing of Christ's comings but also from vain calculations about the rise and fall of the Antichrist. Thankfully, besides the Seven-Day Adventist church, which continues to cling to its Millerite roots, historicism has largely disappeared.[18]

The Rise of Premillennialism and Pretribulationism

The reformers failed to reform end times theology, placed little importance on the timing of the rapture, and made matters worse with the propagation of historicism. To this day, the reformed churches remain largely amillennial, as does the Catholic Church and many liberal denominations and theologians. The implication of this belief is that if there is no literal millennial reign of Christ on earth, then there is no need to spiritually prepare oneself for such a task, nor does one need to take related Bible promises seriously.

One of the first Protestants to revive a belief in such a reign and to study the rapture of the church was Joseph Mede in the early 17th century. A biblical scholar educated at the University of Cambridge, Mede argued that the 1,260 days, the 42 months, and the 3.5 times mentioned in Daniel and the book of Revelation all referred to the same literal time period of 3.5 years.[19] He also affirmed a literal belief of the millennial reign of Christ on earth after His coming at Armageddon, a position that became later known as premillennialism. Premillennialism stipulates that Christ will return before (*pre-*) the millennial reign, meaning the millennium takes place in a future era after the coming of Christ and not in the present church age.[20] This is the literal teaching of Revelation 20 and of many Old Testament prophecies (see chapter 14 for a detailed discussion).

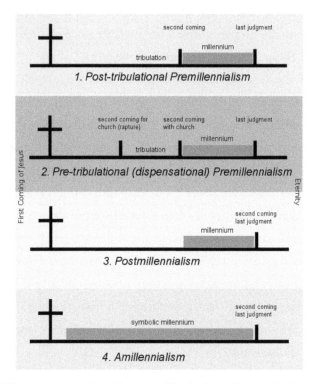

Figure 6. Different views on the millennium. The first two views are both premillennial; they stipulate a literal earthly reign of Christ before the last judgment. These two views differ with regard to when the rapture of the church will take place. The latter two views, postmillenialism and amillenialism, do not teach that Jesus will literally reign on the earth. His reign is either seen as merely symbolic or as being fulfilled in the expansion of the church across the world. Source: Wikimedia Commons.

From this time onward, interest in the prophetic in general and in the second coming of Christ increased. In the early 19th century, Cuninghame, Brooks, Elliott, and others were amongst the outstanding leaders of the prophetic revival, and prophetic conferences began to spring up across Britain.[21] The doctrine of a pretribulational rapture (the rapture occurring before the Great Tribulation) is often attributed to the Anglican clergyman John Darby in the 1830s, although it is also suggested that it originated with Edward Irving's report on the visions of a young Scottish girl named Margaret Macdonald.[22] Darby, however, was arguably the most important promoter of the view, and when the eminent Bible

94

teacher Dwight L. Moody adopted pretribulationism, it quickly became the most popular rapture perspective amongst conservative Christianity. However, back then the doctrine of the pretribulation rapture was still in its infancy and not always clearly understood or distinguished from premillennialism. Gundry, for example, observes regarding Moody's views on these matters:

> Moody adopted the concept of an any-moment return and some of its attendant vocabulary from the dispensationalists. But that he had a carefully thought-out and expressed … distinction between a pretribulational rapture and a post-tribulational coming cannot be demonstrated.[23]

Of particular importance were also the Niagara Bible Conferences between 1879 and 1909, which firmly established the premillennial perspective of a literal reign of Christ on earth together with the believers. Previously, Whitby's postmillennialism had been the prevailing interpretation of the millennial reign in the North American church. The famous preacher Jonathan Edwards held this view. According to postmillennialism, the millennium occurs towards the end of the church age, with Jesus returning after (*post-*) the tribulations of the 70th week of Daniel. The millennium is—like in amillennialism—considered to be merely an earthly reign of the saints, with Jesus still being in heaven. The turn towards premillennialism also marked the rise of a futurist view on end times teachings amongst Bible-believing Christians, as historicism was increasingly considered unscriptural (the first Protestant to proclaim a belief in a future, personal Antichrist was probably S. R. Maitland).[24]

Additionally, as Christians developed an increasing interest in learning Hebrew and began to interact with Jews, they adopted the biblical teaching of God's plans for the future salvation of the Jews based on Paul's teachings in Romans 9–11. Rather than believing that the church had completely replaced Israel (often called Replacement Theology), the dispensationalist view held that many Old Testament prophesies and promises regarding Israel will still be literally fulfilled. This perspective does not contradict the fact that many of God's promises for Israel are now applied to the church (such as all believers being priests in Christ, see 1 Peter 2:9; Revelation 1:6). But it does assert that God has not forgotten about His chosen people and that "it is not as though the word of God has failed" (Romans 9:6). Many Old Testament passages that pertain to the end times can only be understood as literally applying to Israel, for example Zechariah 12–14 (which will be discussed later).

The Emergence of the First Fruits Rapture Perspective

Soon after the advance of pretribulationism, a number of its proponents began to realize that the pretribulation rapture is not an easy promise to the entire church, regardless of its spiritual state. Well-respected Bible scholars and personalities such as R. Govett, G. H. Lang, G. H. Pember, A. Edwin Wilson, J. A. Seiss, Edward Irving, T. Austin-Sparks, the well-known Chinese pastor Watchman Nee, the eminent missionary Hudson Taylor, as well as A. B. Simpson, founder of the Christian and Missionary Alliance (C&MA), all held to what came to be known as the "partial rapture" view, that only those who are spiritually prepared and meet the conditions of the preservation promises will be raptured as "first fruits," while "foolish virgin" believers will have to undergo the tribulations.[25] G. H. Lang wrote:

> The assertion that all believers are overcomers is so plainly contrary to the fact and to Scripture that one wonders it ever has been made.... It avoids and nullifies the solemn warnings and urgent pleadings of the Spirit addressed to believers.[26]

But the first fruits rapture perspective is not merely a historic relic. Recent books include James Harmon's *The Coming Spiritual Earthquake,*[27]

J. W. White's *The Partial Rapture "Theory" Explained*, and Robert Harris' *Midnight's Cry*. They all share the same basic message: the body of Christ must actively prepare itself for the return of their Lord; it cannot just presume to avoid all spiritual refinement and escape all fiery trials through the supposed easy escape provided by an unconditional rapture. Scripture does not promise a pretribulational rapture regardless of one's spiritual readiness; rather, this rapture is directly dependent on one being ready, prepared and alert.

This new end times perspective and the reinvigorated interest in end times events soon began to bear spiritual fruit. A. B. Simpson, a Canadian Presbyterian preacher, was inspired by Jesus' words in Matthew 24:14: "This gospel of the kingdom shall be preached in the whole world as a testimony to all the nations, and then the end will come." Simpson realized that global evangelism was an urgent task for the end times church and subsequently founded a missionary training college in New York as well as the C&MA. Since its inception in the 1880s, the Alliance has planted over 13,000 churches with over 4 million followers in over 80 countries, making a huge impact on world missions.[28] Simpson's beliefs are summarized in his hymn "The Missionary Cry":

> The Master's coming draweth near.
> The Son of Man will soon appear,
> His Kingdom is at hand.
> But ere that glorious day can be,
> The Gospel of the Kingdom, we
> Must preach in every land.[29]

These words and the actions they inspired demonstrate how vital it is that the church develops a correct understanding of end times prophecy and then wholeheartedly embraces it. Throughout history, we have seen how Satan has attempted to suppress and confuse an accurate understanding of end times prophecy in order to confound the spiritual readiness of the saints for the coming of Christ. During the last 200 years, God has actively worked to restore a biblically accurate belief amongst His people, revealing truths that had been overlooked or distorted in the past. Now, He is calling His people to get ready and prepare themselves, so that they are spiritually ready for the first fruits rapture.

The belief in a literal millennial reign of Christ on earth together with the believers, as described in Revelation 20 and promised in Revelation 2:26–27, has been recovered in the form of premillennialism. This perspective is now widely held amongst conservative evangelical Christian circles, although especially in academic circles it continues to face staunch opposition. The idea of Christ reigning as King on earth over the nations together with his saints just does not seem acceptable especially to the more intellectual Christians. Because this is such an important event for us to look forward to and to personally prepare ourselves for, this book devotes a whole chapter to Christ's millennial reign.

Regarding the timing of the rapture, however, we see quite a diverse range of views within the Bible-believing church. While in America pretribulationism emerged as the dominant view during the first half of the 20th century, many conservative European scholars believe in a rapture at the end of the tribulation and wrath of God (posttribulationism). Additionally, the prewrath rapture perspective is gaining popularity amongst North American believers and conservative scholars.[30] Because of this confusion, many Christians believe that the truth about the rapture is an encrypted Biblical secret, encoded in Bible prophecy but not clearly decipherable for the present church.

The problem is that all rapture views have shortcomings—none of them can explain the full picture. Here, the first fruits rapture can bring some much-needed clarity by showing how two of the most popular rapture views can actually complement rather than contradict each other and how each rapture position is, when taken by itself, incomplete. The following chapter will examine scriptural evidence for a conditional first fruits rapture, especially based on the book of Revelation. The two chapters after that will then contrast this perspective with the pretribulation and pre-wrath rapture views, and demonstrate how these two popular rapture teachings can be combined into one comprehensive view on the end times.

Chapter 4 Notes

1. F. Kenton Beshore and R. William Keller, *When?: When Will the Rapture Take Place?* (Costa Mesa, CA: World Bible Society, 2011), ch. 6.
2. A. Roberts and J. Donaldson, *The Anti-Nicene Fathers*, vol. 3 (Grand Rapids, MI: Eerdmans Publishing Company, 1956), quoted in Beshore and Keller, 70 (emphasis added).
3. *Dialogue With Trypho*, ch. CX, quoted in Robert Van Kampen, *The Sign* (Wheaton, IL: Crossway, 2000), 449 (emphasis added).
4. "Didache," in J. B. Lightfoot and J. R. Harmer, trans., *The Apostolic Fathers* (Grand Rapids, MI: Baker Book House, 2000), 129, quoted in Beshore and Keller, 65 (emphasis added).
5. Mal Couch, "History of the Rapture," in Mal Couch, ed., *Dictionary of Premillennial Theology* (Grand Rapids, MI: Kregel Publications, 1997), 345.
6. Ibid., 345.
7. The Shepherd of Hermas, *First Book: Visions*, ch. 2, http://www.earlychristianwritings.com/text/shepherd.html (emphasis added). See also Thomas Ice and Timothy J. Demy, eds., *The Return: Understanding Christ's Second Coming and the End Times* (Grand Rapids, MI: Kregel Publications, 1999), 87.
8. Ice & Demy, 88.
9. Paul N. Benware, *Understanding End Times Prophecy: A Comprehensive Approach*, (Chicago: Moody Publishers, 2006), ch. 7.
10. The doctrine of amillennialism is currently held by the Roman Catholic and Orthodox churches, as well as a majority of Protestant denominations.
11. In 313 AD, the emperor Constantine had previously officially legitimatized the Christian faith, and consequently the social elite began to embrace this new religion.
12. Ice & Demy, 58.
13. A. Maas, "Antichrist," in *The Catholic Encyclopedia* (New York: Robert Appleton Company, 1907), http://www.newadvent.org/cathen/01559a.htm. See also Thomas Ice, Tom's Perspectives, "The Ethnicity of the Antichrist," 2009, http://www.pre-trib.org/articles/view/ethnicity-of-antichrist.

14. *Dr. Martin Luther's Church-Postil: Sermons on the Epistles: for the different Sundays and festivals in the year,* (New Market,VA: New Market Evangelical Lutheran Publishing Co., Henkel & Calvert, 1869), 140.

15. Sammtliche Werke, *The Facts About Luther* (O'Hare:TAN Books, 1987), 63, 169–170, 203.

16. Calculated as 2,520 minus 677, plus one year for the BC/AD conversion: 2,520 - 677 + 1 = 1,844.

17. The 2,300 days refer to Daniel 8:13–14.

18. Ice & Demy, 17.

19. Mal Couch, 250.

20. As opposed to postmillenialism, which holds that the millennium occurs toward the end of the church age before Christ returns. This perspective teaches that when Christ comes, the eternal state (heaven) starts immediately.

21. See George E. Ladd, "The History And Origins Of Pretribulationism," http://www.theologue.org/OriginsOfPretribulationalism-GELadd.htm.

22. Bob Gundry, *The Church and the Tribulation* (Grand Rapids, MI: Zondervan, 1973), 185.

23. Richard Reiter, "A History of the Development of the Rapture Positions," *in Three Views on the Rapture,* ed. G. L. Archer and S. N. Gundry (Grand Rapids, MI: Zondervan, 1996), 13.

24. G.E. Ladd.

25. See the following articles for examples. Gerald McGraw, "Oil in Your Vessel: A.B. Simpson's Concept of a Partial Rapture," http://prophecycountdown. com/wp-content/uploads/2009/09/Oil-In-Your-Vessel.pdf.   A.B. Simpson, "Wholly Sanctified," http://prophecycountdown.com/ wp-content/uploads/2009/09/Wholly-Sanctified.pdf.   Watchman Nee, "Rapture," http://www3.telus.net/trbrooks/Partial_rapture. htm. "Partial Rapture Believers," http://www3.telus.net/trbrooks/ PartialRaptureBelievers.htm. Robert Govett, "The Church and the Tribulation," http://www3.telus.net/trbrooks/THE-CHURCH-AND-THE-TRIBULATION.pdf. In contrast to our position, which holds that the "foolish virgin" believers will be raptured before the wrath of God falls, these first fruits rapture proponents believed that they would have to go through the period of the wrath.

26. G. H. Lang, *The Revelation of Jesus Christ: Select Studies* (London : G.H. Lang, 1945), 91–92.

27. James Harman's books are available for online viewing at http:// prophecycountdown.com.

28. *The Alliance,* http://www.cmalliance.org/region/.

29. From Hymn 338, *Hymns of the Christian Life*, no. 2 (South Nyack, NY: Christian Alliance Publishing Co., 1897), http://www.archive.org/details/hymnsofchristian00simp.
30. This rising popularity is, for example, indicated by the inclusion of the prewrath rapture perspective in the new edition of Alan Hultberg, ed., *Three Views on the Rapture: Pretribulation, Prewrath, or Posttribulation* (Grand Rapids, MI: Zondervan, 2010).

Chapter 5

But the Wise Shall Understand: Scriptural Evidence for the First Fruits Rapture

Many shall be purified, made white, and refined … and none of the
wicked shall understand, but the wise shall understand.
Daniel 12:10 (NKJV)

The prophecies are to be unintelligible to the ungodly but intelligible
to those who are properly instructed.
Blaise Pascal, 17th century mathematician

Setting the End Times Stage: The Final Seven Years

In the introduction we looked at some preliminary scriptural evidence for a conditional rapture. We saw the following points:

- Firstly, that both preservation promises in Revelation 3:10 and Luke 21:36 are conditional on spiritual alertness and faithful obedience to Christ. Scripture simply makes no unconditional pretribulation rapture promise. Jesus tells the church of Philadelphia that they will escape the "hour of testing…which is about to come upon the whole world" because they have "kept the word of My perseverance".

- Conversely, that Scripture gives warnings of severe discipline to those believers who are unready or unrepentant. This group is especially represented in the warnings to Jezebel's followers in Thyatira (Revelation 2:22) and to the lukewarm Laodiceans (Revelation 3:19), but also in Jesus' words to several other compromising churches of Revelation.

We had seen that the contrast between those two groups, the overcomers and the compromised, is vividly depicted in the parable of the ten virgins. It is significant that in this parable, the wise virgins were allowed to go through an *open door*. Jesus promises exactly such a door to the overcoming Philadelphians, the "wise virgin" believers: "I have put before you an *open door* which no one can shut, because you have … kept My word" (Revelation 3:8, emphasis added). Conversely, the foolish virgins faced a door that "was shut" (Matthew 25:10). To the Laodiceans, Christ calls out, "Behold, I stand at the door and knock; if anyone hears My voice and opens the door, I will come in to him and will dine with him, and he with Me" (Revelation 3:20). These passages imply that some end times Christians will get an "open door" that keeps them from the "hour of testing," while others will face a door that is "shut." With His invitation, Jesus is calling on the Laodiceans to become wise and to prepare spiritually for His return. This is precisely what Paul wrote in Ephesians:

> Therefore be careful how you walk, *not as unwise men but as wise*, making the most of your time, because the days are evil. So then *do not be foolish*, but understand what the will of the Lord is. And *do not get drunk with wine, for that is dissipation* [symbolizing the worldliness of the foolish virgins], *but be filled with the Spirit* [symbolized by the oil of the wise virgins].
>
> (Ephesians 5: 15–18, emphases added)

Scripture also gives us other clues that there will be two distinct raptures. However, before we dig deeper, we first need to understand a few basics concerning the end times. These are views that are widely held amongst conservative scholars who believe in a literal reign of Christ on earth after His coming.[1]

The most pivotal time frame for end times events are the so-called 70 weeks of Daniel. In Daniel 9:24–27, Daniel records a vision that spans from his present time far into the future:

> Seventy weeks have been decreed for your people [the Jews][2] and your holy city [Jerusalem], to finish the transgression, to make an end of sin, to make atonement for iniquity [Christ's death on the cross], to bring in everlasting righteousness [Christ's future millennial kingdom], to seal up vision and prophecy and to anoint the most holy place.
>
> So you are to know and discern that from the issuing of a decree to restore and rebuild Jerusalem [destroyed by the Babylonians] until Messiah the Prince [Jesus] there will be seven weeks and sixty-two weeks [together 69 weeks, representing 483 years]; it will be built again, with plaza and moat, even in times of distress [under Nehemiah against much local opposition]. Then after the sixty-two weeks [which occur after the 7 weeks, so after 69 weeks = 483 years] the Messiah will be cut off and have nothing [Jesus crucified], and the people of the prince who is to come [the Romans under General Titus] will destroy the city and the sanctuary [fulfilled in 70 AD]. And its [Jerusalem's] end will come with a flood [picture of complete destruction by the Roman army who "flooded" the city]; even to the end [of the age] there will be war; desolations are determined [the birth pangs and tribulations Jesus predicted in Matthew 24].
>
> And he [the Antichrist] will make a firm covenant with the many [the majority of modern Israel] for one week [7 years], but in the middle of the week [after 3.5 years] he will put a stop to sacrifice and grain offering [temple worship]; and on the wing of abominations will come one who makes desolate [the Antichrist], even until a complete destruction,

one that is decreed, is poured out on the one who makes desolate [Antichrist destroyed at the battle of Armageddon].

Even though this passage seems very cryptic, there is an understanding of it that is rather straightforward. The total time frame of the prophecy is 70 weeks, literally 70 "sevens." From the passage, it is clear that each of the "sevens" refers not to seven days (a literal week), but seven years.[3] Consequently, 70 "weeks" span a period of 490 years. Regarding the 490 years, the prophecy says that there will be 483 years (62 + 7 = 69 "weeks" of seven years each) between the decree to rebuild Jerusalem until the first coming of Jesus, the Messiah (the first seven "weeks" = 49 years which may have referred to the time it took to properly rebuild the city).[4] Indeed, from the time that Artaxerxes Longimanus issued this decree to Nehemiah in the Passover month of Nisan in 444/5 BC (Nehemiah 2:5) to the death of Christ in 32/3 AD[5] just after the Passover celebration (also in the month of Nisan), we can count 483 prophetic years (of 360 days each).[6] What a perfect fit, and what an incredible testimony to the accuracy of Biblical prophecy!

Yet what of the last "week" of seven years that remains of the 70 weeks? This "week" is referred to as the final or the 70th week, and it does not follow chronologically from the death of Christ. This is because when the Jews rejected their Messiah, they stop the prophetic clock and ushered in the "times of the Gentiles" as Jesus Himself described it in Luke 21:24: "[A]nd Jerusalem will be trampled under foot by the Gentiles until the times of the Gentiles are fulfilled."[7] From that time on, the Jews were (again) dominated by the Gentiles, culminating in the complete destruction of Jerusalem by the brutal Roman General Titus in 70 AD, as Jesus predicted in Luke 19:41–44. This gap between weeks 69 and 70 is therefore a direct consequence of the Messiah having been "cut off" by His own people. This explains why the 70 weeks prophecy is specifically addressed to the Jews—referred to as "your people"

105

throughout the book of Daniel, and *not* to us, the saints, who in Daniel are described as "saints of the Highest One."

This is confirmed by Paul, who writes that after the Jews rejected Jesus:

> [A] partial hardening has happened to Israel until the fullness
> of the Gentiles has come in [the times of the Gentiles]; and so
> all Israel will be saved [at the end of the age].
>
> (Romans 11:25–26)

This "partial hardening" is the church age: a time when the vast majority of Jews reject the gospel, while vast numbers of non-Jews ("Gentiles") find salvation. This "hardening" spans from the spread of Christianity after Jesus' death until the future coming of Christ. Such a "gap" was also foreseen by the Old Testament prophet Micah in two key passages. Firstly, Hosea 3 states the following:

> For the sons of Israel will remain for many days without king
> or prince, without sacrifice....Afterward the sons of Israel will
> return and seek the Lord their God and David their king; and
> they will come trembling to the Lord and to His goodness in
> the last days.
>
> (vv. 4–5)

Here, Hosea unambiguously foretells that Israel's royal line will be interrupted as a direct consequence of her unfaithfulness to God. However, "in the last days" their descendants will return to the Lord and "seek" Him with "trembling." Then, in Micah 5, we read the following prophesy:

> But as for you, Bethlehem Ephrathah, too little to be among
> the clans of Judah, from you One will go forth for Me to be

ruler in Israel [Jesus, who was born in Bethlehem]. His goings forth are from long ago, from the days of eternity.

Therefore He will give them up [His people, the Jews] until the time when she who is in labor has borne a child [the woman with child in Revelation 12, the woman being the church, and the child being the overcomers of the first fruits rapture]. Then the remainder of His brethren will return to the sons of Israel [the future gathering of all Jews to the Messiah]. And He [Jesus] will arise and shepherd His flock in the strength of the LORD, in the majesty of the name of the LORD His God [at His millennial earthly reign]. And they will remain [with God], because at that time He will be great to the ends of the earth [Jesus' worldwide millennial kingdom].

(vv. 2–4)

Micah's prophecy foretold that Jesus would be born in Bethlehem. But then, He will "give up" His people, the Jews, to the "partial hardening" that Paul wrote about, until the woman (the church) will be "with child"—the child being the first fruit believers who will be raptured when Jesus comes again. This child cannot refer to Jesus Himself, because His birth is already described in the preceding verse (for more details see the textbox about the woman of Revelation 12 at the end of this chapter). When Jesus returns to reign upon the earth, He will gather His people and establish His Kingdom. It is at this time that "all Israel will be saved."

In the meantime, we are in the church age, the "times of the Gentiles." After Israel regained their land in 1948 and their capital Jerusalem in 1967, the end of this phase is now gradually being ushered in. The stage is set for the final 70th week of the prophecy.

Why the 70th week of Daniel is a literal, future 7-year period

The final confirmation that there is a gap between the 69th and the 70th week comes from the way the angel describes the last "week" or 7-year period in Daniel 9. This last "week" is divided into two 3.5-year sections which refer to future events that occur just before the glorious return of Christ, and therefore cannot have found fulfillment in past historic events. At the beginning of this time, the Antichrist, "the one who makes desolate," will make a false peace treaty with Israel. This is also prophesied in Isaiah 28:14–15:

> Therefore, hear the word of the LORD, O scoffers, who rule this people who are in Jerusalem, because you have said, "We have made a covenant with death, and with Sheol [place of the dead, here symbolizing the forces of darkness] we have made a pact. The overwhelming scourge [God's judgment, directly or through foreign invaders] will not reach us when it passes by, for we have made falsehood our refuge and we have concealed ourselves with deception.

At the mid-point of the 70th week, the Antichrist then turns his back on the treaty and reveals his true colors. He sets up what is called the "Abomination of Desolation" in the rebuilt temple in Jerusalem (details in chapter 10 of this book), and starts the Great Tribulation of the Jewish people, all described by Jesus in Matthew 24:15–22. (Significantly, the period from the beginning of Jesus' ministry in 28 or 29 AD—in the 15th year after the start of Tiberius Caesar's reign in the fall of 14 AD—to his death in the spring of 32 or 33 AD also spanned 3.5 years, and it also ended with the "abomination" of the Messiah being subjected to a criminal's death on the cross!)

This unprecedented tribulation and oppression of God's people lasts for 3.5 years. This is confirmed by multiple Scripture passages:

He will speak out [blasphemy] against the Most High and wear down the saints of the Highest One, and he will intend to make alterations in times and in law; and they [the saints] will be given into his hand for a time, times, and half a time [3.5 years].

(Daniel 7:25)

I heard the man dressed in linen, who was above the waters of the river, as he raised his right hand and his left toward heaven, and swore by Him who lives forever that it would be for a time, times, and half a time [3.5 years]; and as soon as they finish shattering the power of the holy people, all these events will be completed.

(Daniel 12:7)

Then the woman [the church] fled into the wilderness where she had a place prepared by God, so that there she would be nourished for one thousand two hundred and sixty days [3.5 years]…. And when the dragon saw that he was thrown down to the earth, he persecuted the woman [the church] who gave birth to the male child. But the two wings of the great eagle were given to the woman, so that she could fly into the wilderness to her place, where she was nourished for a time and times and half a time [3.5 years], from the presence of the serpent [the devil].

(Revelation 12:6, 13–14)

There was given to him [the beast = Antichrist] a mouth speaking arrogant words and blasphemies, and authority to act for forty-two months was given to him [3.5 years]…. It was also given to him to make war with the saints and to overcome them.

(Revelation 13:5, 7)

All of these passages unilaterally agree that the Antichrist will dominate and overcome the saints for a literal period of 3.5 years (3.5 times/42 months/1,260 days). The distinct ways in which this time period is referred to indicates that the final seven years cannot be taken as symbolic for the entire church age from Jesus' death to His future coming. At the end of that time, Jesus will return for battle at Armageddon, and the "complete destruction" that has been "decreed" will be "poured out on the one who makes desolate [the Antichrist]." As it is written in Daniel 7:26, "his [the Antichrist's] dominion will be taken away, annihilated and destroyed forever."

Altogether, Daniel 9:27 spells out the following elements of the final 7-year period during which the key end times events will take place:

1. The peace treaty between the Antichrist and Israel, which marks the beginning of the final 7-year period.

2. The global rule of the Antichrist over all nations of the world, during which he is given power over the believers. According to both Daniel 7:25 and Revelation 13:5, this period lasts 42 months (3.5 years; in Daniel this is referred to as "a time, times, and half a time," a total of 3.5 times or years).

3. Unprecedented tribulations for God's people: on the one hand, the Antichrist's 3.5-year-long persecution of the saints (the church), starting from His rise early in the 70th week and ending just after the mid-point of this week; on the other hand, an unparalleled time of persecution specifically for the Jewish people, which starts in the middle of the 70th week and continues until its end. Both "Great Tribulations" last for 3.5 years. They overlap for a short period, but they are not the same and must be looked at separately.

4. The return of Christ: both to rapture His church, and then at the end of the seven years to Armageddon to defeat and destroy the Antichrist and to set up his earthly reign from Jerusalem.

Rapture: Christ comes to rapture the church – before the tribulation, before the wrath, or at the end?

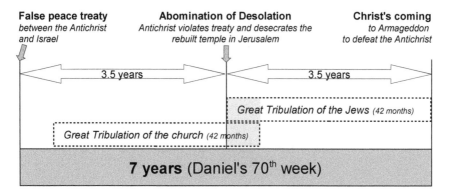

Figure 7. The 70th week of Daniel

Equipped with this foundational knowledge, we can now examine the scriptural evidence for two separate raptures in the context of the final seven years.

The First Fruits in Revelation 14

Revelation chapter 14 is of particular significance, as it represents a mini-summary of the sequence of end times events. The first scene of this chapter is a highly symbolic depiction of a unique group of 144,000 of God's people:

> Then I looked, and behold, the Lamb was standing on Mount Zion, and with Him one hundred and forty-four thousand, having His name and the name of His Father written on their foreheads. And I heard a voice from heaven, like the sound of many waters and like the sound of loud thunder, and the

voice which I heard was like the sound of harpists playing on their harps.

And they sang a new song before the throne and before the four living creatures and the elders; and no one could learn the song except the one hundred and forty-four thousand who had been purchased from the earth.

These are the ones who have not been defiled with women, for they have kept themselves chaste. These are the ones who follow the Lamb wherever He goes. These have been *purchased from among men as first fruits* to God and to the Lamb. And no lie was found in their mouth; they are blameless.

(Revelation 14:1–5, emphasis added)

A popular view is that these 144,000 of Revelation 14 are the same as the 144,000 Jews of Revelation 7. However, we will further compare those two groups below and see that they are in fact quite different. After carefully examining Scripture, we argue that this group is actually the first fruits of the church directly after they have been raptured. The figure 144,000 is a symbolic number that may represent groups from various groups (denominations) of the church. It is arrived at by multiplying 12 (symbolizing the whole church through the twelve apostles) with 12,000, a number used to symbolize the tribes of Israel, as seen in Revelation 7:4–8. To say that the 144,000 is not symbolic suggests that those amongst Christendom who are ready and prepared for Christ's return would only amount to a small number. There are those who take this position, believing that only a total of 144,000 will make it to heaven (such as the Jehovah's Witnesses). We do not believe this view to be scriptural.

Generally, the description of this group is full of symbolic and spiritual (rather than literal) references. The 144,000 are said to stand with the Lamb on spiritual "Mount Zion," which symbolizes the "throne of God" (compare Psalm 125:1; Hebrews 12:22). There, they sing a "new song" that "no one [else] could learn." They are described as spiritual virgins who "kept themselves chaste," meaning morally pure and "blameless." Spiritual purity is often symbolized in the Old Testament through the notion of virginity. Most significantly, they are called spiritual "first fruits," the first of the harvest. In the Old Testament, during the Feast of First Fruits, the Israelites were to offer the first of the barley harvest before the Lord. This was a symbol that we should give the first of everything we own or make to God, putting Him first in all aspects of our lives, as Jesus said in Matthew 6:33, "But seek first His kingdom and His righteousness, and all these things will be added to you." The first fruits are a unique group, representing those who put God first in their lives and who are consequently put first by Him. They are therefore the first of the end times 'harvest' (the rapture), having been "purchased [or "bought," Gr. *agorazo*[8]] from among men as first fruits."

After the first fruits group three angels appear, each with a message to proclaim. The first of the angels signals the spread of the gospel to the ends of the earth, as predicted by Christ in Matthew 24:14, heralding a great harvest of souls. He also heralds the beginning of the "hour of His [God's] judgment." The second angel announces the fall of Babylon, which refers to two distinct events: firstly, the fall of "financial Babylon," meaning the collapse of the world's financial system and economy, paving the way for the rise of the Antichrist. Secondly, the fall points to the destruction of the literal city that Babylon symbolically represents. This "Babylon" city's fall will come through the Antichrist and his alliance towards the end of the 70th week (Revelation 17:16–17, see chapter 12 of this book for details). A third angel then warns those who would worship the image of the beast of God's judgment. At this point in Revelation 14, we are right in the middle of the reign of the Antichrist and the Great Tribulations. What comes next is indeed a call for the perseverance of the saints who are caught in this terrible trial.

The next depiction in chapter 14 logically follows the end times sequence. While the Great Tribulations are running their course, John has the following vision:

> Then I looked, and behold, a white cloud, and sitting on the cloud was one like a son of man, having a golden crown on His head and a sharp sickle in His hand. And another angel came out of the temple, crying out with a loud voice to Him who sat on the cloud, "Put in your sickle and reap, for the hour to reap has come, because the harvest of the earth is ripe." Then He who sat on the cloud swung His sickle over the earth, and the earth was reaped.
>
> (Revelation 14:14–16)

Verse 14 mentions someone "like a son of man." This phrase is also used in Daniel 7:13–14, where Daniel sees "one like a son of man" coming to receive "dominion, glory and a Kingdom, that all peoples ... may serve Him." Clearly, this is none other than Jesus. Just as it is described in the second coming passage in Matthew 24:29–31, He comes on a "cloud" to rapture his church. In Acts, we read that at Jesus' ascension He was "lifted up while they were looking on, and a *cloud* received Him out of their sight" (Acts 1:9, emphasis added). Immediately afterward, two men in white tell the onlooking disciples that Jesus "will come in just the same way as you have watched Him go into heaven" (v. 11b), suggesting He will return on a cloud. This is exactly what Revelation 14:14 states. Here, the rapture is symbolized through the concept of harvesting, just like in the parable of the tares among the wheat in Matthew 13:39b, where it says that "the harvest is the end of the age; and the reapers are angels" (v. 39b).

This "harvest" is described as being "ripe." However, the Greek term for "ripe," *xeraino*[9] is more accurately translated as "over-ripe". It literally means "dried up" or "withered," referring to a harvest that has been in the heat of the sun for so long that it must urgently be gathered. This description clearly implies that this harvest is the late harvest. This autumn harvest occurs toward the end of the dry season that runs from mid-May to September, as opposed to the early, first harvest, which comes in spring and therefore before the heat of the summer (which peaks around July). This summer heat is a picture of the tribulations that those who are raptured at the late harvest must go through—symbolism that Jesus Himself confirmed in Luke 23:31. There, when walking up to Golgotha to be crucified, He said to the women who were mourning for Him: "For if they do these things when the tree is green, what will happen when it is dry [*xeros*,[10] root word for *xeraino*]?" The time when the "tree is green" refers to times of peace and normality for God's people, whereas the season when "it is dry" implies tribulation and persecution, looking forward to the destruction of Jerusalem by the Romans in 70 AD. Likewise, the "dry" harvest in Revelation 14:15 describes a harvest that occurs in the midst of tribulations. From these references, it is evident that this "harvest" (rapture) is not the first fruits harvest of the wise virgin believers, but rather the late harvest of the foolish virgins which occurs after the heat of the tribulations.

This late harvest of the over-ripe produce comes just in time, because the very next image is that of the grape harvest of God's wrath. This second "harvest" symbolizes the fierce outpouring of God's wrath on the entire unbelieving world, as outlined in Revelation 19:15: "From His mouth comes a sharp sword … and He treads the wine press of the fierce wrath of God, the Almighty." The image of the grape harvest as a picture of God's wrath on wicked mankind is also found in Joel 3:13: "Put in the sickle, for the harvest is ripe. Come, tread, for the wine press is full; the vats overflow, for their wickedness is great."[11] Following the promise that God's children are "not destined … for wrath" (1 Thessalonians 5:9), the believers are snatched up just in time to escape this terrible judgment, in which "blood came out from the wine press, up to the horses' bridles, for a distance of two hundred miles" (Revelation 14:20).

Overall, Revelation 14 gives us the following chronological sequence of end times events that will take place during the seven years of the 70th week of Daniel:

1. The 144,000 "first fruits" who stand before God's throne at the very beginning of the unfolding of the end times sequence.
2. The worldwide proclamation of the Gospel and the beginning of God's judgment, starting with the fall of Babylon, the global rule of the Antichrist, and the persecution of the saints (and later the Jews) in the Great Tribulations.
3. The rapture of the church as an "over-ripe" harvest.
4. The outpouring of the wrath of God (a particular part of the hour of His judgment),[12] which climaxes in the battle of Armageddon when Christ defeats His enemies and destroys the Antichrist (Revelation 19).

The Two Raptures Predicted by the Old Testament Harvest Feasts

From this summary chapter it follows that there will be two raptures, both symbolized through the concept of harvesting. It is very interesting to see how the two-fold harvest rapture and the following wrath are confirmed by the harvest feasts that God gave to Moses.

In ancient Israel, there were three harvest seasons: 1) the barley harvest, 2) the wheat harvest, and 3) the autumn grain and fruit harvest. Directly corresponding to those were the three harvest feasts, the "three times in a year when all your males shall appear before the Lord your God" (Deuteronomy 16:16).

The barley was the first of all produce to mature in spring and was therefore the grain offered for the First Fruits Offering (*bikkurim*), celebrated in the Jewish month of Nisan (March–April). In the New Testament, Christ the "first fruits" (1 Corinthians 15:23) was resurrected on the very day of the Feast of First Fruits—the Sabbath after the Passover (Leviticus 23:9–14). This feast and Christ's resurrection consequently represent the *first* "first fruits" resurrection.

Before the First Fruits Offering of the barley harvest, however, God instituted a feast designed to prepare His people for this offering: the Feast of Unleavened Bread, also called the "bread of affliction" (Deuteronomy 16:3). In the Bible, leaven represents compromise and sin, as when Jesus told the disciples to "beware of the leaven of the Pharisees" (Mark 8:15). The Feast of Unleavened Bread follows the Passover, the day on which Jesus died. For us in the present church age, the Feast of Unleavened Bread therefore signifies the sanctification period that follows the Passover blood being sprinkled on us for our justification. During this time of sanctification we are to allow God to refine us through afflictions and trials until Christ comes to take His bride. We are to remain without "leaven," meaning without sin. This is why Paul urges the saints in 1 Corinthians 5:7–8 to "purge out the old leaven ... for Christ our Passover lamb was sacrificed. Let us therefore celebrate the festival ... with the unleavened bread of sincerity and truth." We are currently living in this season as we await the return of our Lord.

Now, if Christ was the first fruits already, then where do the first fruits of the church feature in the harvest feast cycle? The answer is that there are not one but *two* first fruit offerings in the Old Testament! The *second* First Fruits Offering was that of the wheat harvest, which matured soon after the barley crop. This offering was to be performed at the Feast of the Harvest (also called Feast of Weeks), 49 days after the First Fruits Offering of the barley, in the Jewish month of Sivan, which is around May–June (Exodus 23:16; Leviticus 23:15–21). The wheat offering symbolically foreshadows the *second* "first fruits" rapture, which will occur when Christ comes to take the wise virgins. It is no coincidence that John the Baptist specifically identified Jesus' coming with the wheat (and not the barley) harvest in Matthew 3:12: "He will gather His wheat into the barn...."

Here, it is significant that, in contrast to the barley first fruits, the Israelites were not just to bring a sheaf of the grain, but to bake two loafs of wheat bread for the offering. The two breads likely symbolize the combined community of Old Testament and New Testament saints. In 1 Corinthians 10:17, Paul wrote: "Since there is one bread, we who are many are one body; for we all [New Covenant believers] partake of the one bread [Christ]." Moreover, this time, the breads were to be prepared with leaven. This reflects the fact that while Christ the First Fruits was perfect and without sin (without "leaven"), His people will not be perfect until He comes to take them. Also, the head of barley is very soft, reflecting the humility of Christ, whereas the head of wheat is hard, and therefore needs to be threshed and crushed in order to separate wheat from chaff. Likewise, we believers need trials and tribulations to break and mold us before we are ready for the harvest. Those who avoid the refining fires of sanctification (the foolish virgins) therefore need to be refined (threshed) in the fires of the end times tribulation before they are ready to be "harvested."

Interestingly, this First Fruits offering is specifically described as the "first fruits of your labors" (Exodus 23:16), prefiguring the fact that the first fruits rapture of the wise virgins is a reward for bearing fruit for Christ and therefore related to our labors in Christ (God-directed and God-enabled works). In Jewish tradition, the Feast of Weeks is considered to be the day on which God gave the law to Moses—seven weeks after the exodus from Egypt. In the New Testament, the Feast of the Harvest became known as Pentecost.[13] It was the day on which the Holy Spirit was poured out on the disciples (Acts 2). Together, God's law and God's Spirit represent the sanctification period of God's people, our time on earth where we are to walk in the light of God's Word (formerly the law, now Jesus' teachings and commandments) through the enabling and guidance of His Spirit. This is another indication that the second first fruits harvest stands for the rapture of the wise virgins, those who did not run out of the "oil" of the Spirit but kept their lamps burning. They are the ones who have allowed God to sanctify them, making them ready and prepared for the coming of the Bridegroom.

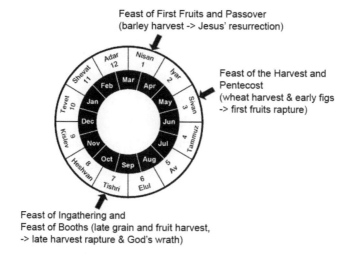

Feast of First Fruits and Passover
(barley harvest -> Jesus' resurrection)

Feast of the Harvest and
Pentecost
(wheat harvest & early figs
-> first fruits rapture)

Feast of Ingathering and
Feast of Booths (late grain and fruit harvest,
-> late harvest rapture & God's wrath)

Figure 8. The Jewish Old Testament harvest cycle and the raptures

After the two first fruit offerings comes the summer period, during which other grains and fruits would gradually ripen in the heat of the near-eastern sun. In relation to the end times, the heat of the summer represents the fiery trials of the tribulations. Those who are not raptured at the first fruits harvest because they are not "ripe" will have to be matured in the heat of the summer, to be taken at the late ("over-ripe") autumn harvest.

This third and final harvest season would be celebrated by the Feast of Ingathering in the Jewish month of Tishri (September-October), when the Israelites would have "gathered in from your threshing floor and your wine vat" (Deuteronomy 16:13). In contrast to the two first fruits feasts, the Feast of Ingathering represented the collecting of everything that had remained and matured during the summer, not only of additional grains, but also of the fruit harvest. This symbolizes that at that point, Christ will "harvest" all the remaining believers.

This timing of the two raptures is also implied in the parable of the fig tree in Matthew 24. Right after describing the events of the end times, Jesus goes on to say:

> Now learn the parable from the fig tree: when its branch has already become tender and puts forth its leaves, you know that *summer is near*, so, you too, *when you see all these things*, recognize that He is near, *right at the door.*
>
> (Matthew 24:32–33, emphases added)

This passage hints at the fact that Jesus' first coming at the end of the age occurs *before* the summer (meaning in late spring). In terms of Jewish harvest feasts, this can only refer to the first fruits of the wheat harvest. Fascinatingly, there are two types of figs. First come the early figs, which are harvested before the heat of the summer, around the time of the first fruits of the wheat. They are considered a particular delicacy. Figuratively, God had intended the Israelites to be like "the first fruit on the fig tree in its first season" (Hosea 9:10 ESV), and in Micah 7:1–2, a "godly person" is compared to a "first-ripe fig." Secondly, there are the late figs, which are harvested after the summer at the late fruit and grain harvest. His exhortation to "recognize that He is near, right at the door," is a clear invitation to be ready for the early fig harvest. He is warning us to be ready so that we will not face a "closed door" as the foolish virgins will and as a result will have to wait until the late fig harvest.[14]

With the Feast of Ingathering, Scripture specifically refers to two kinds of late autumn harvests: that of the threshing floor (fruits and grains), and that of the wine vat, which represents the grape harvest. Likewise, after the heat of the tribulations, Christ will come for the over-ripe late autumn harvest of the foolish virgins, which will then have matured through the refining fires. Immediately afterward follows the grape harvest of the wrath of God for the unbelieving world that remains on the earth.[15]

Confirmation for this sequence of events can be found in the Feast of Trumpets. This feast occurs just before the Feast of Ingathering (Leviticus 23:24). This timing agrees firstly with the fact that the late harvest rapture will be announced by the "trumpet of God" (1 Thessalonians 4:16; see also Matthew 24:31) and secondly with the teaching of Revelation 8 that the trumpet also ushers in the beginning of God's wrath. Of special importance is here the fact that the key rapture passages of Matthew 24:29, 1 Corinthians 15:52, and 1 Thessalonians 4:16 all speak of the rapture occurring at the blast of a trumpet (or the "last trumpet"). However, in the parable of the ten virgins no trumpet call is mentioned, only the shout of the bridegroom's best man (the *krauge* shout that we had examined in chapter 3). This confirms firstly that there will be two *different* raptures (one involving only a shout and the other a trumpet call); and secondly that the second rapture, which is described as a globally-visible spectacle in the three passages listed above, will not occur until after the summer heat of the tribulation, at the time of the Feast of Trumpets (hence it will be announced with a "trumpet call"!).

The "last trumpet" call referred to in 1 Corinthians 15:52 is therefore not the last (seventh) trumpet of Revelation, which announces the final phase of God's wrath and in any case would not have inspired any meaningful associations in the minds of Paul's readership[16] but rather *the last trumpet blow of the Feast of Trumpets*, which occurs right before the late autumn harvest feast. Those who consider 1 Corinthians 15:51, which says that we will "all be changed," to be an argument against two raptures miss the fact that this passage speaks of a two-fold fulfillment. Like Old Testament prophecy that does not clearly distinguish between the first and last comings of Christ, this scripture teaches us about the fact of the rapture without separating the two phases of its realization.

Finally, we know that the Feast of Booths (or Feast of Tabernacles), which is celebrated in conjunction with the Feast of Ingathering, symbolizes the moment when Israel moved out of Egypt and began to dwell in booths (temporary shelters; Leviticus 23:42–43). In Scripture,

Egypt is associated with sinfulness and reliance on the world rather than on God. In the same way, the late harvest rapture signifies the removal of the whole church from an ungodly, unrighteous world and its final entrance into the promised land of heaven. The Feast of Booths is then concluded on the eighth day with a holy assembly (Leviticus 23:36). This is the climax of celebrating God's removal of the Israelites from Egypt, the land of their bondage, and points forward to the final judgments when God will forever separate His children from the unsaved who remain in spiritual bondage. The heat of the 70th week of Daniel tribulations are therefore not only designed to refine the foolish virgins of the church. Like the separating of God's people from idolatrous Egyptian society, the tribulations will sift out the unrepentant and pretenders from truly born-again believers.

It is amazing to see how the Old Testament feasts, especially the three harvest feasts, prefigure the exact sequence of end times events, as depicted in the chart below.

Christ the first fruits resurrected 1 Cor. 15:23	First fruits of the church raptured Rev. 14:1-5	'Heat' of the tribulations Rev. 14:6-13		Late harvest rapture (rest of church) Rev. 14:14-16	Grape harvest of God's wrath Rev. 14:17-20
First Fruits Offering / Passover	Feast of the Harvest / Pentecost	summer heat		Feast of Trumpets	Feast of Ingathering / Feast of Booths
barley harvest	wheat & early fig harvest			harvest of all other grains and fruits	
March-April	May-June	July	August	September	October

Figure 9. Ancient Jewish harvest cycles and feasts and the future comings of Christ

The First Fruits Compared to Other Groups in Revelation

So who are these 144,000 "first fruit" believers? Most theologians have tended to equate them with either the 144,000 sealed Jewish believers depicted in the first half Revelation chapter 7 or the "great multitude" of the second half of that chapter who stand raptured before the throne of God. However, this cannot be. Even though the 144,000 first fruits are, like the great multitude, raptured in heaven before God's throne, both represent two very distinct groups. The first fruits are raptured at the first fruits rapture, which, following the sequence of Revelation 14, occurs at the beginning of the 70th week, before the reign of the Antichrist (after the first seal), and before the beginning of tribulations. In contrast, the great multitude is explicitly said to have "come out of the great tribulation," which means that it must have been raptured at the late autumn harvest.

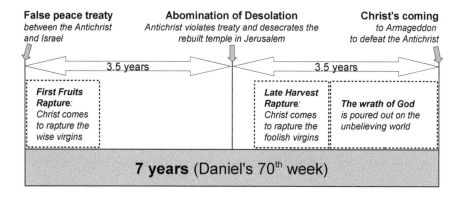

Figure 10. The 70th week of Daniel with rapture timings

When we compare the Revelation 14 first fruits with the great multitude of Revelation 7, we quickly notice how different both groups are. Firstly, the great multitude is described as one "which no one could count" (v. 9). In contrast, the first fruits are numbered at 144,000, which, even though it is almost certainly symbolic, is definitely a countable number. Secondly, the great multitude is depicted as having "come out of the great tribulation" (v. 14), whereas this is not said of the first fruits, whose rapture occurs well before then. Thirdly, we have noted that the first fruits are in numerous ways portrayed as a unique group. They are said to sing a "new song" which no one else could learn, including, of course, the great multitude. They are not "defiled with women" but "kept themselves chaste [lit. are virgins]". This is a reference to spiritual purity in the sense of undivided devotion to God and obedience to His commandments. It does not mean that they cannot be married because the scriptures state in Hebrews 13:4 that "[m]arriage is to be held in honor among all." The Message translation aptly paraphrases Revelation 14:4 as: "They ... lived without compromise, virgin-fresh before God". Having this faithful bride of Christ in mind, Paul wrote to the Corinthians that he sought to "present you [to Christ] as a pure virgin" (2 Corinthians 11:2). The description of the first fruits group therefore matches the spiritual meaning of the Old Testament first fruits harvest: just as the physical first fruits were meant to be a special offering to the Lord, the spiritual first fruits are a distinguished group, set apart by their close walk with God.

This latter point is then reinforced by the observations that they "follow the Lamb wherever He goes," meaning that they were faithful followers and disciples, and that "no lie was found in their mouth; [for] they are blameless" (14:5). Being described as "blameless" (Gr. *amomos*,[17] lit. "without blemish") means that the first fruits represent the truly sanctified bride of Christ, which is to be "blameless [*amomos*]" when her Lord returns (Ephesians 5:27; see Colossians 1:22). In many ways, this description of the first fruits resembles that of the wise virgins in Matthew 25, which is no coincidence, because the first fruits *are* the wise virgins. Moreover, it is abundantly clear that this group meets the conditions of the preservation promises from Luke 21:36 and Revelation 3:10. This is also confirmed by the fact that the first fruits bear the overcomer promise to the Philadelphian church in Revelation 3:12, the names of God and of Christ, on their foreheads, which makes it clear that they *are* these overcomers.

Table 6. Comparing the overcomer descriptions of Revelation 3 and 14

Revelation 3:12	Revelation 14:1
He who overcomes ... *I will write on him the name of My God ... and My new name.*	[A]nd with Him [were] one hundred and forty-four thousand, *having His name and the name of His Father written on their foreheads.*

In contrast, the great multitude is said to "have washed their robes and made them white in the blood of the Lamb" (v. 14b). Being covered by the blood of the Lamb is a reference to salvation, but why is this group said to have "washed their robes"? The Greek word used for washing, *plyno*[18] occurs only three times in the New Testament. It specifically refers to the washing of clothes or other objects such as fishing nets. In Scripture, the robes of the saints symbolize two things. Firstly, the robes symbolize the righteousness of Christ, by which we through grace gain entrance into eternity with God. As the prophet Isaiah wrote, "My soul will exult in my God; For He has clothed me with garments of salvation, He has wrapped me with a robe of righteousness." (61:10). Secondly, as we had seen before, the robes signify the righteous acts of the saints (Revelation 19:8).

In Revelation 3:2, Christ heavily criticizes the spiritually "dead" church of Sardis, saying, "I have not found your deeds completed in the sight of My God." He then points out that some in that church "have not soiled their garments; and they will walk with Me in white, for they are worthy [worthy to escape the tribulations, as stated in Luke 21:36]" (v. 4b). Here, we see that believers can, after receiving garments of righteousness through faith in Jesus, get them soiled through compromise and disobedience. This was the case with the church in Sardis, where soiled clothes symbolize incomplete and compromised sanctification (rather than a loss of salvation). But those who followed Christ closely and are commended for their faithfulness had not "soiled" their robes and are therefore considered "worthy" to be part of the first fruits rapture.

Similarly, Isaiah laments that "all our righteous deeds are like a filthy garment" (64:6b). Here, Isaiah is not talking about his or the Israelites' lack of salvation, since salvation was provided under the Old Testament law, which looked forward to Jesus' atoning death. Rather, these supposedly "righteous deeds," which are in reality like "filthy garments," are works done out of self-effort and not from abiding in Christ. Therefore, the soiling of the garments we received from Christ not only results from outright sin but also when we do things *for* God out of our own strength, rather than doing them *in* Him and *through* Him.

The same meaning is shown in Zechariah's vision of the high priest Joshua before the throne of God. As a high priest under the Old Testament law, Joshua was commanded to wear a white linen tunic (Exodus 28:39), symbolizing his righteous status (salvation) before God by observing and administering the law. However, in the vision Joshua was "clothed with filthy garments," and so God orders him to be clothed with "festal robes" instead (Zechariah 3:4), affirming that "If you will walk in My ways and if you will perform My service, then you will also govern My house" (v. 7). By symbolically giving Joshua new, clean clothes, God put him back on the track of sanctification and faithful service. Importantly, God's promise to Joshua was conditional on his faithful and obedient service.

This helps us to understand the picture used in Revelation 7 with the great multitude: they enter the Great Tribulation with soiled garments, spiritually compromised and unfit to meet their Lord. In both Revelation 7:14 and 22:14, the verb "to wash" (*plyno*) is in the active voice, meaning the washing is performed by the subject (the believers in question), and not by someone else. This directly points to the fact that this washing is not done by Christ (although certainly with His enabling), but is expected of these saints, whose robes got soiled through compromise with the world. This group therefore represents the foolish virgins who ran out of (spiritual) oil. When they first got saved, they had received new garments of righteousness. Now, through the refining fires of the tribulations, their robes are washed and again "made white," not through self-righteousness, but through the righteousness that comes from the blood of Christ. The fiery trials they go through therefore effect the sanctification that they had previously shunned as they had preferred the easy lifestyle of spiritual compromise with the world. This refinement process will therefore be a direct fulfillment of the prophecies contained in Daniel 12:10 (NKJV, emphasis added): "Many shall be purified, *made white*, and refined" as well as in Daniel 11:35 (NKJV, emphasis added): "And some of those of understanding [saved believers who understand the gospel] shall fall, to refine them, purify them, and *make them white*, until the time of the end." We will further present reasons why this multitude is not just made up of "tribulation saints" in chapter 6.

The Church First Fruits and the Jewish First Fruits

Another common interpretation of the first fruits is to equate them with the 144,000 Jewish believers from the first half of Revelation 7, presumably because their number is the same. But, as Dr. William R. Newill in his book on Revelation stated, "The repetition of the number 144,000, one of governmental completeness and fullness, is not necessarily conclusive proof that the two companies are one and the same."[19] The one thing that they have in common is that they are both first fruits: the 144,000 from Revelation 14 are the first fruits of the church, while the 144,000 Jews are the first fruits of Israel, who believe when they see Jesus come in the clouds and realize that He is their Messiah (compare Revelation 1:7).

But here, the similarities end. While the first fruits are clearly standing in heaven before the beginning of the tribulations, the Jewish group is being sealed while still on earth, just before the outpouring of God's wrath:

> And I saw another angel ascending from the rising of the sun,
> having the seal of the living God; and he cried out with a
> loud voice to the four angels to whom it was granted to harm
> the earth and the sea, saying, "Do not harm the earth or the

sea or the trees until we have sealed the bond-servants of our
God on their foreheads."

(Revelation 7:2–3)

The reference to the harming of earth, sea, and trees points to the wrath of God as described in the subsequent chapter: the first trumpet judgment burns a third of the earth and the trees, and the second trumpet turns a third of the sea into blood (Revelation 8:7–9). Rather than being raptured before the Great Tribulation, or during it like the great multitude, this group receives a special seal in order to *protect them through* the time of God's wrath. In Revelation 9, which is in the middle of the wrath, it says that the army of locusts sent by God to torment the unbelieving world could only touch "the men who do not have the seal of God on their foreheads" (v. 4). This implies that those who receive the seal are still on the earth at that time; otherwise the locusts would not be given such specific instruction. Moreover, in contrast to the first fruits believers, we note that these 144,000 Jews receive a protective *seal*, while the first fruits have the actual *names* of both God and the Lamb written on their foreheads.

Another distinctive feature of the Jewish first fruits is their explicit identification with Jewish tribes. They are depicted as groups of 12,000 from each of the 12 tribes of Israel. Even though the number 12,000 is likely symbolic, just as the division of Israel into 12 tribes is full of symbolic significance,[20] it makes no sense to view them as "spiritual tribes" that supposedly represent different sections of the church. After all, God has a clear plan to bring redemption to Israel in the end times (Romans 9–11), and it seems reasonable that this group of 144,000 sealed Jewish servants has a key role to play in it. From this perspective, it would then make sense that these servants continue to witness on the earth to their fellow Jews while God's wrath is in full force, although nothing is said about their role as witnesses or their ability to even gain any converts. However, everything that is stated about them points to the fact that they are a unique group of God's servants from amongst the

Jews, chosen to carry out God's purposes on earth in relation to Israel while the church has already been removed.

In contrast, the 144,000 from Revelation 14 are said to be "purchased from the earth" [Gr. *ge*,[21] land, ground, the whole inhabited earth], indicating that they are taken from all nations (and there is certainly no indication in the text that they are Jewish). Consequently, all three groups in Revelation 7 and 14 are not only *described* in very different ways, they *are* in fact different and cannot be equated with each other.

Table 7. Comparing the three groups of Revelation 7 and 14

	First Fruits *(Revelation 14:1–5)*	Great multitude *(Revelation 7:9–17)*	Jewish Servants *(Revelation 7:1–8)*
General setting and description	"Then I looked, and behold, the Lamb was standing on Mount Zion, and with Him one hundred and forty-four thousand, having His name and the name of His Father written on their foreheads." (v. 1)	"After these things I looked, and behold, a great multitude which no one could count, from every nation and all tribes and peoples and tongues, standing before the throne and before the Lamb, clothed in white robes, and palm branches were in their hands." (v. 9)	"After this I saw four angels standing at the four corners of the earth, holding back the four winds of the earth, so that no wind would blow on the earth or on the sea or on any tree. And I saw another angel ascending from the rising of the sun, having the seal of the living God; and he cried out with a loud voice to the four angels to whom it was granted to harm the earth and the sea, saying, "Do not harm the earth or the sea or the trees until we have sealed the bond-servants of our God on their foreheads." (vv. 1–3)
Where they came from	"These have been purchased from among men as first fruits to God and to the Lamb." (v. 4b)	"These are the ones who come out of the great tribulation.... They will hunger no longer, nor thirst anymore; nor will the sun beat down on them, nor any heat; for the Lamb in the center of the throne will be their shepherd, and will guide them to springs of the water of life; and God will wipe every tear from their eyes." (vv. 14a;16–17)	*The context implies that they are on the earth and will remain there during the outpouring of God's wrath. Compare Revelation 9:3–5:* "Then out of the smoke came locusts upon the earth, and power was given them, as the scorpions of the earth have power. They were told not to hurt the grass of the earth, nor any green thing, nor any tree, but only the men who do not have the seal of God on their foreheads."

Distinctive spiritual or other characteristics	"And they sang a new song before the throne and before the four living creatures and the elders; and no one could learn the song except the one hundred and forty-four thousand who had been purchased from the earth. These are the ones who have not been defiled with women, for they have kept themselves chaste. These are the ones who follow the Lamb wherever He goes.... And no lie was found in their mouth; they are blameless." (vv. 3; 4a; 5)	"[A]nd they have washed their robes and made them white in the blood of the Lamb." (v. 14b)	"And I heard the number of those who were sealed, one hundred and forty-four thousand sealed from every tribe of the sons of Israel: from the tribe of Judah, twelve thousand were sealed, from the tribe of Reuben twelve thousand, from the tribe of Gad twelve thousand, from the tribe of Asher twelve thousand, from the tribe of Naphtali twelve thousand, from the tribe of Manasseh twelve thousand, from the tribe of Simeon twelve thousand, from the tribe of Levi twelve thousand, from the tribe of Issachar twelve thousand, from the tribe of Zebulun twelve thousand, from the tribe of Joseph twelve thousand, from the tribe of Benjamin, twelve thousand were sealed." (vv. 4–8)

Table 8. Four kinds of first fruits

Christ **(1 Corinthians 15:20, 23)**	Christ is the first fruits of those who are "asleep" (meaning Jesus was the first to be resurrected to eternal life).
All believers (James 1:18)	The believers are the first fruits of all creation, meaning they are the first to be saved and regenerated during this age, whereas the rest of creation awaits its redemption from decay and sin during Jesus' millennial reign and then the eternal state (compare Romans 8:19–23). Likewise, present believers will enter the millennium in their eternal, glorified bodies, whereas the perfect state of creation will only be partially restored at that time.
The wise virgins (Revelation 14:4)	The 144,000 believers of Revelation 14 are the first fruits of the church, to be resurrected and raptured at the first fruits rapture. They are the first to stand before the throne of God.
The Jewish bond-servants (Revelation 7:1–8)	The 144,000 born-again Jews of Revelation are the first fruits of Israel. They recognize Him as the Messiah when He comes in the clouds to rapture the rest of the church.

The First Fruits Revealed in the 24 Elders

Another depiction of the first fruits can be found in Revelation 4–5. Here, we see a group of 24 elders seated around the throne of God:

> Around the throne [of God] were twenty-four thrones; and
> upon the thrones I saw twenty-four elders sitting, clothed in
> *white garments*, and *golden crowns* on their heads.
>
> (Revelation 4:4, emphases added)

The Greek word for elder, *presbuteros*,[22] literally refers to an older man or elder and therefore to a person of dignity and authority. In the New Testament, a *presbuteros* is a church elder or overseer (Titus 1:5; compare the English word "presbyter"). Many commentators, and especially the vast majority of pretribulational theologians, consider these elders to symbolize the raptured church in heaven. The reason for this is that they possess three key characteristics that reflect promises to overcoming believers in the letters to the seven churches: white garments,[23] crowns, and thrones.

- "He who overcomes will thus be clothed in *white garments*." (Revelation 3:5)
- "Be faithful until death, and I will give you the *crown of life*." (Revelation 2:10b).
  Also: "[to the Philadelphian church] hold fast what you have, so that no one will take your *crown*" (Revelation 3:11).
- "He who overcomes, I will grant to him to sit down with Me on My *throne*, as I also overcame and sat down with My Father on His *throne*." (Revelation 3:21). Note how in Revelation 4:4 the 24 elders sit on thrones that are arrayed right around the throne of God Himself.
  (emphases added)

Although some scholars believe that the elders represent angels or heavenly beings, such an interpretation is unscriptural. Angels are "ministering spirits" that are sent out to serve God's people (Hebrews 1:14). Nowhere in Scripture are angels referred to as "elders" or are said to wear crowns, sit on thrones, or have been promised to reign with Christ.

The crowns that Jesus promised to overcomers are not like the royal crowns that He Himself is depicted to wear at His glorious return for Armageddon (Revelation 19:12). The Greek word for Christ's royal crown is *diadem*[24]. In contrast, the crowns mentioned in the letters to the churches are *stephanos*[25] crowns—the victory wreaths that were awarded to victorious athletes at the Olympic Games. *Stephanos* is also the term used for the crown of thorns that Jesus wore on the cross, where he won the victory over the evil one, and so it is fitting that those who overcome Satan by Christ's power will receive the same victory wreath that He once wore.

Significantly, the 24 elders are described as wearing *stephanos* crowns, which identify them as overcoming believers. Moreover, just like the first fruits, the elders sing about themselves a "new song" (we could call it the "first fruits song") about reigning with Christ. In this "new song," they declare themselves to have been "purchased … to God," which is the same Greek word (*agorazo*), carrying the same meaning as the first fruits of Revelation 14. The song also reveals the group to be reigning on the earth, which is Christ's promise to the overcoming churches of Revelation:

> And they sang a new song, saying:
> "You are worthy to take the scroll,
> And to open its seals;
> For You were slain,
> And have redeemed [lit. purchased, *agorazo*] us to God by
> Your blood
> Out of every tribe and tongue and people and nation,
> And have made us kings and priests to our God;
> And we shall reign on the earth."
>
> (Revelation 5:9–10 NKJV)

Clearly, this "new song" closely identifies the elders with the raptured first fruits—both are one and the same group.[26] It is important to note that the 24 elders are already in heaven before the beginning of the 70th week of Daniel (the Antichrist does not arise until the first seal in Revelation 6). This is why the popular pretribulational position assumes that they represent the raptured church. However, that is a contradiction, because the majority of the church is constituted by the great multitude of Revelation 7. Since an elder is standing there describing to John who this great multitude is and where they have come from, the elder and the multitude cannot be the same. Additionally, the great multitude does not belong to those singing the "new song."

Rather, the 24 elders symbolize the first fruits, who are those amongst the believers who are victorious in their faith at the time Christ returns for the first rapture: those from the Old Covenant (law-abiding Israelites) through the 12 tribes of Israel and those from the New Covenant (followers of Christ) through the 12 apostles. Together, they represent the two "breads" of the wheat harvest first fruits offering—the combined community of overcomer saints. Throughout Scripture, 12 is a number that symbolizes authority and apostolic government (12 patriarchs, 12 tribes, 12 leaders under Moses and Aaron,[27] 12 judges, 12 governors under Solomon,[28] 12 apostles). This fits with the fact that these elders will "reign on the earth." Taken together, both numbers add up to the symbolic figure of 24, which exactly corresponds to the number of Old Testament priestly divisions recorded in 1 Chronicles 24. Therefore, overcomers from Old and New Covenants together represent the "royal priesthood" (1 Peter 2:9) that Christ redeemed for Himself at the cross. After the rapture, they are standing around the throne of God, just as those who will be "worthy to escape" in Luke 21:36 are promised to "stand before the Son of Man."

Conclusion

In this chapter, we have seen that the first fruits of Revelation 14 are a distinct group from all other groups mentioned in the book of Revelation. These first fruits represent the wise virgins of the church that are raptured right before the start of the tribulation period. Together with the first fruit believers of the Old Testament, they are symbolized by the 24 elders of Revelation 4–5. But these passages in Revelation are not the only indications that there will be more than just one rapture. The next two chapters will carefully examine other important end times passages throughout especially the New Testament, and point out some significant contradictions within pretribulationist thinking that are resolved as we take into account the complete picture of God's teaching on the end times.

The Woman and the Overcomer-Child

Another biblical reference to the first fruits rapture can be found in Revelation 12, a chapter full of symbolisms which describes a woman and the birth of her child:

> A great sign appeared in heaven: a woman clothed with the sun, and the moon under her feet, and on her head a crown of twelve stars; and she was with child; and she cried out, being in labor and in pain to give birth.
>
> Then another sign appeared in heaven: and behold, a great red dragon having seven heads and ten horns, and on his heads were seven diadems. And his tail swept away a third of the stars of heaven and threw them to the earth. And the dragon stood before the woman who was about to give birth, so that when she gave birth he might devour her child.
>
> And she gave birth to a son, a male [Gr. *arren*[29]] child, who is to rule all the nations with a rod of iron; and her child was caught up [Gr. *harpazo*[30]] to God and to His throne.
>
> (Revelation 12:1–5)

The common interpretation is that the woman represents Israel, and her child is Christ, because Christ was born to an Israelite woman. However, both immediate and wider contexts contradict such an interpretation. As we had stated before, the book of Revelation clearly defines itself as being about the future, about "things which must soon take place" (Revelation 1:1). By the time John had written this book, the birth and death of Christ were already past. The wider context therefore suggests that the woman and the child are future events from John's perspective.

The other argument for the historic perspective is that the fall of Satan from heaven, which is described later in this chapter, was witnessed by Jesus as described in Luke 10:18–19:"I was watching Satan fall from heaven like lightning. Behold, I have given you authority ... over all the power of the enemy." But even though Satan was indeed defeated at the cross after these words were spoken, the description of the fall of Satan in Revelation 12 is quite clearly a future event:

> And there was war in heaven, Michael and his angels waging war with the dragon. The dragon and his angels waged war, and they were not strong enough, and there was no longer a place found for them in heaven. And the great dragon was thrown down, the serpent of old who is called the devil and Satan, who deceives the whole world; he was thrown down to the earth, and his angels were thrown down with him. Then I heard a loud voice in heaven, saying,
>
> "Now the salvation, and the power, and the kingdom of our God and the authority of His Christ have come, for the accuser of our brethren has been thrown down, he who accuses them before our God day and night. And they overcame him because of the blood of the Lamb and because of the word of their testimony, and they did not love their life even when faced with death.
>
> For this reason, rejoice, O heavens and you who dwell in them. *Woe to the earth and the sea, because the devil has come down to you, having great wrath, knowing that he has only a short time."*
>
> (Revelation 12:7–12, emphasis added)

The clue to the timing of this event lies in the last verse. The devil exhibits great wrath because his time is "short." For the devil, 2,000 years are not a short amount of time. If his fall did indeed happen before the death of Christ, then this statement would make little sense. Moreover, he is described as having "great wrath." Although the devil is always wrathful against the children of God, this description carries a particular emphasis. The exclamation "woe to the earth" indicates that this is indeed an unprecedented time of Satan's wrath on the earth: the reign of his minion, the Antichrist, which will be an unparalleled time of evil and persecution of God's people, both Jews and Christians.

The immediate context equally contradicts the historic perspective. In verses 4–5 we hear that the devil positions himself in front of the woman in order to "devour her child," who is then "caught up to God." But Christ was not raptured after His birth; his family fled to Egypt, and He was not taken up to heaven until after his death. Moreover, this taking up was not a last-minute escape from the devil, as depicted in this passage. Rather, it was a glorious ascension in front of His disciples after he had appeared to them and others for many days—all without any interference by Satan. Consequently, the description of the child does not fit with the events surrounding the birth of Jesus.

Equating the child with Christ is typically based on the fact that the child is said to "to rule all the nations with a rod of iron" (v. 5), a prophecy from Psalm 2:9 that finds its fulfillment in Revelation 19:15 at Christ's coming at Armageddon. However, such a promise of authority over the nations is also given to overcoming believers in the letter to Thyatira:

> He who overcomes, and he who keeps My deeds until the end, TO HIM I WILL GIVE AUTHORITY OVER THE NATIONS; AND HE SHALL RULE THEM WITH A ROD OF IRON, AS THE VESSELS OF THE POTTER ARE BROKEN TO PIECES, as I also have received authority from My Father.
>
> (Revelation 2:26–27)

When we consider all of these facts in their totality, only one conclusion is possible: the child in Revelation 12 symbolizes those in the church who have been faithful to Christ and have "overcome" the temptations and devices of the evil one. As it is written, "You are from God, little children, and have overcome them; because greater is He who is in you [Jesus] than he who is in the world [the devil]." (1 John 4:4). The woman who symbolically gives "birth" to the child is the whole church. Like a mother considers her children to be part of her, the woman of Revelation 12 is said to bring forth a part of her in birth: her child is both her product and also an intrinsic part of who she is. Just like children are related to their parents yet are also distinct from them, the overcomer-child depicted here is a separate entity: part of the church yet also set apart in a spiritual sense.

This child is symbolically (not literally) said to be a "male child" (*arren*), a firstborn son, which further emphasizes the special status of that child, as stipulated in Old Testament law and cited in the Gospel of Luke: "EVERY firstborn MALE [*arren*] THAT OPENS THE WOMB SHALL BE CALLED HOLY TO THE LORD" (Luke 2:23). Just like Christ is "the firstborn of all creation" (Colossians 1:15), His followers who are symbolized by the child are spiritual firstborn children. These are none other than the first fruits believers described in Revelation 14.

After having been "born," this child is then "caught up" to God. The Greek word for this, *harpazo*, literally means "snatched away" or "carried off by force." Very importantly, *harpazo* is the term used to describe the rapture in 1 Thessalonians 4:17, which is the most specific and detailed rapture passage in all of Scripture. This means that Revelation 12:5 outlines a rapture—not the ascension of Christ, who was "lifted up" (Gr. *epairo*[31]), which also carries the meaning of being exalted, and is therefore very different from *harpazo*) in Acts 1:9, nor the rapture of the entire church, but the rapture of the overcomer-child, which symbolizes the first fruits, the 144,000 of Revelation 14.

Finally, we see how Revelation 12 closely parallels the sequence of events in Revelation 14. After the first fruits are taken, the woman, who symbolizes the remainder of the church, goes through the Great Tribulation:

> Then the woman fled into the wilderness where she had a place prepared by God, so that there she would be nourished for one thousand two hundred and sixty days.
>
> (Revelation 12:6)

The time period given here is exactly the same as the 42 months (3.5 years) duration of the global rule of the Antichrist over "every tribe and people and tongue and nation," during which the saints are given into his hands (Revelation 13:5, 7; Daniel 7:25). Consequently, the majority of the church, which was not raptured, will be persecuted by the Antichrist. But rather than being left alone to their own devices, God has already "prepared" a place for them, where they will be nourished and sustained in the midst of fiery trials and seemingly overpowering adversity. God never abandons His church, though they be foolish virgins. No, quite the contrary, it is in the most trying of times that the church will find His provision to be of greatest abundance. In the process of needing to rely entirely on their Lord and Father, the unprepared, carnal believers who missed the first fruits rapture are being transformed into powerful witnesses—even martyrs—who, having now become overcomers, are like a shining spotless bride, ready to meet their Master.

Chapter 5 Notes

1. This position, dispensationalist premillennialism, had been discussed in chapter 3.

2. In the book of Daniel, the expression "your people" refers to Daniel's ethnic group, the Jews. In contrast, the future church saints are called the "saints," or literally the "holy ones" (Aramaic: *qaddish*, equivalent to the Hebrew *qadosh, Strong's Concordance,* H6918).

3. According to the day-year principle of Old Testament prophecy, one day represents one prophetic year of 360 days (see Leviticus 25:6, Ezekiel 4:6).

4. The building of the wall under Nehemiah only took 52 days (Nehemiah 6:15).

5. The exact year of the death of Christ is debated. Scholars place it in the 28–33 AD date range. However, the most reliable way to determine it is to calculate from the year in which Jesus was baptized and began His public ministry. According to Luke 3:1, Jesus was baptized in the 15th year of the reign of the Roman Emperor Tiberius Caesar. This emperor ascended the throne on September, 14 AD, meaning that the first year of his reign was 14 AD and the 15th year was therefore from autumn 28 AD to autumn 29 AD. Jesus' public ministry lasted for 3.5 years, which takes us to the Passover of 32 or 33 AD. It cannot have been 31 AD for two reasons. Firstly, John's Gospel records that Jesus saw at least three Passovers after His baptism. Secondly, the Passover celebration is in spring, and 28 + 3.5 as the earliest possibility takes us at least to the summer of the year 31 AD, which is already after the Passover. When counting from autumn 28 or 29 AD, Jesus' death must therefore have been in 32 or 33 AD.

    The advantage of 33 AD is that in that year the Passover fell on a Friday. This fits with the statement of Scripture that His triumphal entry into Jerusalem was five days before the Passover, which was a Sunday (John 12:1, "six days before the Passover," was counted from *the day before* the triumphal entry). Another reason that the Passover must have been on a Friday is that Jesus celebrated the Passover with His disciples a day early, on Thursday evening. This is because the day after His crucifixion was a Sabbath (Saturday), and so the bones of the thieves were broken so that they would die sooner and the bodies could be removed before the onset of the Sabbath on Friday evening. That is also why the women could not embalm His body after He was placed in the tomb (during the Sabbath) but had to wait until the day after the Sabbath (the Sunday), when they found the tomb empty (Jesus resurrected on Sunday morning). All four Gospels agree that Jesus was crucified on a Friday and before the Sabbath. After being crucified on Friday, the day of the Passover, Jesus then remained in the grave for "three days." According to Jewish custom, each part of a 24-hour period would count as a full "day." Therefore, the "three days" in the grave were Friday, Saturday, and Sunday, each counted as a "day" (as opposed to measuring the "three days" as three complete 24-hour periods, as we in our modern era would do). Additionally, recent research confirms that an earthquake occurred on Friday, April 3, 33 AD, just as described in Matthew 27:51 (see http://news.discovery.com/history/jesus-crucifixion-120524. html). See also http://www.gotquestions.org/length-Jesus-ministry.html.

6. They are equivalent to 476 solar years of 365.25 days each (483 * 360 / 365.25 = 476.06), plus one additional year to make up for the changeover from BC to AD time which skips the zero (1 BC jumps straight to 1 AD, therefore a total of 477 solar years), which takes us exactly from 444/5 BC to 32/3 AD. Earlier decrees, such as the one made by Cyrus to Zerubbabel in 538 BC or the one given by Artaxerxes to Ezra in 457 BC, did not mandate the reconstruction of the wall and establishment of Jerusalem as a politically self-governing city, which is indicated in Daniel's prophecy by the reference to the rebuilding of gates and walls—structures of military, and therefore of political, significance. Also, these edicts do not have the 483-year period end in the year that Jesus was put to death ("cut off"). Measured from Artaxerxes' decree to Nehemiah, it is significant that the 483 years may have ended exactly on Palm Sunday with the entrance of Christ into Jerusalem, since that was a public, political event, which marked Jesus" position as "Messiah the Prince."

7. The "times of the Gentiles" could not have begun in 586 BC with the capture of Jerusalem by Babylonian king Nebuchadnezzar, because Jesus' prophecy concerns the future and could therefore only have been fulfilled after His death.

8. *Strong's Concordance*, G59.

9. Ibid., G3583.

10. Ibid., G3584.

11. Compare also Isaiah 63 for the symbolism of the grape harvest as God's wrath against the nations.

12. The difference between the hour of judgment and the wrath of God will be explained in chapter 6.

13. *Pentecost* is Greek for "fifty," referring to the 50-day period between the Passover Sabbath and the Feast of the Harvest.

14. The time period between the first fruits of the wheat harvest (Pentecost) and the Feast of Ingathering just over 4 months, from the 6th of Sivan to the 15th of Tishri (approx. late May to the beginning of October).

15. This wrath starts with the seventh seal of Revelation 8.

16. Paul's audience at Corinth received his letters several decades before the book of Revelation was written. However, they would have been aware of the Jewish feasts prescribed in the Old Testament, and almost certainly

associated the last trumpet with the Feast of Trumpets. Today's messianic Jews acknowledge this same link.

17. *Strong's Concordance*, G299.

18. Ibid., G4150.

19. William R. Newill, *Revelation Chapter-By-Chapter: A Classic Devotional Commentary* (Grand Rapids, MI: Kregel Publications, 1994), 157.

20. In the Old Testament there are at least 19 different lists of Israelite tribes, which record anywhere from 10 to 13 tribes. In the list of 12 tribes in Revelation 7, the tribes of Dan and Ephraim are omitted, while Joseph and Manasseh are listed as separate tribes (usually, the OT lists either include Joseph and omit his two sons Ephraim and Manasseh, or they omit Joseph and include the two sons; see Genesis 49 and Ezekiel 48). The symbolic character of this list is heightened by the fact that modern Israelites are usually no longer able to clearly trace their ancestry to a particular tribe.

21. *Strong's Concordance*, G1093.

22. Ibid., G4245.

23. The Greek term for garment in Revelation 3:5 and 4:4 is *himation* (*Strong's Concordance*, G2440), which is quite distinct in use and meaning from the term for robe (*stole*, G4749) used for the "white robes" of the great multitude in Revelation 7. The *himation* is the garment promised to overcomers, whereas the *stole* is the robe that became filthy and must be washed clean (compare also Revelation 22:14). See chapter 11 for more details.

24. Ibid., G1238.

25. Ibid., G4735.

26. The elders who are said to be present when the first fruits arrive before the throne (Revelation 14:3) are the symbolic "12" elders that represent the first fruits of the Old Covenant saints. This throne scene depicts the heavenly reunion of overcoming first fruits from both Old and New Covenants.

27. See Numbers 1:44.

28. See 1 Kings 4:7.

29. *Strong's Concordance*, G730.

30. Ibid., G726.

31. Ibid., G1869.

Chapter 6

Pretribulation Versus Prewrath
Part I: Why There Will Be Two Raptures

*For the Lord Himself will descend from heaven with a shout, with
the voice of the archangel and with the trumpet of God, and the
dead in Christ will rise first.*
*Then we who are alive and remain will be caught up together with
them in the clouds to meet the Lord in the air, and so we shall
always be with the Lord.*
1 Thessalonians 4:16–17

Even though we will deal here with essential end times scriptures, it is not necessary to read this or the next chapter in order to understand the main points of this book. These two chapters are primarily written for those who hold specific and clear views of the rapture and its timing and find it hard to believe that there should be two separate raptures plus the coming of Christ at Armageddon (three appearances in total). If that is you, then with these two chapters we humbly seek to challenge your current understanding of end times prophecy, especially of key rapture passages.

If you feel you get bogged down while working through these sections, you can always skip ahead and return to them later on. But we do encourage you to engage with the Scripture passages below; they are the "meat" of end times prophecies. If you want to grow in your understanding of the end times, then do not be afraid to dig in and study the Word of God. Be like a Berean: don't trust what we say until you find it confirmed by the Word!

The Pretribulational Rapture View

The pretribulational perspective of the end times rests on the following key assumptions:[1]

1. The entire church is raptured at the beginning of the 70th week, the final 7-year period (pretribulationists usually call this period the "tribulation period"). This whole period is considered to be the wrath of God.

2. Those believers who do go through the tribulation are those who are saved during this 7-year period without any witness by the church (since the church has been completely removed). They presumably convert to Christianity because of the shock of seeing so many people disappear, and at the witness of the 144,000 Jewish evangelists (they are presumed to be evangelists) described in Revelation 7:1–8. These conversions apparently occur without any involvement of the Holy Spirit, since the Spirit is the "restrainer" who currently prevents the Antichrist from exerting his full power (2 Thessalonians 2:6–8). Once the Holy Spirit is removed from the earth, the Antichrist can rise to achieve world domination. The "great multitude" described in the second half of Revelation 7 (which we discussed in the previous chapter) is therefore only made up of these "tribulation saints."

3. The raptured church will return together with Jesus for his "coming in glory" to the battle of Armageddon. The church therefore represents the "armies which are in heaven" of Revelation 19:14. The rapture of the church and the second coming of Christ are therefore two distinct events: the rapture occurs at the beginning of the 7-year period, while the second coming occurs at the end.[2]

4. Most pretribulationists believe that both "tribulation saints" and the raptured church will then reign with Christ over the post-Armageddon world for 1,000 years before the eternal state (the new heaven and the new earth) begins. This is the premillennial perspective which we had discussed before and which the early church believed.

Our intention here is to demonstrate from Scripture that points 3 and 4 are correct (besides the fact that there is a second rapture), point 1 is partially correct, and point 2 is basically unscriptural.

The primary challenges to the pretribulational rapture view come from posttribulationism and a more recent approach which is called the prewrath rapture. Posttribulationism simply teaches the opposite of pretribulationism: the rapture of the church occurs after (*post-*) the tribulation, meaning the rapture and the second coming of Christ at Armageddon are one and the same event. The entire church must experience not only the tribulation of the Antichrist but also the wrath of God, although it is asserted that the believers are being "protected" during this time so that the wrath will not hurt them.

The prewrath rapture position only differs from posttribulationism in that it believes that the whole church will be raptured at the end of the Great Tribulation of the church, just before the wrath of God is poured out on the world (hence the "prewrath" rapture). This is because God has promised that his people are "not destined … for wrath" (1 Thessalonians 5:9). According to these two views, the great multitude from Revelation 7 therefore represents the entire church. As we had seen previously, the majority position of the early church was either posttribulational or possibly prewrath.[3]

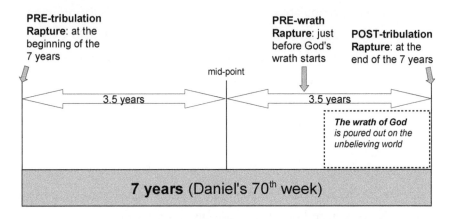

PRE-tribulation Rapture: at the beginning of the 7 years

PRE-wrath Rapture: just before God's wrath starts

POST-tribulation Rapture: at the end of the 7 years

mid-point

3.5 years

3.5 years

The wrath of God is poured out on the unbelieving world

7 years (Daniel's 70ᵗʰ week)

Figure 11. The 70ᵗʰ week of Daniel showing various rapture timing views

Recently, the prewrath rapture position has gained increasing popularity, and is posing a rising challenge to pretribulationism. Why? Because the prewrath view on key rapture and second coming passages has managed to challenge a number of arguments that pretribulationists are forced to make in order for their view to be consistent with Scripture. Now, we will take a closer look at these assertions and where they may turn out to be problematic or even unscriptural.

We will establish from Scripture, particularly from Matthew 24, that there will be two raptures: 1) the first fruits rapture, which is pretribulational, and 2) the late harvest rapture, which is very similar to the prewrath rapture (we assert that all believers will be taken from the earth before the wrath of God starts, which differs from most 19th century proponents of the first fruits rapture perspective). Together with Christ the first fruits, who was raptured (taken up) 40 days after His resurrection, there will therefore be a total of three raptures throughout history.

Likewise, there will be three resurrections for the believers: Firstly, the resurrection of the first fruits of the Old Testament saints, which happened right after Jesus' resurrection. Matthew 27:52 teaches that "many bodies of the saints who had fallen asleep were raised"—"many," but not all of them. Therefore, it is likely that only the Old Testament first fruits saints were raised at that time, together with Christ the first fruits. Secondly, it is equally likely that the first fruits rapture will coincide with the resurrection of the deceased first fruits of the church. After all, the 24 elders in Revelation 4 and 5 represent all first fruits throughout history up to this point, and not only those who will be alive at Jesus' coming. Thirdly, 1 Thessalonians 4:16 clearly teaches that "the dead in Christ will rise first [meaning before the rapture]." In our view, this passage refers to the late harvest (or prewrath) rapture of the "foolish virgin" believers of the church. Consequently, the late harvest rapture will likely involve the resurrection of all remaining Old Testament and New Testament saints who were not first fruits.

Comparing Matthew 24 With Revelation 6–8: The First Five Seals

Matthew 24 poses a particular problem for the pretribulation rapture position. As Stanley Toussaint put it, "pretribulationists would find it disconcerting to have either the church or the rapture in Matthew 24."[4] The reason for this is quite simple: in Matthew's account, the coming of Christ to "gather together His elect" (v. 31) comes *after* the Great Tribulation of the church. Therefore, if Matthew 24 talks about a rapture of the church, then this rapture is most evidently *not before* the tribulation! Consequently, posttribulationists and prewrath advocates both understand Matthew 24 to teach the rapture of the church. Let us examine the text from the beginning:

> As He was sitting on the Mount of Olives, the disciples came to Him privately, saying, "Tell us, when will these things happen, and what will be the sign of Your coming, and of the end of the age?"

And Jesus answered and said to them, "See to it that no one misleads you. For many will come in My name, saying, 'I am the Christ,' and will mislead many. You will be hearing of wars and rumors of wars. See that you are not frightened, for those things must take place, but that is not yet the end. For nation will rise against nation, and kingdom against kingdom, and in various places there will be famines and earthquakes. But all these things are merely the beginning of birth pangs.

Then they will deliver you to tribulation, and will kill you, and you will be hated by all nations because of My name. At that time many will fall away and will betray one another and hate one another. Many false prophets will arise and will mislead many. Because lawlessness is increased, most people's love will grow cold. But the one who endures to the end, he will be saved. This gospel of the kingdom shall be preached in the whole world as a testimony to all the nations, and then the end will come."

(Matthew 24:3–14)

In this passage, Jesus is describing the "sign of [His] coming" in response to the disciple's questions. These signs include wars, rumors of wars, famines, earthquakes, and deceptions. Jesus calls these things "birth pangs." Already here, we notice a remarkable similarity between this passage and the description of the first five seals in Revelation 6. We can view them side by side in Table 9.

Table 9. Mathew 24 compared with the first five seals of Revelation 6

Seal	Matthew 24	Revelation 6
1st seal: Deceptions/ Rise of the Antichrist	4 And Jesus answered and said to them, "See to it that no one misleads you. 5 For many will come in My name, saying, 'I am the Christ,' and will mislead many."	1 Then I saw when the Lamb broke one of the seven seals, and I heard one of the four living creatures saying as with a voice of thunder, "Come." 2 I looked, and behold, a white horse, and he who sat on it had a bow; and a crown was given to him, and he went out conquering and to conquer.
2nd seal: wars	6 And you will hear of wars and rumors of wars. See that you are not troubled; for all these things must come to pass, but the end is not yet. 7 For nation will rise against nation, and kingdom against kingdom.	3 When He broke the second seal, I heard the second living creature saying, "Come." 4 And another, a red horse, went out; and to him who sat on it, it was granted to take peace from the earth, and that men would slay one another; and a great sword was given to him.
3rd seal: economic depression and famines	7 ... and there will be famines....	5 When He broke the third seal, I heard the third living creature saying, "Come." I looked, and behold, a black horse; and he who sat on it had a pair of scales in his hand. 6 And I heard something like a voice in the center of the four living creatures saying, "A quart of wheat for a denarius, and three quarts of barley for a denarius; [outrageously high prices for basic staples] and do not damage the oil and the wine."
4th seal: death, plagues, disasters	7 ... pestilences, and earthquakes in various places.	7 When the Lamb broke the fourth seal, I heard the voice of the fourth living creature saying, "Come." 8 I looked, and behold, an ashen horse; and he who sat on it had the name Death; and Hades was following with him. Authority was given to them over a fourth of the earth, to kill with sword and with famine and with pestilence and by the wild beasts of the earth.
5th seal: martyrs	9 Then they will deliver you to tribulation, and will kill you, and you will be hated by all nations because of My name. 10 At that time many will fall away and will betray one another and hate one another.	9 When the Lamb broke the fifth seal, I saw underneath the altar the souls of those who had been slain because of the word of God, and because of the testimony which they had maintained; 10 and they cried out with a loud voice, saying, "How long, O Lord, holy and true, will You refrain from judging and avenging our blood on those who dwell on the earth?" 11 And there was given to each of them a white robe; and they were told that they should rest for a little while longer, until the number of their fellow servants and their brethren who were to be killed even as they had been, would be completed also.

Wonderfully, we perceive how Scripture confirms itself as Jesus' statements are explicitly matched by John's prophetic vision. Scholars across different camps interpret the white rider of the first seal to symbolize the rise of the Antichrist, the master of deception. Some scholars believe that he is Christ, because of some similarities with the coming of Jesus in Revelation 19 (white horse, crown, conquering), but this misinterpretation itself only shows how effectively the Antichrist will mimic the real Christ! Jesus Himself never makes a direct reference to the Antichrist; instead, He describes him, his false prophet and others who work deception in his name as those who say "I am the Christ." The Greek word *anti-*[5] does not just mean "against" but also "in place of" or "instead." The Antichrist does not just simply try to openly fight against Jesus and the believers—he wants to replace Jesus and be an alternative savior!

The second to fifth seals also closely match Jesus' description of the birth pangs. The martyrs of the fifth seal refer to those believers who are killed during the "tribulation" of the birth pangs. Correspondingly, Jesus says that we will be "hated by all nations," a precise description of the Great Tribulation of the church. But the fifth seal martyrs do not yet represent all of the saints who will be killed during the Great Tribulations, because the "number of their fellow servants and their brethren who were to be killed" is not yet "completed" (v. 11). These "fellow brethren" are other believers who will be martyred until the removal of all remaining saints at the late harvest rapture. The rise of the Antichrist at the first seal marks the beginning of the 42-month (3.5-year) Great Tribulation of the church, whereas the Great Tribulation for the Jews begins at the mid-point of the 70th week of Daniel, with the setting up of the Abomination of Desolation. Then, from the mid-point until the late harvest rapture, both Great Tribulations will be occurring at the same time, and it is likely that this marks the period when the church saints are under the greatest pressure.

Comparing Matthew 24 with Revelation 6–8: The Sixth and Seventh Seals

We now move on to demonstrate that chapters 6, 7, and 8 of Revelation match the chronological sequence of Matthew 24, with only one exception: in Revelation, the Great Tribulation of the church is described in a separate chapter (13) that, together with the preceding and the following chapter, does not fit into the general chronology of the whole book. In Matthew 24, the Great Tribulation comes immediately after the birth pangs, starting with the setting up of the Abomination of Desolation in the reconstructed temple in Jerusalem, exactly as Daniel's prophecy foretold it (Daniel 9:27). After this, Jesus continues to describe the "sign of [His] coming," and now the sequence again matches that of Revelation 6, where the next seal, the sixth, closely correlates with Jesus' account—even in the smallest details:

Table 10. Matthew 24 compared with the sixth seal of Revelation 6

Seal	Matthew 24	Revelation 6
6th seal: sign of the Day of the Lord	29 But immediately after the tribulation of those days THE SUN WILL BE DARKENED, AND THE MOON WILL NOT GIVE ITS LIGHT, AND THE STARS WILL FALL from the sky, and the powers of the heavens will be shaken. 30 And then the sign of the Son of Man will appear in the sky, and then all the tribes of the earth will mourn.	12 I looked when He broke the sixth seal, and there was a great earthquake; and the sun became black as sackcloth made of hair, and the whole moon became like blood; 13 and the stars of the sky fell to the earth, as a fig tree casts its unripe figs when shaken by a great wind. 14 The sky was split apart like a scroll when it is rolled up, and every mountain and island were moved out of their places. 15 Then the kings of the earth and the great men and the commanders and the rich and the strong and every slave and free man hid themselves in the caves and among the rocks of the mountains; 16 and they said to the mountains and to the rocks, "Fall on us and hide us from the presence of Him who sits on the throne, and from the wrath of the Lamb; 17 for the great day of their wrath has come, and who is able to stand?"

The references to heavenly signs in the form of a darkening of sun and moon, the falling of the stars from the sky, and a powerful shaking of creation, are clearly taught in both passages. The sixth seal and the words of Jesus about His coming describe what Old Testament prophecy calls the "Day of the Lord":

> Behold, the *day of the* LORD is coming, cruel, with fury and burning anger, To make the land a desolation; and He will exterminate its sinners from it. For the *stars of heaven and their constellations will not flash forth their light;* The *sun will be dark* when it rises and the *moon will not shed its light.* Thus I will *punish the world for its evil* and the wicked for their iniquity; I will also put an end to the arrogance of the proud and abase the haughtiness of the ruthless.
>
> (Isaiah 13:9–10, emphases added)

> Blow a trumpet in Zion, and sound an alarm on My holy mountain! Let all the inhabitants of the land tremble, for the *day of the* LORD *is coming;* Surely it is near, *a day of darkness and gloom, a day of clouds and thick darkness....* Before them the *earth quakes, the heavens tremble, the sun and the moon grow dark and the stars lose their brightness....* I will display *wonders in the sky and on the earth, blood,* fire and columns of smoke. The sun *will be turned into darkness* and the *moon into blood* before the great and awesome *day of the* LORD comes.
>
> (Joel 2:1–2, 10; 30–31, emphases added)

> Near is the *great day of the* LORD ... a *day of wrath* is that day, a day of trouble and distress, a *day of destruction and desolation*, a *day of darkness and gloom*, a *day of clouds and thick darkness, a day of trumpet and battle cry* against the fortified cities and the high corner towers. I will bring distress on men ... because they have sinned against the LORD; and *their blood will be poured out like dust and their flesh like dung.* Neither their silver nor their gold will be able to deliver them on the *day of the* LORD'S

wrath; and *all the earth will be devoured* in the fire of His jealousy,
for *He will make a complete end, indeed a terrifying one, of all the*
inhabitants of the earth.

(Zephaniah 1:14–18, emphases added)

God's Wrath and Satan's Wrath

Now, what is the Day of the Lord? From Scripture, it is evident that
this is the beginning of the outpouring of God's wrath on an unrepentant
world. It is a day of "darkness and gloom," an "awesome day" of terror
and dread (not a literal 24-hour period, but a period of time). Its focus
is to "punish the world for its evil and the wicked for their iniquity"
(Isaiah 13:11), and its outcome will be the "complete end … of all the
inhabitants of the earth" (Zephaniah 1:18). This is most certainly not
something that God's people must go through, a fact that is taught by
Paul in 1 Thessalonians 5:

> For you yourselves know full well that the *day of the Lord*
> will come just like a thief in the night. While they are saying,
> "Peace and safety!" then destruction will come upon them
> suddenly like labor pains upon a woman with child, and they
> will not escape. *But you, brethren, are not in darkness, that the day*
> *would overtake you like a thief…. For God has not destined us for*
> *wrath.*
>
> (1 Thessalonians 5:2–4, 9, emphases added)

Similarly to the Old Testament prophets, Paul states that the Day
of the Lord will consist of sudden destruction, and there will be no
escape.

Pretribulationists assert that the entire 70th week of Daniel, including
birth pangs, the Antichrist, and the Great Tribulation, is the "Day of
the Lord" and therefore the wrath of God. But Paul's words are not

a description of the Antichrist's reign, which will promise to bring peace to people, but rather of God's terrible wrath. The Antichrist will unite the world under a false, satanic peace by posing as a benevolent ruler. The unbelieving world will be saying "Peace and safety!" when the sudden destruction that Paul talks about here will come on them. The Old Testament passages cited above confirm that the Day of the Lord is a time of utter destruction and desolation against the ungodly, a time of darkness and not of the deceptive peace brought about by the Antichrist's global rule. The work of the Antichrist is the *wrath of Satan* against God's people: "Woe to the earth and the sea, because the devil has come down to you, having great wrath" (Revelation 12:12). It will bring great suffering to God's people, both Jews and saints. In contrast, the Day of the Lord is the *wrath of God* against (and only against) Satan's people. God's wrath is entirely destructive, a fierce, punitive judgment on the whole unrepentant world, and is never destined for His people. Both are therefore entirely different.

The birth pangs, the Great Tribulations for saints and Jews, and the reign of the Antichrist—as opposed to the actual wrath of God—cannot be treated as the same thing. This assertion is confirmed by the fact that the wrath is not actually recorded in the birth pangs passage in Revelation 6. Instead, we find it in a separate section beginning from Revelation 8. The very word "wrath" (Gr. *orge,*[6] from which we get the English word "orgy") does not occur in the entire book of Revelation until the sixth seal (Revelation 6:16), and in the next verse (v. 17) is written, "for the great day of their [God and the Lamb's] wrath has come…" This "great day of their wrath" is none other than the Day of the Lord, whose coming is announced coinciding with the late harvest rapture in chapter 7.

In contrast, the birth pangs and disturbances created by the fall of Babylon are referred to as the beginning of the "hour of His [God's] judgment" (Revelation 14:7). The Greek word used for judgment here is *krisis,*[7] which implies a separating and dividing. This designation perfectly suits the reign of the Antichrist, since it will divide the world's population into those who worship the image of the beast and receive its mark and those who refuse to submit to his deceptive rule. The "hour" in Revelation 14:7 is the same as the "hour of testing" in Revelation 3:10. The Greek word for testing is *peirasmos*,[8] which refers to a testing, a trial, or an experiment—as we would understand a scientific experiment (for example, in classical Greek, this could refer to a medical experiment).[9] Both "hours" denote the birth pangs and the Great Tribulation, which are a process of testing (*peirasmos*) where the spiritually unready—who nevertheless end up siding with God—will be separated (*krisis*) from those who reject God.

Judgment and wrath therefore must not be confused with each other. The fact that they are not the same is clearly reflected in the mini-summary of the whole book of Revelation contained in chapter 14. After the "hour of His [God's] judgment" (v. 7) is announced, those who worship the beast are threatened with the wrath of God (vv. 9–11), which obviously has not been poured out yet because it is described as a future event. Only after the harvest of the earth by the Son of Man (the late harvest rapture) does the "wrath of God" (v. 19) begin.

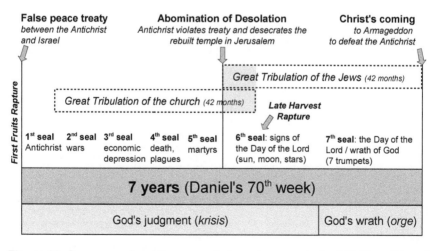

Figure 12. Sequence of end times events based on our study of Matthew 24 and Revelation 6–8

Matthew 24 and the Chronology of all Seven Seals

From the above, it is evident that the signs that herald the coming of the Day of the Lord are all contained in the sixth seal, rather than already starting with the first seal as pretribulationists are forced to assert. Moreover, these are only the *signs*; the actual Day of the Lord begins *after* these signs in Revelation 8. This timing is confirmed by Acts 2:20, where Peter says: "the sun will be turned into darkness and the moon into blood, *before* the great and glorious Day of the Lord shall come" (emphasis added). The chronology of both Matthew 24 and Revelation 6–8 shows clearly that the heavenly signs of the Day of the Lord (God's wrath) occur *before* the late harvest (prewrath) rapture. But the actual beginning of this Day, the outpouring of the wrath of God, starts *right after* this rapture.

Table 11. Matthew 24 compared with the events of Revelation 6–8

Seal/Event	Matthew 24	Revelation 6–8
6th seal: sign of the Day of the Lord	Verses 29–30 (cited above)	Chapter 6:12–17 (cited above) All men will shake in terror as they see the Lamb (Jesus) coming in glory, knowing that the hour of His wrath has come.
Rapture (the late harvest rapture, not the pretribulation rapture)	30 ... and they will see the SON OF MAN COMING ON THE CLOUDS OF THE SKY with power and great glory. 31 And He will send forth His angels with A GREAT TRUMPET and THEY WILL GATHER TOGETHER His elect from the four winds, from one end of the sky to the other.	Chapter 7 9 After these things I looked, and behold, a great multitude which no one could count, from every nation and all tribes and peoples and tongues, standing before the throne and before the Lamb.... 13 Then one of the elders answered, saying to me, "These who are clothed in the white robes, who are they, and where have they come from?" 14 I said to him, "My lord, you know." And he said to me, "These are the ones who come out of the great tribulation [of the saints]....
7th seal: beginning of the Day of the Lord (God's wrath)	The wrath is not mentioned in Matthew 24	Chapter 8 1 When the Lamb broke the seventh seal, there was silence in heaven for about half an hour. 2 And I saw the seven angels who stand before God, and seven trumpets were given to them.... [The seven trumpets represent the whole wrath of God, climaxing at Armageddon]

Here, we have a natural chronology of all seven seals: the first five seals represent the birth pangs before God's wrath, the sixth seal signals the beginning of God's wrath, and the seventh seal is the beginning God's wrath. During the sixth seal we have the late harvest rapture, as well as the sealing of the 144,000 Jews: "After this I saw four angels …" (Revelation 7:1). These four angels are temporarily holding back the wrath of God, which is about to be poured out on "earth," "sea," and "trees," in order to protect the group of Jews through the wrath by sealing them on their foreheads. While the 144,000 are set to go through the wrath, the great multitude will have already been raptured just in time before God's wrath falls.[10]

Pretribulationists are forced to argue that this multitude does not represent the church, but only the so-called "tribulation saints," those who supposedly were saved after the rapture of the church. But a key argument against this view is that the multitude is by far the largest of all the groups described in Revelation. The great multitude is again depicted in Revelation 19 at the beginning of the marriage supper of the Lamb with the believers. How can it be that this vast group only consists of those who are saved during the 3.5 years of the Great Tribulation? Even worse, according to pretribulationism, this innumerable assembly is supposed to have been saved not only without any Christian witness left on earth but also with the Holy Spirit having been fully removed. This is completely unscriptural, because the Holy Spirit plays a central role in salvation: "[God] saved us, not on the basis of deeds, but … by the washing of regeneration and renewing by the Holy Spirit" (Titus 3:5); "Truly, truly, I say to you, unless one is born of water and the Spirit he cannot enter into the kingdom of God" (John 3:5).

Pretribulationists often assert that the mere shock of the believers having disappeared will somehow cause people to turn to God. However, Scripture itself tells us that salvation is primarily a spiritual and individual process. External events even as dramatic as the disappearance of a vast part of the world's population is by no means guaranteed to lead to the profound, transformational heart changes that salvation requires. In the parable of Lazarus, the rich man begs Abraham to tell Lazarus to warn his brothers, arguing that "if someone goes to them from the dead, they will repent!" (Luke 16:30). But Abraham's reply is telling: "'If they do not listen to Moses and the Prophets, they will not be persuaded even if someone rises from the dead'" (v. 31). We should therefore be careful about assuming that a particular event—even an exceedingly spectacular one—will by itself cause people to turn to God. When God's wrath is being poured out on the world, people can plainly perceive that these supernatural judgments are from the Creator of the universe. But will this unprecedented spectacle cause them to repent? Not at all! John's account states: "they blasphemed the name of God who has the power over these plagues, and *they did not repent* so as to give Him glory" (Revelation 16:9, emphasis added).[11]

Moreover, the multitude is described as having "washed their robes and made them white" (7:14). As we saw before, this is not a picture of salvation, which is symbolized by receiving new clothes, but of sanctification: washing the pure, white clothes that one received at salvation which subsequently became stained through one's lukewarm, carnal Christian walk. The great multitude is therefore not just a group of new believers (although many new ones are certainly added), but of spiritually-unprepared Christians who were sanctified in the tribulation.

To summarize these findings, our comparison of Matthew 24 with Revelation 6–8 yielded the following five facts:

1. Matthew 24:1–31 closely corresponds to Revelation 6–8 in almost every respect. Both passages record a chronological sequence of events of all of the seven seals.
2. The birth pangs of Matthew 24:4–12 correlate to the first five seals of Revelation, while the Day of the Lord signs of Matthew 24:29 match the sixth seal of Revelation 6:12–16.

3. Matthew 24:30–31 describes the late harvest rapture: the rapture of the foolish virgins and of the tribulation saints (who get saved during the tribulations) after 42 months of Great Tribulation for the church.

4. No pretribulational rapture account can be found in Matthew 24:1–31. This means that the saints who miss the first fruits rapture will be the key witnesses for Jesus during the tribulations.

5. The wrath of God starts after the late harvest rapture. The unrepentant Jews continue to suffer in the Great Tribulation of the Jews, while the 144,000 Jewish servants of God continue to remain on the earth with God's special protection.

Chapter 6 Notes

1. See for example John Walvoord, *The Revelation of Jesus Christ* (Chicago: Moody Bible Institute, 1989). See also Tim LaHaye and Ed Hindson, eds., *The Popular Encyclopedia of Bible Prophecy* (Eugene, OR: Harvest House, 2004).

2. See for example John F. Walvoord, *Prophecy in the New Millennium* (Grand Rapids, MI: Kregel Publications, 2001), 126–7.

3. The early church did not have a clear, well-established theology on the exact timing of the rapture. Most of its leaders and scholars anticipated that the church would have to face the Antichrist's persecutions, but the writings we have are usually not specific on whether the rapture will take place before or after the seven trumpet judgments (God's wrath).

4. Stanley Toussaint, "Are the Church or the Rapture in Matthew 24?" in Thomas Ice and Timothy J. Demy, eds., *The Return: Understanding Christ's Second Coming and the End Times* (Grand Rapids, MI: Kregel, 1999), 122.

5. *Strong's Concordance*, G473.

6. Ibid., G3709.

7. Ibid., G2920.

8. Ibid., G3986.

9. See Colin Brown, *New International Dictionary of New Testament Theology* (Grand Rapids, MI: Zondervan, 2000), Olive Tree Bible Software, Inc., entry *peirasmos* (under the heading "tempt, test, approve").

10. The passage clearly states that they have "come out of the great tribulation" (v. 14).

11. Compare also Revelation 9:20–21.

Chapter 7

Pretribulation Versus Prewrath
Part II: Rapture, Battle, and the
Appearances of Christ

Say to the daughter of Zion,
"Behold your King is coming to you,
Gentle, and mounted on a donkey,
Even on a colt, the foal of a beast of burden."
Matthew 21:5

Rapturing the Church or Coming for Battle? A Close Look at Matthew 24:30–31

Matthew's account poses a real problem to the pretribulational rapture view, because if the coming of Christ described in it represents a rapture of the church, then we have two raptures: one before the 70th week of Daniel and one after the Great Tribulation of the church, right before the outpouring of God's wrath.

Consequently, some pretribulation scholars such as Thomas Ice or Renald Showers argue that Matthew 24 only talks about the Jews (although others such as Walvoord disagree with this idea).[1] They assert that the coming of Christ described there refers to His coming to battle at Armageddon, and not to His coming to rapture the church. According to them, the rapture is only taught in 1 Thessalonians 4. Let us compare those passages and see for ourselves:

Table 12. Matthew 24 compared with 1 Thessalonians 4

Matthew 24	1 Thessalonians 4
30 ... and they will see the <u>Son of Man coming</u> on the <u>clouds</u> of the sky with power and great glory. 31 And He will send forth His <u>angels</u> with a great <u>trumpet</u> and they will <u>gather together</u> His elect from the four winds, from one end of the sky to the other.	16 For the <u>Lord Himself will descend from heaven</u> with a shout, with the voice of the <u>archangel</u> and with the <u>trumpet</u> of God, and the dead in Christ will rise first. 17 Then we who are alive and remain will be <u>caught up</u> together with them in the <u>clouds</u> to meet the Lord in the air, and so we shall always be with the Lord.

Pretribulationists argue that these passages describe two separate appearances, and point to minor details in the accounts that would make them seem to differ. But from the comparison above, it becomes evident that the similarities far outweigh the differences. Jesus comes on the clouds, and at the sounding of the trumpet His people are gathered to Him. In both accounts, this coming is described as a public spectacle; no secret rapture is in view here, as the pretribulation view asserts. In Scripture, blowing the trumpet is always an official signal, intended to be widely heard and perceived. In 1 Thessalonians 4 both the Lord and His archangel are said to raise their voices to attract everyone's attention to this important event.

In Matthew 24, the angels are described as doing the gathering. In 1 Thessalonians 4, it simply says that the saints will be "caught up" without giving details of how this is done. This does not preclude the possibility of it being done by angels as depicted in the Matthew account. Similarly, the fact that in Matthew Christ is said to be "on the clouds" (v. 30), while in 1 Thessalonians 4 the believers are caught up "in the clouds" simply means that once they are raptured, they will be in the clouds where their Lord already is. Therefore, some of the supposed differences that pretribulationists point out are easily resolved when we see how unmentioned details are simply implied. The different Greek terms used for the taking up, *episunago*[2] ("gathering") in Matthew 24 and *harpazo*[3] ("caught up") in 1 Thessalonians 4, which are often cited as a reason for why these two accounts talk about different events, also pose little headache. The same root word of *episunago* (translated as "gathering" in Matthew 24:31) is used in 2 Thessalonians 2:1, a passage that pretribulationist scholars also believe to refer to the rapture of the church: "Now we request you, brethren, with regard to the coming of our Lord Jesus Christ and our gathering together [*episunagoge*] to Him …" Both Matthew 24 and 1 Thessalonians 4 therefore describe the same event: the coming of Christ for the rapture of His church.

The similarities between Matthew 24 and 1 Thessalonians 4 become even more obvious when we contrast these two passages with the two main sections in Scripture that describe Christ's coming for the battle of Armageddon: Zechariah 14 and Revelation 19.

Table 13. Zechariah 14 compared with Revelation 19

Zechariah 14	Revelation 19
3 Then the LORD will go forth and fight against those nations, as when He fights on a day of battle. 4 In that day His feet will stand on the Mount of Olives, which is in front of Jerusalem on the east.... Then the LORD, my God, will come, and all the holy ones with Him! ... ... 12 Now this will be the plague with which the LORD will strike all the peoples who have gone to war against Jerusalem; their flesh will rot while they stand on their feet, and their eyes will rot in their sockets, and their tongue will rot in their mouth. 13 It will come about in that day that a great panic from the LORD will fall on them; and they will seize one another's hand, and the hand of one will be lifted against the hand of another.... 15 So also like this plague will be the plague on the horse, the mule, the camel, the donkey and all the cattle that will be in those camps.	11 And I saw heaven opened, and behold, a white horse, and He who sat on it is called Faithful and True, and in righteousness He judges and wages war. 12 His eyes are a flame of fire, and on His head are many diadems; and He has a name written on Him which no one knows except Himself.... 14 And the armies which are in heaven, clothed in fine linen, white and clean, were following Him on white horses. 15 From His mouth comes a sharp sword, so that with it He may strike down the nations, and He will rule them with a rod of iron; and He treads the wine press of the fierce wrath of God, the Almighty.... ... 17 Then I saw an angel standing in the sun, and he cried out with a loud voice, saying to all the birds which fly in midheaven, "Come, assemble for the great supper of God, 18 so that you may eat the flesh of kings and the flesh of commanders and the flesh of mighty men and the flesh of horses and of those who sit on them and the flesh of all men, both free men and slaves, and small and great."

These coming-for-battle passages have the following aspects in common: 1) they very clearly and graphically depict a battle, 2) the saints ("holy ones") fight alongside Jesus, and 3) the enemy's army is decisively defeated. Do any of these two passages have anything at all in common with the coming of the Lord in Matthew 24:30–31? The answer is clear: absolutely nothing. In these battle passages, the Lord is not coming on the clouds and there is no gathering of any sorts. Conversely, in Matthew 24:30–31, there is not even the slightest hint of the Lord coming in battle, punishing, and destroying His foes. We can therefore conclude that Matthew 24 and 1 Thessalonians 4 both talk about the rapture of the church (specifically, those who missed the first fruits rapture, who are said to be "alive and remain" in 1 Thessalonians 4:17). In contrast, the coming of Christ for battle at Armageddon is depicted in Zechariah 14 and Revelation 19.

Pretribulationists go on to suggest that the "elect" in Matthew 24 are not Christians but Jews, and that this therefore refers to the "gathering" of the Jews from the nations.[4] However, the Greek word for elect, *eklektos*,[5] is nowhere used in the New Testament to refer specifically to the Jews as an ethnic group; instead, it always refers to the believers, regardless of ethnicity. Below are just a few of the many passages that conclusively demonstrate this fact:[6]

> For many are called, but few are chosen [*eklektos*].
>
> > (Matthew 24:14)

> [N]ow, will not God bring about justice for His elect [*eklektos*] who cry to Him day and night, and will He delay long over them?
>
> > (Luke 18:7)

> Who will bring a charge against God's elect [*eklektos*]? God is the one who justifies.
>
> > (Romans 8:33)

In Matthew 24:22, the term "elect" likely includes Jews chosen by God for salvation at the end of the Great Tribulation, when the appointed number of Jews will be brought into a covenant relationship with God (see chapter 11 for details).

Some pretribulationists make the blanket assertion that Matthew 24 was exclusively written for a Jewish audience and therefore cannot be addressing the church. But this cannot be. Almost the exactly same rapture account can be found in Mark 13:24–27, as well as a similar one in Luke 21:25–28. New Testament scholarship universally agrees that Mark's Gospel, together with the Q document (called Q for the German word *quelle* or "source"), was the source from which both Matthew and Luke were written. Therefore, even if we would say that Matthew 24 was specifically written for a Jewish audience, it is unreasonable to say that Mark 13 and Luke 21 were also limited to an Israelite readership (Luke was written by a Gentile!). The parallel passage of the rapture in Luke is clearly addressed to the disciples of Jesus:

> There will be signs in sun and moon and stars ... for the powers of the heavens will be shaken. Then they will see the Son of Man coming in a cloud with power and great glory. But when these things begin to take place, straighten up and lift up your heads, because your redemption [or deliverance,[7] meaning being rescued out of tribulation with the late harvest rapture] is drawing near.
>
> Luke 21: 25–28

There is nothing in this account that indicates an exclusive reference to Jewish followers of Jesus. Instead, the generic term "you," referring to the disciples, is an indication that this refers to all followers of Christ regardless of ethnicity.

Not surprisingly, the updated version of the popular book *Three Views on the Rapture* features a defense of the pretribulation rapture written by the Matthew expert Craig A. Blaising, which no longer claims that the coming of Christ in Matthew 24 is only addressed at a Jewish audience.[8] Rather, it is more appropriate to consider the Abomination of Desolation, which is mentioned in Matthew 24 but absent in Luke 21, to be specifically Jewish in nature. We can therefore conclude that the "gather[ing] together" in Matthew 24 refers to the (late harvest/prewrath) rapture of the saints (the "elect").

Does Matthew 24 Teach a Rapture of the Wicked?

Other pretribulationists (and some posttribulationists) argue that the "gathering" in Matthew 24:31 does not refer to a bringing together of the Jews before their Messiah, but of Jesus taking the unsaved for judgment. This is supposedly confirmed by the verses in Matthew 24:40–41 that talk about "one will be taken and one will be left," which is assumed to mean that the ones "taken" will be taken up for judgment. However, this reasoning is contradicted by the fact that the "taking" of some and "leaving behind" of others is said to be like the days of Noah and Lot:

> And just as it happened in the days of Noah, so it will be also in the days of the Son of Man: they were eating, they were drinking, they were marrying, they were being given in marriage, *until the day that Noah entered the ark* [which removed him], *and the flood came and destroyed them all* [those who stayed behind]. It was the same as happened in the days of Lot: they were eating, they were drinking, they were buying, they were selling, they were planting, they were building; *but on the day that Lot went out from Sodom it rained fire and brimstone from heaven and destroyed them all* [those who stayed behind, whereas Lot was removed]. It will be just the same on the day that the Son of Man is revealed.
>
> (Luke 17:26–30, emphases added)

Even though in the Matthew version it says that the flood "took them all away" (v. 39), this cannot mean that those who are taken by Jesus are taken away for judgment and the saints are left behind. The very reverse is the case. With both Noah and Lot, the righteous were *removed* from the place of judgment just before the judgment came (flood/fire from heaven).[9] Lot and his family were told to flee Sodom in order to avoid the judgment that would befall the city and *destroy those who were left in it* (Genesis 19). Similarly, the book of Revelation depicts the saints as having been raptured and in heaven just before the wrath of God falls on the unbelievers who are left behind on the earth for their judgment (Revelation 8–9; 15–16).

Another passage commonly cited in support of a rapture for judgment are the parable of the tares and the wheat and of the dragnet, both in Matthew 13. The parable of the tares concludes with these words:

> First gather up the tares and bind them in bundles to burn them up; but gather the wheat into my barn. . . . So it will be at the end of the age; the angels will come forth and take out [lit. separate, Gr. *aphorizo*[10]] the wicked from among the righteous, and will throw them into the furnace of fire.
>
> (vv. 30b, 49–50)

The parable of the dragnet makes a similar point:

> Again, the kingdom of heaven is like a dragnet cast into the sea, and gathering fish of every kind; and when it was filled, they drew it up on the beach; and they sat down and gathered the good fish into containers, but the bad they threw away. So it will be at the end of the age; the angels will come forth and take out the wicked from among the righteous, and will throw them into the furnace of fire.
>
> (vv. 47–50)

In both cases, the argument is that the wicked (tares, or bad fish) are raptured before the saints (wheat, or good fish).

There are several problems with this line of reasoning. Firstly, even within the parables themselves, not all details always agree. The dragnet parable first mentions a gathering of good fish into containers and then secondly talks about the bad being thrown away. This sequence would contradict that of the wheat and the tares. Likewise, John the Baptist's account of the judgment states that Jesus "will gather His wheat into the barn, but He will burn up the chaff with unquenchable fire" (Matthew 3:12), also implying the gathering of the wheat (believers) will take place before Christ deals with the chaff (the lost). If we take these statements literally, they actually contradict each other! Additionally, the wheat-tares rapture timing clashes with the sequence of the two harvests of Revelation 14, which places the over-ripe harvest rapture before the reaping of the grape harvest of God's wrath. Finally, we had seen that Jesus' teaching about the rapture in Matthew 24:30–31 clearly speaks of the taking up of the "elect." As discussed before, this can only refer to God's people and not to the wicked, which are never described as "elect" or "chosen" by God.

But of course, there is no contradiction at all between Jesus' analogies, John the Baptists' statement, and the teachings of Revelation. The answer is simple: Jesus' sayings of the wheat and the tares, and the good and bad fish, are parables. Parables use illustrations from daily life to put across a spiritual point. The details they contain are intended to illuminate the main story, in order to making it easier to relate to. It is therefore improper textual analysis to take such details in an overly literal manner. Rather than making theological statements about rapture chronologies, Jesus' parables in Matthew 13 simply focus on the fact of the final judgment. They cannot be taken as doctrinal statements about rapture timings, which must instead be inferred from passages such as Matthew 24, Luke 21, 1 Thessalonians 4, and the book of Revelation in general. All of these teachings must line up in their totality, and a summary of these passages contradicts any assertions that the wicked will be taken up for judgment. Our treatment of the parable of the ten virgins follows these principles: firstly, we focus on the parable's primary point (not all virgins are admitted to the feast when the groom returns), drawing on details only as they illuminate this main message; secondly, we combine and align it with other rapture passages and end times scriptures, and obtain our theological framework from the latter texts rather than from the parable.

But even if one would try to extract theological foundations from the details of parables, the judgment rapture interpretation stumbles over the fact that the literal meaning of *aphorizo* is not to "take up," but to "separate," as in Matthew 25:32 where Christ is said to "separate [*aphorizo*] them [the nations] from one another, as the shepherd separates [*aphorizo*] the sheep from the goats." The "separating" of the wicked from the righteous in Matthew 13 is therefore in no way a teaching about a "taking up" of the wicked, but a parallel passage to the sheep and goat judgment which again shows the righteous being judged first, and the wicked second. This is consistent with John 5:28–29, which affirms that first the saints will be resurrected and judged and then the wicked. (The fact that the sheep and goat judgment is not a judgment about who enters the millennium, but a judgment about who enters eternity, will be discussed in detail in chapter 13).

In fact, there is no precedent anywhere that unbelievers are raptured for judgment while the believers remain. Rather, as in the cases of Lot and Noah, God's people are taken out before the judgment falls, while those who reject God are left behind in order to face His wrath. This is confirmed by the prophet Isaiah:

> The righteous man perishes, and no man takes it to heart; and *devout men are taken away*, while no one understands. *For the righteous man is taken away from evil*, he enters into peace.
>
> (Isaiah 57:1–2, emphases added)

Finally, there is another, more personal, reason why there cannot be a rapture of the wicked. The very act of rapture implies a personal relationship between the one who takes and those who are taken. Jesus takes His people to Himself as a sign of their honor and of His humility. From a cultural perspective of ancient times, it was completely unthinkable that a high dignitary or king would go out to meet his subjects. Quite to the contrary, if he wanted to see them, he would simply summon them to himself. It was the inferior subject's responsibility to go and see their master, rather than the reverse. Therefore, Jesus' listeners would have been stunned to hear that the King Himself would leave His throne in heaven to come down to earth for the rapture of His people. This act will testify to the Master's intimate relationship with His people, and will greatly honor the raptured saints—similar to the picture of the returning Master who ends up serving His faithful servants in Luke 12. From this background, we can be certain that Jesus would never bestow the same distinction on the unrighteous by making a special appearance for them!

Having evaluated these Scripture passages and arguments, we can conclude that it is impossible to interpret away the church or the rapture from Matthew 24 (or from Mark 13). This being the case, it becomes evident that there must be a second rapture of the believers, which occurs during the sixth seal (the signs of the Day of the Lord) and just before the seventh seal (the wrath of God). The parallels between Matthew 24, 2 Thessalonians 2 (see the section below), Revelation 6–8, and Revelation 14, which all teach this same sequence, show how wonderfully Scripture confirms itself.

The Rapture Timing in 2 Thessalonians 2

The final argument that Matthew 24 refers to a rapture of the church after the Great Tribulation of the church comes from 2 Thessalonians 2. Here, Paul admonishes the believers that the coming of Christ to gather His people is *not* imminent, because *first* the "man of lawlessness," the Antichrist, has to ascend to power:

> Now we request you, brethren, with regard to the coming of our Lord Jesus Christ and our gathering together to Him [the rapture of the church], that you not be quickly shaken from your composure or be disturbed either by a spirit or a message or a letter as if from us, to the effect that the day of the Lord has come. Let no one in any way deceive you, for it will not come unless the apostasy [lit. falling away] comes first, and the man of lawlessness [Antichrist] is revealed, the son of destruction, who opposes and exalts himself above every so-called god or object of worship, so that he takes his seat in the temple of God, displaying himself as being God [the Abomination of Desolation]....
>
> For the mystery of lawlessness is already at work; only he who now restrains will do so until he is taken out of the way. Then that lawless one [Antichrist] will be revealed whom the Lord will slay with the breath of His mouth and bring to an end by the appearance of His coming [for battle to Armageddon]."
>
> (2 Thessalonians 2:1–4, 7–8)

This passage clearly states that the "day of the Lord"—which we noted is the wrath of God—will "not come unless ... the man of lawlessness," which is the Antichrist, "is revealed" to all and the Abomination of Desolation described by Jesus is set up in the reconstructed temple in Jerusalem. Moreover, the "coming of our

Lord Jesus Christ and our gathering together to Him," which refers to the rapture, is linked with these events. In contrast, the "coming" of the Lord described in the last verse of the quote above refers to Christ's coming to battle at Armageddon. Here, it says that Christ will "slay [the Antichrist] with the breath of His mouth." In Revelation 19:15, Christ is depicted very similarly: "From His mouth comes a sharp sword, so that with it He may strike down the nations."

The sequence taught here is therefore exactly the same as in Matthew 24 and Revelation 6–8:

1. First the rise of the Antichrist.
2. Then the rapture of the remaining church (the "foolish virgins").
3. Then the wrath of God, climaxing at Armageddon.

Combining Pretribulation and Prewrath Raptures: Where Does the First Fruits Rapture Fit In?

Our exegesis of end times Scripture passages shows that the pretribulation and the prewrath perspectives are in many ways complementary. Neither of them possesses the complete truth but both have important truths to contribute. This also explains why both sides hold so passionately to each of their views. Yet it is only when we combine them that we see how the various end times scriptures fall into place and the two raptures taught in Revelation 14 become clear.

The great weakness of the prewrath perspective is that it cannot account for the conditional preservation promises of Luke 21:36 and Revelation 3:10, which we had discussed previously. It also fails to explain the first fruits from Revelation 14, which is a group set apart and distinct from the great multitude of Revelation 7 (which is made up of saints coming out of the Great Tribulation). Neither can it adequately interpret the 24 elders in Revelation 4–5 or the woman and her child in Revelation 12.

Prewrath and posttribulation scholars seek to explain the promise of Revelation 3:10 in light of John 17:15 where Jesus prays to the Father for His disciples: "I do not ask You to take them out of the world, but to keep them from the evil one." The argument is then that this "keeping" is in fact a "keeping through," and not a literal removal, because Satan can still attack us. But the Greek words *tereo...ek*[11] literally mean to "keep from" or "keep out of," and this is also what Jesus, in effect, asks of his Father. Although we are within the realm of Satan's influence, God "rescued us from the domain of darkness, and transferred us to the kingdom of His beloved Son" (Colossians 1:13). Therefore, we are "kept from" the enemy, rather than being "kept through." In the context of the "hour of testing," the only valid interpretation is a literal removal of the spiritually-prepared believers, since there is no need for them to undergo any testing. Moreover, this promise was literally fulfilled for the historic Philadephian church, who will never have to go through the tribulations. The Luke 21:36 promise is even more blunt: to "*escape* all these things" certainly cannot mean being preserved through them!

But the pretribulation position also has two major weaknesses. Firstly, it fails to take the conditional nature of the preservation promises seriously, applying them indiscriminately on all believers regardless of whether they met these conditions or not. Secondly, this oversight gives pretribulationism no choice but to find the rapture in the wrong scriptures. The result is that a pretribulational blueprint is forced on end times prophecies, regardless whether it fits or not. That which does not fit is explained away, with the consequence that pretribulational interpretations are scripturally unconvincing.

Now if Matthew 24 and 1 Thessalonians 4—the two classical rapture passages—talk about the same event, namely the second late harvest rapture, then where is the pretribulational first fruits rapture taught? Pretribulationists argue that this rapture is a secret event where Jesus will not make a glorious, spectacular public appearance. Yet in both Matthew 24 and 1 Thessalonians 4 we saw a description of a highly noticeable coming of the Lord: visible to "all tribes of the earth" (Matthew 24:30) and announced with a trumpet and proclaimed with a mighty "shout" (1 Thessalonians 4:16). This description does not qualify as a secret rapture. So where can we find evidence for such a secret coming of Christ for His bride?

In Matthew 24, Jesus says that He will come like a thief in the night and that we must be alert and awake for this event:

> Therefore be on the alert, for you do not know which day your Lord is coming. But be sure of this, that if the head of the house had known at what time of the night the thief was coming, he would have been on the alert and would not have allowed his house to be broken into.
>
> (Matthew 24:42–43)

How does a thief break into a house? Does he cause a great commotion and try to alert everyone to his coming? No, a thief will attempt to break in without anybody noticing his coming and going. In Jesus' times, it would be largely up to the head of the house to defend his property. If the thief aroused the members of the household, he would almost certainly be attacked by them and their neighbors and might even get killed in the process. Jesus' description of His coming as a thief therefore clearly refers to the secret first fruits rapture.

Similarly, at the ascension the disciples are told that Jesus "will come in just the same way as you have watched Him go into heaven" (Acts 1:11). His ascension occurred on a lonely mountaintop (Mount Olivet) with only the eleven apostles present (and therefore not all of His disciples), without trumpet calls or shouts of command. Likewise, His first return will be an unobtrusive occasion that will only be witnessed by His closest followers (the first fruits). In contrast, His coming to "gather together His elect" will be a highly public event, alerting the entire world that the wrath of God is about to fall on those who are left behind on the earth.

When Jesus appeared approximately 2,000 years ago, he revealed Himself in three different ways. He first showed Himself at His birth in a manger in Bethlehem—unspectacular, unexpected, and hidden from most. Only the "wise" knew about it by following the star, and nearby shepherds were alerted by angels, forming an unlikely audience to this otherwise very unobtrusive event. When Jesus' family went to Jerusalem for His circumcision, Simeon and the prophetess Anna recognized that He was the Messiah, because God had supernaturally revealed it to them (Luke 2). Again, only those with God-given insight and the indwelling of the Holy Spirit could see who this little boy really was.

Then, until age 30, Jesus was simply part of His family. He most likely practiced carpentry under His father Joseph (as was common for young men back then), and no one really knew about His status as Savior and Son of God, except for His parents. We are not even sure if Mary still truly believed the angel's testimony 30 years later. Only then did Jesus officially begin His ministry. He came out into the public, beginning with His reading of Isaiah at the synagogue of Nazareth, His hometown (Luke 4). Virtually overnight, He became famous:

> The news about Him spread throughout all Syria; and they brought to Him all who were ill, those suffering with various diseases and pains, demoniacs, epileptics, paralytics; and He healed them. Large crowds followed Him from Galilee and the Decapolis and Jerusalem and Judea and from beyond the Jordan.
>
> (Matthew 4:24–25)

Jesus' second revelation of Himself (as part of His first coming 2,000 years ago) was therefore a "coming out" with the start of His public ministry.

Then, three years later, Jesus revealed himself in a third way. Prefiguring His coming in glory at the end of the age, he rode on a donkey as King into Jerusalem on Palm Sunday.[12] At that point, many expected Him to proclaim His earthly reign and drive out the Romans. Especially His disciples hoped He would finally ascend to His throne. But instead, Christ died on the cross, was resurrected, and caught up into heaven. In total, His first "coming" consisted of three stages or revelations: hidden, publicly visible, and as King to defeat the enemy (by His death on the cross).

Therefore, it should not surprise us that at the end of the age, Jesus' return will also have three phases to it. The Bible does not actually teach such a thing as a "second coming," and no such expression can be found anywhere in Scripture. Christians used the term "second coming" over the centuries until it became a classic phrase. Rather, the Word of God says that Christ will "return," and from the totality of end times prophecy we know that this return involves more than one aspect. One element is the gathering of saints, symbolized by "harvests"; another is the return of Jesus as King.

Each future appearance will mirror His appearances 2,000 years ago. His first appearance at the first fruits harvest will be secret, and only the wise and understanding will discern it and be ready for it. This will fulfill Daniel's prophecy that only "the wise shall understand." Then, Jesus' second gathering at the late harvest (or prewrath) rapture, like His coming out for public ministry in Nazareth and Galilee, will be a highly public and extremely spectacular event. This time, not only the masses in Israel will see Him, but "every eye shall see him" (Revelation 1:7). Then, they will mourn, because it will be too late to turn to Him.

Finally, Christ's third appearance, His return as King, will represent the beginning of His earthly reign. Unlike His royal entry into Jerusalem on a donkey, Christ will then ride on a dazzling white horse, with "many crowns" on His head, and be surrounded by the "armies in heaven." Back then, He defeated Satan spiritually by submitting to a humiliating death on the cross. At Armageddon, Christ will physically and literally defeat Satan's army and His minion, the Antichrist, in order to set up His literal millennial Kingdom on earth. Just as His first coming was threefold in nature, so will be His future return.

Table 14. Comparison of Jesus' appearances

Appearances	Jesus' coming as Servant	Jesus' coming as King
First appearance in secret	Obscure birth in a manger, only foreseen by the wise men, and prophetically foreknown by Simeon and Anna (Luke 2)	Obscure rapture of His first fruits, only foreseen by those with insight (Revelation 12:5, 14:1–5)
Second appearance in public	Beginning of His public ministry in Nazareth (Luke 4:14–30)	Public, globally-visible coming on the clouds to rapture the rest of the church (Matthew 24:30–31; 1 Thessalonians 4:16–17)
Third appearance as a King riding to victory	Riding on a donkey into Jerusalem to defeat Satan on the cross (Luke 23:44–46)	Riding on a white horse to Armageddon to defeat Antichrist and False Prophet (Revelation 19:11–21)

But who are the ones that will be raptured to the Lord as first fruits? Not a tiny super-elite, a handful of "ultra-spiritual" elect, nor just members of a particular church or exclusive movement. Rather, they are simply like those in the Philadelphian church who faithfully walked with Jesus through their God-given trials. They will be those who "overcome" because Jesus overcame the one who is in the world, who have kept themselves spiritually pure in keeping His word and obeying it, and who have closely followed their Lord where He led them. All believers are called to be overcomers and first fruits, and Christ daily gives us everything we need to overcome. Whether we follow this high calling or not is entirely our own choice.

Chapter 7 Notes

1. Thomas Ice, "Matthew 24:31: Rapture Or Second Coming?" *Rapture Ready*, http://www.raptureready.com/featured/ice/Matthew24_31_Rapture OrSecondComing.html. Renald Showers, *Maranatha: Our Lord, Come!* (Bellmawr, NJ: The Friends of Israel, 1995), 182. John Walvoord, *Every Prophecy in the Bible* (Colorado Springs: David C. Cook, 1999), 389–390.
2. *Strong's Concordance*, G1996.
3. Ibid., G726.
4. See for example Thomas Ice, "Matthew 24:31: Rapture Or Second Coming?" *Rapture Ready*, http://www.raptureready.com/featured/ice/ Matthew24_31_RaptureOrSecondComing.html.
5. *Strong's Concordance*, G1588.
6. See also Craig Keener, *The Gospel of Matthew: A Socio-Rhetorical Commentary* (Grand Rapids, MI: Wm. B. Eerdmans, 2009), 586.
7. The Greek term *apolutrosis* can mean deliverance, release, or redemption (release on payment of ransom). *Strong's Concordance*, G629.
8. Craig A. Blaising, "A Case for the Pretribulation Rapture," in *Three Views on the Rapture: Pretribulation, Prewrath or Posttribulation*, ed. Stanley Gundry and Alan Hultberg (Grand Rapids, MI: Zondervan, 2010).
9. Compare also Isaiah 57:1–2: "The righteous man perishes, and no man takes it to heart; and devout men are taken away, while no one understands. For the righteous man is taken away from evil, he enters into peace."
10. *Strong's Concordance*, G873.
11. Ibid., G5083 and G1537.
12. In Old Testament times, the donkey was used by royalty to ride on, especially when they came in peace and not in war—see also 2 Samuel 16:2.

Chapter 8

Become an Overcomer:
Focus on the Spirit

Everyone who has been born of God overcomes the world.
1 John 5:4

For the mind set on the flesh is death, but the mind set on the Spirit is
life and peace....those who are in the flesh cannot please God.
Romans 8:6–8

Two Kinds of Natures: The Flesh and the Spirit

The parable of the ten virgins narrows different levels of discipleship and spiritual maturity down to two types: "wise" and "foolish" disciples. Is this distinction merely found in this parable, or can we find the idea of two kinds of believers in other parts of Scripture?

We can indeed. A similar concept is found in Paul's first letter to the Corinthians, where he distinguishes "spiritual men" from those who are "fleshly" or "carnal" (1 Corinthians 3:1–3).[1] In fact, throughout his letters, and especially in the book of Romans, Paul speaks about two primary opposites in the Christian life: the spirit (Gr. *pneuma*[12]) on the one hand, and the flesh (Gr. *sarx*[3]) on the other.

In the past, Christians have mistakenly assumed that Paul was distinguishing between the spiritual and the bodily, as if "flesh" referred to our physical bodies, or to all material things in general. But such an understanding of reality is borrowed from Greek philosophy, which considers the spiritual to be superior to the bodily or physical. In contrast, Paul's distinction is about something completely different. He is speaking about the conflict between old nature and new nature (or "old man"

178

versus "new man"). Jesus taught about this in John 3, when he revealed to Nicodemus that we must be spiritually born again:

> Truly, truly, I say to you, unless one is born of water and the Spirit [*pneuma*] he cannot enter into the kingdom of God. That which is born of the flesh [*sarx*] is flesh [*sarx*], and that which is born of the Spirit [*pneuma*] is spirit [*pneuma*]. Do not be amazed that I said to you, "You must be born again."
>
> (John 3:5–7)

Like Paul, Jesus contrasts two things: our old, sinful nature, which we inherited from Adam as soon as were conceived and began to grow in our mother's womb; and the new spirit nature which we receive when we are born again. The old nature is described as "flesh" (*sarx*), and the new born-again nature as "spirit" (*pneuma*). Jesus is telling Nicodemus that whatever comes from our old sinful "flesh" nature cannot be anything but "flesh," meaning that it cannot bear any spiritual fruit for God. Only the new "spirit" nature, which is born of God's Spirit, has the ability to be spiritually fruitful and pleasing to God. Later, Jesus told His disciples: "It is the Spirit who gives life; the flesh profits nothing" (John 6:63). In Romans, Paul affirmed this truth:

> For the mind set on the flesh [old nature/*sarx*] is death, but the mind set on the [s]pirit [new nature/*pneuma*] is life and peace, because the mind set on the flesh [old nature] is hostile toward God; for it does not subject itself to the law of God, for it is not even able to do so, and those who are in the flesh [old nature] cannot please God."
>
> (Romans 8:6–8)[4]

When Jesus argued that we must not try to "put new wine into old wineskins" (Matthew 9:17), He was telling us that it is no use to try to convert or revive our old sinful nature that we inherited from Adam. Being "born again" is not a revival of the old; it does not mean that our old nature is somehow born again and receives new life. Our old self is totally unable to contain God's life—as Paul said, it is spiritually dead, utterly "hostile toward God," and those who walk in it "cannot please God." If we try to bear fruit for God through our old natures, it is like filling old wineskins with new wine. The result is that they are "ruined."

No, the new "wine" of the spirit nature that we receive when we are born again must be poured into our new nature. The old nature can only produce "dead works" (Hebrews 9:14). Like Sardis, one of the seven churches of Revelation, it can put on an appearance of life and spirituality, but in reality its deeds are totally worthless in God's eyes, and its supposed righteousness like a "filthy garment" (Isaiah 64:6). In contrast, the new spirit nature naturally desires to do God's will as it is made "in the likeness of God [having] been created in righteousness and holiness" (Ephesians 4:24). If we walk by it, we will "not carry out the desire of the flesh" (Galatians 5:16).[5] This is why the New Testament always calls us Christians "saints"—literally "holy ones"—and not sinners![6]

Many of the very drastic statements of John make sense when we perceive them from this new nature perspective: "No one who lives in him [walks after his new nature] keeps on sinning.… No one who is born of God [spiritually born again] will continue to sin, because God's seed [the new nature] remains in him; he cannot go on sinning, because he has been born of God" (1 John 3:6, 9 NIV).[7] Indeed, as we walk after our new self, we tune out of sin's frequencies, because contrary to the old flesh nature (or "soulish" nature, the literal meaning of the Greek term *psychikos* in 1 Corinthians 2:14), our new nature is like Jesus in that it has no actual desire to sin.

This is then how we can understand spiritual versus carnal Christianity, or wise versus foolish virgins: carnal Christians ("foolish virgins") try to follow Christ based on their old flesh nature. This is an impossible task, doomed to failure, and the primary reason why many Christians feel like they are spiritual underachievers. The old nature is only capable of pseudo-religiousness: it can neither resist the lure of sin's temptations, nor truly carry out God's will. God does not intend to "fix" our old nature. No, He wants us to walk with Christ in the power of the new spirit nature that He gave us. When we do that, it is like putting on the easy yoke that Jesus talked about (Matthew 11:30): suddenly, bearing the fruit of the Spirit becomes a light burden and a natural desire, and all our human striving ceases as we allow God to produce His fruit through our born-again lives. As Roy Hession wrote: "only life that pleases God and that can be victorious is His life."[8]

> **Overcomer Principle #1:** If you are born again, you already have a perfectly sinless, victorious, and fruitful new spirit nature inside of you!

Everyone who has been born again through faith in Jesus—by accepting and submitting to Him as the King of his life—has received a new spirit nature. If you do not have this new nature, then you are not saved (see Romans 8:9). But why do we still struggle so much in our daily Christian walk? Quite simply, victorious and fruitful living for Jesus in the power of our new nature does not come automatically. Ephesians challenges us to actively "lay aside the old self" and to "put on the new self" (4:22, 24). Similarly, Romans 8 exhorts us to set our minds on and walk according to the spirit (new nature) and not the flesh (old nature). Why is this so difficult?

When we are born again and receive the new nature, our old nature is still alive and well and immediately begins to attack its new competitor. Paul describes this ongoing struggle:

> For the flesh [*sarx*] sets its desire against the [s]pirit [*pneuma*], and
> the [s]pirit against the flesh; for these are in opposition to one
> another, so that you may not do the things that you please.
>
> (Galatians 5:17)

This passage is typically understood as the struggle of our sinful nature against God's Holy Spirit. But the Greek word *pneuma* can refer to any kind of spirit: God's Spirit or our own spirit. Which one is implied must be inferred from the context. In this verse and in much of Romans 8, the translators simply decided to translate *pneuma* as God's Spirit (with a capital 'S'). But what Paul is talking about here is not a struggle between us and God but a battle that is occurring *within* us: between our old nature (flesh/*sarx*) and our new nature (spirit/*pneuma*). Both are in opposition to each other. Our old flesh nature continually paralyzes our new spirit nature, preventing it from doing "the [good] things that you please." This is the desperate inner battle that Paul also described in Romans 7: "for I am not practicing what I would like to do, but I am doing the very thing I hate" (v. 15).

This statement of Paul's refers to the time before he was born again and had no chance to overcome sin. However, it also applies to some degree to the lives of all born-again believers: if we give the old nature the room and space it needs, it will rise up and strangle the spiritual life and fruitfulness of the new nature.[9] We are literally unable to do what we know to be right. Many Christians even believe that we are doomed to continually fail, that while we are not yet glorified we remain utterly enslaved to sin, continually needing to rely on God's grace and forgiveness. God does indeed forgive us, but His grace is much more powerful than that: He did not save us so that we would be stuck in perpetual failure until we reach heaven. No, Jesus' death on the cross destroyed the works of the devil (1 John 3:8)! He overcame the very power of sin in us, enabling us to live victoriously for Him. But how can this actually be put into practice?

Old and New Nature as Spirit Versus Soul Life

Scripture also distinguishes between old and new nature by referring to them as soul and spirit. Soul and spirit are different from our physical body. Just as God is three (Father, Son, Spirit), so we have three parts, as taught in 1 Thessalonians 5:23: "Now may the God of peace Himself sanctify you entirely; and may your spirit and soul and body be preserved complete, without blame at the coming of our Lord Jesus Christ."

Paul writes in 1 Corinthians 15:45, "So also it is written, 'The first man, Adam, became a living soul.' The last Adam [Jesus] became a life-giving spirit." Here, the soul life refers to the old fallen human nature, whereas the spirit life that came through Jesus is the new nature. Paul goes on to say that the "natural [lit. soulish] man does not accept the things of the Spirit of God, for they are foolishness to him; and he cannot understand them, because they are spiritually appraised" (1 Corinthians 2:14). Both "flesh/fleshly" and "soul/soulish" are therefore contrasted with the spirit, the new nature, and the spiritual power and revelation that comes through it. At times, the process of sanctification—the death of the old and the growth of the new—is therefore referred to as the "salvation of the soul", for example in James 1:21:

> Therefore, putting aside all filthiness and all that remains
> of wickedness, in humility receive the word implanted,
> which is able to save your souls.

Enforcing the Old Nature's Death Sentence—Nourishing Our New Nature

When we are born again, new spirit nature is like a newborn infant: it must slowly grow up through extensive nurture, protection, and continual care. At that point, our old self is still much stronger than the new self and easily grabs away all focus, attention, and energy from our baby-like new nature. There is only one solution to this problem: if our new spirit nature is to grow and mature, the old flesh nature must gradually be cut off and die.

Thankfully, Jesus' death not only provides us with a new nature, it also takes care of our old one. At the same time that we received our new self, our old self incurred the death penalty. In Romans 6, Paul plainly tells us that in the symbolic act of baptism, our old flesh man died with Christ on the cross: "[O]ur old self was crucified with Him … so that we would no longer be slaves to sin" (v. 6).

So we are set free from our bondage to the old sin nature. But this is a positional truth. A positional truth is a spiritual fact that will not have any real-life effects until it is implemented. Practically, this means that even though God has issued the old self's death penalty, this penalty must actually be executed! Our old body is like a sentenced criminal who has not yet been put to death, but who is still at large, wreaking havoc inside of us.

The execution of this death sentence is done by God within us, not suddenly but gradually. Jesus said that he who seeks to follow Him "must deny himself, and take up his cross daily" (Luke 9:23). Likewise, Paul told the Corinthians that "I die daily" (1 Corinthians 15:31). Both speak of the same thing: our old self must die every day on the cross so that we will ultimately have "crucified the flesh" (Galatians 5:24), meaning that the death sentence over the old self is being executed. The outcome of this process is aptly summarized in one of the most-cited verses of the entire New Testament:

I have been *crucified with Christ*; and it is *no longer I who live*
[through the old nature], *but Christ lives in me* [through the
new nature].

(Galatians 2:20, emphases added)

The secret of Paul's powerful spiritual life in Jesus lies in the first
part: "I have been crucified with Christ." Putting to death our old self so
that our new nature can flourish is the single most important aspect of
following Jesus. But how does that work?

The death of the old nature won't happen automatically—it requires
our active and willing cooperation. Discipleship is a process of feeding
the new while starving the old. God has given us powerful spiritual
disciplines, such as fasting, giving, and sacrificial service to others, which
are effective tools for starving the old nature to death. At the same time,
God's power through our new nature will cut off old sin habits and
thought patterns, which are the lifeline of our old self. As we walk in our
new nature and progressively let God crucify these old nature habits, and
as we stop feeding on the things of the world, our old fallen self will lack
the fuel it needs to flourish. Then, it will gradually die off.

However, these disciplines must be done in a God-directed way
or, ironically, the old nature can also benefit from them! The Pharisees
practiced these disciplines as legalistic acts of self-righteousness that made
them "feel good" about their spirituality rather than bringing glory to
God alone. We must be careful to realize that disciplines do not make us
more righteous or acceptable to God. Instead, they are simply spiritual
tools that allow God to crucify our old self so that the new self has more
room to grow. Neglecting these tools stifles our spiritual development:
the old nature remains well-fed, sin habits continue, and the result is a
lukewarm spiritual life.

As the old nature is progressively being put to death, we must
continually feed and nurture our new nature. As we connect to God
in prayer and through His Word, as we abide in Christ and have our

minds renewed through immersion in His Word, our new nature receives the spiritual food it so badly needs to grow. Paul wrote that "[o]ne who speaks [prays] in a tongue edifies himself [his new nature]" (1 Corinthians 14:4), meaning that speaking in tongues is—in appropriate contexts—an effective tool for building up the new self. Similarly, Jesus told the devil: "It is written, 'Man [our new nature] shall not live by bread alone, but by every word that proceeds from the mouth of God'" (Matthew 4:4 NJKV). Our new nature starves if we don't feed it! A daily quiet time—that is, a protected, regular, and undisturbed quality time with God through His Word and His presence—cannot be replaced by anything else. Just as human marriages flourish or wither depending on the amount of quality time and communication they receive, the development of our marriage with our heavenly Husband-to-be greatly depends on the time we invest in it! Likewise, prayer and Bible reading must be done *with* God, with His active enabling and guidance—not as a one-way monologue but a two-way dialogue.

> **Overcomer Principle #2:** Starve your old flesh nature to death through spiritual disciplines! Feed your new spirit nature by abiding in God's Word and presence. Both are God's work in us that we can't do ourselves, but our active and willing cooperation is required.

Walking by Faith Destroys the Power of the Old Nature

However, spiritual disciplines and regular quiet times are not enough to cut off the life force of our Satan-empowered old nature. For that, we must wield God's Word in faith before we can gain victory over the forces of darkness that continue to operate through our old self. Positional truths must be enforced by firmly standing on and proclaiming God's promises over our lives!

In Romans 6, Paul tells us how to appropriate Christ's victory over the old self: we must "consider [our]selves to be dead to sin, but alive to

God in Christ Jesus" (v. 11). This is not an empty name-it-and-claim-it practice; God's Word has not promised us a luxury car or an apartment, but it gives us the certain promise that "sin shall not be master over you" (v. 14). Whenever we are tempted to sin, we must activate our God-given faith, wield the sword of God, which is His Word, and stand on these promises. Jesus said: "If you abide in my word ... you will know the truth, and the truth will set you free" (John 8:31–32). We must abide in these scriptures, meditating on them and memorizing them, so that they become firmly engrafted into our new spirit. We must proclaim the truth that we have received a new nature, which has no desire to yield to sin, and that our old sinful nature has died with Christ on the cross. It is a fact. Express your unreserved faith in God's promises, and the spiritual powers of the old nature will fade away!

After receiving the death sentence, our old self, although being a sentenced criminal, still pretends to be innocent and continues to roam around. Satan primarily operates through deception, because he knows that he has in fact already been defeated. But when we declare the truth in faith and affirm that the old has been condemned to die, then we move it along on its way to the executioner until its death sentence is gradually enforced. This is why faith is so important, as John wrote:

> *Everyone* who has been born of God overcomes the world. And this is the victory that has overcome the world—*our faith.*
>
> (1 John 5:4, emphases added)

It is no surprise therefore that faith is one of the primary things that Jesus will be looking for when He returns: "when the Son of Man comes, will He find faith on the earth?" (Luke 18:8). Faith is a decisive factor in the victory of our new nature over the old flesh!

> **Overcomer Principle #3:** Allow God to enforce the death sentence of your old flesh nature by proclaiming and standing on His promises in faith! Remember that this is not your work—God provides the faith you need.

It is like a man who inherited a huge debt of $10 million from his predecessors. They never managed to pay it back to the bank, and neither can he. But the bank demands payment in full and keeps threatening him. Then, suddenly, a wealthy nobleman appears and pays off the man's entire debt. In a moment, the crushing burden that weighed him down is gone! As if that wasn't enough, the nobleman gives the man a chest of refined gold.

The man is now free; he no longer owes a single penny. However, an enemy has set up a counterfeit bank, which looks like the real bank. Through this deceptive operation, he sends angry, threatening letters to the man, letters which almost look like those of the real bank, demanding full payment of the debt. Imagine what would happen if that man is deceived by the counterfeit letters into believing that his old debt still exists. As the letters pile in, he starts to doubt that the nobleman ever came and paid it off. Finally, the man gives in, contacts the counterfeit bank and seeks to appease them by promising to repay a small amount at a time. Before long, the man is again in bondage but this time to a counterfeit bank that has no real claim over him! By acting like this, he gives credibility to a deceiver, he empowers his enemy, and he makes the generous nobleman look totally foolish. Moreover, his worries make him completely forget about the chest of gold that the nobleman gave him.

Likewise, whenever we tell ourselves that we are still in bondage to this or that sinful habit or thought pattern, we are committing the absurd mistake of that doubting man. When we say that we can't help but sin, and make all kinds of excuses, we affirm the deception of the devil and extend the lifespan of our old nature. If we justify our sin, we rob the Holy Spirit of the opportunity to destroy its power over our lives. The truth is that Satan no longer has any claim over us, and he cannot keep us in bondage if we do not let him. Our debts have been paid in full at the cross, and our sinful old nature was put to death there alongside Jesus. We must through His grace confess this truth every day and tear apart the letters from the counterfeit bank! Then, we will have space in our lives to receive the fullness of the riches that the heavenly nobleman has already given us!

Do you want to empower Satan or God in your life? If you make excuses or hide sin before God and others, you empower Satan; if you openly and freely confess your sin and bring it before God and thank Him that He has set you free from it through His Son, then you allow God to enforce the death of your sinful self. Then, your new nature has won another decisive victory! Jesus told the disciples, "you will receive power when the Holy Spirit has come upon you" (Acts 1:8). This is the power that gives us victory over sin and the forces of darkness. The Holy Spirit is more than able to enforce the death of the old and prosper the life of the new if we just let Him do it! When we know the truth and believe it, it will indeed set us free, because God's power can now work in our lives and change us.

Lord, bend that proud and stiff necked I,
Help me to bow the head and die;
Beholding Him on Calvary,
Who bowed His head for me.[10]

> **Overcomer Principle #4:** Don't excuse your sin, but expose and confess it so that God's Spirit can set you free from it! Remember, sin can no longer make you do what you don't want to do!

Nurturing the New Nature: The Importance of Tribulation for Spiritual Growth

An important way in which God enforces the gradual death of our old nature is by graciously allowing various forms of suffering and tribulation in our lives. Paul's life is a testimony of the significance of suffering for spiritual growth and the main reason why he had every reason to rejoice in his tribulations. He summarized his experience in this way:

> [W]e are afflicted in every way, but not crushed; perplexed, but not despairing; persecuted, but not forsaken; struck down, but not destroyed; *always carrying about in the body the dying of Jesus, so that the life of Jesus also may be manifested in our body.* For we who live are constantly being delivered over to death for Jesus' sake, so that the life of Jesus also may be manifested in our mortal flesh....
>
> ... Therefore we do not lose heart, but *though our outer man [old nature] is decaying, yet our inner man [new nature] is being renewed day by day.*
>
> (2 Corinthians 4:8–11, 16, emphases added)

Paul and his helpers regularly experienced the death of their old selves. But rather than literally dying or becoming discouraged by constant tribulation, they knew that this "death" was bringing about the "life of Jesus" in them. Consequently, they did not "lose heart" but were conscious that their new nature, the "inner man," was being "renewed day by day." Through outward tribulation, they were being blessed with true inner spiritual life.

The reason for this is clear: the more the old nature withers away, the more the new nature can blossom and bear fruit for God. Paul and Barnabas plainly told the young believers that "[t]hrough many tribulations we must enter the kingdom of God" (Acts 14:22), and so prepared them for spiritual growth. In John 15, Jesus compared this process with pruning. However, God's pruning greatly depends on our active cooperation. We can allow Him to progressively crucify our old habits and character traits, but we can also actively hamper His efforts. Every time we stubbornly resist God's discipleship work, we prolong the life of our old nature and stifle our spiritual growth.

Death of the Old Nature – Growth of the New Nature

1. Starve it to death	2. Let God crucify it	3. Feed your new Nature
- Stop sinful behaviors	- Submit to the trials and	- Immerse yourself in God's
- Stop carnal (worldly)	tribulations that God brings	Word and Spirit through
activities that are not	to your life	regular quiet times, home
directly sinful but are	- Allow God to prune you,	group, and times of worship
spiritually unproductive	removing unproductive or	- Walk in the "good works"
- Practice spiritual	harmful habits, activities	that God places in your path
disciplines such as fasting,	and thought patterns	- Exercise the spiritual gifts of
which temporarily remove	- Walk in the light—be	your new nature
worldly pleasures	accountable to others	

Figure 13. From the death of the old nature to the growth of the new nature

But unlike Paul, many contemporary church leaders sadly tend to avoid the topic of suffering, giving their followers the wrong impression that the decision to follow Jesus will bring them a life of blessing and comfort (and even material wealth if they believe in the prosperity gospel). Much of the spiritual lukewarmness in the Western church is due to a tendency to steer away from the trials that God lovingly brings in our paths. But Scripture says that if we do not experience persecution, there is something wrong with our walk: "Indeed, *all* who desire to live godly in Christ Jesus will be persecuted" (2 Timothy 3:12, emphasis added). It is telling that Sardis and Laodicea, the only two churches of Revelation who apparently did not suffer persecution, were also the only congregations that received exclusively negative appraisals. If we are not facing some form of rejection because of our faith, and even if this rejection comes from fellow Christians who do not appreciate the radical nature of our discipleship, we must ask ourselves whether we are actually allowing God to crucify our old nature!

> **Overcomer Principle #5:** Let God crucify your old nature daily by submitting to the trials and tribulations that He brings in your way!

What happens if we do not allow God to put our old self to death? The results are sobering:

> Do not be deceived, God is not mocked; for whatever a man sows, this he will also reap. For the one who sows to his own flesh [old nature] will from the flesh reap corruption [moral decay/spiritual death], but the one who sows to the [s]pirit [new nature] will from the [s]pirit reap eternal life.
>
> (Galatians 6:7–8)

> For the mind set on the flesh is [spiritual] death …
>
> (Romans 8:6)

> [F]or if you are living according to the flesh [old nature], you will die [spiritually]; but if by [God's] Spirit you put to death the deeds of the body, you will live.
>
> (Romans 8:13 NKJV)

If we prevent God from crucifying our old self, we will have to face the consequences, a spiritually dry and dead life that bears little fruit for God, full of meaninglessness and devoid of joy and purpose. Such a life is a sham; even when it has an outward appearance of liveliness, on the inside it is spiritually dead.

Even worse, seeking after the old self leads us back into bondage to Satan, robbing us of the freedom that Jesus achieved for us through His death on the cross:

> Do you not know that when you present yourselves to someone as slaves for obedience, you are slaves of the one whom you obey, either of sin resulting in [spiritual] death, or of obedience resulting in righteousness?
>
> (Romans 6:16)

This stands in stark contrast to the freedom from sin that is ours. Through His death, Jesus has purchased for us all we need to lead a powerful, victorious, and God-glorifying Christian life, as Paul wrote of: "For sin shall not be master over you, for you are not under law but under grace" (Romans 6:14).

But we tend to make one of two mistakes. We may strive for this new life on our own strength, forgetting that it is something we must pursue and desire but can only obtain through God's strength and grace. Or, when God graciously provides us with opportunities to die to our self, we become stubborn and stiff-necked, much like the Israelites did when they wandered in the desert. Later, we wonder why our spiritual life is so dry and unfruitful, why God seems increasingly distant, and why we do not experience His full blessings. Whenever we seek to escape the tribulations that God brings our way, we forgo important discipleship opportunities. This is precisely the mistake of the foolish virgins.

The irony of such carnal strategies is that the foolish virgins' active avoidance of God's spiritual training will cause them to face a much worse tribulation than the sufferings that God uses for His regular discipleship program! If we do not by His grace embrace the death-to-self opportunities that God gives us now, we will end up going through the greatest tribulation that humanity will ever witness. As Roy Hession writes,

But dying to self is not a thing we do once for all. There may be an initial dying when God first shows these things, but ever after it will be a constant dying, for only so can the Lord Jesus be revealed constantly through us (2 Cor 4:10).

All day long the choice will be before us in a thousand ways. It will mean no plans, no time, no money, no pleasure of our own. It will mean a constant yielding to those around us, for our yieldedness to God is measured by our yieldedness to man. Every humiliation, everyone who tries and vexes us, is God's way of breaking us, so that there is a yet deeper channel in us for the Life of Christ.[11]

From Bondage to Freedom: Entering and Taking Our Promised Land

The spiritual truths of deliverance from our old self and the development of our new spirit nature are symbolized by Israel's exodus from Egypt and its entrance into the Promised Land. When the Israelites were freed from slavery and led out of Egypt, their exodus was symbolic of salvation, in which the believer is set free from bondage to Satan. Their crossing of the Red Sea is like us passing from death to life when we believe in Christ and is therefore a picture of the waters of baptism.

After this miraculous deliverance, God did not bring His people directly into the Promised Land but first into the Sinai desert. There, He gave them His law and spiritually prepared them to conquer the land of His promise, a land "flowing with milk and honey" (symbolic for spiritual abundance and fruitfulness). They went through years of discipleship, eating only manna and walking only where God led them by pillars of smoke (during the day) and of fire (during the night). This desert "boot camp" training was designed to teach them to depend not on themselves but on God alone. As Jesus said, "[T]he Son can do nothing of Himself, unless it is something He sees the Father doing" (John 5:19). By giving them only manna and not meat (in a sense, a kind of fasting even while maintaining a regular calorie intake), God wanted their old self to die and their new self to grow. By needing to rely on God to provide their physical nourishment, the Israelites were to learn to daily seek spiritual food from Him.

However, they stubbornly rebelled against this discipleship program and even wanted to return to Egypt, their place of slavery. Therefore, when the time had come to take the Promised Land, these people showed a severe lack of faith in the God who had supernaturally delivered them out of Egypt. Being spiritually unprepared, they were thoroughly intimidated by the spies' report that the land was inhabited by tall and fierce warriors. Only trusting in their own strength, they chose to remain in the desert. What should have been a historic moment of great joy turned out to be a major spiritual defeat! God had spent all this time preparing the Israelites to become true first fruits, being like "the first fruit on the fig tree in its first season" (Hosea 9:10 ESV). But instead, like the foolish virgins who are unready to meet their "husband," the Israelites were woefully unfit to enter the Promised Land.

Then, 40 years later, when this entire stiff-necked and unbelieving generation had passed away, God commanded Joshua to lead the younger Israelites across the river Jordan into the Promised Land as wise virgins who are spiritually ready for battle. This group did indeed trust God and obey Him, marching around Jericho instead of trying to attack this impregnable fortress. When God caused the city's walls to crumble and Joshua's army entered, He exhorted them to put to death everything in it, young and old—even its cattle—and to take no spoil from the remains. This was symbolic of the spiritual principle that God's people must never compromise with the enemy by lusting after the fruit of sin. Likewise, if we want to enter God's Promised Land for us, we must be willing to let go of the "Egypt" in our hearts!

Achan, however, disobeyed and hid gold and silver from Jericho in his tent. As a consequence, he and his clan were stoned to death, symbolizing the spiritual death that comes through compromise and following the desires of the old nature (Joshua 7). In contrast, Caleb, one of the original spies who had in faith urged the people to conquer the land, lived to see and claim his rightful inheritance, receiving the reward for his faith and dedication (Joshua 14).

After Joshua's death, there was no longer a faith-driven, God-fearing leader to complete the conquest of the Promised Land, and the Israelites never managed to take all of the regions that God had promised them. The tribe of Judah, for example, was unable to defeat the Jebusites (Joshua 15:63), with the consequence that David was later on left with the task of driving them out of Jerusalem (2 Samuel 5). But even Joshua was at times spiritually inattentive; he let himself be deceived by the Gibeonites and ended up making a peace treaty with them rather than destroying them (Joshua 9). In the long run, these failures all had serious consequences, because all the nations that were left in the Promised Land would later provide a powerful source of temptation for the Israelites to follow other gods.

Spiritual Lessons for Overcomers

In summary, the Israelites give us an example of seven key spiritual mistakes that we must seek to avoid:

1. After having been delivered, the Israelites again desired to return to Egypt and pursue the carnal pleasures (food/meat) they had enjoyed there rather than being part of God's desert-based discipleship program. We, after being born again, must refrain from lusting after the sinful and worldly pursuits that we used to revel in. If we continue in sin, we feed the old nature and keep it alive.

2. While in the desert, God tested and tried the Israelites in order to refine them. However, they repeatedly rebelled against God's pruning efforts and therefore failed to grow spiritually. The challenge we face is to willingly submit to God's spiritual refinement process so that the old nature is being pruned away while the new nature can grow and flourish.

3. The Israelites became tired of the manna that God provided for them to eat and instead craved meat. But manna was God's chosen food for them. Likewise, we must come to God daily and eat from the spiritual manna that He has for us by partaking of His Word and His presence—as Jesus told us to pray, "Give us this day our daily bread [physical and spiritual nourishment]" (Matthew 6:11; see also 4:4). Our new nature will never get tired of spiritual manna, but our old nature will long for the "meat" of the old days (the sinful and worldly things that we used to feed on before we came to Christ). By God's grace, we must persist in eating "manna," and refrain from the sin-stained "meat" that only feeds the old fleshly self. This also means that we must by His grace practice spiritual disciplines, including fasting.

4. The Israelites' lack of discipleship resulted in spiritual lukewarmness, which in turn meant that they didn't develop much faith. When the spies who scouted out the Promised Land told them about the giant warriors who lived there, they did not act as wise virgins in faith and spiritual preparedness but as foolish virgins in fear and spiritual slackness. As a consequence, that generation never set foot on the Promised Land. Similarly, if we do not allow God to grow our faith, we will tend to be driven by fears and self-reliance. That may mean that we will never get to see the spiritual abundance and fruitfulness that God has in store for each of us in our very own "Promised Land."

5. Sadly, even the new generation of Israelites under Joshua made some serious mistakes by engaging in spiritual compromises with

the enemy. They were tempted to keep some of the possessions of the enemy. Achan secretly took some of the booty, and immediately, the Israelite army faced defeat at the battle of Ai against an inferior enemy. Similarly, we risk spiritual defeat even in situations that we consider to be "easy" when we compromise with the enemy by lowering our standards. Every time we give in to the lusts of the old self, we obstruct the victorious life of the new nature. Also, if we notice that we are spiritually weak and are not sure why, then we should act like Joshua did after the defeat at Ai and humbly ask God why He did not give victory. God graciously responded to his submission by revealing to Joshua where the sin problem was.

6. The Israelites did not root out all of their enemies. Joshua imprudently allowed himself to be deceived by the Gibeonites, who pretended that they were a distant people who were just passing through. Rather than checking back with God, Joshua went ahead in his own wisdom, believed them and readily made a peace treaty with them. Similarly, the people of Judah battled the Jebusites in their own strength and consequently failed to conquer them. In contrast, we must by His grace be constantly on our guard, not acting independently from His leading. The enemy still "prowls around like a roaring lion, seeking someone to devour" (1 Peter 5:8). More often than not, Satan works through deception rather than outright attack. The Gibeonites used flattery when deceiving Joshua, telling him how great and wonderful his people were.

> **Overcomer Principle #6:** Never rely on your own understanding. Always consult God first, and act in His strength!

7. The long-term consequence of the Israelites' failures was that many of God's enemies were never driven out of the

Promised Land. God's people settled down around them and accommodated their presence. When their spiritual zeal had declined just one generation after Joshua's death, the Israelites were soon tempted to follow these peoples' gods. We may ask what is so tempting about worshiping a god made of stone or wood. But even though most modern people will not readily worship a literal "god" statue, we have many other idols in our lives. A "god" or an idol is anything that we put our trust in and depend on for any aspect of our lives; in short, anything that replaces God. For some, a large savings account will prove to be an idol, because they put their trust more in it than in God's provision. For others, it will be something else.

> **Overcomer Principle #7:** Do not make peace agreements with your spiritual "enemies" (sin habits)! Instead, be uncompromising and allow God to root them out.

To the extent to which we refuse to let God put our old self, the "enemy" within us, to death and fail to take the spiritual "land" that He promised to us, we will sooner or later succumb to these idols. The more spiritual compromises we enter into, the more room we give for the enemy to rob us of true spiritual riches. But when we cooperate with God to ruthlessly root out the enemy within us, we will reap the abundant fruit of the Promised Lands that is now ours.

Like the Israelites, all of us must pass through "deserts" of trials and tests, and we all are called to conquer our "enemies" (sin habits) in God's strength (His grace). Our freedom from bondage, our degree of victory over the enemy, and our spiritual fruitfulness all greatly depend on how uncompromisingly we root out the enemies' forces and on how much of our personal Promised Land we take together with Him. Then, our newborn spirit nature will grow and mature as we feed on the lush green pastures of God's Word instead of the bug-infested mud pools of the world. The more our new nature grows and matures, the more God can give spiritual authority and responsibilities to it. Then, when Jesus comes to take up His kingdom, those with a more mature new spirit nature will naturally receive more spiritual power and authority under His reign than those whose new selves never grew beyond the infant stage.

The Importance of Works for Christians, Who Are Saved by Grace Alone

Because of the salvation-by-works doctrine that has bedeviled God's church for centuries, many evangelical fellowships avoid the word "works" and do not exhort their members to actively pursue them. The perception is that because we are saved by grace alone, teaching believers about works is problematic, because it might cause them to fall back into a "works mindset."

But this is a dangerous practice. Even though we are indeed saved by faith through grace alone, we are by His grace to walk in the "good works" that God prepared beforehand for us (Ephesians 2:10). If we minimize the significance of works in discipleship, we render our Christian walk void of meaning and purpose and stifle the new life that we received. Our new spirit nature naturally wants to do God's will and is entirely able to do so. In fact, God created it for this very reason, because when we obey God and do His will, He gets the glory. As Jesus said, "My Father is glorified by this, that you bear much fruit, and so prove to be My disciples" (John 15:8). A quick look at what God's Word says about "good works" should settle the discussion on this topic:

> Let your light shine before men in such a way that they may see your good works, and glorify your Father who is in heaven.
>
> (Matthew 5:16)

> For we are His workmanship, created in Christ Jesus for good works, which God prepared beforehand so that we would walk in them.
>
> (Ephesians 2:10)

Instruct them [the rich] to do good, to be rich in <u>good works</u>, to be generous and ready to share.

(1 Timothy 6:18)

[I]n all things show yourself to be an example of <u>good deeds</u>.

(Titus 2:7)

[A]nd let us consider how to stimulate one another to love and <u>good deeds</u>.

(Hebrews 10:24)

Keep your behavior excellent among the Gentiles, so that in the thing in which they slander you as evildoers, they may because of your <u>good deeds</u>, as they observe them, glorify God in the day of visitation.

(1 Peter 2:12)

[C]oncerning these things I want you to speak confidently, so that those who have believed God will be careful to engage in <u>good deeds</u>.

(Titus 3:8)

Scripture plainly tells us that God expects us to do "good works" in His strength, because they glorify Him and show the world that we, His people, have truly received His power and grace. A Christian life steeped in sin and devoid of acts of blessing towards others is a poor witness to the new spirit nature for which Christ paid so dearly at the cross! The world evaluates us not by our talk, but by our walk. If the two do not match up, people will rightly consider us to be hypocrites: those who say they possess virtues or character qualities but fail to exhibit them in their actual lives.

Hypocrisy is nothing but deceit. If we say we follow Jesus but do so through our old nature, we are lying to the people around us. We tell them that we are "Christians" but our walk does not match up with our talk. This is a poor witness and a major reason why many unbelievers do not turn to God. But when we allow God to crucify our old self and live in the power of the new nature, then we glorify God by our "good works." Our works are our primary testimony of our faith to others. To minimize their importance is to belittle our role as ambassadors for Christ to an unregenerate world. No one can be saved through works, but all who have been saved were saved so that they would do works for the glory of God.

Chapter 8 Notes

---

1. The KJV and NKJV translate *sarkikos* (*Strong's Concordance,* G4559), the adjective of the noun *sarx* ("flesh"), as "carnal."
2. Ibid., G4153.
3. Ibid., G4561.
4. Compare also 1 Corinthians 2:14.
5. Our new nature is also called a "new creation" in Galatians 6:15. We know that whatever God creates, He makes perfect!
6. For example, every introduction in the New Testament epistles refers to the local believers as "saints" (Gr. *hagios, Strong's Concordance,* G40). Literally, *hagios* means "holy ones." Even Jesus is at times referred to as a "holy one" (*hagios,* for example Acts 3:14). An exception is James 4:8, which talks about "sinners," but a strong argument can be made that his passage is an exhortation to those who perhaps believe they are Christians, but who are not truly born again. In either case, this usage in James is an absolute exception and not found elsewhere in the New Testament. Likewise, in the Old Testament, the word "sinner" (Hebr. *chatta,* ibid., H2400) is never used for God's people (see for example Psalm 1).
7. The Greek term translated as "keeps on sinning," *amartanon* (*Strong's Concordance,* G264), is a present active participle, which denotes an on-going action that does not come to an end, and therefore a habitual action that will not change.
8. Roy Hession, *The Calvary Road* (London: CLC Publications, 2009), 6.
9. This inner spiritual struggle of old against new does not mean that we are both sinners and saints at the same time. The Bible makes it clear that we have only ONE identity: we are saints. But we have TWO competing natures within us which war against each other. However, if we let God keep us on the narrow path of discipleship, the new nature will soon be much more powerful than the old nature, whose power was broken by Jesus' death on the cross. God plainly tells us that we can be victorious!
10. Hession, 6.
11. Hession, 6.

Chapter 9

Stay an Overcomer:
Focusing on the Narrow Path

In the world you have tribulation, but take courage;
I have overcome the world.
John 16:33

We Are All Called to Be Overcomers

After understanding all these truths about victoriously and fruitfully living with Jesus, we can now begin to appreciate what it means to be an "overcomer." The Greek word for overcoming, *nikao*,[1] means to subdue, conquer, prevail, or gain the victory. This refers precisely to the process of taking the Promised Land that we just looked at! An overcoming Christian is one who continually overcomes (conquers) the enemy of sin within him as he enters his Promised Land, taking hold of the freedom and fruitfulness that Jesus purchased for him through his blood. The overcoming believer achieves this not by his own strength but because Christ overcame and defeated the adversary at the cross, once and for all. John wrote, "You are from God, little children, and have overcome them [lying spirits]; because greater is He who is in you than he who is in the world" (1 John 4:4). Then he proclaims, "*Everyone* who has been born of God overcomes the world" (1 John 5:4 ESV, emphasis added). John didn't say that the spiritual supermen amongst us overcome the world. No, *everyone* who is born of God and therefore has the new spirit nature will do so!

All of us have been assigned a Promised Land by God, and we are all called and enabled to be overcomers and conquer this land. This is not something that God reserves for a blessed few. No, all Christians can and must overcome by walking after the new nature, letting God crucify their old selves. The Bible makes it clear that whether we overcome or not is entirely our choice, because God continually gives us everything we need to overcome. Christ's death has set you free from sin. Whether you "go on presenting the members of your body to sin as instruments of unrighteousness," or whether you "present yourselves to God ... and your members as instruments of righteousness to God" (Romans 6:13) is now totally up to you, not to God.

Consequently, overcoming is not an optional high-achiever level of discipleship, like icing on the cake. Aiming at anything less than overcoming means heading toward certain failure. God expects and requires all of us to overcome. He still loves us if we do not, but there will be consequences in the form of losing eternal rewards.

The letters to the seven churches of Revelation described in Revelation chapters 2 and 3 show us some particular areas in which Christians must be careful to prove themselves as overcomers. They tell us which strategies the enemy employed back in the first century AD in order to keep God's people from fruit-bearing, overcoming discipleship. We can be sure that he will employ them again in the times before the first fruits rapture. With Satan, as with humanity, there is "nothing new under the sun."

Learning From the Strengths and Weaknesses of the Seven Churches of Revelation

In the first century AD, the letters to the seven churches provided an appraisal of the contemporary spiritual landscape, showing how different churches were plagued with different issues. But more than that, these letters point to typical problems that have hampered God's church throughout history up to this day. Attempts have been made to categorize church history according to these letters, assuming that the early church after Jesus' death was like Ephesus, while our contemporary end times church is characterized by Laodicea's woes.

However, such a scheme is overly simplistic. No single church age can be fully described by just one type of church.[2] Throughout the ages, churches have suffered from the Ephesus phenomenon (loss of first love), the Thyatira phenomenon (false teachings), the Sardis phenomenon (outward show without inner qualities), and the Laodicea phenomenon (lukewarmness and a wrong focus on material over spiritual riches). Especially now, during the end of the age, we find all of these predicaments simultaneously bedeviling the contemporary global church.

Even among American Christianity, Laodicean lukewarmness is by no means the only problem. False doctrines, such as an acceptance of homosexuality or the belief that even unbelievers will ultimately be saved (the doctrine of universalism), a loss of first love and first passion for Christ, false teachers tearing apart unprepared churches, as well as spiritual superficiality and an emphasis on show over substance are all equally serious issues. In European Christianity, a liberal interpretation of the Word of God and compromise with the spirit of the age are arguably the greatest temptations. In other areas such as Asia, persecution often keeps the church spiritually alive and materially poor, but heresy frequently creeps in as especially underground churches have been lacking reliable study materials and solid doctrinal teaching.

Consequently, Jesus does not want us just to be preoccupied with the letter to the Laodiceans, as if that should be our primary "church age" focus. No, He wants us to carefully examine all seven churches and to learn from all of their mistakes as well as their strong points! Taken together, they show us what the church will look like when Christ returns to rapture His first fruits.

In the letters to the churches of Revelation, Jesus dishes out stinging criticism as well as lavish praise, bold exhortations as well as encouraging commendations. From these letters, it is evident that the spiritual condition of these churches differed greatly. In particular, we notice that some of them only receive criticism while others only get praises, and yet others are given some of both. Noticeably, Philadelphia, the church that obtained the promise of being kept from the "hour of testing," is amongst the two who secured an entirely positive appraisal.

From Jesus' evaluation of the seven churches and the lack or presence of praise and criticism, we can discern a model of overcoming discipleship. They can be divided into three major categories: 1) two congregations that are well on the overcomer path, one of which has already reached overcomer status; 2) three endangered overcomer churches; and 3) two non-overcomer churches.

Table 15. Three categories of churches of Revelation

Description	Churches	Jesus' appraisal	Church characteristics	Future prospects
1. Overcomer churches	Philadelphia, Smyrna	No criticism, only praise	Face persecution and have spiritual fruit. Focus on Jesus.	**Smyrna**: will receive its reward once it passes the upcoming trial. **Philadelphia**: already passed the test and therefore already possesses a reward (crown).
2. Endangered overcomer churches	Ephesus, Pergamum, Thyatira	Both criticism and praise	Were steadfast under persecution and have spiritual fruit. However, all three suffer from dangerous compromises and internal problems.	**Ephesus**: will no longer be fit for being used by God if they don't recover their first love. **Pergamum**: Jesus will war against them if they don't judge those amongst them who hold to false teachings. **Thyatira**: church is controlled by a false prophetess, whom Jesus will strike with sickness and will put her spiritual children to death.
3. Non-overcomer churches	Sardis, Laodicea	No praise, only criticism	Do not face persecution. Full of compromise, wrong priorities and false doctrines.	**Sardis**: Jesus will come against them like a thief if they don't repent. **Laodicea**: they will face God's discipline and reproof if they don't change their ways.

Of all seven fellowships, only two were without compromises. The other five were troubled by serious issues that had the potential to destroy them—even though three of these possessed multiple overcomer qualities. But each of these five churches had allowed themselves to be overcome by the enemy in one way or another, and all the devil initially needs is a foot in the door. In every instance, Satan had gotten strategic footholds because these congregations did not closely watch their spiritual walk or their doctrine.

Examining Each Church in Detail

Sardis: At Sardis, the emphasis was on putting on a show. It all looked good, and the church had a reputation of being "alive." Maybe they had professional worship but Jesus was not at the center; maybe the preaching style was impressive, but the truth of God's Word was not being taught; maybe they practiced spiritual gifts but God's Kingdom was not the focus; or perhaps they had a congregation who was active and excitable but not spiritually mature or discerning. Here, discipleship was likely a form of pseudo-spiritual entertainment but without the substance of Christ. As a result, only a few in Sardis had "not soiled their garments" (Revelation 3:4). The rest walked in spiritual compromise. There is no mention of the church facing persecution—a sure sign that something was wrong.

Laodicea: This fellowship is often seen as the worst of all seven. But the words of Jesus primarily indicate a fatherly concern over its utterly wrong spiritual focus, which is less severe than the harsh threats He makes against Sardis, Thyatira or Ephesus. Laodicea was totally immature because it got all its priorities wrong! It was materially rich, yet spiritually bankrupt. They thought they were doing great, but in reality they were spiritually blind. For them, discipleship was all about wellness and wealth, and no persecution touched them. As a result, their whole Christian walk was thoroughly lukewarm, and their new spirit natures were utterly underdeveloped. Jesus' reaction to this church is a mixture of disgust and pity. This church's only way out of its predicament is a complete turnaround of its understanding of what it means to progress along what Roy Hession so aptly termed "Calvary Road"—the narrow path of true discipleship.

Pergamum and Thyatira: Both of these churches faced the same problem but to different extents. Jesus accuses them of eating "things sacrificed to idols" and of committing "acts of immorality." In their society, eating things sacrificed to idols meant to participate in feasts given to honor local gods. Such deity worship was an intrinsic part of social and economic life. When business contracts were signed or important decisions made, feasts were held during which these gods would be consulted and worshiped in order to obtain their blessings. Food would be spiritually offered to them and then put on the table for everyone to eat. To join such occasions and eat the food basically meant to take part in worshiping the local idol. But refusing to do so resulted in one's exclusion from social, cultural, and economic life. Social isolation and material poverty were the harsh but typical consequences of keeping oneself away from such idolatry. The first century Christians in Asia Minor therefore paid a high price for their faith.

But Pergamum and Thyatira apparently developed a new kind of theology that "permitted" them to engage in idolatrous behaviors. Pergamum is criticized for holding to the "teaching of Balaam" (Revelation 2:14). This teaching falsely argued that because Christians live under the New Covenant (as opposed to the Old Covenant that God gave through Moses), they have the "freedom" to do whatever they want—including sinful activities. This false freedom teaching had previously been condemned by Jude, who wrote of "ungodly persons who turn the grace of our God into licentiousness" (v. 4). Such spiritual compromise with the enemy does not remain without severe consequences. Thyatira was especially hard-hit as it had come to be completely dominated by Jezebel, a false prophetess who effectively controlled both church practice and doctrine. This is an additional lesson in watchfulness: a church must be extremely careful about whom it allows to assume positions of power and influence over its congregation.

Ephesus: Paul visited the Ephesians in 53 AD and wrote in his epistle to them how incredibly thankful he was for "your love for all the saints" (1:15). John compiled the book of Revelation around 90 AD, one or two generations later. By then, their love for each other and for their Lord had unfortunately markedly declined. Jesus' letter to this church praises their faithfulness to God's word, commending them for rejecting false apostles who sought to infuse the church with heretical teachings. But He also has one very important thing against them: "you have left your first love" (Revelation 2:4). After several decades, the Ephesians' initial love and passion for Jesus had gradually subsided. Now, Christianity was just a dull routine, a passionless expression of duty. This has happened to many churches and believers. One reaches a certain level of maturity and discipleship, but then, there is a gradual loss of passion. That first love slowly and quietly slips away. Then, following Jesus has been reduced to being "religious," and the danger of legalism rises dramatically.

Where there is no genuine love, the letter of the law quickly replaces the sincere grace that used to permeate a church. A place dominated by duty-driven religiousness is a perfect breeding ground for joyless legalism and hypocrisy, both of which feed on the old self. Ephesus had rejected heretical doctrines, including the false freedom teaching of Balaam. But if Satan cannot lead a fellowship into outright sin or heresy, he will try to move it toward a spiritually dry exercise of religious routine that lacks the true power of the new nature. Without its first love and passion for Jesus, a church loses the primary reason for everything it is and does. This is exactly what had happened to the Ephesian church.

Sadly, all five of these churches developed skewed views of discipleship as a consequence of their compromises and loss of focus. For them, following Jesus became a form of pseudo-spiritual entertainment, a self-centered pursuit of wellness and wealth, an unfettered false "freedom" that permitted compromise with the spirit of the age, or a loveless, legalistic performance of duty that was based on rules rather than on relationship.

Table 16. Discipleship forms of endangered and non-overcoming Revelation churches

Sardis	Discipleship as pseudo-spiritual entertainment
Laodicea	Discipleship as wellness and wealth
Pergamum & Thyatira	Discipleship as limitless freedom
Ephesus	Discipleship as loveless duty

Two Common Incorrect Views on Discipleship

In the previous chapter, we had shown the importance of trials and tribulations for spiritual growth, which clearly indicates that the focus of Sardis and Laodicea was wrong. In this section, we will focus on the other two false understandings of discipleship found among the seven churches: discipleship as limitless freedom and discipleship as loveless, legalistic duty. All of us are liable to practice these incorrect forms of discipleship because the enemy continually seeks to deceive us into pursuing them.

Pergamum and Thyatira had come to a skewed understanding of the freedom that we have in Christ as New Testament believers. Even though many of us would not take it as far as they did, justifying the open practice of sexual immorality, there is a fair bit of confusion among Christian circles when it comes to the question of fixed, mandatory rules and commandments. Does the New Testament even contain any commandments? Does it teach us anything that we absolutely must do? Is it perhaps only about love, because Jesus declared loving God and others to be the greatest of all commandments (Matthew 22:37–40)?

A common perception is that because we are no longer under the law given through Moses, we are now set free from any "rigid" and "legalistic" rules, because following Jesus is all about "love" and "grace." But what does that actually mean? Because we are not under the law, does that mean we are free to make up our own rules as we go along, just as postmodern relativism proclaims? A key problem in this confusion is our incomplete understanding of grace. Romans 6:14 says that we are "not under law, but under grace." Here, our old self tends to interpret "grace" as a license to do what we want—or at least as the "freedom" to keep on sinning and asking God for forgiveness without actually overcoming our sin habits and developing transformed character. Or perhaps we are led to believe that because there are no longer hard and fast commandments, we can treat them with some "flexibility." This perspective would, for example, argue that Jesus' commandment against divorce should not be viewed too "legalistically" and that divorce should therefore be permissible, based on our situation and needs. This kind of thinking can also work the other way round: one might say that one's situation is so desperate that one "must" divorce, but because Jesus loves us, it's okay, and there won't be negative consequences.

The other end of the spectrum is represented by the Ephesians and the loveless legalism that would likely have developed in their church. In reaction to the less-than-holy lifestyles of the grace-oriented freedom advocates, there are those who lament that Christians are too lax in their spiritual lives. These holiness-oriented believers feel that true discipleship requires a return to a more law-abiding Christianity. Some of them advocate keeping most of the Old Testament law (except for animal sacrifices). Others compile long lists of do's and don'ts that they feel true Christians must follow. Both approaches are ultimately very similar, because they seek to place us under a comprehensive system of written commandments.

Finally, a majority of Christians aimlessly wander somewhere between the two extremes, wondering what exactly they are supposed to do and how they are to understand the significance of the Mosaic law and Jesus' extremely demanding interpretations of some of its commandments in the Sermon on the Mount. Their feelings are often dominated by a mix of inner bondage and guilt, unsure as to what and how much they ought to "do" in order to please God.

What It Means to Be "Not Under Law but Under Grace"

When Jesus died on the cross, two things died with Him. Firstly, our old sin nature inherited from Adam died. Secondly, we died to the Old Testament law, which had then been the only way under which sinful humans could approach a perfectly holy God. In the Old Covenant, the Israelites were under the law. However, because they only had the old flesh nature, they were unable to keep it. According to Paul, the purpose of the law was to give God's people a standard of righteousness that would make them aware of their sinfulness. In Romans 3:20 he tells us that "through the Law comes the knowledge of sin" (see also Romans 7:7). By learning God's righteous requirements expressed in the Law, the Israelites were to develop an awareness of right and wrong.

However, the law was entirely powerless to change their sinful natures—not because there was anything wrong with the law, which Paul describes as "holy and righteous and good" (Romans 7:12). Rather, the problem lies with the old nature, which is utterly incapable of meeting the standard of righteousness set by the law. Being under the law therefore caused a real dilemma for Old Covenant believers: they knew that the law was "good," but they could not keep it. As a consequence, the law proved to be a "ministry of condemnation" (2 Corinthians 3:9), even a "ministry that brought death" (3:7 NIV). It revealed the spiritually dead condition of the old self but was not able to transform it into spiritual life. Consequently, instead of bringing freedom and life, the Old Covenant kept those under it in a state of condemnation and spiritual death.

So why did God give the law when it only reinforced the deadness of fallen human nature? Scripture says that He mandated it in order to keep God's people "captive under the law, imprisoned until the coming faith would be revealed" (Galatians 3:23 ESV). Therefore, the law was "our guardian until Christ came; it protected us until we could be made right with God through faith" (3:24 NLT). The purpose of the law was therefore to make God's people aware of their sinfulness and to show them their need for a savior. The resulting state of condemnation was designed to prepare them for Jesus' coming. Then, when Jesus had died for them, they would be released from the law, ready to experience the spiritual power and freedom of the new nature. The problem was therefore not with the law itself but rather with the legalistic and unspiritual way in which the fallen nature responded to it.

The Two Purposes of the Law:
1. To make God's people aware of God's standards and therefore of their sinfulness.
2. To make God's people aware of their inability to keep God's standards.

Both purposes showed them that they needed a savior.

When Christ came, He not only caused us to die to our old self, but also to die to the law. Paul wrote, "But now we are released from the law, having died to that which held us captive" (Romans 7:6 ESV). Why did we have to die to the law, so that we are no longer under it? Because our new spirit nature is not designed to operate under the law. The law only served its purpose in conjunction with our old nature, and even then, it did not actually enable us to keep it but only held us captive so as to prepare us for receiving the new nature. The mistake of the Galatians whom Paul so harshly condemned was trying to put the new nature back under the old law. But that doesn't work—the two must not be combined! In fact, attempting to do so only stunts the growth of the new self, promoting a return to relying on our old self. Why does this impede the growth of the new self?

We Are Under the Law of the Spirit of Life

The reason for this is that our new nature requires another system under which to operate. The Romans 7:6 quote from above continues as follows: "[we died to the law] so that we serve in the new way of the Spirit and not in the old way of the written code." In 2 Corinthians 3:6, Paul writes that "[God] made us ... servants of a new covenant, not of the letter but of the Spirit; for the letter kills, but the Spirit gives life." He could not have been clearer than that. The old system, the written code or "letter," could only produce spiritual death through our old nature, but the new system, the "law of the Spirit of life" (Romans 8:2) or "law of Christ" (1 Corinthians 9:20), brings forth true spiritual life through our new nature.

In 1 Corinthians 9, Paul further explains that he is not "under the Law ... though not ... without the law of God but under [lit. in] the law of Christ" (vv. 20–21). Although Paul is not under the old law, he is clearly under something. He somewhat mysteriously refers to this something as the "law of Christ." This term also appears in Galatians 6:2, where Paul exhorts the Galatians to "[b]ear one another's burdens, and thereby fulfill the law of Christ." Paul therefore links the "law of Christ" with the "royal law," that we are to love our neighbors as ourselves (James 2:8). Similarly, James describes the Word of God as a "law of liberty" (1:25) and therefore as the very opposite of the old law which kept those under it imprisoned. Therefore, the new system we are under has three different names:

1. The "law of Christ"
2. The "law of the Spirit of life"

3. The "law of liberty"

Romans 7:4 affirms that we died to the law, not so that we would be our own masters but so that we "might be joined to another, to Him who was raised from the dead, in order that we might bear fruit for God." We are therefore still under a system or "law" as Scripture calls it, but clearly under a very different one than that given to Moses. Most importantly, this "law" does not operate in a legal manner but in a spiritually-inspired and personal way—it is about being in God's will through a living relationship to our Heavenly Father. Consequently, this new "law" is full of spiritual power and life, perfectly designed by God to empower our new spirit nature.

This new system was foreseen by Jeremiah's famous prophesy of the New Covenant that God would make when He sending His Son:

> "But this is the covenant which I will make with the house of Israel after those days," declares the LORD, "I will put My law [not the law of Moses but the new 'law of Christ'] within them [into the new nature] and on their heart I will write it; and I will be their God, and they shall be My people."
>
> (Jeremiah 31:33)

Likewise, Ezekiel prophesied:

> Moreover, I will give you a new heart and put a new spirit within you [the new nature]; and I will remove the heart of stone [the old nature's heart] from your flesh and give you a heart of flesh [the new nature's heart]. I will put My Spirit within you and cause you to walk in My statutes [Jesus' commandments or the "law of Christ"], and you will be careful to observe My ordinances.
>
> (Ezekiel 36:26–27)

Both prophecies are saying the same thing: under the New Covenant, we receive a new spirit nature, which is entirely capable of walking in God's ways and following His perfect "statutes"—the will of God revealed in the Old and especially in the New Testaments. This time, God's law is not something external, written on tablets of stone like the Ten Commandments. Now, it is actually "within us," written on our "heart[s] of flesh;" it is like a living law placed right into our very hearts. Paul referred to these prophetic truths when he told the Corinthians, "You show that you are a letter from Christ ... written not with ink but with the Spirit of the living God, not on tablets of stone [symbolic of the old nature] but on tablets of human hearts [the new nature]" (2 Corinthians 3:3).

Now, under the New Covenant, God's Word and will are no longer outside of us but are right inside us, written *within* our new nature hearts. This is why the "law of Christ" is said to be "in" us: *ennomos*,[3] translated by the NASB as "under the law [of Christ]," comes from the words *en* ("in") and *nomos* ("law"), together meaning "in the law [of Christ]." The result is that now we are fully able to "walk in [God's] statutes, and [are] careful to observe [God's] ordinances," as Ezekiel wrote.

Practically, this means that God directly guides our newborn spirit by His Spirit through a personal relationship. The New Testament has two Greek terms for God's "Word": *logos*,[4] which refers to the universal Word of God, eternal and universally applicable for all of God's people, and *rhema*,[5] which denotes God's spoken Word that His Spirit flexibly speaks into specific situations and contexts.

For example, the angel's message to Mary that she would give birth to the Savior, Jesus' predictions of His own death, Jesus' prophetic word to Peter that he would deny Him three times, or His command to Peter and his fellows that they should let down their fishing nets in the deep water, were all *rhema* words: specific and personal words of knowledge. Likewise, prophetic words spoken by God through His prophets are referred to as *rhema* (for example, 2 Peter 3:2).

Table 17. God's *logos* Word compared with His *rhema* Word

	God's *logos* Word	God's *rhema* Word
What it is	God's written Word to all His people of all generations	God's spoken Word, spoken by His Spirit to each of His sheep
Validity	Eternally and universally valid for all believers	Valid for specific individuals (or groups of individuals such as churches), times and contexts
Scope	General and universal	Specific and individual/personal/contextual
How it works	Contains commandments, exhortations and promises which function as general signposts, giving us general principles for how we must live in order to grow spiritually.	Takes commandments or promises from God's *logos* word and applies them to our lives and specific situations. The result may be a specific promise, exhortation, or commandment to us.
Rules and principles that govern its use	Nothing must ever be added to or taken away (Matthew 5:18; Revelation 22:19).	Must be in agreement with and following the same principles as God's *logos* word, being in line with God's revealed character. All *rhema* Words spoken by God through believers must be tested (1 Thessalonians 5:19–22; 1 John 4:1).

Jesus said, "My sheep hear My voice, and I know them, and they follow Me" (John 10:27). Under the New Covenant, our new spirit nature relies not only on universal commandments (*logos*) but also depends on God guiding us continually through moment-by-moment promptings (*rhema*). Suddenly, general scriptural commandments such as "you shall not steal" or "do not hate your brother" become specific to our personal situation. Like the rich ruler, we thought that we kept them, but now the Spirit reveals to us how we have in fact been espousing behaviors and attitudes that He wants to transform. Jesus told His followers, "the words [*rhema*] that I have spoken to you are spirit and are life" (John 6:63). "If you abide in Me, and My words [*rhema*] abide in you, ask whatever you wish, and it will be done for you" (John 15:7). This is what it means to be living within the "law of the Spirit of life."

> **God guides our new nature**
> a) through His universal, written word (*logos*), and
> b) through His personal, context-specific spoken word (*rhema*).
> Together, the *logos* and the *rhema* are God's tailor-made, Spirit-empowered "law" for us.

This new, Spirit-empowered method is much more advanced than the previous system of merely reading, understanding, and following a written code. Now, we can read any part of God's Word, and God can use that Word to speak to us, teaching, guiding, exhorting, rebuking, encouraging, and setting us free. By His Spirit, He can take a Word spoken to one of His people or prophets long ago and apply it to our personal situations. Now, He can take us much deeper than before, revealing to us the spirit behind a commandment, just as Jesus did in the Sermon on the Mount, when He re-interpreted Moses' commandments and showed the people how much higher God's standards really are.

Being under the "law of the Spirit of life" takes us far beyond the Law of Moses, revealing to us a much greater level of righteousness and truth. Most importantly, it has the power to transform us so that we can actually walk in it. This Spirit-empowered law is therefore the perfect fulfillment of the Old Testament law, following Jesus' words that He came not to "abolish but to fulfill" (Matthew 5:17). This new "law" does not lead us back under the "old written code" given by Moses. Instead, it keeps us in Jesus and empowers us to bear fruit for God! Therefore, being under the "law of Christ" or the "law of the Spirit of life" is exactly the same as being "under grace" or being "in Christ": they all refer to the wonderful new existence that we can have as our new nature is firmly rooted in God's Word and will for our lives.

Table 18. The Old Covenant versus the New Covenant

	Old Covenant (Moses)	New Covenant (Christ)
Our nature	Old sinful nature inherited from Adam.	New spirit nature inherited through Christ.
Which kind of law/ system this nature is designed to operate under	Designed to operate under the law of Moses (the "old written code").	Designed to operate under the "law of Christ"/"law of the Spirit of life."
How does this law/ system work?	A written code to be read, understood, and obeyed. Culturally and historically specific for the nation of Israel during Old Testament times.	God's Spirit applies the written Word of God (*logos*) together with His spoken Word (*rhema*) to our personal situations, guiding us into His will for our lives.
Outcome of being under this system	Our old self is exposed as sinful and helpless, leading to condemnation.	Righteousness, obedience, and fruitfulness resulting in freedom and true life.
Significance for us	• Some of the laws of Moses are eternally valid (especially the Ten Commandments). However, they must be spiritually discerned through our new nature so that we can understand their full spiritual depth. • Other laws are specific to ancient Jewish culture, but the principles behind them are still important for us. • The sacrificial and ceremonial laws have been explicitly revoked because they were fulfilled in Christ (Hebrews 9–10). They must never be reinstated.	This is the new system or "law" that we live under. It has its roots in the Old Covenant, but is far more powerful, designed to work with our new nature.

Universal Commandments and Personal Spiritual Guidance

Now we understand that a return to an *exclusive* focus on a written universal law, be it the literal law of Moses or similar lists of commandments extrapolated from the Bible, represents a fatal step back into a system which was never designed to bring true life. Our new spirit-self fails to benefit from a return to such a written code. Even worse, self-made lists of do's and don'ts tend to replace and hinder a continual abiding in Jesus by the Spirit, hampering our desire and ability to continually discern His voice. That is precisely the reason why the New Testament has not sought to replicate a comprehensive written legal system such as the Mosaic law. The living "law of the Spirit of life," the only system under which our new nature can tap into its full spiritual potential, requires that our immersion in God's *logos* Word is empowered by His *rhema* words of knowledge, guidance, and inspiration. The *rhema* words that we believe we have received from God must be tested and found to correspond to the written teachings of His *logos* word.

Jesus' general commandments must be complemented by God's personal, tailor-made discipleship program for us. When we replace the personal leading and empowering of the Holy Spirit with our own universal, one-fits-all written code, we ultimately empower our old sin nature. Because this nature cannot submit to God's Spirit or discern His directions, it tends to justify itself by superficially obeying the letter of the law but actually fails to meet God's true standard that the law points to. The results are legalism, hypocrisy, and self-righteousness, while the new nature is sidelined.

Loving Jesus Means Keeping His Commandments

Moreover, we now also perceive what it means to be "not under law, but under grace." Grace is not a mere bundle of fuzzy emotions. Grace is the Spirit's power in us through our new nature, power to overcome sin and the works of the evil one in us. Being under grace does not mean that we are no longer under any system or "law." Not at all! Instead, Jesus' death transferred us from being under the old law to being under a new system or "law." So we are still under a "law"—but under a very different one! Those Christians who ignore this and think they are "free" to do as they please (that is, they believe there are no more universal commandments) are in a very dangerous place. Like Pergamum and Thyatira, they are back on the path of bondage into sin because they fail to place themselves under the new system that our new nature needs for its spiritual growth.

If we only know the truth but do not practice it, we cannot experience the freedom it brings. This is why Jesus continually talked to His disciples about the need to keep His commandments (plural!) in the decisive hours before His arrest:

> If you love Me, you will keep My commandments.
>
> (John 14:15)

> He who has My commandments and keeps them is the one who loves Me.
>
> (John 14:21)

> If you keep My commandments, you will abide in My love; just as I have kept My Father's commandments and abide in His love.... This is My commandment, that you love one another, just as I have loved you.
>
> (John 15:10, 12)

Affirming and deepening this truth, John later wrote:

> By this we know that we have come to know Him, if we keep His commandments. The one who says, "I have come to know Him," and does not keep His commandments, is a liar, and the truth is not in him; but whoever keeps His word, in him the love of God has truly been perfected.
>
> (1 John 2:3–5)

Jesus' universally-valid commandments that we are all called to walk in are like major signposts that mark the narrow path along which the personal *rhema* words of the Spirit lead us. To ignore or disobey them means to leave the narrow way of discipleship and to walk back into bondage to sin. Whatever God tells us through His Spirit has become His personal and specific "law" for us—as Ezekiel's prophecy says, "… and you *will* be careful to observe my ordinances" (36:27, emphasis added).

In the same spirit, Paul wrote, "For you were called to freedom, brethren; only do not turn your freedom into an opportunity for the flesh, but through love serve one another" (Galatians 5:13). If we say that we "love" but do not keep Jesus' commandments, our "love" is meaningless. It is impossible to love God and others through our old, self-centered sin nature. Therefore, if we keep walking in that nature by continuing in our sin habits, we cannot be practicing true love. As the German theologian Dieter Schneider put it, "Human love towards God is not a vague emotion, but concrete obedience to His commandments."[6] In Matthew 24:12, Jesus teaches us that lawlessness invariably leads to lovelessness. Likewise, Jesus' appraisal of the Philadelphian overcomer church makes no mention of love. Rather, He focuses on them having "kept the word of My perseverance." This is a clear reference to them having been faithful to Jesus' commandments, which is equivalent to loving Jesus. Therefore, there was no need for Christ to mention "love." Faithful endurance and commitment to His word implies that true love must be present.

Likewise, we cannot abide *in* Christ without being *under* His will or "law," the system that must govern our new nature.[7] True discipleship requires long-term obedience to both God's universal *logos* Word (such as Jesus' commandments) and His specific *rhema* words to us. Overall, we must be careful to stay clear of both legalism and lawlessness and instead remain *in* Christ and *under* the authority of His Word, so that we can experience the abundance of true life and rich spiritual fruit that God wants to produce through our new nature.

How to Stay on the Overcomer Path

Discipleship is about continually overcoming through God's grace, and overcoming requires that we follow Jesus as His disciples. Both are like a life-long marathon. Overcoming is a progressive path, the narrow path of "Calvary Road" that we must follow and stay on. The two overcomer churches that received only praise clearly had the right focus. Smyrna was about to experience spiritual refinement in the fiery furnace of tribulation for "10 days." Philadelphia, the very place that Jesus described as having only "little power" (3:8), had faithfully kept His "word of … perseverance" (3:10), and had run the marathon of discipleship in God's strength. Both churches had developed a correct understanding of discipleship as enduring spiritual growth through continual pruning and refinement.

Table 19. Discipleship forms of the two overcomer churches of Revelation

Smyrna	Discipleship as a fiery furnace of spiritual growth and refinement
Philadelphia	Discipleship as a marathon of overcoming through God's strength

When we look at all seven churches in regard to their place on the overcomer path, we can make the following observations:

- **Sardis and Laodicea** never even moved onto the overcomer path. Instead, they were continually being overcome by the enemy and thereby kept in a state of spiritual fruitlessness.
- **Ephesus, Pergamum, and Thyatira** had gotten on the overcomer path and had made some significant progress but then developed several dangerous issues. One of them (Thyatira) became so fatally compromised in the hands of its false prophetess that the church was almost entirely lost to the Kingdom.
- **Smyrna** had already been on the path for awhile and now received the opportunity to prove itself and pass the final overcomer test.
- **Philadelphia** had already passed this test and now primarily needed to hold on to what it already had so that it would not

lose its overcomer status (and related reward). Similarly, Jesus tells a faithful minority in Thyatira who had not followed Jezebel that He will "place no other burden on you." Like the Philadelphians, they had passed the test, and consequently God promises to send them no further tribulation. Just as at Philadelphia, Christ exhorts them to "hold fast [to what you have] until I come" (Revelation 2:25).

Several lessons can be learned from the seven churches' starkly differing performance on the overcomer trail. Firstly, being an overcomer requires one to be part of an established local church. The Bible makes no provisions for individualists who attempt to run the race alone. The letters to the seven churches make it very clear that we are strongly influenced by the church community that we are in. If we are not firmly planted in a local church, we cannot flourish and grow spiritually. This is a strong and clear message to the individualistic Western church, where many people refuse to commit to a single home church. Now, the seven examples also sadly show that the church itself can persecute the faithful few within it, but Jesus did not tell any of them to get out and become lone rangers, or to branch off and form a splinter movement. Instead, God promised these overcomer minorities protection and strength in the midst of their trials.

Secondly, we can play Christianity like Sardis and Laodicea without ever moving on the path of overcoming. If our understanding of following Jesus centers on our own emotional, material, or pseudo-spiritual well-being, and we are expecting a life of comfort and ease, then we are not even headed toward Calvary Road. Instead, our old self is alive and well, pampered and entertained by worldly hobbies, polished church environments, professionally-performed worship, and entertainment-focused sermons. This may be church membership, but it is not discipleship, and it bears little resemblance to the life and ministry of the early church. Of course, worship should aspire to a high level of musical performance and sermons can (and even should) be funny and engaging, but there must be much more to a functioning body of Christ than that. God's Word is a double-edged sword, designed to cut apart and divide the fleshly from the spiritual. Church is not a place to pamper the old self, but to bring out and feed the new self while the old nature is being nailed to the cross. As Ajith Fernando put it, rather than entertain, "sermons should disturb, convict, and motivate to radical and costly obedience."[8]

Thirdly, when we are on the overcomer path—exerting our faith based on God's promises, engrafting His Word into our hearts, allowing Him to crucify our old nature, and coming to Him daily for spiritual food—we must be very careful to stay on it. This is again not a work of our own, but requires close dependence on God. God cannot tempt anyone, but "each one is tempted when he is carried away and enticed by his own lust" (James 1:14). However, He permits temptations to enter our path in order to test and refine us. The Psalmist wrote, "For you, O God, tested us; you refined us like silver" (Psalm 66:10).

But God won't let us be overwhelmed or crushed. He "will not allow you to be tempted beyond what you are able, but with the temptation will provide the way of escape also, so that you will be able to endure it" (1 Corinthians 10:13). God's testing is designed to evaluate whether we will choose to follow the old nature and yield to temptation or whether we will opt for the new self and endure in God's strength. Whenever we pass such a test, we are rewarded with spiritual growth and greater spiritual authority. Each wrong choice, however, leads us down the slippery slope of spiritual compromise towards eventual defeat (not loss of salvation but spiritual ineffectiveness and loss of eternal rewards). God's endurance tests for us are designed to increase dependence on Him and to promote the focus, priorities, and attitudes of the new nature.

> **We can overcome, because of the following:**
> 1. We are "under grace"—God's power in us over sin and death.
> 2. We are in the "law of Christ" and therefore "in Christ," God's will for our lives that keeps us on the narrow path through His universal word (*logos*) and specific, personal guidance (*rhema*).
> 3. We have the "law of the Spirit of life," a new spiritual principle that operates within us, defeating the "law of sin and death" and enabling freedom and fruitfulness.

Conclusions: Watch and Pray

When Jesus spent the last night before His death on the cross in the Garden of Gethsemane with His disciples, he told them, "Keep watching and praying that you may not enter into temptation; the spirit [our new nature] is willing, but the flesh [our old nature] is weak" (Matthew 26:41). Contrary to what we may think, Jesus' advice was not so much about physical tiredness as it was about the need to follow Him in the power of our new spirit nature. Moreover, it was not limited to that particular night. Although we have a perfectly-created new spirit nature inside of us—willing to follow Him and to do His will—the fallen flesh nature can continually hold us back.

If we want to remain in Jesus and on the overcomer path, we need to "keep watching and praying." Especially in these last days before Jesus' return, we must beware of the subtle but powerful ways in which the enemy tries to deceive and defeat us. The example of the seven churches shows that even those who are well along the overcomer path can be deceived into spiritual compromise; their discipleship can degenerate into a passionless, legalistic performance of religious duty. But God Himself will keep us on the narrow road if we remain in Him. The Philadelphian overcomer church obtained its preservation promises because of its continual and patient endurance: "Because you have kept the word of My perseverance [or: patient endurance], I also will keep you from the hour of testing" (Revelation 3:10).

As we keep watching and praying, patiently submitting to God's discipleship course for our lives, He Himself will keep us on the narrow path of victorious, overcoming discipleship. This is the path of the wise virgins, who, through total dependence on God, will be prepared and ready when their Lord comes for His first fruits. Let us have the same attitude as Paul, who wrote:

> Indeed, I count everything as loss because of the surpassing worth of knowing Christ Jesus my Lord. For his sake I have suffered the loss of all things and count them as rubbish, in order that I may gain Christ and be found in him ... that I may know him and the power of his resurrection, and may share his sufferings, becoming like him in his death....
>
> ... Not that I have already obtained this or am already perfect, but I press on to make it my own, because Christ Jesus has made me his own. Brothers, I do not consider that I have made it my own. But one thing I do: forgetting what lies behind and straining forward to what lies ahead, I press on toward the goal for the prize of the upward call of God in Christ Jesus.
>
> (Philippians 3:8–10, 12–14 ESV)

Chapter 9 Notes

1. *Strong's Concordance,* G3528.
2. Much more can be said about the shortcomings of the church-ages model. Since the letters to the churches were written to actually existing churches, the first church age cannot just be understood through the letter to the Ephesians. After all, several of the other churches that John wrote to received commendations for their passionate commitment to Christ! Moreover, it is hardly a compliment to the reformers (Luther, Calvin, etc.) to describe the reformation age through the church of Sardis, which received no praise at all and was given an overall very negative appraisal. Sardis was said to be spiritually dead, to have put on an empty show that gave no glory to God. In contrast, the reformation period witnessed the growth of many spiritually sincere church movements, which culminated in the birth of evangelical Christianity throughout the western world. Additionally, God gave the preservation promise to the Philadelphian and not to the Laodicean church, which would imply that the time window for the first fruits rapture already passed by with the end of the (supposed) Philadelphian church age! Overall, we can see that throughout history, all the features and characteristics of the seven churches of Revelation have existed in God's church.
3. *Strong's Concordance,* G1772.
4. Ibid., G3056.
5. Ibid., G4487.
6. Dieter Schneider, "Liebe," in Fritz Grünzweig, *Biblisches Wörterbuch* (Wuppertal: R.Brockhaus, 1992).
7. Compare the statement of the Roman centurion in Matthew 8:9, who understood himself as a man under the authority of his superiors. In the same way, we are to be under the authority of Christ, which in turn gives us authority and power over the works and devices of the enemy. If we move outside of Christ's authority, we will experience defeat instead of victory in our Christian walk.
8. Ajith Fernando, *Jesus Driven Ministry* (Wheaton, IL: Crossway, 2002), 23.

Chapter 10

The Origin and Rise of the Antichrist

The beast that you saw was, and is not, and is about to come up
out of the abyss and go to destruction. And those who dwell on the
earth, whose name has not been written in the book of life from the
foundation of the world, will wonder when they see the beast, that
he was and is not and will come.

Revelation 17:8

The Stage Is Set: The Global Economy and the Rise of the Antichrist

In the first century AD, the apostle John wrote to his fellow believers:

> Children, it is the last hour; and just as you heard that antichrist
> is coming, even now many antichrists have appeared; from
> this we know that it is the last hour.
>
> (1 John 2:18)

With these words, John makes an important point: even though the one antichrist that will appear at the very end has not yet come, "many antichrists" are already active in our world. This means that the spirit of the antichrist, the spirit of deception that is preparing the way for the final antichrist, has already infiltrated the way our society works. As Paul wrote: "For the secret power of lawlessness is already at work…" (2 Thessalonians 2:7 NLT). This secret power is continually preparing the way for the ultimate antichrist, whose rise to power will come at a time when society's lawlessness has reached an unprecedented peak.

It is our belief that we are now very close to this time. Human society has never been so ready to be dominated by the power of the enemy than now. Never in human history have ordinary people been more ready and willing to show profound irreverence toward their Maker, to openly promote all types of immoralities, and to view themselves as the ultimate authorities over their own lives. This development has not come by coincidence. We previously saw how the rise of the final antichrist has been prepared by successive intellectual movements from enlightenment to modernism to postmodernism. These movements have:

a) instilled an anti-authoritarian, rebellious worldview into humanity, creating an environment where lawlessness is not only acceptable but even encouraged

b) made humanity self-confident and independent from God in response to scientific progress and industrialization

c) fattened it with the temptations of materialism in an age of utilitarian consumerism

d) given the deceptive worldview of postmodernism a sophisticated intellectual basis and a false humility through relativism and tolerance thinking

e) prepared for the global rule of the Antichrist through an efficient system of global communication, transportation, and technological advancement

At present, therefore, the stage is fully set for the Antichrist to arise.

Now, there is just one thing missing. Revelation 13 clearly teaches that the earth will willingly worship and submit to the Antichrist. But how is it that the world will actually surrender all power and control to one person or organization? Why would the nations and their citizens empower such a person as the Antichrist? After all, don't we live in a world that worships individual freedom and despises any form of tyranny?

To answer these questions it is important to understand that the New World Order that emerged after the end of World War II is more driven by economic and financial power than by military might. In fact, money increasingly determines military power, because modern warfare depends far more on expensive weapons technology than on large numbers of soldiers. Much of the United States's huge budget deficit is not just due to Obama's financial rescue efforts but is also a consequence of the costly wars in Iraq and Afghanistan. The nation's financial weaknesses are directly threatening its current and future military capabilities.

In our time, world domination is about gaining control over the world's economic and financial affairs. Increasingly, the one in charge is not he who holds the guns in his hands but he who finances their technological development, acquisition, and deployment. Consequently, it is very likely that the rise of the Antichrist will be facilitated by a major global financial meltdown that will significantly alter the global balance of power and create the need for a "savior" to step on the scene. This will be the Antichrist's moment: he will promise to protect the world's middle classes' affluent lifestyles, and in exchange for this, the world will relinquish significant control over their affairs to him.

This meltdown will be much worse than the financial crash that started in September 2008, but it will be based on the same root causes. One possible scenario that appears increasingly likely is the fall of heavily indebted Eurozone[1] nations such as Greece, Spain, Italy, Portugal, Ireland, and perhaps even France. Whereas Greece's debts amount to 350 billion Euro, a sum that is still covered by the EU's rescue fund, Italy's 2 trillion Euro and Spain's 900 billion Euro debts are far too large for the other Eurozone nations to shoulder.[2] Should these nations suffer a financial breakdown, they would almost certainly take down the entire Eurozone and, together with France's, Portugal's and Ireland's financial frailties, could achieve a devastating multiplying effect. This would have severe ramifications for the world economy, whose recovery from the 2008-2009 financial crisis is still very fragile. In November 2011, the

EU drastically cut its growth forecast for 2012 from 1.8 down to just 0.5 percent. However, by September 2012 the anticipated growth rate for the Eurozone nations for that year was as low as -0.8 percent.[3] This leaves its economies little leeway to weather another financial crisis. Likewise, expected United States growth for 2012 was revised down to 1.9 percent, which is inadequate for a sustained turnaround of the weak job market.[4]

In 2008, governments around the world went on a huge spending spree in order to cushion the impact of the economic meltdown and boost domestic growth. As a consequence, debts ballooned everywhere and have now reached very dangerous levels. United States debt alone increased by 66 percent between 2007 and 2011, exceeding $16 trillion in September 2012 and surpassing a critical mark when it overtook the value of the nation's entire economic output or Gross Domestic Product (GDP). When a second global financial crisis hits, neither the United States nor the EU will have the financial means to deal with it. Though China has huge financial reserves, it cannot save the world either. The Chinese economy depends largely on exports—three times more so than the United States.[5] If a crisis hits and global demand for goods plummets, China will also be affected. The country's worse-than-expected January 2012 export and import figures—which mark the first decline in two years—are already indicating a negative trend.[6] Ting Lu, an economist of Bank of America Merrill Lynch, rightly argues that "the major drag and biggest risk to China's growth in 2012 is weaker external demand caused by the ongoing Eurozone debt crisis."[7]

Altogether, the combined weaknesses and interdependencies of the United States, the EU, and the major Asian economies such as China and Japan could create a fatal global economic downward spiral, sparking a second economic crisis that would be far more severe than that of 2008–2009. Whether such a global meltdown will occur sooner or later is of course difficult to predict, the structural conditions for it to occur are certainly in place.

Already, the economic turmoil in the Eurozone is promoting an increasing centralization of power in the hands of EU bureaucrats. Since November 2011, the EU government has significantly increased authority over the approval of each member state's national budget, effectively reserving for itself the right to control national spending patterns. Greece's budget is additionally supervised by the International Monetary Fund (IMF). As the EU's ability to rescue itself weakens, the IMF's influence over the EU's national budgets will also be bolstered. When the financial crisis spins out of control, it is quite likely that the G-20 nations, the "ten horns" of the Axis beast, will establish a global super-institution or use existing ones such as the IMF in order to regulate each nation's financial behavior. Such a centralization of economic, financial, and ultimately political power is precisely what the Antichrist needs to achieve global dominion. In exactly this vein, in June 2012 Germany's finance minister Wolfgang Schäuble announced that as a consequence of the financial turmoil, Germany and other European nations would soon need to hold country-wide constitutional referendums that would transfer considerable national sovereignty to the centralized European parliament.[8] This proposition is a clear indication of how economic chaos will lead to the kind of political centralization that the Antichrist is waiting for.

The Antichrist's Miraculous Appearance as a King Raised From the Dead

Apart from becoming the earth's financial savior, the second major factor behind the world's worship of the Antichrist is his supernatural healing. In Revelation 13:3 it says, "I saw one of his heads as if it had been slain, and his fatal wound was healed.[9] And the whole earth was amazed and followed after the beast." What does that mean? The answer is given in chapter 17, where John receives an explanation of the seven heads of the beast:

> And the angel said to me, "Why do you wonder? I will tell you the mystery of the woman and of the beast that carries her, which has the seven heads and the ten horns. "The beast that you saw *was*, and *is not*, and *is about* to come up out of the abyss and go to destruction. And those who dwell on the earth, whose name has not been written in the book of life from the foundation of the world, will wonder when they see the beast, that he *was* and *is not* and *will come*.
>
> Here is the mind which has wisdom. The seven heads are seven mountains on which the woman sits, and they are seven kings; five *have* fallen, one *is*, the other has *not yet* come; and when he comes, he must remain a little while. The beast which was and is not, *is himself also an eighth and is one of the seven*, and he goes to destruction.
>
> (Revelation 17:7–11, emphases added)

Here, John is told that the Antichrist will in fact be a revived ruler of a former empire. The beast "was" (meaning it used to exist) but "is not" (it is not alive at the present). However, it "is about to come up out of the abyss" (Gr. *abyssos*, the bottomless pit of the underworld that functions as a prison for demons[10]), which implies that it will be raised from the dead. This is nothing less than a counterfeit of Jesus' resurrection. When it says in Revelation 13 that "one of its heads had been slain" (v. 3) using a "sword" (v. 14), but that this fatal wound was healed, it does not mean that the Antichrist will recover from a deadly wound to his physical head. The angel clearly tells John that the seven heads don't represent literal heads but kings. One of the "heads" (kings) had been "slain" but was healed. This means the same as the statement that the beast "was … and is about to come," pointing to the fact that this beast is a former king who will be brought back to life. This is confirmed by the fact that he is "one of the seven" yet also "an eighth"—a revived member of the seven kings sequence (v. 11). When he appears, the whole world will therefore truly be "amazed" and follow him, because no such thing has ever happened before!

There have been many unsuccessful attempts to decode this mysterious seven-king sequence. One of its most difficult aspects is that the first five kings had already fallen at John's time, and the sixth is said to be king during the time John received God's revelation. Only two more kings were to come, the seventh, who would only "remain a little while," and then the Antichrist as the eighth. Here, it is important to notice that "king" does not just refer to a human ruler, but also to the kingdom or empire that this ruler represents (see Daniel 7). This rules out vain attempts to try to identify the seven kings with a sequence of Roman emperors (all of which have failed). We are therefore faced with the challenge of identifying a sequence of seven world empires prior to the rise of the Antichrist, with the Antichrist being a revived king from one of these historic empires. Clearly, this sequence is different from the empire visions of Daniel, who received two revelations that each spoke of four empires. There, the first four empires from the statue vision of Daniel 2 began with Nebuchadnezzar's Babylonian empire, while the second set of empires from Daniel 7 related only to ones that would arise in Daniel's future (after the fall of Babylon).

As Robert van Kampen suggested, the long historical gap between the sixth and the eighth "king" (empire) in John's vision can be explained in the same way as the gap in Daniel's vision of the 70 weeks in chapter 9: because the Jews refused their Messiah, God permitted an intervening period, the times of the Gentiles.[11] This period is now drawing to a close with the return of the Jews to their land in 1948 and to their capital, Jerusalem, in 1967. Moreover, just as this intervening period was gradually phased in— spiritually with the death of Christ in 32 AD and nationally with the destruction of Jerusalem and the dispersion of the Jews in 70 AD—it is now being gradually phased out: nationally with the events of 1948 and 1967 and spiritually with the final (late harvest) rapture of all remaining saints and the national salvation of the Jews. This sequence—first the national restoration, followed by the spiritual restoration—is well-documented in several prophetic passages such as Ezekiel 11:17–19, 36:24–27, and 37:1–14. Van Kampen also argues that the seven-empire sequence in Revelation 17 extends further back than Daniel's time, including two older empires that had already vanished by Daniel's time.[12]

The Mysterious Seven Empire Sequence

When we put Daniel's and John's visions next to each other, the mysterious empire sequence comes into focus.

Table 20. Empire sequences from Daniel and Revelation

King no.	Empire visions from Daniel 2 & 7	Empire sequence from Revelation 17	These empires' relationship to Israel and the church
1st	(before Daniel's time)	Egypt (3150–343 BC)	Joseph was promoted by a pharaoh, possibly a ruler from the Hyksos peoples. A subsequent pharaoh from a new line of kings (possibly Tuthmosis III, 15th century BC) uses the Israelites as slaves in his massive building projects. He then seeks to destroy them by killing all male infants until the Exodus (either 1440s BC or 1260s BC).[13]
2nd	(before Daniel's time)	Assyria (including older Akkadian and Sumerian empires, ca. 2330–608 BC)[14]	Under Shalmaneser V and Sargon II, Israel's northern kingdom is captured and Judah becomes an Assyrian vassal (8th century BC). In 701 BC Sennacherib threatens to destroy Jerusalem, but following God's promise to King Hezekiah and the prophet Isaiah, his armies are destroyed by God's messenger.
3rd	Golden head = Babylon	Babylon[15] (612–539 BC)	From 605 BC, Nebuchadnezzar II subdues Judah and demands tribute. When Judah's King Jehoiakim rebels against him, he conquers Jerusalem in 597. In 586, he attacks again, destroying the first temple, and exiling most of the Jewish population. He later makes Daniel the second-highest ruler in his empire.
4th	Silver chest = Medo-Persia	Medo-Persia (539–339 BC)	Cyrus the Great permits the Jews to return to their land in 538 BC, but most remain. Under King Ahasuerus (Xerxes I, 486–465 BC), Haman almost succeeds in destroying the exiled Jews, but Esther's brave intervention saves them (474–473 BC). In 445 BC, Artaxerxes Longimanus permits Nehemiah to rebuild Jerusalem's wall.

5th	Bronze belly = Greece	Greece and its subsequent four empires (336–30 BC)	Antiochus IV Epiphanes, ruler of the Seleucid empire, becomes the prototype of the Antichrist when he desecrates the temple with abominations, outlaws the Jewish religion, and slaughters those who continue to worship God (175–164 BC).
6th	Iron legs = Rome	Rome (ca. 200 BC[16]–476 AD [Western Roman Empire]/1453 AD [Eastern Roman Empire])	In 70 AD, Titus destroys Jerusalem and the temple, and brutally murders most survivors (an estimated 1.1 million Jews die). While earlier emperors tolerate Judaism and Christianity, Nero and Domitian in particular viciously persecute them. More persecutions occur in the 2nd and 3rd centuries, until the emperor Constantine grants special freedoms for Christians and returns seized church property in 313.
FIRST CONVERGENCE FROM ANTIQUITY TO MODERNITY *The feet and the "10" toes symbolize the full number of nations that arises out of the fallen Roman empire. These mark the beginning of the modern era, and set the stage for the rise of the subsequent four beast-empires of Daniel 7 and the rise of the Antichrist.*			
---	Lion with wings = British Empire & USA	Times of the Gentiles (British Empire: 1593-1950s/ USA as empire or superpower: 1898–present)	
---	Bear = Russian empire, especially Stalin's Russia	Times of the Gentiles (1721–1991)	These three empires and the animals (beasts) that symbolize them describe the characteristics of the Antichrist and his reign.
---	Leopard = Enlightenment/ French Revolution / Napoleon's French Empire → Postmodern era	Times of the Gentiles (mid-17th to mid-20th century)	
7th	Terrible fourth beast = Axis beast (Hitler's Germany, Italy, Japan)	Axis powers (lasted only a "little while" from 1936 to 1945, their fall facilitated the end of the times of the Gentiles)	Under Hitler, an estimated 5-6 million Jews are exterminated between 1938 and 1945. Hitler also persecutes faithful Christians, a well-known martyr being Dietrich Bonhoeffer. Hitler's genocide of the Jews results in a worldwide resettling of Jews to Palestine, culminating in the founding of Israel in 1948.

239

SECOND CONVERGENCE FROM MODERNITY TO POSTMODERNITY			
*"10" horns = the full number of nations that arise out of the fall of the fourth beast-empire. Taking the figure "10" symbolically, these kingdoms or nations represent the New World Order after World War II, culminating in global super-unions such as the G-20. This is an intermediate phase between the seventh and the eighth empire, which prepares the stage for the rise of the Antichrist (the eighth king). **This is the phase that we are currently living in.***			
8th	Small horn = Antichrist	Antichrist's world dominion (together with "ten" kings under him)	The Antichrist will implement the worst-ever persecution of God's people, set up an abomination in the temple in Jerusalem, have those killed who do not worship his image, and prevent those who do not accept his mark from being able to buy or sell.

What is the identity of the seventh empire, which is said to only last for a "little while"? Of all of the empires, the Axis beast fits the bill perfectly. Firstly, the Axis alliance only lasted from 1936–1945, with Hitler's reign also spanning only 12 years from 1933–1945, historically-speaking an extraordinarily short time frame (only Napoleon's French Empire comes close to it). Secondly, this fourth beast-empire rose to power at the very end of the times of the Gentiles, and its fall directly resulted in the spiritual ending of these times. Thirdly, this empire, like no other before, centered around the systematic persecution of the Jews. It reflected Satan's ultimate attempt to destroy them before God could fulfill his promise of gathering them from all nations and bringing them back into their own land. Therefore, the sixth (Roman) and the seventh (Axis) empires bracket the intermediate times of the Gentiles: they began with the Romans and ended with the fall of the Axis beast.

Overall, it becomes clear that this seven-empire sequence refers to history's major world powers that Satan used to persecute or destroy the Jews. This also explains why the dragon in Revelation 12, who symbolizes Satan, is described as having seven royal diadems (Gr. *diadema*, a symbol of royal authority) on his seven heads, whereas the beast (Antichrist) is said to have a diadem on each of his ten horns (Revelation 12:3; 13:1). The meaning behind this difference is that the dragon has had authority over all seven historic beast empires, whereas the beast will control the final (8th) world empire, which will give him authority over "ten" kings that will reign together with him and be in complete submission to his will (Revelation 17:12–13).

All of these seven historic empires of Satan facilitated his attempts to completely annihilate God's people, even if some of them had rulers who were at times benevolent towards them:

1. **Egypt**: the Pharaoh at the time of Moses orders the death of all Jewish male infants.

2. **Assyria**: successive Assyrian kings invade and ravage the Northern Kingdom and Samaria. King Sennacherib threatens to destroy Jerusalem at Hezekiah's time, arrogantly asserting that Hezekiah's trust in God is foolish.

3. **Babylon**: Nebuchadnezzar II conquers Israel and Judah and destroys Jerusalem and its first temple, virtually emptying the city by leading much of its population into exile. Daniel's account shows that the Jewish captives were given Babylonian names (often names with pagan meanings) in order to assimilate them (Daniel 1). Nebuchadnezzar demanded to be worshiped like a God, and that those who did not submit were put to death (Daniel 3).

4. **Medo-Persia**: under King Ahasuerus, Haman the Agagite, a high-ranking advisor of the king, almost succeeds in wiping out the Jewish populations in exile, which represent the vast majority of all Jews at that time (only a few had returned to Israel by then). Some view this as the first historic case of anti-Semitism—the persecution of a Jewish minority in another nation.

5. **Greece and the four subsequent Hellenistic kingdoms:** The Seleucid ruler Antiochus IV Epiphanes desecrates the temple and slaughters thousands of Jews in an attempt to eradicate Jewish culture and religion, in order to assimilate the Jews into Greek culture.

6. **Rome**: the general and later emperor Titus destroys Jerusalem and the temple, and kills or enslaves its survivors. According to the historian Josephus, about 1.1 million Jews die in the process. Many subsequent Roman emperors viciously persecute both Jews and Christians.

7. **Axis powers**: under Hitler, unprecedented millions of Jews are systematically annihilated, the largest genocide of Jews ever and one of the worst genocides in human history.

The Ancient Origin of the Antichrist

Which revived ruler the Antichrist will be is difficult to assess, because there are so many possibilities. Van Kampen believes that it will be Hitler, who committed suicide with a military weapon (pistol) that could in John's time be represented by a sword. But apart from the fact that a raised Hitler would hardly be popular in the current day and age, van Kampen's conjecture is impossible. In Revelation 17:8, it specifically says that the beast "*was*, and *is not*, and is about to come up." The "*is not*" means that the beast was not alive at John's time and won't be alive until it arises from the abyss. Likewise, the "*was*" directly implies that it did live (and can only have lived) at a time *before* John, meaning prior to Roman rule. This excludes any post-Roman modern empire, meaning that the Antichrist must be a raised ruler from a time between the Egyptian and the Greek empires.

Even though many kings have lived during this long time span, there is only one of them who—according to God's Word—died through a sword wound. Moreover, God even prophesied that this king would meet death in this way and decreed it as a judgment for this king's arrogant defiance of His name. In fact, he is the only major foreign ruler in the entire Bible who is directly described as having "blasphemed" God Himself.[17] This is all the more remarkable because "speaking arrogant words and blasphemies" (Revelation 13:5) is one of the most notable characteristics of the Antichrist. Additionally, historic records testify to the extraordinary brutality of this king's armies towards their captives, flaying them (removing their skin) while they were still alive. Finally, God supernaturally wiped out this king's army before it could destroy His holy city, Jerusalem, and ravage His people. This, again, is precisely what God will do at Armageddon, when Jesus is prophesied to annihilate the forces of the Antichrist and bring deliverance to His besieged Jerusalem (Zechariah 14, Revelation 19).

Some of you will by now have guessed that the ruler in question is the Assyrian King Sennacherib, who in 701 BC besieged Jerusalem under King Hezekiah. Before assaulting the city, Sennacherib sent his representative to Hezekiah to intimidate him, saying, "Do not let your God in whom you trust deceive you.... Did the gods of those nations which my fathers have destroyed deliver them...?" (Isaiah 37:10, 12). God's response through Isaiah to Sennacherib's arrogant railing is uncompromisingly clear:

> I will make him fall by the sword in his own land....
>
> ...Whom have you reproached [*charaph*] and blasphemed [*gadaph*]? And against whom have you raised your voice and haughtily lifted up your eyes? Against the Holy One of Israel! Through your servants you have reproached [*charaph*] the Lord....
>
> ... But I know your sitting down and your going out and your coming in and your raging against Me. Because of your raging against Me and because your arrogance has come up to My ears, therefore I will put My hook in your nose and My bridle in your lips, and I will turn you back by the way which you came. (Isaiah 37:7, 23–24a, 28–29)[18]

This is the only instance in the entire Bible that the Hebrew words for blasphemy, *charaph*[19] and *gadaph*,[20] are applied to a foreign king, who is said to have blasphemed not just God's people, but God Himself![21] As judgment for this unprecedented act of defiance, God engaged in an unparalleled act of retribution: the "angel of the LORD went out and struck 185,000 in the camp of the Assyrians" (v. 36). Never before in Scripture did God send an angel to wreak such terrible wrath, nor will it ever again occur until the outpouring of God's wrath and the end of the age.[22] Traumatized, Sennacherib returned to Nineveh, his capital, but even after this humiliation he never admitted his defeat in his records, which only boast of his successes and victories. But he could not escape God's judgment. When worshiping his god Nisroch, two of his own sons killed him with the sword.

In contrast to his father Sargon (whom he never even mentioned in his writings), Sennacherib's era was not primarily characterized by military advances. His reign also had a decidedly cultural focus, as reflected in his architectural pursuits. Even though His father had just built a brand new capital city, Sennacherib surprisingly decided to move the capital back to Nineveh and undertook extensive reconstruction work in the city. Nineveh was later judged by God because of its rampant evil, lies, bloodshed, and sorcery (Nahum 2–3). Sennacherib turned the city into what was probably the largest metropolis of ancient times. He built a vast "palace without rival" for himself, the area of which was nearly twice that of Europe's largest palace of Versailles[23] and established a sophisticated irrigation system for both palace and city (he is credited with designing the world's oldest aqueduct). As a consequence, secular appraisals of his rule are predominantly positive—just as they will be of the Antichrist's future reign.

But beneath this seemingly benevolent and sophisticated rule was a heart of evil that was capable of unbelievable brutality. Amongst all ancient peoples, the Assyrians are especially renowned for their savage brutality, and Sennacherib is said as having "surpassed his predecessors in the grisly detail of his descriptions."[24] One example reads:

I [Sennacherib] cut their throats like lambs. I cut off their precious lives (as one cuts) a string. Like the many waters of a storm, I made (the contents of) their gullets and entrails run down upon the wide earth. My prancing steeds harnessed for my riding, plunged into the streams of their blood as (into) a river. The wheels of my war chariot, which brings low the wicked and the evil, were bespattered with blood and filth. With the bodies of their warriors I filled the plain, like grass. (Their) testicles I cut off, and tore out their privates like the seeds of cucumbers.[25]

ASSYRIANS FLAYING THEIR PRISONERS ALIVE.

Figure 14. Assyrian depiction of their soldiers flaying their prisoners alive. Sennacherib's stone tablets that portray his conquest also show Hebrew men of Lachish having been stripped naked and impaled on wooden stakes. Another practice of the Assyrian soldiers was to erect piles of the severed heads of their enemies next to their feet. Source: Wikimedia Commons.

As part of his bloody campaign against the rebellious province of Babylon, Sennacherib recorded:

The people of the city of Hirimme ... I cut down with the sword. Not one escaped. Their corpses I hung on stakes, surrounding the city with it.[26]

He later did the same at Lachish with his Hebrew captives. There, archaeologists discovered a mass grave with the bones and decapitated human skulls of over 1,500 Hebrews, apparently all civilians rather than soldiers.[27] Not surprisingly, the Expositor's Bible Commentary notes that:

> In Isaiah's day, Assyria was feared by every little nation....Their brutality made them more of an object of general hatred than any other nation of antiquity. The Egyptians, Babylonians, and Persians were all capable of inhuman acts, *but the Assyrian record for callous cruelty is difficult to parallel.*[28] (emphasis added)

But despite all this carnage, Sennacherib sought to portray himself as moral and loving, referring to himself as one "who protects the truth, who loves the right, who comes to the help of and lends assistance to the weak."[29] One of his titles described him as the "expert shepherd" and "shepherd of mankind."[30] This reminds us of Satan's appearance as an "angel of light" in the last days. Sennacherib's claim to being a benevolent, wise, and peaceful ruler who secures the prosperity of all mankind mirrors the rhetoric of the Antichrist.

Overall, Sennacherib's personality and achievements are surprisingly similar to all key characteristics of the future Antichrist, as shown in Table 21.

Table 21. Sennacherib's characteristics compared with the characteristics of the Antichrist

Criterion	Sennacherib	Antichrist
Arrogance & blasphemy	He spoke arrogantly and boastfully and blasphemed God.	"And he opened his mouth in blasphemies against God, to blaspheme His name and His tabernacle, that is, those who dwell in heaven." Revelation 13:6
Brutality	He acted with incredible brutality and mercilessness towards his victims.	The Antichrist will have "feet like those of a bear," reflecting his relentless cruelty.
Without respect	He showed no regard to his father, never mentioning him, and abandoning his father's new capital city.	Daniel 11:37 prophecies that the Antichrist will go even further in his disrespect of his predecessors: "He will show no regard for the gods of his fathers...."
Enlightened leader	He is credited with significant architectural and other cultural and scientific achievements, which have drawn much praise from historians. In his own historic records, he portrayed himself as an enlightened and benevolent ruler.	The Antichrist will be cunning like a leopard; to the worshiping world, he will not appear as a brutal tyrant but as an enlightened and wise leader.
World domination	He ruled almost the entire ancient world, except for Egypt, which his son Esarhaddon later also subdued.	The Antichrist will rule over the entire world.
Threat to God's people	He threatened to destroy Jerusalem, God's city.	The Antichrist will also seek to destroy Jerusalem.
Supernatural defeat	His army was supernaturally destroyed by God.	The Antichrist's armies will be annihilated at Armageddon.
Sword wound	He received a fatal wound by a sword at the hands of his own sons.	The Antichrist has a fatal sword wound, which will be healed.
Death ordained by God	Because of his blasphemy and arrogance, God specifically ordained and predicted his death.	Because of his blasphemy and arrogance, God has specifically ordained and predicted his death: the Antichrist, also called "son of destruction" in 2 Thessalonians 2:3, will be thrown into the lake of fire after his defeat at Armageddon.

Connecting Nimrod, Sennacherib, and the Antichrist

The book of Micah contains a chapter which helpfully summarizes the entire history of Satan's attack on God's people and contrasts it with the first and final comings of Jesus. Previously, we had already looked at the first few verses of Micah 5, which predict the first coming of Christ (born in Bethlehem) and the "giving up" of the Jews during the times of the Gentiles until the "woman" (the church) gives birth to a "child" (the first fruits of the church, see Revelation 12). Then "He" (Jesus) will come again and be "great to the ends of the earth" at the millennial kingdom (v. 4). The passage continues as follows:

> This One [Christ] will be our peace. When the Assyrian invades our land [successive Assyrian kings, especially Sennacherib], when he tramples on our citadels, then we will raise against him seven shepherds and eight leaders of men. They will shepherd the land of Assyria with the sword, the land of Nimrod at its entrances; and He [Christ] will deliver us from the Assyrian when he attacks our land and when he tramples our territory.
>
> (Micah 5:5–6)

After the final coming of Christ to the battle of Armageddon depicted in Revelation 19, the Antichrist will send to "the kings of the earth and of the whole world, to gather them to the battle of that great day of God ... to the place called in Hebrew, Armageddon" (Revelation 16:14, 16 NKJV). In Micah's prophetic passage, this final battle is compared to the Assyrian invasions, the most notable of which was of course Sennacherib's. In that way, Sennacherib is again linked to the future Antichrist. But there is another important detail in the text: Sennacherib is also connected backward in history, with the ancient figure of Nimrod, a great-grandson of Noah.

Genesis 10 ambiguously describes Nimrod as a "mighty hunter" (the name Nimrod means "rebel"). He founded a kingdom in the region of Mesopotamia, the fertile land between the two rivers of the Euphrates and the Tigris, where both the Assyrian and the Babylonian kingdoms were later located. His initial realm was in central and southern Mesopotamia, the region of Babylon, where he established the city of Babel or Babylon (the Hebrew word *Babel* is the same word that the Bible uses for Babylon). Babel/Babylon was the site of the Tower of Babel, humanity's first organized attempt to become as great as God, and it is probably no coincidence that the Akkadian word *Babili* after which it was named means "gate of God." According to archaeological estimates, this tower was erected between 3500 and 2400 BC (archaeological evidence shows that Babylon has been a settlement since 3500–4000 BC).[31] It may have been a *ziggurat*—an ancient religious structure used for the worship of Babylonian and Assyrian gods, designed as a platform between the gods in heaven and the inhabitants of the earth.[32]

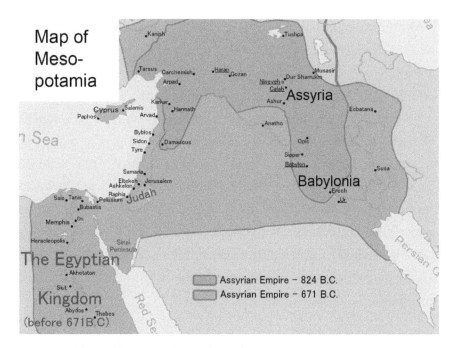

Figure 15. Map of Mesopotamia. Asshur in the north later became Assyria. Genesis 10 states that Nimrod founded the cities of Babel (Babylon), Erech (Uruk, north of Ur), Accad, Nineveh, Calah and Resen (location unknown). Later, Abraham went from Ur to Haran, and then into the Promised Land. Source: Wikimedia Commons (map edited by the authors).

But Nimrod also ruled over northern Mesopotamia, which later became Assyria, and Genesis 10 credits him with establishing Nineveh, the city that Sennacherib later established as his capital. This is why the Jews typically viewed Assyria as "the land of Nimrod." From Nimrod's time, the histories of Babylon and Assyria were closely intertwined, and the city of Babylon was also part of Sennacherib's empire.

Micah's prophecy therefore links Nimrod, Sennacherib,[33] and the Antichrist. Like Sennacherib, the Antichrist will directly blaspheme God and launch a brutal invasion of Israel, which will again be repelled through God's supernatural intervention at the battle of Armageddon. Like Nimrod, he will be a "mighty one" who "exalts himself above every so-called god or object of worship" (2 Thessalonians 2:4). He will accept the world's worship through a speaking image, which the world will erect under the influence of the false prophet (Revelation 13:14). Back in Nimrod's time, when humanity made its first concerted attempt to supplant their Creator, God graciously stopped their efforts before the Tower of Babel could be completed. This time, God will permit the Antichrist to succeed for a while, allowing him to complete Nimrod's evil plan. Through the worship of his image, the world will be united in a greater way than ever—just as Nimrod had envisioned it. Yet this time, it will not just center around one city and its tower, but around one global ideology (postmodern relativism), one world empire (the Antichrist's reign), one object of worship (the Antichrist), and one method of worship (the image of the beast). Then, humanity's rebellion against its Maker since the dawn of history will have come full circle.

Anti-Christ: The Replacement-Christ

Perhaps the most satanic act of Sennacherib was not even his open blasphemy and opposition to God. Rather, it was a cunning promise that he made to God's people if they would surrender to him:

[F]or thus says the king of Assyria [to the Jews], "Make your peace with me and come out to me, and eat each of his vine and each of his fig tree and drink each of the waters of his own cistern, until I come and take you away to a land like your own land, a land of grain and new wine, a land of bread and vineyards."

(Isaiah 36:16–17)

This offer was nothing short of an alternative "Promised Land," an attempt to replicate the promise of a "land flowing with milk and honey" which God gave the Israelites. But of course, the land promised by Sennacherib would be in Assyria, a place of spiritual exile, where the Israelites would have had no place to worship the true God. Instead, they would have gradually shifted toward worshiping the Assyrian idols, especially the chief god Ashur, to which Sennacherib attributed his glory and power. Sennacherib was effectively presenting himself as an alternative false savior of God's people who would provide and care for them in his own land.

Many think of the Antichrist as someone who will openly oppose Christianity. While this will probably be true, it only represents a partial picture. The English term "Antichrist" comes from two Greek words: *anti* and *christos*, which can mean either "against Christ" or "instead of Christ." When examining the scriptural record, it seems that the Antichrist will come into power as a "replacement Christ," a world savior who seeks to obviate humanity's need of God. Table 22 shows how the Antichrist will in some ways be the very opposite of Christ. However, in many other respects, his strategy is to imitate Jesus in order to completely replace him.

Table 22. The original Christ compared with the imitation "Christ"

	The Original (Jesus Christ)	The Imitation/Replacement (Anti-Christ)
Differences		
Origin	"came down from heaven" (John 3:13 NKJV)	Will "come up out of the abyss" (Revelation 17:8)
Identity	Son of God (Luke 1:35)	Son of destruction (2 Thessalonians 2:3)
Source of his power	"All things have been handed over to Me by My Father." (Matthew 11:27)	"And the dragon gave him his power and his throne and great authority." (Revelation 13:2)
Relationship to sin	Set us free from sin (Romans 3:24)	Deceives those who perish (2 Thessalonians 2:10)
Manner of speech	"Like a lamb that is led to slaughter, and like a sheep that is silent before its shearers, so He did not open His mouth." (Isaiah 53:7)	"... this horn possessed eyes like the eyes of a man and a mouth uttering great boasts." (Daniel 7:8)
Similarities		
Raised from death	A king resurrected from the dead	A king raised from the dead (Revelation 13:3; 17:8,11)
Legitimizes his status and claims with signs and wonders	"But if I do his work, believe in the evidence of the miraculous works I have done, even if you don't believe me." (John 10:38 NLT)	"He [the false prophet] performs great signs, so that he even makes fire come down out of heaven to the earth in the presence of men." (Revelation 13:13)
Breathes life into things	"Then the LORD God formed man of dust from the ground, and breathed into his nostrils the breath of life; and man became a living being." (Genesis 2:7)	"And it was given to him to give breath to the image of the beast, so that the image of the beast would even speak...." (Revelation 13:15)
Unites both worldly and spiritual power (king and priest)	Is both king and priest, just as Melchizedek (Hebrews 7)	Antichrist and False Prophet together possess both worldly (Revelation 13:2–7) and spiritual powers (Revelation 13:13–15).
Demands everyone's worship in order to honor his own ultimate authority	"... so that at the name of Jesus every knee will bow, of those who are in heaven and on earth and under the earth." (Philippians 2:10)	"And the whole earth was amazed and followed after the beast ... they worshiped the beast ..." (Revelation 13:3–4) "... so that the image of the beast would ... cause as many as do not worship the image of the beast to be killed." (Revelation 13:15)
Member of a trinity	Father – Son – Holy Spirit	Satan – Antichrist (beast) – False Prophet (second beast)

Seals his followers	"Do not grieve the Holy Spirit of God, by whom you were sealed for the day of redemption." (Ephesians 4:30)	"And he causes all, the small and the great, and the rich and the poor, and the free men and the slaves, to be given a mark on their right hand or on their forehead." (Revelation 13:16)
Arrives riding on a white horse, wearing a crown or diadem, and coming to conquer	"And I saw heaven opened, and behold, a white horse, and He who sat on it is called Faithful and True, and in righteousness He judges and wages war. His eyes are a flame of fire, and on His head are many diadems...." (Revelation 19:11–12)	"I looked, and behold, a white horse, and he who sat on it had a bow; and a crown was given to him, and he went out conquering and to conquer." (Revelation 6:2) "Then I saw a beast coming up out of the sea, having ten horns and seven heads, and on his horns were ten diadems...." (Revelation 13:1)

From this long list of similarities, it is clear that the Antichrist will not present himself as a beastly tyrant or a direct enemy of God. Quite to the contrary, he will actively seek to deceive even Christians to follow and worship him. According to Jesus, the deceptive powers of the Antichrist and his miracle-working team will be so effective that they will "mislead, if possible, even the elect [God's people]" (Matthew 24:24). This means that we believers must be extremely watchful and base our assessments on the guidance of God's Spirit rather than our own wisdom. You may think that the Antichrist will be an ugly, mean guy whom we will all instantly recognize for who he is really is. But the picture of him that the Bible gives us shows him as a deceptive angel of light. The dangerous implication of this is that only those who walk closely with the true Jesus will be able to distinguish Him from His false imitation.

Learning From Hezekiah's Encounter With Sennacherib

The Bible's description of Sennacherib occurs primarily in his attempt to subdue Judah's King Hezekiah. Hezekiah was not just any king, but perhaps the most important spiritual reformer of the entire Old Testament. He purified and strengthened the remaining priesthood, restored temple worship, re-instituted the celebration of the Passover, and removed all of Judah's idols, making God's temple the only legitimate place of worship. God gave Hezekiah success in everything he did, because he was wholeheartedly devoted to his Maker:

> He [Hezekiah] trusted in the Lord, the God of Israel; so that after him there was none like him among all the kings of Judah, nor among those who were before him. For he clung to the Lord; he did not depart from following Him, but kept His commandments.
>
> (2 Kings 18:5–6)

After thoroughly purging Judah's idolatrous religious practices, Hezekiah then decides to rebel against the Assyrian overlordship. His predecessor, the unfaithful King Ahaz, had made the grave mistake of inviting the Assyrians to help him against his enemies. As a result, Judah became subject to the Assyrian king. Ahaz went even further and changed the manner of temple worship in accordance with Assyrian practices in order to appease his new masters (2 Kings 16; 2 Chronicles 28).

Scripture does not comment on the wisdom or folly of Hezekiah's rebellion against Assyria, and we can perhaps assume that it was part of his spiritual reform process and a God-sanctioned act to revert Ahaz's idolatrous actions. Israel's (the northern kingdom's) ungodly King Hoshea also secretly plots against Assyrian rule, but the Assyrian King Shalmaneser V captures him and leads hundreds of thousands of Israelites into exile (2 Kings 17). Later, Sennacherib also moves against the northern kingdom and conquers all its fortified cities. So far, Hezekiah has not been affected. Because of his faithfulness, God will be on his side and deliver him from all evil.

But when Sennacherib's vast army moves against Judah and Jerusalem, Hezekiah's faith and spiritual zeal suddenly begins to falter. Doubtlessly, he and his advisers are greatly intimidated by the vicious cruelty of the Assyrians, especially in their capture of Lachish, the second most heavily fortified town in the whole country. Because

Lachish had fallen and its occupants had been killed, tortured and exiled, the same fate might befall Jerusalem. 2 Kings 18:7 tells us that "the Lord was with him [Hezekiah]; wherever he went he prospered." But now, Hezekiah's faith slips. Gripped with fear, he sends envoys to Sennacherib, telling him that he has "done wrong" and entreating him to withdraw his troops in return for paying a heavy fine. Sennacherib demands 300 talents of silver and 30 talents of gold. Hezekiah apparently deliberately goes even beyond what was asked of him in order to appease the enemy:

> Hezekiah gave him all the silver which was found in the house
> of the Lord, and in the treasuries of the king's house. At that
> time Hezekiah cut off the gold from the doors of the temple
> of the Lord, and from the doorposts which Hezekiah king of
> Judah had overlaid, and gave it to the king of Assyria.
>
> (2 Kings 18:15–16)

This act of distrust in God's sovereign protection is one of the greatest mistakes that Hezekiah ever commits. Seeing that the Jews eagerly meet his demands, Sennacherib is emboldened and immediately sends his envoy to Jerusalem to demand the city's unconditional surrender. Hezekiah's fears had led him to act on his own accord. By willingly compromising with the enemy rather than trusting in God's providence, he only promotes the enemy's advance against him.

What then follows is perhaps Scripture's most brilliant and ingenious example of psychological warfare, rivaled only by the craftiness of the snake in the Garden of Eden. Sennacherib's representative first deliberately highlights Hezekiah's weaknesses. He sarcastically offers him 2,000 horses "if you are able on your part to set riders on them." In those days, horse-drawn chariots were the equivalent of modern battle tanks and were instrumental for military success. Judah's armies scarcely had any. They did not even have enough skilled riders to man the horses that the Assyrians are sarcastically offered to them. Point-for-point, the officer reveals Hezekiah's supposed strong points as weak spots, even arguing that his spiritual reforms had robbed him of the vital support of the gods whose altars he removed!

Sennacherib's final assault is then on God Himself. Within hearing distance of the people of Jerusalem, his representative exclaims,

> Do not let Hezekiah deceive you, ... nor let Hezekiah make
> you trust in the Lord, saying, "The LORD will surely deliver
> us, and this city will not be given into the hand of the king of
> Assyria. Do not listen to Hezekiah, for thus says the king of
> Assyria, 'Make your peace with me and come out to me....'"
>
> (2 Kings 18:29–31)

After thus undermining the trust of the people in both their king and their God, the officer then delivers the flowery promise of an alternative "Promised Land" in Assyria, the "land of grain and new wine ... and honey" (v. 32) that we cited earlier.

Knowing the Enemy's Tactics

Our readers may feel that Sennacherib as the Antichrist's precursor is not as spectacular or impressive as a Nero or Hitler. But there is an important reason for why it is a revived Sennacherib whom we will have to reckon with: neither Nero nor Hitler are in the Bible, but Sennacherib's encounter with God's people has been preserved—not just in any history book but in God's infallible Word! This is a great advantage for us end times believers. Because of God's special providential grace, we can learn valuable spiritual lessons and avoid the mistakes of the past.

Sennacherib's dealings with Hezekiah are a chilling preview of the future Antichrist's strategies against God's church. Let us summarize them in their sequence:

1. **Fear**: Sennacherib's extremely brutal dealings with those who do not surrender to him (his slaughter of the Hebrew defenders of Lachish) serve to intimidate those he has not yet conquered. The enemy's strategy of fear is a step up from Satan's scheming in the Garden of Eden. Back then, humanity was still secure in God and did not know fear or intimidation. But now, in our fallen state, fear is the second most powerful emotion that humans can have, with faith being the strongest one. If we do not stand strong in our faith, we will succumb to fear. In Sennacherib's case, his psychological warfare succeeds. Hezekiah's confidence crumbles, and he reaches out for a dangerous compromise with the enemy.

2. **Exploiting any sign of weakness**: As soon as his victim seeks to appease him by compromising and giving in to his demands, Sennacherib knows that his chance has come, and he moves out in full force. Any show of weakness will immediately be exploited and later on used against the victim. Even though Sennacherib's army was later destroyed by God, the royal annals in his palace in Nineveh only focus on the spectacular capture of Lachish and on the tribute that he exacted from Hezekiah. Had Hezekiah remained uncompromising and had the northern kingdom of Israel trusted in God, then Sennacherib's shame and defeat would have been complete. But as it stood, he managed to hold on to power for another 20 years[34] after the slaughter of his army.

3. **Intimidation and promises**: Rather than immediately assaulting the victim, Sennacherib first attempts to achieve an easy surrender through negotiation. His negotiating tactics involve a clever carrot-and-stick approach, seeking to simultaneously intimidate the victim while at the same time making deceitful

offers of peace and prosperity. The main purpose of this strategy is to make the consequences of continued resistance appear far worse than living in "Promised Lands" under Assyrian rule. The people were greatly intimidated by this, but thankfully Hezekiah's response at this point was a prayer of faith to God.

4. **Undermining trust**: Above all, Sennacherib's strategy centered on undermining his victim's trust in God. If the victim could be led to believe that his God had left him to his own devices, his resolve was undermined, and his resistance would soon crumble. An especially dangerous aspect of Sennacherib's tactics was the implication that Hezekiah made a serious mistake in removing the altars of other gods. The Assyrians always avoided offending other gods and simply integrated the gods of conquered nations into their own pantheon of deities. Sennacherib's representative basically asserted that his master's attack against Hezekiah was a justified act of revenge on behalf of the gods that Hezekiah had purged. Thankfully, Hezekiah remained strong, because he believed in God's promises delivered through the prophecies of Isaiah.

5. **Brute force conquest**: If the victim cannot be deceived into surrender, a brute force attack is the last resort. The Assyrians were experts at military technology, deploying sophisticated siege and battering rams and placing archers behind movable towers. Once the victim had been surrounded and cut off from all supply lines, his defeat was usually only a matter of time. If God had not supernaturally intervened, Jerusalem would eventually have fallen into Sennacherib's hands.

6. **Spiritual defeat through exile**: Once the victim either willingly surrendered or suffered defeat in battle, Assyrian policy was to deport large sections of the local population, resettling them in Assyrian heartlands. Through forced exile, the conquered peoples were to be assimilated into the empire's culture and

religion. This is basically how Israel's ten "lost tribes" became "lost" until today: many of the exiled Jews from the northern kingdom (the ten tribes) were resettled in the Mesopotamian region and presumably became so thoroughly assimilated into local society that they completely lost their "Jewishness," being indistinguishable from those around them (Israel's deportation was later completed by the Babylonian kings). They were now "Assyrians" under the care of Sennacherib the "expert shepherd" rather than their true heavenly Shepherd. Then, their spiritual defeat would be complete. While Hezekiah was able to avert such a fate, under his faithless successors, the people of Judah were later deported to Babylon by Nebuchadnezzar.

Countering the Enemy's Schemes

Satan used Sennacherib to employ six steps against Hezekiah, God's king, and Judah, the remaining faithful people of God. In Scripture, six is the number of man[35] and a triple six is the number of the Antichrist. But thankfully, God always speaks the final word. The seventh and final phase of Sennacherib's encounter with Hezekiah ends in God's decisive victory over the Assyrian forces. God acts in response to Hezekiah's prayer of faith and utter dependence to Him, and it is He who fights and wins our battles for us. Disaster is averted and Jerusalem rejoices in the power of its Maker. Likewise, God will show Himself sovereign at the end of the age, decisively defeating the Antichrist and his armies.

But until then, we are called to stand strong in our faith. In this present age, the postmodern spirit is replicating Sennacherib's strategy: postmodernism believes that the more gods humanity worships, the better, and those who do not accept other beliefs as true will face persecution (the "revenge of the gods" so to speak). By doing so, postmodernism asserts its own "righteousness" over God's absolute demand for the spiritual purity of His people, a demand that does not tolerate compromise and sin in the church. Just like Sennacherib, it employs clever psychological rhetoric to "peacefully" appeal to people's moral consciences. But it will end up intimidating and crushing those who will not bow to its idolatrous relativistic beliefs.

The historic events of Israel and Judah under the Assyrian Empire are a forceful warning to us end times believers. King Ahaz, who prostrated himself before the Assyrians in order to gain their favor, ended up hopelessly enslaving his entire nation to the Assyrian king. This is a picture of today's liberal church but also of liberalizing sections of the more conservative church who are trying to appease the enemy through compromise. Yet those within conservative Christianity who are more faithful to God's Word are also in danger of repeating Hezekiah's mistake. Like Ahaz, Hezekiah also sought to placate the enemy. Although he did not go as far as Ahaz, he gave in to doubts and fears and opened himself up for attack and emboldened the enemy. Only faith is stronger than fear. The years to come will be a time of great trial and of the testing of our faith. Only those who fully throw themselves into God's arms will be able to withstand Satan's schemes.

Chapter 10 Notes

1. The Eurozone comprises the 16 of the 27 EU nations that have the Euro as their currency.
2. Spain's 2012 debt is forecasted to reach 85.9 percent of its GDP, which equates to just under 900 billion Euro, and will increase to 90.5 percent of its GDP in 2013 (see "Spain's debt-to-GDP ratio to rise to 90.5 percent in 2013 versus 85.3 percent in 2012," *Reuters*, http://www.reuters.com/article/2012/09/29/us-spains-debt-gdp-idUSBRE88S05420120929). See also http://www.statista.com/statistics/167461/national-debt-of-spain and http://www.nationaldebtclocks.org/national_debt_of_italy.
3. "S&P lowers forecast for eurozone GDP growth in 2012 and 2013," *Reuters*, http://in.reuters.com/article/2012/09/25/idINWLA370920120925.
4. "Business Economists Reduce U.S. GDP Growth Forecasts," *Bloomberg News*, http://www.bloomberg.com/news/2012-10-15/business-economists-reduce-u-s-gdp-growth-forecasts.html.
5. In 2011, about 26 percent of China's GDP came from exports, whereas the US figure stood at 10 percent.
6. "China's Exports and Imports Dip Raising Growth Concerns," *BBC News*, http://www.bbc.co.uk/news/business-16977202.
7. Ibid.
8. "Germany Debates a Euro Bailout Referendum," *Spiegel Online*, http://www.spiegel.de/international/germany/germany-debates-referendum-over-euro-zone-integration-a-841014.html.
9. The expression "as if it had been slain," which might make us wonder whether it had actually been slain, carries the same meaning as the description of Jesus the Lamb, who appears "as if slain" (Revelation 5:6). Just as Jesus was actually slain, and raised from the dead, so it will be with his counterfeit, the Antichrist.
10. See the entry *abyssos* (*Strong's Concordance,* G12) in Colin Brown, "Hell, Abyss, Hades, Gehenna, Lower Regions," *New International Dictionary of New Testament Theology* (Grand Rapids, MI: Zondervan, 2000), Olive Tree Bible Software, Inc.
11. The times of the Gentiles cannot have started with the Babylonian king Nebuchadnezzar capturing Jerusalem in 586 BC, as is asserted by Walvoord and other dispensational scholars. From 142–63 BC, the Jewish state under the Hasmonean dynasty was recognized as an independent state even by the Roman Empire. During this time, no gentile nation ruled over Jerusalem. Most importantly, Jesus foretold the "times of the Gentiles" as a future event that would take place *after* his death. In Luke 21:24, He prophesied, "and Jerusalem will be [Gr. *estai*, future tense, *Strong's Concordance,* G1510] trampled under foot by the Gentiles until the times of the Gentiles are fulfilled." Therefore, the time of the Gentiles can only have started with

the utter destruction of both the city (Jerusalem) and the temple in 70 AD by the Romans, which also wiped out the Jewish nation until its re-establishment in 1948.

12. Our list differs from van Kampen's, because he follows the popular thesis that the four empires in Daniel 7 are the same as those in Daniel 2. We had argued against this assumption in chapter 2.

13. The early dating of the Exodus (1446 BC) under Tuthmosis III, first proposed by the American missionary and archaeologist Edwin R. Thiele, is supported by biblical passages such as 1 Kings 6:1, 1 Chronicles 6:33-37 and Judges 11:26.

14. Initially it was called the Akkadian, then the Sumerian, and then the old and middle Babylonian empire, which included cities such as Babel and Nineveh that were founded by Nimrod according to Genesis 10. Shalmaneser V, Sargon II, and Sennacherib were kings of the Neo-Assyrian Empire, which began in 911 BC. The Assyrian region was settled from about 5500 BC and began to have significant cities from 3500 BC.

15. More precisely, the Neo-Babylonian or Chaldean empire.

16. Strictly speaking, the Roman Republic began in 508 BC, while the Roman Empire started in 27 BC. However, in the 2nd century BC Rome conquered many European regions (including Greece and Spain) and therefore became a superpower.

17. Quite a few figures in the Bible did revile God's people (for example Goliath or the nation of Moab) but not God's name itself. Ezekiel is led to prophesy against Edom because of the "revilings [ne'atsah, Strong's Concordance, H5007] which you have spoken against the Mountains of Israel" (35:12). The Jews themselves are said to have "blasphemed [gadaph, ibid., H1442] Me [God] by acting treacherously against me" (Ezekiel 20:27), to have "committed great blasphemies [ne'atsah]" during their 40 years in the desert of Sinai (Nehemiah 9:18), and God laments that because of their disobedience "My name is continually blasphemed [or: spurned, despised, na'ats, ibid., H5006] all day long" (Isaiah 52:5). Balak hired Balaam to curse (qabab, ibid., H6895) God's people (Numbers 22–23). But there is only one instance in which a foreign king is directly said to have "blasphemed" God.

18. Compare also Isaiah 10:12-13: "I [God] will punish the fruit of the arrogant heart of the king of Assyria and the pomp of his haughtiness. For he has said, "By the power of my hand and by my wisdom I did this…."

19. Charaph also means to taunt or reproach. Strong's Concordance, H2778.

20. Gadaph carries the meanings of blasphemy, reviling, or verbal abuse. Ibid., H1442. In Numbers 15:30, God determines that the punishment for blaspheming (gadaph) Him is spiritual death (being cut off from the people of God).

21. Other descriptions of blasphemy in the Old Testament usually refer to other nations blaspheming against Israel, for example the Edomites in Ezekiel 35:12 (the word for reviling here is *na'ats*, *Strong's Concordance*, H5006).

22. God helped Gideon and his men by causing the Midianites and Amalekites to turn on each other. Together with those killed by the pursuing Israelites, 120,000 enemy forces fell (Judges 7–8). However, in contrast to Sennacherib's army, these deaths were not directly caused by God, but by human beings killing each other. The "angel of the Lord" also appeared to destroy Jerusalem as punishment for David's pride, but God stopped him. By then, 70,000 Israelites had died of a "pestilence" (2 Samuel 24:15).

23. The floor space of Versailles measures 721,206 square feet, whereas that of Sennacherib's palace stood at an incredible 1,285,110 square feet. See http://en.wikipedia.org/wiki/World's_largest_palace and Craig S. Keener, *IVP Bible Background Commentary, Old Testament* (Downer's Grove, IL: IVP Academic, 1993), 790.

24. Erika Belibtreu, "Grisly Assyrian Record of Torture and Death," *Biblical Archeological Society*, http://www.cojs.org/pdf/grisly_assyrian.pdf, 7.

25. Ibid.

26. Saul Kussiel Padover, *Confessions and Self-Portraits: 4600 Years of Autobiography* (North Stratford, NH: Ayer Publishing, 1957), 11.

27. Keener, 2 Chronicles 32:11.

28. Kenneth L. Barker and John R. Kohlenberger III, *The Expositor's Bible Commentary Abridged Version* (Grand Rapids, MI: Zondervan, 2004), Isaiah 19:23–20:1, notes on verse 23.

29. Padover, 12.

30. John Malcom Russell, *Sennacherib's Palace Without Rival at Nineveh* (Chicago, London: University of Chicago Press, 2001), 242, 246.

31. See Paul Seely, "The Date of the Tower of Babel and Some Theological Implications," *Westminster Theological Journal* 63 (2001), http://faculty.gordon.edu/hu/bi/ted_hildebrandt/otesources/01-genesis/text/articles-books/seely_babel_wtj.pdf.

32. See "Ancient Babylonia – The Ziggurats," http://www.bible-history.com/babylonia/BabyloniaThe_Ziggurat.htm.

33. Sennacherib here represents the Assyrian kings.

34. From 701 to 681 BC, when he was murdered by two of his sons.

35. Man was created on the 6th day, and 6 is one less than 7, the number of divine perfection. Therefore, man falls short of the perfection of God.

Chapter 11
The Tribulations Begin

Then another angel, a third one, followed them, saying with a loud
voice, "If anyone worships the beast and his image, and receives a
mark on his forehead or on his hand, he also will drink of the wine
of the wrath of God.... Here is the perseverance of the saints who
keep the commandments of God and their faith in Jesus."
Revelation 14:9–10, 12

The "Hour" of Tribulation: God's Process of Separation and Refinement

When we think of the tribulations of the end times, Satan's purpose and authority over the world are usually in the forefront of our minds. But in this chapter, we want to demonstrate how the final seven years before the establishment of Jesus' Kingdom on earth are not only permitted but also actively controlled and guided by God Himself. Even though Satan has definite plans for this time and will be able to carry them out, God will remain in complete sovereign control at all times, even in the greatest of darkness. His purposes in the tribulations are the primary reason for why these events will take place. Let us examine them.

After the rapture of the first fruits, Revelation 14 depicts an "angel flying in midheaven," who "said with a loud voice":

> Fear God, and give Him glory, because the hour of His judgment has come; worship Him who made the heaven and the earth and sea and springs of waters.

> (v. 7)

Here, the tribulations of the 70th week are described as the "hour of … judgment [Gr. *krisis*[1]]." In Revelation 3:10, they are talked about as the "hour of testing [Gr. *peirasmos*[2]]." Both expressions refer to the same event, but they express the two distinct purposes that God will pursue during this decisive final 7-year period (or "hour") of human history: firstly, a testing and refining, secondly a judging or separating. On the one hand, God will subject His people to testing in the sense of refining, as one refines gold in order to make it pure. This refers to the refining of the "foolish virgin" believers. On the other hand, God will test the world in order to sift out pretenders from those with saving faith, separating the wheat from the chaff (Matthew 3:12) and giving the undecided a final chance to make a definite commitment. As Jesus put it so aptly in His parable of the sower:

> Those on rocky soil are those who, when they hear, receive
> the word with joy; [but] these have no firm root; they believe
> for a while, and in time of temptation [or: testing, *peirasmos*]
> fall away.
>
> (Luke 8:13)

Many who say they "believe" seem to be truly excited about Jesus, and at first they cannot be distinguished from those who are truly born-again. It is only in times of testing that the difference will gradually be revealed. When Paul challenges all believers in 2 Corinthians 13:5 to "[t]est [*peirazo*] yourselves to see if you are in the faith," he employs *peirasmos* in its verb form *peirazo*[3] in that exact sense. For those who are found to be without true spiritual "roots," the "hour of judgment" will then lead to the "day of judgment [*krisis*]" when all unbelievers will face eternal punishment in the lake of fire (Revelation 20).

The exact duration of the tribulation during the Antichrist's global reign, given by Scripture as 42 months or 3.5 years, points towards these

265

multiple purposes. Throughout the Bible, the numbers 40 and 42 are periods of testing and refinement, judgment and punishment:[4]

Testing and refinement:

- The 12 spies that spied out the Promised Land did so for **40 days**. This was a time of testing their faith, a test that 10 of them failed (all except for Joshua and Caleb) because they were intimidated by the giants of the land (Numbers 13–14).
- Moses lived **40 years** in the wilderness of Midian before God appeared to Him in the burning bush and commissioned Him to rescue God's people (Acts 7:30). This was a time of preparation and refinement for him. Later, God tested the Israelites during the **40 days** when Moses was on Mount Sinai where he received the Ten Commandments (Exodus 34:28). Sadly, they failed this test when Aaron made a golden calf at their insistence.
- God prophesied through Jonah that Nineveh had **40 days** to repent before He would utterly destroy the city because of all its evil (Jonah 3:4). Nineveh passed the test and repented, and the city was spared God's judgment and punishment (which came on it later in the time of the prophet Nahum).
- Jesus fasted in the wilderness for **40 days** before He was tempted or tested (*peirazo*) by the devil (Luke 4:1–2).

Judgment:

- As judgment for their unbelief, God made the Israelites wander in the desert for **40 years**—one year for each day that the spies were in the land—until that entire generation had passed away (Numbers 14:33–34). This period is also expressly described as a time of "testing" (Septuagint: *ekpeirazo*,[5] to prove or test thoroughly, from *ek*, "out of," and *peirazo*) in Deuteronomy 8:2. God tested them in order "to know what was in your heart."

During all their wanderings, they made a total of **42 stops** (linking the numbers 40 and 42 together).

- When Israel repeatedly turned against God during the times of the Judges, God gave them into the hands of the Philistines for **40 years** (Judges 13:1). Later, Goliath taunted the Israelite army for **40 days**, until he was defeated by David (1 Samuel 17:16).

- After rejecting and killing their Messiah, God graciously gave Jerusalem nearly **40 years** before its utter destruction by the Romans in 70 AD. During this time, the early church grew and witnessed in Jerusalem, but the vast majority of Jews refused the message and failed the test, and so God's judgment was executed.

- In the end times, Jerusalem will be given over to the nations who will "tread under foot the holy city for **forty-two months**" (Revelation 11:2).

Punishment:

- During the great flood, which destroyed evil humanity except for Noah's family, it rained for **40 days** and nights (Genesis 7:4, 12, 17).

- Under Mosaic Law, a convicted transgressor was liable to be punished with up to **40 lashes** (Deuteronomy 25:3). Compare Luke 12:47–48, which says that unfaithful servants (Christians) who knew God's will but did not do it will "receive many lashes," whereas those who did not know it will "receive but few."

- When a group of youths taunted the prophet Elisha, he cursed them, and two bears killed **42** of them (2 Kings 2:24).

- Likewise, Jehu, who had been called by God to utterly destroy King Ahab of Israel's extended family and to stamp out Baal worship, seized and killed **42 relatives** of Judah's King Ahaziah, who had come to pay their respect to Ahab's royal family and worship their gods (2 Kings 10:12–14).

- The apocalyptic slaughter of God's enemies at Armageddon is symbolically described through a flow of blood from the "great winepress of the wrath of God ... as high as a horse's bridle, for 1,600 stadia" (Revelation 14:19–20 ESV). One thousand six hundred is the **square of 40**, again as a number of judgment or punishment.

More specifically, the number 42, the duration of the reign of the Antichrist, is derived by multiplying the number of man (six) with the number of God (seven), pointing to the interaction of humanity with their Maker. Therefore, 42 symbolizes the rebellion of fallen mankind against God—culminating in the world domination of the Antichrist. But it also stands for God's salvation plan for us: Matthew's genealogy from Adam to Christ was purposely constructed[6] as consisting of 42 generations.

In addition, the number 3.5 (3.5 years) also signifies a period of testing: the Israelites were tested by God for 3.5 centuries from the end of King Solomon's reign and the division of Israel to the Babylonian exile (approx. 930 BC to 586 BC). This time frame was an opportunity to repent from idol worship and to return to God. However, the Jews failed the test, persisting in idolatry, and therefore had to successively go into exile. Likewise, God sent a drought during the time of the prophet Elijah that lasted 3.5 years (James 5:17). The purpose of this drought was the same: God gave Israel a chance to repent from Baal worship, to remember their dependence on Him as the ultimate provider, and to cry out so that He would hear them.

All four of these aspects of the biblical numbers of 40, 42, and 3.5—testing, refining, judging and punishing—will also be part of the 42 months of great tribulation. Here, the punishment aspect will not apply to God's born-again people, but only to unsaved "Christian" pretenders and the unbelieving world.

God's Testing and Refining Produces "Patient Endurance"

Tests, trials, and temptations, all of which are meanings of the noun *peirasmos*, are a normal part of Christian life. God "tested [*peirazo*[7]]" Abraham by commanding him to sacrifice his only son (Genesis 22:1). The Queen of Sheba came to King Solomon to "test [*peirazo*] him with difficult questions" until she saw for herself that Solomon's famed wisdom was real (1 Kings 10:1). Even Jesus was "tested [*peirazo*]" both by the devil and by the Pharisees, as well as others who sought to make Him stumble (Luke 4:13; Matthew 16:1). Likewise, we are to expect temptations and trials and even welcome them with "all joy" (James 1:2).

Why are we told to have joy during these difficulties? The reason for this exhortation to rejoice in all trials is that God's testing ultimately "produces endurance [*hupomonei*]," so that we "may be perfect and complete, lacking in nothing" (James 1:3, 4). James emphatically states:

> Blessed is a man who perseveres [*hupomeno*] under trial [*peirasmos*]; for once he has been approved, he will receive the crown of life which the Lord has promised to those who love Him.
>
> (James 1:12)

The Greek term for "endurance" in James 1:3 is *hupomonei*,[8] which can be translated as patience, steadfastness, or patient endurance. In James 1:12, its verb form *hupomeno*[9] is translated as "persevere." *Hupomonei* also occurs in other important passages such as Romans 5:3–4, where Paul writes that "we also exult in our tribulations, knowing that tribulation brings about perseverance [*hupomonei*]; and perseverance [*hupomonei*], proven character ..." *Hupomonei* comes from the two root words *hupo* and *meno. Hupo* simply means "under," as in being under someone's authority and is used in that sense in Jesus' encounter with the Roman centurion in Matthew 8:9. *Meno* is a very important word. It means to "remain" or to "abide" and is extensively used in John 15 where Jesus says, "Abide [*meno*] in me, and I in you" (v. 4). Together, the meaning of *hupomonei* is a remaining or abiding in Jesus by remaining under His authority and will for our lives. *Hupomonei* as "patient endurance" reflects this attitude of utter dependence on God: a faithful and enduring waiting on Him, much like Jesus in the garden of Gethsemane, when He looked ahead to His ultimate trial with a patient endurance that only faith can give.

The fact that *hupomonei* is an essential overcomer quality is underlined by its prominent use in the preservation promise of Revelation 3:10:

> Because you have kept the word of My perseverance [*hupomonei*], I also will keep you from the hour of testing [*peirasmos*], that hour which is about to come upon the whole world, to test [*peirazo*] those who dwell on the earth.

The ultimate purpose of God's testing, either through trials (sufferings, persecutions, etc.) or through temptation to sin, is therefore to develop patient endurance, which in turn produces essential spiritual character qualities such as faith, hope, and ultimately, love. God-given tests and tribulations enforce the death of the old sin nature, powerfully promoting the growth of our new born-again nature and causing us to bear abundant spiritual fruit. The link between *hupomonei*-endurance and fruit-bearing discipleship is vividly highlighted in the parable of the sower:

> But the seed in the good soil, these are the ones who have heard the word in an honest and good heart, and hold it fast, and bear fruit with perseverance [*hupomonei*].
>
> (Luke 8:15)

Endurance will be especially important during times of tribulation and will be a characteristic sign of those who ultimately decide to follow Jesus and refuse the mark of the beast:

> Many false prophets will arise and will mislead many. Because lawlessness is increased, most people's love will grow cold. But the one who endures [*hupomeno*] to the end, he will be saved.
>
> (Matthew 24:11–13)

> He who leads into captivity shall go into captivity; he who kills with the sword must be killed with the sword. Here is the patience [or endurance; *hupomonei*] and the faith of the saints.
>
> (Revelation 13:10 NJKV)

Finally, Scripture marks *hupomonei* as a precondition for reigning with Christ:

> If we endure [*hupomeno*], we will also reign with Him....
>
> (2 Timothy 2:12)

Because such co-regency is an overcomer promise (Revelation 2:26–27)—the overcomer church of Philadelphia is promised to be spared the tribulation because of its *hupomonei*—it is abundantly clear that "patient endurance" is an essential character trait of any overcoming believer.

How God Tests Us: The Examples of Abraham and Job

God's primary way to build *hupomonei*-style endurance into our character is by tribulations. Paul says in Romans 5:3, "[W]e also exult

271

in our tribulations, knowing that tribulation brings about perseverance [*hupomonei*]...." Tribulations and testing are two sides of the same coin, because God often tests His people through trials and tribulations.

Two examples of God's testing and the wonderful spiritual fruit that results from it are found in the Old Testament. After God fulfilled His promise to Abraham and Sarah and gave them a son, Abraham was about to face his ultimate test. God asked him to sacrifice this very son of promise. This must have seemed so crazy! After many years of waiting, Abraham had finally received his own offspring, the heir through which God's word would be fulfilled that one day "many nations" would come from his line and his descendants would be as numerous as the stars in the sky (Genesis 12; 15). God's test for Abraham was therefore to take away the very thing that was needed for His promise to come true.

In the same way, God often forces us to die to the very vision that He gave to us in the first place and to let go of the very promises that He has given us. He does this to make sure that what we are ultimately after is not His promises or His blessings to us, but He Himself. God wants to be first in our lives, and that means that we even have to die even to the very dreams He has placed in our hearts!

Another instance of God's testing is found in the story of Job. Job was a righteous man, more so than any other at his time, and God had blessed him richly. But Satan challenged Job's devotion to God, saying,

> Yes, but Job has good reason to fear God. You have always put a wall of protection around him and his home and his property. You have made him prosper in everything he does. Look how rich he is! But reach out and take away everything he has, and he will surely curse you to your face!
>
> (Job 1:9–11 NLT)

God accepted Satan's challenge and allowed him to put Job to the test in order to publicly prove whether Job's love and respect for God was dependent on His blessings or not. By God's enabling grace, Job passed the test with flying colors, confounding Satan's accusations and confirming God's positive assessment of his character. Scripture says, "In all of this, Job did not sin by blaming God" (Job 1:22). God's testing of Job was therefore not a needless act of torturing a faithful disciple, as some wrongly believe. Rather, it represented the height of His spiritual development, made him a spiritual hero, and ended with abundant blessings (Job 42).

God wants to do the same kind of testing with all of his children. He permits sufferings and trials to come our way in order to burn away the dross of the old nature and bring out the pure spiritual power and fruitfulness of the new nature. Peter writes to the scattered believers across Asia Minor,

> These trials [or tests, *peirasmos*] will show that your faith is genuine. It is being tested as fire tests and purifies gold—though your faith is far more precious than mere gold. So when your faith remains strong through many trials, it will bring you much praise and glory and honor on the day when Jesus Christ is revealed to the whole world.
>
> (1 Peter 1:7 NLT)

Likewise, Jesus' appraisal of the seven churches of Revelation is directly linked to the extent to which they passed the tests that He had brought their way. The lukewarm Laodicean church appears to have been cushioning themselves against any discomforts, and consequently Jesus strongly exhorts them to "buy from Me gold refined by fire" (Revelation 3:18). By this, He means that they should willingly submit to the trials and tribulations that are an inevitable part of committed discipleship. Likewise, the fellowship in Smyrna is told that as part of their refinement process designed by God to turn them into overcomers, they "will be tested [*peirazo*], and you will have tribulation for ten days. Be faithful until death, and I will give you the crown of life" (Revelation 2:10).

The entire message of both Old and New Testaments is that testing, trials, and sufferings are such an essential aspect of discipleship that no major Bible figure, including Jesus Himself, could do without it. Hebrews 5:8 says, "Although He was a Son, He learned obedience from the things which He suffered." Without testing there can be no overcoming. Jesus told His disciples,

> You are those who have stood by Me in My trials [*peirasmois*]; and just as My Father has granted Me a kingdom, I grant you that you may eat and drink at My table in My kingdom, and you will sit on thrones judging the twelve tribes of Israel.
>
> (Luke 22:28–30)

That is precisely the problem of foolish virgin believers. Instead of submitting to God's testing, they evade it as much as they can. Like the Laodiceans, their discipleship is more about pampering the old self than nourishing the new. Like the Sardians, their walk with Jesus is more a pseudo-spiritual show than the self-denying path along Calvary Road. Rather than submitting to testing, they may end up putting God to the test, as the stubborn Israelites did (Psalm 78:40). As a sad consequence, these believers never develop *hupomonei*-style endurance and character, never become overcomers, and miss out on the first fruits rapture because they are so utterly unprepared for the coming of their Groom.

This is where the tribulation comes in. The "hour of testing" that the foolish virgins must go through is their unique God-given chance to "get their act together" and begin to take their discipleship seriously. This does *not* mean that they embark on a frenzy of "spiritual" self-effort! However, it does mean that they now actively pursue their relationship with Jesus, obeying His universal Word (*logos*) and His personal directives (*rhema* words) to them. Now, they view sufferings and privations as a God-given opportunity to grow spiritually. They gladly forsake the things of the world, willingly accepting "the loss of all things, and count[ing] them but rubbish so that [they] may gain Christ" (Philippians 3:8). Finally, Jesus will become the single most important focus of their lives. All this, they will do "under grace" (God's constant enabling) and the knowledge that God "will not allow you to be tempted [or tested, *peirazo*] beyond what you are able, but with the temptation will provide the way of escape also, so that you will be able to endure it" (1 Corinthians 10:13).

The fact that the foolish virgins will be refined and transformed into overcoming saints is not a hopeful speculation, but a sure prophetic word of Scripture. Revelation 12:11 assures us of this:

> And they overcame him because of the blood of the Lamb
> and because of the word of their testimony, and they did not
> love their life even when faced with death [lit. until death].

The second half of this verse directly corresponds to the overcomer promise in Revelation 2:10, meaning that the saints in the tribulation have now become overcomers!

The Tribulation: God's Sovereign Work Executed Through Satan

It is commonly thought that the evil events of the final seven years represent humanity's final act of rebellion against God—in short, a time when Satan reigns supreme. God is said to tolerate all this through His permissive will, allowing it to occur even though it is entirely contrary to His perfect will. Somehow, we think, God will try to make the best of this situation and manage to use evil for good.

Now, there is some truth to this perspective. Human evil and rebellion were certainly never part of God's perfect will. But we must beware of believing that the final seven years of history are a time when

God just passively observes the world's most severe calamities and is then left with picking up the pieces caused by this mess when he wipes "every tear" from the eyes of His saints. Quite to the contrary, the Bible teaches us that God actively uses acts of evil and the works of Satan, even that He ordains evil to occur in order to fulfill His perfect will. As Wayne Grudem in his well-known *Systematic Theology*[10] explains, this does not mean that God approves of evil but rather that he "causes all things to work together for good to those who love God" (Romans 8:28). This means that evil can be actively ordained by God for the accomplishment of His will, even though these acts are carried out by Satan or human beings.

The same applies for the tribulations of the 70th week. 2 Thessalonians 2:8–12 explains why God not only allows the rise of the Antichrist to occur but even decrees it as part of His grand purpose for humanity:

> Then that lawless one [Antichrist] will be revealed ... the one whose coming is in accord with the activity of Satan, with all power and signs and false wonders, and with all the deception of wickedness for those who perish [the unbelievers], because they did not receive the love of the truth so as to be saved. For this reason God will send upon them a deluding influence [the Antichrist] so that they will believe what is false, in order that they all may be judged [Gr. *krino*] who did not believe the truth, but took pleasure in wickedness.

Amazingly, God has preordained the rise of the Antichrist from the beginning of history. Why? So that all those will be "judged who did not receive ... the truth so as to be saved." The Greek term for "judged" is *krino*,[11] the verb of the noun *krisis* that we met in the phrase "hour of judgment." Basically, God will judge the unbelieving world that rejects His truth by sending them the Antichrist as a "deluding influence." This will lead them even further away from the truth, resulting in their judgment. In short, from God's perspective the rise of the Antichrist is His act of judgment on those who refuse salvation through Christ, and this judgment comes in the form of a deceptive influence. This judgment is His will for the unbelieving world.

This will certainly not be the first time that God sends deception to the wicked: in 1 Kings 22:21–23, we are told of how God authorizes and empowers a "deceiving spirit" to "entice" and mislead Israel's disobedient King Ahab. As with the Antichrist, this deceptive spirit was God's judgment against those who refuse to submit to Him. Even Sennacherib, the Antichrist's historic manifestation, was preordained and empowered by God to move against Israel and other nations as an act of God's punishment. In Isaiah 10:5, God calls Assyria the "rod of My anger." Sennacherib himself knew of this when he told the Israelites, "Have I now come up without the LORD's approval against this land to destroy it? The LORD said to me, 'Go up against this land and destroy it'" (Isaiah 36:10). God, however, did not approve of Sennacherib's arrogance or brutality and held him fully responsible for his acts of wickedness.

Of course, God will not condone the acts of the Antichrist, whose authority is not from God but from the "dragon," who is Satan (Revelation 13:2). But neither is God a passive observer in all this. Quite to the contrary, the reign of the Antichrist is God's active act of judgment on the world in order to reinforce the separation (*krisis*) of wheat (believers) and chaff (unbelievers). To put it differently, God will use the Antichrist's reign of terror to make the world more black-and-white: "black" being the evil deeds of the unbelieving, and "white" being the righteous acts of the saints. People will either take the mark of the beast or they will refuse it and suffer the consequences—there will be no choice in-between the two. Moreover, as we said before, God also uses the terrible persecutions that will ensue to purify and refine the foolish virgin believers, so that they also will become the spotless bride which Jesus is returning for. Therefore, rather than being in charge, the Antichrist, Satan, and the tribulations they are causing *are merely God's tools* to bring about His will in the end times.

God is sovereign. This means that at all times everything is always under His full control. With God, there are no coincidences, no accidents, and no nasty surprises. God's complete and perfect sovereignty will especially be evident during the events of the 70th week of Daniel. As we will soon see, not only the rise of the Antichrist, represented in the first seal of Revelation 6, but also the global disasters that follow suit (seals two to four) are ordained by Him. This is reflected in the fact that in Revelation 5, Jesus, the Lamb, will first have to open the book with all seven seals before they can come to pass. Moreover, the four apocalyptic riders that symbolize these terrors of the first four seals are called forth by none other than the four living creatures that stand around the throne in the very presence of God. Through these servants of His, God Himself calls these catastrophic events into being. Likewise, in Amos 3:6 the prophet exclaims, "If a calamity [*or: evil*][12] occurs in a city has not the LORD done it?"[13] This, however, does not contradict the fact that the four riders themselves are agents of Satan and that Satan (and not God) is morally responsible for all the evil that comes through them. God is so much in control of everything—both good and evil—that He even claims authorship of both (Isaiah 45:7). But He Himself never does evil, and neither does He approve of evil deeds.[14] Scripture does not construe this to be a contradiction, and therefore neither should we.

Seals 1–4: The Opening of the First Four Seals

The Antichrist's rise to global dominion occurs right at the start of the final 7-year period with the opening of the first seal (Revelation 6:2). He is described as a white rider who "went out conquering and to conquer," carrying a bow but no arrows. This symbolism corresponds to the description of the beast in Revelation 13: rather than overpowering the world with military might, the Antichrist will achieve global dominion as a charismatic "savior," impressing the world with his supernaturally resurrected nature, his amazing abilities, and his powerful speech. Described as a "little horn" in Daniel 7, he will rise to power from a position of smallness and obscurity, surprising his opponents who will at first think little of him. The unbelieving world will hail his coming as a miracle and willingly offer their worship (Revelation 13:3–4). Therefore, right at the first seal and soon after the start of the 7-year period, the Antichrist will be empowered by Satan to rise into a position of world domination that will last for 3.5 years (42 months).

The other seals will unfold as follows:

1. **Red horse (2nd seal):** This seal will bring warfare, strife, and anarchy, as "nation will rise against nation" (Matthew 24:7). A more literal translation would be "people group [*ethnos*] will rise against people group [*ethnos*]," because *ethnos*[15] is the Greek term from which the English word "ethnic" or "ethnic group" is derived. The Antichrist will likely use the chaotic conditions that ensue in order to implement further policies designed to tighten his rule over the world. This situation of global unrest is likely related to the increased "lawlessness [*anomia*]" that Jesus predicted would overtake the world, and as a consequence "most people's love will grow cold" (Matthew 24:12).

    The Greek Sophist philosophers, who first coined the term *anomia*,[16] understood it not just as referring to moral evil (in the sense of transgressing God's will) but also as general lawlessness in society—for example, when mobs rage out of control, and governments are powerless to enforce law and order.[17] This two-fold sense is likely what Jesus meant in this passage. The resulting anarchy will play into the hands of the Antichrist. This shows how deceptive his reign will be: he will come into power as a "man of peace" yet fully knowing that as soon as he is in charge, Satan, his sponsor, will bring about widespread war-like conditions in order to empower him even further.

- **Black horse (3rd seal):** Global unrest will be followed by economic disaster, inflation, and famine. This will most likely come as a direct consequence of the conditions of anarchy and strife that will befall the world. These conditions will in turn spark even greater disorder, this time over scarce food supplies. The result will be the same as in the second seal: the Antichrist will use these disturbances to further tighten his grip over the world. In Revelation 14:8, the severe economic depression that will usher the Antichrist into power, is described as the economic and financial fall of "Babylon," with "Babylon" symbolically representing the world's global economic system (capitalism): "Fallen, fallen is Babylon the great ..." This is the first phase of the fall of "Babylon." The second phase (literal physical destruction of the city "Babylon"), which is described in Revelation 17–18, will come towards the end of the 70th week.

Table 23. Three major economic crises of the end times

2008–09 financial crisis	Caused the U.S. and Europe to incur huge debts and thereby prepared the way for subsequent crises.
Economic crisis right before the rise of the Antichrist	Will cause the world to hand over control to the Antichrist as their financial (and eventually spiritual) "savior." Will greatly reduce the autonomy and sovereignty of individual nations.
Economic turmoil of the third seal (perhaps 1–2 years after the previous crises)	Will worsen the widespread anarchy and unrest, thereby further strengthening the grip of the Antichrist over the world. By now, all peoples will be utterly enslaved to him. This crisis could mark or prepare the establishment of the image of the beast.

- **Pale horse (4th seal):** After warfare, strife, starvation, and deprivation, humanity will face a rider called "Death," accompanied by "Hades," the two places that will at the very end "g[i]ve up the dead which were in them" at the Great

White Throne judgment (Revelation 20:13). They will receive authority "over a fourth of the earth," where they will wreak havoc with the sword (warfare), famine, pestilence (rampant contagious diseases), and wild beasts (likely a reference to the secondary causes of death that arise from the chaos created by political and economic turmoil). In this seal, we now have a combination of man-made disasters and natural disasters.

In many ways, the disasters of the fourth seal are similar to those of the previous two seals, with warfare resulting in economic deprivation, conditions of economic scarcity, and political anarchy, which in turn create the ideal context for the spread of diseases. Therefore, it seems that in this particular area of the globe, the deadly trail of the previous two seals will unfold with even greater intensity. It is likely that Satan will implement the fourth seal in regions where he specifically wants to reinforce the power of the Antichrist or as a means to intimidate and defeat God's people who live in these nations. Like a place inhabited by "wild beasts," these regions will be very dangerous and hostile and full of terror, anguish, and the horrors of death.

The Israelites, like other ancient peoples, believed that the earth had four corners. Consequently, the number four in Scripture symbolizes global reach—events that affect the farthest corners of the earth. Taken together, these four seals will indeed spell global disasters that will affect every single person on the planet. They are an expression of God's testing and judgment, and there is still a chance to repent and be born again.

Therefore, the seals are different from God's wrath (*orge*), which are executed from chapter 8 and unleashed not by the four living creatures but by four angels "standing at the four corners of the earth" (Revelation 7:1). The calamities of the four seals are God's means to refine the foolish virgins and to separate the wheat from the chaff. As they run their terrible course, "most people's love will grow cold" (Matthew 24:12), meaning that they close their hearts towards God and His people. This explains why the first fruits rapture will be a secret and quiet affair. After it will take place, people will still have a chance to repent—but only based on faith in an invisible Christ. Their salvation by faith must occur on essentially the same terms as the present-day saints, who also must believe without seeing Christ in all His glory. But when Jesus comes at the late harvest, the final opportunity to believe in Him will have passed, and He will openly reveal His full glory to the world. Once the wrath starts, it will be too late to turn to God, and those who are killed during the wrath are headed for eternal damnation. Those who are allowed to survive will subsequently enter the millennial era, where they graciously receive another chance to follow Jesus.

Seal 5, Part I: The Great Tribulations of the 70th Week

The fifth seal represents the voices of the martyrs, the foolish virgins who missed the first fruits rapture but were refined in the fires of the tribulation. In the midst of great trials, they remained faithful to Jesus and maintained the "testimony" of His Word. The fact that these martyrs are foolish virgins and not first fruits is confirmed by the fact that they are given a "white robe" (v. 11), the same kind of robe worn by the great multitude that came out of the tribulation (Revelation 7:9).[18] These saints' martyrdom has been occurring all along since the first fruits rapture and intensifies as the Antichrist comes into power. This time marks the 42-month period during which he will "make war with the saints and … overcome them" (Revelation 13:7). The timing of the fifth seal corresponds to Jesus' words in Matthew 24:9: "Then they will deliver you to tribulation, and will kill you, and you will be hated by all nations because of My name." This will occur during the whole of the Antichrist's 42-month reign and therefore throughout all of the first five seals.

We must be careful to note that this is not yet the Great Tribulation of the Jews that Jesus talked about in Matthew 24. That tribulation will not start until the mid-point of the seven years when the Antichrist turns his back on his covenant with Israel. Instead, the Great Tribulation of the foolish virgins of the church spans the 3.5 years from the first seal, when the Antichrist comes to control the world, until soon after the mid-point of the 70th week, when Jesus rescues them at the late harvest rapture.[19] Both "Great Tribulations" must therefore be distinguished, even though they do overlap for a period of time.

Seal 5, Part II: The Woman in the Wilderness

Revelation 12 tells us that after the rapture of the first fruits—symbolized by the "son" of the woman—the woman herself (the remaining church) flees into the wilderness.[20] This flight is directly enabled by God, who gives her "the two wings of the great eagle" (v. 14), to a "place prepared by God" for her (v. 6), where she is "nourished for a time and times and half a time, from the presence of the serpent" (v. 14). Subsequent verses describe how the dragon tries to destroy the woman at her God-given hiding place through a "flood"—symbolic in Old Testament language of a large army or destructive force (for example Jeremiah 47:2). However, the "earth" (ge,[21] earth, land or soil) comes to the aid of the woman and swallows up the dragon's flood. This "swallowing" is a picture of utter defeat of the enemy's forces. In Numbers 26:10 God caused the earth to swallow up rebellious Korah and his followers. Similarly, Exodus 15:12 describes Pharaoh and his army as having been "swallowed" by the "earth." Likewise, the earth swallowing the flood of the dragon could refer to such a supernatural act of God against the forces of the Antichrist.[22]

Alternatively, it could refer to a region or nation ("land") that protects God's people, perhaps even through guerrilla tactics that are aided by the many hideouts that a wilderness terrain can provide. Along with others, we believe that this could include regions of the United States, where locals or parts of the armed forces refuse to cooperate with the Antichrist and his henchmen. Those in army leadership who are believers, or who are at least committed to the constitution, which commands them to protect the people, may take sides against the Antichrist and his henchmen and at least partially thwart their plans to completely eradicate God's people. Additionally, it may be that certain regions in other nations are less amenable to execute the Antichrist's orders than others and will end up protecting the Christians who live there. This protection may not be complete, but it would be sufficient to at least enable them to continue to follow Jesus without being martyred.

Clearly, the woman in the wilderness is in a safe place. God himself is said to "nourish" her there. The Greek term, *trepho*,[23] refers not only to physical feeding but also to a nurturing or bringing up of children (see Luke 4:16). The Old Testament word for wilderness, *midbar*,[24] describes not just uninhabited wastelands but also remote pastures, as well as areas with oases and even towns (for example Joshua 15:61). Throughout Scripture, the wilderness is a place of testing and refining but also of spiritual growth and character development. It is a place of spiritual feeding for the foolish virgin believers, who are like spiritual infants, so that they can grow up and mature in Christ. Jesus himself was tested and refined in the wilderness, where he fasted for 40 days.

Likewise, the believers in the wilderness will undergo significant deprivation and discomfort, but through this they will experience significant spiritual growth. At the same time, they will certainly receive God's supernatural provision of their bodily needs, much like Elijah, who was fed by ravens when he hid in a remote place from the wrath of King Ahab (1 Kings 17). Later on, Elijah again retreated into a wilderness, where he received provisions from an angel. The passage says that "he arose and ate and drank, and went in the strength of that food forty days and forty nights to Horeb, the mountain of God" (1 Kings 19:8). Thankfully, 40 is not only a number of trial and testing but also a number of rest and provision. God repeatedly gave Israel rest and peace for 40 years in the times of the judges, such as after Gideon defeated the Midianites.[25]

This raises the question of why there are two groups of saints during the tribulation: firstly, the woman in the wilderness, away and protected "from the presence of the serpent," and secondly, the saints against whom the Antichrist will make war for 42 months, described in Revelation 12:17 as "the rest of her children, who keep the commandments of God and hold to the testimony of Jesus." In Daniel 7:25 it says that they "will be given into his hand." One possibility is that the saints who are on earth during the tribulation will be given a choice, either to flee into the "wilderness" or to take up arms and fight: "he who kills with the sword must be killed with the sword" (Revelation 13:10 NKJV). Another possibility is that God purposefully separates those two groups of believers in order to refine and test them in different ways: those in the wilderness through the need to depend on God for protection and provision of life's necessities (like the Israelites in the wilderness) and the others through the fierce persecution that they will face in the regions controlled by the Antichrist (likely especially urban and other non-remote areas). It is probable that pretenders who are not born-again will not be amongst those in the wilderness but that they will be sifted out through the threat of direct persecution and the benefits of compromise.

Seal 5, Part III: The Mid-Point of the 70th week and the Abomination of Desolation

One of the most significant events of the first half of the seven years is the Antichrist's treaty with Israel. In Daniel 11:25–27, Daniel received a prophecy about the "king of the north" coming against the "king of the south." The King of the North, also called the "prince of the covenant" (v. 22) because of his covenant with Israel from Daniel 9:27, is the Antichrist. In Daniel 7, he is said to start out as a small horn, but then becomes larger in appearance than the other horns (kings/kingdoms). Likewise, in 11:23

it says that "he will practice deception ... and gain power with a small force of people." This strategy of deceitfulness continues in his exploits against the King of the South—possibly a league of Arab or Middle Eastern nations against Israel (for example, this would be confirmed by the fact that during the "Arab Spring" revolutions of 2011, Egypt, a former ally of Israel under the U.S.-friendly Mubarak regime, is now becoming its enemy, being led by a democratically-elected government of Muslim parties; this prophecy also complicates assertions that the Antichrist will be a Muslim).[26] Even though the King of the South's army is said to be greater ("extremely large and mighty," v. 25) than that of the Antichrist (or "King of the North"), he will be defeated by betrayal from within, by those who "eat his choice food" (v. 26). By triumphing over the King of the South, the Antichrist will then be in a position to deceitfully offer peace and protection to Israel. The covenant he makes with the nation will enable the Israelites to regain the Jerusalem temple site, and soon after the newly-erected third "tribulation" temple will be a place where Old Testament-style sacrifices will be offered.

However, right at the mid-point of the seven years, the Antichrist will betray his treaty with Israel and set up the "abomination of desolation" (as Jesus called it in Matthew 24:15) in the third temple in Jerusalem. The New Living Translation rendering of Daniel 9:27 puts it this way:

> The ruler will make a treaty with the people for a period of one set of seven, but after half this time, he will put an end to the sacrifices and offerings. And as a climax to all his terrible deeds, he will set up a sacrilegious object that causes desecration, until the fate decreed for this defiler is finally poured out on him.
>
> (Daniel 9:27 NLT)

The Hebrew word for "abomination," *siqqus*,[27] is essentially a synonym for an idol. Consequently, the "abomination of desolation" almost certainly refers to the speaking image of the beast, which the false prophet makes the world set up in honor of the Antichrist. This is described in Revelation 13:

> And he [the False Prophet] deceives those who dwell on the earth because of the signs which it was given him to perform in the presence of the beast, telling those who dwell on the earth to make an image [Gr. *eikon*] to the beast who had the wound of the sword and has come to life. And it was given to him to give breath to the image of the beast, so that the image of the beast would even speak and cause as many as do not worship the image of the beast to be killed.
>
> (Revelation 13:14–15)

The Greek term for image, *eikon*,[28] signifies the exact representation of something. In Colossians 1:15, Jesus is said to be "the image [Gr. *eikon*] of the invisible God," meaning that He perfectly reflects God's nature. In Jesus' time, there were many images (*eikon*) of Roman emperors, either in the form of coins or as statues. *Eikon* likewise referred to statues of gods as objects of worship; it corresponds to the Hebrew term *selem*,[29] "image," which typically refers to an idol—for example, the golden image of Nebuchadnezzar that Daniel refused to worship. The precedent for this horrendous deed occurred in 167 BC, when the Seleucid ruler Antiochus Epiphanes set up an image of Zeus in the temple and ordered pigs to be sacrificed on its altar. The image of the beast will therefore be an exact representation of the Antichrist's being and nature. Whether this will end up being a literal depiction of his physical appearance or rather a reflection of his spiritual character will remain to be seen.

2 Thessalonians 2 predicts that in the future, the Antichrist "takes his seat in the temple [Gr. *naos*] of God, displaying himself as being God" (v. 4). This verse refers to the image of the beast, which will be in the likeness of the Antichrist, and therefore it will be as if the Antichrist personally

sat in the temple. The Greek term for temple used in this verse, *naos*,[30] refers to the inner temple or holy place, as opposed to *hieron*,[31] which designates the entire temple complex. This choice of terms corresponds to Jesus' assertion that the Abomination of Desolation will be set up in "the holy place" (Matthew 24:15). In Paul's letters, *naos* is almost exclusively used in a symbolic way, to describe the body of Christ: "For we are the temple [*naos*] of the living God" (2 Corinthians 6:16). A second, symbolic meaning of the Antichrist taking up his seat in the *naos* is therefore that he will come to dominate God's church, infiltrating and corrupting it with his false doctrines and ultimately coming to control it from within.

Even more terrifying is the fact that the image of the Antichrist will be given "breath" (Gr. *pneuma*, breath or spirit), a satanic imitation of God breathing the "breath of life" into Adam (Genesis 2:7). It is said that the image will "even speak and cause as many as do not worship [Gr. *proskyneo*] the image of the beast to be killed" (Revelation 13:15). This must mean that it will have the ability to know whether people just pretend to worship but are secretly holding on to other views. Therefore, the speaking image will be the ultimate differentiating device between true believers, those who "keep the commandments of God and hold to the testimony of Jesus," and those who are just pretenders but "in time of temptation [or testing, *peirazo*] fall away" (Luke 8:13). The Greek term for worship, *proskyneo*,[32] literally means to kiss, which in antiquity referred to the kissing of a superior's hand as a token of worship and respect. *Proskyneo* was used in classical Greek to denote the act of prostrating oneself before the gods, because such worship often involved kissing the ground, and it was also employed in connection with the Roman emperor worship cult.[33]

The common belief is that the image can only identify and condemn God's people when they stand directly in front of it, which would of course greatly limit the numbers of believers that could feasibly be found out in this way and subsequently be put to death. Some, such as van Kampen, have therefore suggested that the Antichrist will in fact erect many of such images across the globe. However, it does not actually say in the chapter that the image requires personal presence for its satanic spiritual detection to work. It is therefore equally possible that the image can be told ID numbers or names of persons throughout the globe, and based on its satanic knowledge can then discern whether these persons truly worship the beast or not. The image would then work like a remote scanner that can detect whether a person carries the mark of the Antichrist. If that will be the case, the agents of the Antichrist may be equipped with communication devices that can directly log into the image's all-knowing prophetic "brain," accessing it like a remote database. Then, even though the image is placed in the temple in Jerusalem, its global reach will play a crucial role in the persecution of God's people.

Seal 6: Starting the Second Half of the 70th Week

For the church, the time of the Abomination of Desolation will be towards the end of the 42 months of the tribulation of the saints. Fairly soon after the mid-point of the 70th week, Christ will come to rapture them at the late harvest rapture. Jesus' coming in glory on the clouds, which will be a global spectacle, will end the 42-month world domination of the Antichrist (Revelation 13:5) and usher in the wrath of God. This is the sixth seal, which not only includes the rapture of the foolish virgins but also the cry of terror of the unbelieving world, who knows that their end is near. This is when all those who did not confess the name of Jesus during the tribulation period will exclaim,

> Fall on us and hide us from the presence of Him who sits on the throne, and from the wrath of the Lamb; for the great day of their wrath has come, and who is able to stand?
>
> (Revelation 6:16–17)

For the Jews, however, the mid-point of the seven years and the erection of the Abomination of Desolation mark the beginning of what Jesus referred to as their Great Tribulation, an intense process of testing and refinement that all of them—except for the seal-protected 144,000 Jewish first fruits—will have to go through. Zechariah describes this process in dramatic words:

> "It will come about in all the land," declares the LORD, "that two parts in it will be cut off and perish; But the third will be left in it. And I will bring the third part through the fire, refine them as silver is refined, and test them as gold is tested.
>
> They will call on My name, and I will answer them; I will say, 'They are My people,' and they will say, 'The LORD is my God.'"
>
> (Zechariah 13:8–9)

This is God's ultimate fulfillment of His promise to the Jews in Romans:

> The Deliverer will come from Zion,
> He will remove ungodliness from Jacob.
> This is My covenant with them,
> when I take away their sins.
>
> (Romans 11:26b–27)

For the Jews, therefore, the wrath of God will prove to be both a blessing and a curse: for those who belong to the one third that will be refined in God's fiery furnace and will end up obtaining salvation, ultimately, it will be a blessing. For those who are "rebels" and transgressors (Ezekiel 20:38) and who will perish in the process, a curse. According to Scripture, God's refining process will wipe out all unbelieving Jews who refuse to come to Christ and leave only born-again Israelites to enter the millennial reign of Christ. In addition to Zechariah 13:8–9 and Romans 11:26–27, this is also clearly taught in Ezekiel:

> "As I entered into judgment with your fathers in the wilderness of the land of Egypt, so I will enter into judgment with you," declares the Lord God. "I will make you pass under the rod, and I will bring you [the one-third of Jews] into the bond of the covenant; and I will purge from you the rebels and those who transgress against Me."
>
> (Ezekiel 20:36–38)

Also amongst the Jews, there will be a group of first fruits, the symbolic "144,000," who, like the wise virgins of the church, will be spared this arduous refinement process. Their salvation occurs at the late harvest rapture, at the blast of the trumpet when Jesus comes on the clouds in His full glory. This deliverance is described in Revelation and Zechariah:

> Behold, He is coming with the clouds, and *every eye will see Him, even those who pierced Him*; and all the tribes of the earth will mourn over Him.
>
> (Revelation 1:7, emphasis added)

> I will pour out on the house of David and on the inhabitants of Jerusalem, the Spirit of grace and of supplication, so that *they will look on Me whom they have pierced; and they will mourn for Him*, as one mourns for an only son, and they will weep bitterly over Him like the bitter weeping over a firstborn. In that day there will be great mourning in Jerusalem, like the mourning of Hadadrimmon in the plain of Megiddo.
>
> (Zechariah 12:10–11, emphasis added)

The timing of this event is confirmed to be the late harvest rapture by two other coming-of-Christ passages:

> And then the sign of the Son of Man will appear in the sky, and then *all the tribes of the earth will mourn, and they will see* the Son of Man coming on the clouds of the sky with power and great glory.
>
> (Matthew 24:30, emphasis added)

> Then the kings of the earth and the great men and the commanders and the rich and the strong and every slave and free man hid themselves in the caves and among the rocks of the mountains; and they said to the mountains and to the rocks, "Fall on us and hide us from the presence of Him who sits on the throne, and from the wrath of the Lamb; for the great day of their wrath has come, and who is able to stand?"
>
> (Revelation 6:15–17, emphasis added)

When Jesus comes in the clouds, He will be seen by His people, the Jews. Some of them, the Jewish first fruits, will immediately believe in Him, while the rest will have to go through the time of God's wrath without God's seal of protection.

Now, it is interesting that there is no promise of a rapture for the Jews in the Bible. God's Word only talks about Jesus rapturing (or "harvesting") the church, and therefore, the Jewish harvest feasts are of such particular significance for the saints. For the Jews, however, God instituted other feasts that uniquely relate to His plans for them.

To this day, devout Jews observe the Ten Days of Repentance, beginning with the Feast of Trumpets (Rosh Hashanah) on the first of the seventh Jewish month (Tishri) and ending with the Day of Atonement (Yom Kippur) on the 10th of the month. During this time, they send each other greeting cards with this text: "May you be inscribed [in the Book of Life] for a good year."[34] This is because the Day of Atonement is considered to be symbolic of God's final Day of Judgment, when those who are not found in the Book of Life will be thrown into the eternal lake of fire (Revelation 20). Until the destruction of the temple in 70 AD, this feast was the only time of the year when the high priest could enter the Holy of Holies in the temple in order to make atonement for the entire nation.

The Ten Days of Repentance will be of great significance for the salvation of the Jews. In particular, it is possible that the ultimate moment of their deliverance will occur on the Day of Atonement itself. In Leviticus 23:26–32, this feast is distinguished from all the other feasts in three ways. Firstly, all persons were to humble themselves before the Lord, the posture of humility representing a special openness toward God and an acknowledgment of one's need to be saved. Secondly, even though God commanded the Israelites to abstain from work on all of the feasts, on the Day of Atonement they are particularly exhorted to "do no work at all" (v. 31). Thirdly, the one who violated these commandments of humbling himself and refraining from any kind of work was to be "cut off from his people" (v. 29). The only other feast-related offense that attracted this severest of all punishments (equivalent to damnation) was for those who ate anything with leaven (leaven symbolizes sin) in it during the Feast of Unleavened Bread (Exodus 12:15). Therefore, the Day of Atonement was clearly instituted to point to a future time of decision: either to humble oneself before God and be saved; or to remain proud and continue in the ways ("work") of the world, pursuing man-centered, works-based salvation, and be condemned.

Based on the sequence of the Feast of Trumpets, the Day of Atonement, and the Ten Days of Repentance in between those two feasts, it is possible that the salvation of the Jews will occur in a two-fold cycle:

1. **First cycle:**

- Firstly, at the sound of the trumpet (the trumpet call of the late harvest rapture described in Matthew 24:30 and 1 Thessalonians 4:16), Jesus will come in the clouds. This is represented by the **Feast of Trumpets**.

- During the subsequent period of repentance, possibly a literal time span of 10 days, the 144,000 Jewish first fruits will come to accept their Messiah. This is finalized on the last day of this period, equivalent to the **Day of Atonement**, and therefore potentially the day on which these first fruits will receive the seal of God (Revelation 7).

- This Jewish first fruits harvest is not raptured. Instead, the Jewish first fruits are protected with a seal and remain on the earth during the wrath. This is symbolized by the feast that comes right after it, the **Feast of Booths or Tabernacles**. Just as this feast commemorates the wanderings of the Israelites in the wilderness in God's presence, the Jewish first fruits are now going to fulfill their God-given mission in the "wilderness" that they are sent to. After all, God has said that He will bring His people, the Jews, "into the wilderness of the peoples, and there I will enter into judgment with [them] face to face" (Ezekiel 20:35). This third phase of the first cycle therefore prepares the next, the second cycle, which will see the salvation of the "one third" of Israel that will turn to God.

2. **Second cycle:**

- Again, the trumpet will sound, just as on the **Feast of Trumpets**. This time, it will be the seventh trumpet of the wrath of God, which is blown near the end of the outpouring of God's wrath (Revelation 11:15). Soon afterward, Jesus will ride with His heavenly armies to Armageddon to defeat the Antichrist.

- This time, the ensuing period of repentance will lead to the salvation of the one-third of Jews that God brought through the fires of His refining judgment. It is possible that right before riding into battle, Jesus will reveal Himself to these refined Jews, and that their salvation will be confirmed at the end of this symbolic or literal "ten day" period, again following the pattern of the **Day of Atonement** feast. In fact, there is a 30-day period between the end of Daniel's 70th week and the defeat of the Antichrist at Armageddon. Daniel 12:11 states that "[f]rom the time that the regular sacrifice is abolished and the abomination of desolation is set up [at the mid-point of the seven years], there will be 1,290 days." These 1,290 days exceed the 1,260 days that extend from the mid-point of the 70th week until its end by 30 days. Therefore, it is likely that the Abomination of Desolation will actually last for 1,290 days even though Jesus' return will already occur after the 1,260 days, right at the end of the 70th week. The implication is that the destruction of the Antichrist (and his abominable image) described in Daniel 9:27 will not occur until 30 days after Jesus returns.[35] Consequently, there is a 30-day period during which Jesus will likely be with the Jews, finalizing their prophesied salvation in the "wilderness."

- This national salvation of Israel is now followed by Jesus defeating the armies of the world at Armageddon and setting up His millennial Kingdom on earth from Jerusalem (Zechariah 14). Then, it is likely that the eternal New Jerusalem will also descend from heaven and co-exist with the millennial Jerusalem (see chapter 14 for a detailed discussion). Both events will be a direct fulfillment of the subsequent feast, the **Feast of Booths or Tabernacles**, which joyfully anticipates God's very presence amongst His people. This feast was to be first and foremost a time of rejoicing before the Lord (Deuteronomy 16:13–14). In the millennium, all nations will be required to celebrate it

(Zechariah 14:16–19). This may be due to the fact that of all the feasts, it most closely relates to the enthronement of Jesus as King over the earth[36] and to the presence of Christ on earth, as reflected in John 1:14: "… the Word became flesh, and dwelt [lit. tabernacled, Gr. *skenoo*[37]] among us. In Revelation 21, it says,

> And I saw the holy city, New Jerusalem, coming down out
> of heaven from God, made ready as a bride adorned for her
> husband. And I heard a loud voice from the throne, saying,
> "Behold, the *tabernacle* [Gr. *skene*] of God is among men, and
> He will *dwell* [lit. tabernacle, Gr. *skenoo*] among them, and
> they shall be His people.…"
>
> (vv. 2–3, emphases added)

Based on this pattern, the Jews will go through the period of atonement twice: first, the Jewish first fruits, second, the rest of the Jews (the one third) who will find salvation. While for the church, the greatest end times significance is found in the harvest feasts, for the Jews it lies in these three fall feasts. Ultimately, God's purpose for all His people will find complete fulfillment before Jesus will reign over all the earth.

Chapter 11 Notes

1. *Strong's Concordance,* G2920.
2. Ibid., G3986.
3. Ibid., G3985.
4. Even though 40 and 42 are not exactly the same numbers, their significance is essentially the same, just like the meaning of the numbers 70 and 72 is very much comparable.
5. Ibid., G1598.
6. It was constructed in the sense that not all generations were actually listed, a practice that was common in Jewish culture and that God used to arrive at this symbolically significant number.

7. The Greek term *peirazo* in Genesis 22:1 (and other Old Testament passages) occurs in the Septuagint.

8. *Strong's Concordance,* G5281.

9. Ibid., G5278.

10. Wayne Grudem, *Systematic Theology: An Introduction to Biblical Doctrine* (Grand Rapids, MI: Zondervan, 1994), 322–327.

11. *Strong's Concordance,* G2919.

12. The Hebrew word here, *ra'* (*Strong's Concordance,* H7451), is most commonly translated as "evil." Compare Genesis 2:9, in which is discussed the "tree of the knowledge of good and evil [*ra'*]".

13. In Isaiah 45:7, God puts it even more bluntly: "I form the light, and create darkness: I make peace, and create evil [*ra'*]: I the LORD do all these things" (KJV). Compare also Lamentations 3:38. The fact that God considers Himself to have created [*bara'*, to create, ibid., H1254] everything, both good and even that which is evil, does not mean that He condones evil or commits evil deeds. Rather, through this statement, God affirms His full and complete sovereignty over all things, even the works of Satan and of wicked humanity. It means that God is ultimately in complete control and that without His active permission even acts of evil could not be committed. This knowledge of God's complete control over evil is especially important in the coming end times.

14. Previously, we had seen that even though the disasters that struck Job were directly caused by Satan, Job correctly interprets these satanic acts of evil as ultimately being acts of God: "The LORD gave and the LORD has taken away. Blessed be the name of the LORD" (Job 1:21). God is not morally responsible for them (that responsibility falls on Satan), but He has preordained them to happen as part of His sovereign will for humanity, in order to bring about His divine purposes and to glorify His name. The fact that God ordains evil to happen does not mean that He condones evil or is morally responsible for it (compare the fact that Job "did not sin by charging God with wrongdoing" even though all his children had died and his health was broken, Job 1:22, NIV). Scripture does not view this apparent contradiction as problematic or unreasonable, and therefore neither should we. For a good discussion of this topic, see for example John Piper, "Is God Less Glorious Because He Ordained that Evil Be?" based on the writings of the famous puritan preacher Jonathan Edwards, available online at http://www.desiringgod.org/resource-library/conference-messages/is-god-less-glorious-because-he-ordained-that-evil-be. See also "God's Providence," Grudem, ch. 16.

15. *Strong's Concordance,* G1484.

16. Ibid., G458.

17. The Sophists understood *anomia* as both a breakdown of moral standards and a breakdown of societal order resulting in strife and civil war. See Maroney, Eric, "Anomie," in *Encyclopedia of Identity*, ed. Ronald Jackson (London: Sage Publications, 2010), 20.

18. In both passages, the Greek word for robe is *stole* (*Strong's Concordance,* G4749). This word is also used to describe the long robes of the Pharisees or scribes (Mark 12:38), the robe which the father puts on the lost son after welcoming him back (Luke 15:22; besides reflecting salvation, this is also a great picture of a refined "foolish virgin"), and the washing of robes in Revelation 22:14. *Stole* mostly occurs in Revelation. The 24 elders of Revelation 4 are also described as wearing "white garments" (v. 4). However, the word here is *himation* (ibid., G2440), the same term used for the robe of the high priest (Matthew 26:65), the garments put on Jesus' donkey and in front of His path as He rode into Jerusalem (Mark 11:7–8), the garment that became "exceedingly white" during His transfiguration (Mark 9:3), and the "robe [*himation*] dipped in blood" which He will wear at Armageddon (Revelation 19:13). Perhaps most importantly, *himation* describes the "white garments" promised to overcomers in Revelation 3:5, such as the few in Sardis who are said to have "not soiled their garments [*himation*]" (Revelation 3:4). The *himation* can therefore aptly be regarded as a first fruits garment that was by God's enabling grace not soiled at the coming of Christ because those wearing it put on their new spirit nature. It is not a garment of salvation or self-righteousness but of sanctification and preparedness. In contrast, the *stole* is described both in Revelation 7:14 and 22:14 as that which first had to be "washed" in the blood of Christ. In both of these passages, the verb "to wash" (Gr. *plyno*) is in the active voice, meaning the washing is to be performed by the subject (the "foolish virgins"). This represents their active co-operation in their God-enabled sanctification process.

19. The 42-month period of war against the saints described in Revelation 13:7 uses the term *hagios* (*Strong's Concordance,* G40) for saints, which in the NT always refers to Christian believers (regardless of ethnic background). This is almost certainly not the same event as the Great Tribulation described in Matthew 24:15, even though both tribulations do overlap at one point, which is why Jesus says that "for the sake of the elect [Gr. *eklektos* (ibid., G1588), the saints or God's chosen people in general] those days will be cut short" (v. 22).

20. Gr. *eremos* (ibid., G2048), the same word used for the wilderness where the Israelites wandered (Septuagint version), and where Jesus was led by the Spirit.

21. Ibid., G1093.

22. Compare Hebrews 11:29, which uses the same Greek term *katapino* (ibid., G2666), to "drink up" or to "swallow," as Revelation 12:16 to describe the destruction of Pharaoh's army in the Red Sea.

23. *Strong's Concordance,* G5142.

24. Ibid., H4057.

25. Moreover, the nation enjoyed success and prosperity under the reigns of David and Solomon, both of which lasted for 40 years each.

26. The Democratic Alliance for Egypt, also called the Muslim Brotherhood, and the Islamic Bloc together obtained over 50 percent of the votes, with secular parties trailing far behind.

27. Ibid., H8251.

28. Ibid., G1504.

29. Ibid., H6754.

30. Ibid., G3785.

31. Ibid., G2411.

32. Ibid., G4352.

33. See Colin Brown, "Proskyneo," under Prayer, in *New International Dictionary of New Testament Theology* (Grand Rapids, MI: Zondervan, 1980), Olive Tree Bible Software, Inc.

34. "Feast of Trumpets," in *Feasts of the Bible* (Torrance, CA: Rose Publications, 2011).

35. Compare Robert Van Kampen, *The Sign* (Wheaton: Crossway, 2000), ch. 19.

36. See Craig S. Keener, entries under Zechariah 14:16 and 1 Kings 12:32, *IVP Bible Background Commentary, Old Testament* (Downer's Grove, IL: IVP Academic, 1993), Olive Tree Bible Software, Inc.

37. *Strong's Concordance,* G4637.

Chapter 12

God's Wrath and the Fall of Babylon

*Then I saw another sign in heaven, great and marvelous, seven
angels who had seven plagues, which are the last, because in them
the wrath of God is finished.*

*After these things I saw another angel coming down from heaven,
having great authority, and the earth was illumined with his glory.
And he cried out with a mighty voice, saying, "Fallen, fallen is
Babylon the great!"*
Revelation 15:1; 18:1–2a

Seal 7: The Wrath of God Falls

The seventh seal unleashes the wrath of God on the world. By now,
all born-again Christians will have been removed from the earth, and
there is no indication that anyone else repents and turns to God. Quite
to the contrary, throughout the period of the wrath there are statements
that show that the remainder of humanity is so hardened that they can
only curse their Maker and persist in their godless idolatry:

The rest of mankind, who were not killed by these plagues,
did not repent of the works of their hands, so as not to worship
demons, and the idols of gold and of silver and of brass and of
stone and of wood, which can neither see nor hear nor walk;
and *they did not repent* of their murders nor of their sorceries
nor of their immorality nor of their thefts.

(Revelation 9:20–21, emphasis added)

Men were scorched with fierce heat; and they blasphemed the name of God who has the power over these plagues, and *they did not repent* so as to give Him glory....and they blasphemed the God of heaven because of their pains and their sores; and they did not repent of their deeds.

(Revelation 16:9, 11, emphasis added)

The fact that God's final wrath no longer has any redemptive aspect to it is confirmed by the exclamations of the angels and other beings. In Revelation 14, the three angels still offer a message of hope, proclaiming the "eternal gospel" and warning those who would worship the beast of dire consequences (vv.6–10). This, however, occurs before the late harvest rapture and the outpouring of the wrath. In contrast, during the wrath an eagle "flying in midheaven" exclaims, "Woe, woe, woe to those who dwell on the earth, because of the remaining blasts of the trumpet of the three angels who are about to sound!" (Revelation 8:13). This is no longer a message of repentance or redemption, but one of divine judgment, retribution, and vengeance.

The wrath of God is the ultimate expression of His justice and righteousness, two of His most important attributes. It represents His righteous anger at the abominations and ungodliness of a deceived world. Moreover, God's wrath comes in response to the cry of the martyrs of the fifth seal, who exclaim:

How long, O Lord, holy and true, will You refrain from judging and avenging our blood on those who dwell on the earth?

(Revelation 6:10)

Likewise, the angels and even the altar praise God during the wrath for His righteousness and justice, punishing those who had so mercilessly persecuted God's people:

301

> "Righteous are You, who are and who were, O Holy One, because You judged these things; for they poured out the blood of saints and prophets, and You have given them blood to drink. They deserve it." And I heard the altar saying, "Yes, O Lord God, the Almighty, true and righteous are Your judgments."
>
> (Revelation 16:5–7)

The destructions of this unprecedented wrath "orgy" will be beyond imagination. They will be all the more shocking, because after the furious disasters of the first four seals during the first half of the 7 years, the world will apparently enjoy a period of prosperity and security. 1 Thessalonians 5:3 says that right before the day of the Lord (the wrath of God), people will be totally unsuspecting of the fact that the worst is yet to come. Utterly deceived about the fate of the world, they will rejoice in the reign of the Antichrist, saying "Peace and Safety!" just before the wrath hits them.

How the Wrath Will Unfold

Much of the description of God's wrath in Revelation involves powerful symbolisms, often expressed through numbers. Especially important for the wrath are the numbers three, its fraction (1/3), and seven. All of these reflect the very nature and perfection of God: God is three (a trinity), and Jesus is described as a Lamb with seven horns and seven eyes (which are said to be the seven spirits of God in Revelation 5:6). Likewise, all events of the 70th week (itself a multiple of seven) are contained in the book with seven seals. Finally, God's wrath is said to unfold through seven trumpets, which in turn contain three woes and seven bowls. At the same time, the first four of these judgments involve the destruction of one third of whatever is in view. None of these symbolisms are coincidental. Rather, they communicate profound truths about God's nature, and convey to us how perfect and good and right the outpouring of His wrath will be.

The structure of God's wrath shows that it will become progressively more intense. The first four trumpets bring about the destruction or poisoning of "a third" of firstly, the land (earth, trees, grass), secondly, the sea (including sea creatures and ships), thirdly, sources of potable water (springs and rivers becoming bitter), and fourthly, the entire universe (sun, moon, stars). As we had seen before, the number 4 symbolizes globality (global reach), whereas "one third" indicates a partial (as opposed to a complete) judgment. The first four trumpets therefore merely represent the first phase of God's wrath, a foretaste of the full horrors of what is yet to come. In total, we can distinguish three phases of God's wrath:

Table 24. The three phases of God's wrath

Trumpets	1st	2nd	3rd	4th	5th	6th	7th
Woes					1st	2nd	3rd
Bowls							1st to 7th
Passages	Revelation 8:7	Revelation 8:8–9	Revelation 8:10–11	Revelation 8:12	Revelation 9:1–12	Revelation 9:13–19	Revelation 11:15; 16

1. **The first four trumpets**, the "one third" judgments on the universe. They will greatly impact on humanity, but this impact is not especially highlighted.

2. **The three woes** (5th to 7th trumpets). All of these directly and primarily affect people, and these judgments represent powerful forms of torture. The passage says that "in those days men will seek death and will not find it; they will long to die, and death flees from them" (Revelation 9:6). The apocalyptic riders of the sixth trumpet kill "one third" of mankind.

3. **The seven bowls** (contained in the 3rd woe or 7th trumpet). These represent an increased intensity compared to the judgments of the first phase: the first four bowl judgments closely match

the first four trumpet judgments, but this time the impact is complete, not just "one third." The people are said to recoil in pain and anguish from them, and there is a sense that they rapidly follow each other, much like a shock treatment. The similarities between the seven bowls and the seven trumpets are shown in the table below.

Table 25. Similarities between the seven bowls and the seven trumpets

First phase: Four Trumpets	Third Phase: Seven Bowls
1st: 1/3 of the *land* (burning)	1st: All the *land* (sores on people)
2nd: 1/3 of the *sea* (blood)	2nd: All of the *sea* (blood)
3rd: 1/3 of *springs* and *rivers* (poisoning bitterness)	3rd: All *springs* and *rivers* (blood)
4th: 1/3 of the *sun/universe* (darkness)	4th: *Sun* scorches humanity (heat)
Second Phase: Three Woes	
5th (1st woe): Locusts from bottomless pit torment humanity for 5 months	5th: Kingdom of beast darkened, humanity gnaws in pain
6th (2nd woe): Four angels bound by the Euphrates kill a third (1/3) of mankind with 200 million riders on horses	6th: Great river Euphrates dries up to pave the way for the kings from the east. Antichrist gathers armies of the world to Armageddon.
7th (3rd woe): The seven bowls (third phase), accompanied by lightnings, voices, thunders, earthquake, and great hail.	7th: Voices, thunders, lightning. The greatest earthquake ever causes all cities to fall. Babylon the Great falls. Huge hailstones.

The intensity of the judgment gradually increases from phase one to phase three, climaxing in a huge earthquake that causes all of the world's cities to fall and a torrential hail consisting of "huge hailstones, about one hundred pounds each." By comparison, the heaviest hailstone ever recorded in the United States merely weighed just under two pounds, less than 1/50th of this end times hail![1] The hail plague will cause men to "blaspheme God ... because its plague was extremely severe" (Revelation 16:21). However, the most severe judgment is probably the slaughter of the world's armies of the earth at Armageddon, symbolically described in Revelation 14:20 as a massive river of blood.

The implementation of these judgments, which are often called "plagues," resemble in many ways the ten plagues against Egypt. These also started at a lower intensity (blood, annoying frogs, and hungry insects) and then gradually became more severe (death of all livestock, deadly hail, locusts eating up anything green). Similar to the "plagues" of the end times, the Egyptian plagues at first only affected part of the land (for example, flies eating up produce) and then became devastatingly comprehensive (locusts devouring all remaining vegetation). In Egypt, the worst plague was the death of all Egyptian first-born children. Likewise, at Armageddon the best of the world's men will fall in the battle against Christ and His heavenly armies.

The Fall of Babylon: The Harlot and the City

During the time of God's wrath, another important event occurs: the fall of the "harlot Babylon." The interpretation of John's vision of Babylon is a very complicated matter and has been subject to much debate. The reason for this is that her description is very complex. Babylon is not one thing but three, reflected in three distinct themes in Revelation 17 and 18.

Firstly, Babylon is said to be a "harlot" (prostitute), full of abominable things, who has been seducing the earth with her immoralities. John writes:

> I saw a woman sitting on a scarlet beast, full of blasphemous names, having seven heads and ten horns. The woman was clothed in purple and scarlet, and adorned with gold and precious stones and pearls, having in her hand a gold cup full of abominations and of the unclean things of her immorality, and on her forehead a name was written, a mystery, "BABYLON THE GREAT, THE MOTHER OF HARLOTS AND OF THE ABOMINATIONS OF THE EARTH. *And I saw the*

woman drunk with the blood of the saints, and with the blood of the
witnesses of Jesus.

(Revelation 17:3–6, emphasis added)

Secondly, Babylon is described as a powerful commercial center, a hub of trade and wealth. Scripture says that "all who had ships at sea became rich by her wealth" (Revelation 18:19), and "your [Babylon's] merchants were the great men of the earth" (v. 23). The harlot herself is said to be extremely rich, "clothed in purple … and adorned with gold and precious stones" (v. 4). Revelation 18 goes into great detail about her significance and power as a hub of world finance and trade.

Thirdly, this trade empire is identified as a literal, geographical "city," the "great city," which will be literally destroyed by fire. Even though this destruction is identified as God's judgment, it will be executed by the Antichrist and his "ten"-king alliance:

And the ten horns which you saw, and the beast, these will hate the harlot and will make her desolate and naked, and will eat her flesh and will burn her up with fire.

(Revelations 17:16)

The woman whom you saw is the great city, which reigns over the kings of the earth.

(Revelation 17:18)

And the kings of the earth, who committed acts of immorality and lived sensuously with her, will weep and lament over her when they see the smoke of her burning, standing at a distance because of the fear of her torment, saying, "Woe, woe, the great city, Babylon, the strong city! For in one hour your judgment has come."

(Revelation 18:9–10)

The first two descriptions of Babylon point to her as a *system* or *principle*: she symbolically stands for a system of power, wealth, and seduction that has enthralled all the mighty ones ("kings") throughout the entire globe. More specifically, we can distinguish between two aspects of this system: on the one hand, its visible side, which are the presently existing structures of power, wealth, and finance. The visible system is made up of international financial institutions (IMF, World Bank, G-20), national banks and the entire banking system, stock markets, currency exchanges, hedge funds and investment firms, and other economic structures. This also includes the media and the Internet and any place or forum that controls the production and dissemination of opinions and ideologies. These manipulative institutions are the cornerstones of the deceptive power of the system. On the other hand, there is an invisible, hidden side that drives these tangible structures from behind the scenes. This side is the one that is really in charge and which control's the world's most powerful institutions: it is the spiritual aspect, the powers of greed, lust, self-esteem, and independence from God that have been in existence since mankind's expulsion from the Garden of Eden.

Therefore, it is obvious that Babylon has controlled all nations and peoples of the world, not just at present but throughout history. The harlot sits on "seven heads," symbolically said to be "seven mountains," which are "seven kings." These "mountains" are therefore not literal but entirely symbolic in character, just as the woman is not literally a "woman" and does not literally ride on a seven-headed, ten-horned beast. In chapter 10, we had identified these "kings" as a sequence of seven world empires that Satan used against God's people. The harlot "sits" on them, meaning that she has been at the heart of every empire in human history. Moreover, she is "sitting" on the beast, the Antichrist. Both the harlot and Antichrist are described as being dependent on each other.

The harlot represents the seductive powers of money, sex, and power, or, as John wrote, "the lust of the flesh ... the lust of the eyes and the boastful pride of life" (1 John 2:16). In this era of fast-paced globalization, she stands for the world's ever-accelerating drive for more and for the growing levels of stress and anxiety that this insatiable craving is producing. The world is literally drunk with the intoxicating wine of Babylon's abominable lusts. People are head-over-heels in love with the harlot, unable to realize in what utterly blind and deceived state that this fateful alliance has gotten them into. But now, it is too late. The power of the harlot literally does make "the world go round." Without her, global society as we know it would grind to a complete halt and perhaps wake up from its drunken stupor.

The Antichrist is dependent on the harlot, because he must seize upon humanity's desperate craving for all that the harlot offers in order to achieve world domination. The world will worship him because he will promise them all these things, promoting sexual "freedom" (the unrestrained and godless practice of all sexual behaviors, including homosexuality), control over their affairs (independence from God), and he will vow to maintain people's standard of living. The nations will believe that they are in control, riding on the harlot and reaping her benefits, whereas in reality they are utterly enslaved to both her and the Great Deceiver. Even the Great Deceiver, the Antichrist, is ridden by the harlot. Nobody can do without her, because she represents the very heart of Satan's deception of and control over mankind.

Thirdly, the harlot is not just a satanic spiritual world system that controls every human authority, nation and people group, but also a literal and specific location: a global city, a "great city" that represents a powerful hub of commerce and trade, as well as a place of ostentatious wealth, spiritual seduction and deception, occultism and "sorcery" (18:23). It is this city that the Antichrist will hate and utterly destroy by fire towards the end of the wrath as part of an internal power struggle amongst Satan's minions. Therefore, "Babylon" is not just one but three: two systems—one visible, one behind the scenes—and a city that completely represents and embodies these systems. This city is a perfect representation of the idolatrous system, Satan's model city that showcases and broadcasts the harlot's value system to the world.

The Literal City of Babylon and Its Demise

Some scholars try to avoid these interpretative complexities by saying that "Babylon" is not literally a "city." For them, it is only the spiritual system that the city represents. But John sees the city as being literally destroyed by the Antichrist and the "ten" kings who will unconditionally yield their power to him:

> And the ten horns [kings] which you saw, and the beast [Antichrist], these will hate the harlot and will make her desolate and naked, and will eat her flesh and will burn her up with fire....
>
> ... And every shipmaster and every passenger and sailor, and as many as make their living by the sea, stood at a distance, and were crying out as they saw the smoke of her burning, saying, "...Woe, woe, the great city, in which all who had ships at sea became rich by her wealth, for in one hour she has been laid waste!"
>
> (Revelation 17:16; 18:17–20)

The only sensible interpretation of these passages is that in the last days, the Antichrist will physically and literally destroy a "city" or major metropolitan area that represents the global spiritual, economic, and political forces symbolized by the harlot Babylon.

There is a historical precursor for such an event, which again amazingly confirms the link between the Antichrist and Sennacherib. The ancient city of Babylon was a center of rebellion against Sennacherib's rule. Consequently, the king laid siege against it, and in 689 BC he razed it to the ground. His own records state:

> Its [Babylon's] inhabitants, young and old, I did not spare, and with their corpses I filled the streets of the city … the town itself and its houses, from their foundations to the roofs, I destroyed, I devastated, by fire I overthrew….[2]

For several years, Babylon remained uninhabited. Never before had the city been subjected to such destruction, and neither would it ever again (its end came gradually as its importance declined after the death of Alexander the Great, the last emperor who sought to reside in Babylon).[3] Prior to this, Sennacherib had tried to use political means to reign in Babylon's rebelliousness, because even though it was not the capital of his empire, the city was an important center of religion, trade, and commerce. The peoples of his realm were therefore shocked at the thoroughness and viciousness with which he destroyed Babylon.[4] These historic events closely correspond to John's prophetic vision, which includes a lengthy lament of the kings and merchants of the earth who watch the destruction of the "great city" with a great sense of shock and disbelief. Like the historic Babylon, the end times "Babylon" will never be rebuilt. It will forever remain a deserted monument to humanity's idolatry.

There are even more parallels between ancient Babylon and the Babylon of Revelation. Just as Revelation 17:3 describes the harlot as riding on the beast (Antichrist), meaning that one needs the other, Assyria and Babylon depended on each other in Sennacherib's time. Just as Sennacherib angered many of his people and significantly weakened his empire by destroying Babylon, the Antichrist will equally risk cutting himself in his own flesh when he moves against the harlot. There must be a really important reason for him to make this decision. John says that he and his "ten" king alliance[5] will "hate" or "detest" (*miseo*[6]) the harlot—a strong word conveying intense negative emotions. It may be that the rationale behind this act will be similar to that of Sennacherib: even though useful and important, the harlot will eventually pose an obstacle to the Antichrist's unchallenged global rule. The fact that he is prophesied to "hate" her so much suggests that she will greatly provoke him through rebellion or betrayal.

Because the destruction of the Great City will be accompanied by the shock and grief of the onlooking world, it is likely that the Antichrist and his henchmen will bring about her doom in a secretive way. They may even make this event appear to be an accident or an act of evil performed by someone else. Babylon's destruction could, for example, be achieved by a nuclear device, perhaps detonated by a terrorist with the support of the Antichrist—or made to look like an act of terrorism so that he will not receive the world's blame for such an infamous act. He would certainly have the ability to carry out such an insidious plan. But this is of course purely speculative. What we do know is that the Great City will be utterly destroyed. However, by satisfying his rage, the Antichrist will be unsuspectingly carrying out God's will. He will be a tool of God's judgment against the idolatrous Great City.

The Phases of Babylon's Judgment

This explains why Babylon's fall will occur over several phases. In Revelation 14:8, an angel cries out, "Fallen, fallen is Babylon the great," right before another angel warns those on the earth not to worship the beast. This timing is confirmed by the angel's call to God's people in Revelation 18:4: "Come out of her, my people, so that you will not participate in her sins and receive of her plagues." This can only refer to "foolish virgin" believers and new converts during the tribulation, in short, those who are left during the tribulations. But the destruction of the actual city that is called "Babylon" is not until Revelation 16:19, at the final (seventh) bowl judgment, which comes after the great tribulation, the late harvest rapture, and the very last phase of God's wrath. It is only then that this monstrous city is given the "cup of the wine of His [God's] fierce wrath." How can this be explained?

The first fall of Babylon, announced in Revelation 14:8, will occur right before the rise of the Antichrist to global domination. This fall pertains to the visible financial and economic system of the world. In total, this system will fall three times, as we had outlined in the previous chapter: firstly, at the world financial crises that began in 2008; secondly, just before the rise of the Antichrist; and thirdly, during the third seal. The most significant of these falls is the second one, because this event will play a key role in bringing the Antichrist into power (the third fall will further cement his grip on the world). Therefore, this occasion is especially highlighted in Revelation 14: there, the announcement of this second fall comes just before the warning against taking the mark of the beast, which confirms that this event will take place before these marks are being administered.

The fall of the spiritual system that drives the visible financial-economic system begins, in a sense, with the demise of its model city, the literal physical "great city" of "Babylon." Its destruction will then occur gradually during Christ's millennial reign but will not be completed until the final destruction of Satan, Death and Hades in the lake of fire—after the millennium and right before the eternal state (Revelation 20).

The call of the angel in Revelation 18:4 to the church to come out and refuse to be part of "Babylon" as a deceptive spiritual system applies to God's people of all ages. However, it is also especially directed at our end times generation. One of the crucial mistakes of the foolish virgin believers is to fail to heed this call and to remain entangled in the things of the world. Once the tribulations begin, these Christians will literally be called to quit the careers and positions that are rooted in the harlot's financial and economic system and to enter the wilderness where God has prepared a place for them. Believers who are destined to be protected in the wilderness are then literally required to leave the physical city. Finally, the very last call to "come out of her, my people" will be addressed to the Jews, the last group of God's people to be saved. This call will go forth during the wrath of God.

Those who will not heed these two final calls (firstly to the last believers before the late harvest rapture and secondly to the Jews during the wrath) are the undecided and the pretenders. The fact that they remain in the system and in the city will show that they have not put their faith in God alone. Then, they will be like Lot's wife, who longingly looked back to the city of Sodom that she still loved within her heart and turned into a pillar of salt (a powerful picture of spiritual death). Likewise, those who will not heed the call to leave "Babylon" will perish together with the unbelieving world.

Babylon, Rome, and the Role of Catholicism

Since the Reformation, many Protestant scholars have interpreted all three aspects of "Babylon" as being represented by the city of Rome. The harlot is said to sit on "seven mountains," and Rome has long been called the "city on seven hills." Also, most Christian persecution at John's time was initiated by Roman emperors, and so his contemporaries certainly associated "Babylon" with Rome. The reformers in particular believed that the harlot symbolized, on the one hand, the corrupt religion of pagan Rome, and on the other hand the "false religion" of papal Rome (the Catholic Church). At that point in history, this association was indeed almost perfect:

- The harlot represents the powers that persecuted God's people as described in Revelation 18:24: "And in her was found the blood of prophets and of saints and of all who have been slain on the earth." Both the Roman emperors and the Catholic Church killed many of God's true followers and were strongly anti-Jewish.

313

- The harlot represents the spiritual powers of deception and idolatry (18:23). Both pagan and papal Rome did represent such corrupt, man-exalting religious systems.

- The harlot embodies wealth and extravagant luxurious living. Most of chapter 18 is devoted to a description of her incredible riches and lavish lifestyle. Again, both Rome pagan and Rome papal were extremely wealthy and economically powerful at their peaks, but not always.

- She is said to be "the great city." Rome was the greatest city of the ancient world, the seat of power of the Roman Empire. In a spiritual sense, it was the religious powerhouse of Europe during the era of Catholicism's supreme reign.

However, when we attempt to apply Revelation's Babylon to contemporary Rome and today's Catholicism, there are at least four major flaws. Firstly, even though the Catholic Church was a major enemy of God's people during the times of the reformers, its political and economic influence began to wane after the Reformation and is becoming increasingly insignificant. In regards to spiritual influence, the church's moral authority even in Catholic heartlands such as Ireland, Spain,

Figure 16. Illustration of the harlot Babylon. Source: Wikimedia Commons.

or Italy is rapidly declining, accelerated by the scores of child abuse cases that have come to light in recent years. If anything, the dogmas of the Catholic Church are severely at odds with postmodern relativism and its pluralistic tolerance thinking, which explains why the church's active membership in Europe has tumbled. In Germany, regular Sunday mass attendance declined from 50 percent in 1950 to 13 percent in 2009. In Ireland, it fell from 82 percent in 1982 to 48-45 percent in 2006, and the influence of the church over society is being actively pushed back in the wake of a major child abuse scandal.[7]

Especially under the present Pope Benedict XVI, Catholicism is poised to maintain its traditional understanding of the Word of God as absolute truth that must not bow to the spirit of the age. Overall, the church's theological positions are certainly contradictory. On the one hand, it continues to uphold its own extra-biblical traditions, such as the worship of Mary and church saints, or the practice of celibacy, over scriptural teachings. But on the other hand, those scriptural truths that Catholicism does uphold it seems determined to defend against the onslaught of postmodern relativism. Pope Benedict himself published several apologetics books that defend the absolute divine authority of Scripture. Therefore, while the Catholic Church continues to believe in the false doctrine of purgatory, it staunchly upholds the truth that those who are not saved in Christ will be eternally damned to hell. Likewise, it affirms that extra-marital relations, divorce, and homosexuality are sinful. Overall, as Protestantism is liberalizing on all sides, the Catholic Church is now increasingly looking more faithful to the Bible than many Protestant denominations! At present, large sections of Protestantism are readily compromising the authority of God's Word as they bow to the spirit of the age, and the first doctrine they often sacrifice on the altar of postmodernist relativism is that of eternal damnation of the unbelievers. These parts of God's church are easily manipulated by the Antichrist. By comparison, if the Catholic Church maintains its current doctrines and continues to reject the postmodern spirit, the Antichrist will end up having to destroy Catholicism because it will not bow to his demands.

Secondly, the overall description of the harlot Babylon far exceeds the total influence of pagan or papal Rome even at the height of their power. The harlot sits on the beast and its seven heads. She is said to have made *all nations and kings* drunk with the wine of her spiritual idolatry and to be reigning (present tense!) "over the kings of the earth." It is evident that she symbolizes Satan's entire spiritual, economic, and political power over all empires and nations, both past and present. The harlot's description is so comprehensive, and her influence so all-encompassing, that she cannot possibly be just one empire, institution, or religion. She represents Satan's spiritual world system, which includes every Christian or non-Christian ideology (including atheism) that sets itself up against God's true Word and persecutes God's true people. Because Babylon is the force behind all attacks on God and his followers, all the blood of God's people that was ever spilled from the dawn of humanity is symbolically said to be found in her. This cannot apply to a single belief or power system such as the Roman Empire or the Catholic Church, not even at their peak, and especially not at the present time.

Thirdly, when Babylon is said to be a "great city," her description in fact invokes not one but two great cities, both of which have been centers for the work of Satan against God and His people. Her depiction of sitting on "seven mountains" clearly points to Rome, the supreme world power of John's time. But John also calls her "Babylon," a symbolism that speaks especially to a Jewish audience and the fate of the Jewish nation in the Old Testament. From the times of Nimrod to the days of Nebuchadnezzar, whose army exiled God's people and destroyed God's temple, Babylon has embodied the satanic world power that sought to destroy God's redemptive plan for humanity. For the Old Testament prophets, Babylon, not Rome, was the epitome of evil and idolatry. And like Rome, ancient Babylon was the seat of the world's most dominant empire at the time. From this perspective, the picture of the harlot Babylon is inherently symbolic of *not one but of two* great cities: Babylon (as well as all Mesopotamian empires of the region, including Assyria and Nimrod's ancient kingdom), which stands for the anti-Christian world power of the Old Testament era; and Rome as the anti-Christian empire of the New Testament (early church) era. Therefore, even as a city, the harlot cannot be reduced to just Rome.

Fourthly, neither of these two cities can—as of today—fit the requirements of all that the Babylon of Revelation stands for. Present-day Rome is neither a city of great political and economic power (it plays no role whatsoever in the governance of the EU and is not likely to take on such a role), nor does it have a major spiritual hold over current world ideologies such as postmodernism that will play a major role in an Antichrist-dominated world. Right now, there are no indications whatsoever that this will change. If one would view the European Union as a major anti-Christian force of the end times, one would have to focus on Berlin, seat of Europe's most powerful national government and economy, or Brussels, headquarters of the European Parliament and the European Commission.

Likewise, speculations that the ancient city of Babylon in today's Iraq will again be rebuilt into the Antichrist's world capital seem completely utopian. At present, the city does not even exist (apart from ruins). There are tentative plans to reconstruct it, but almost nothing has been done so far. Moreover, compared to other non-Western contenders such as Russia, China, or India, the nation of Iraq is extremely unlikely to become a major player in the global affairs of the end times. It commands no significant military or financial power and is not even a member of the G-20.

Can a Rebuilt Ancient Babylon be the "Babylon the Great"?

Those who irrefutably believe in the future rise of literal ancient Babylon point out that the Antichrist will somehow be able to accomplish the amazing feat of lifting this city to a position of world dominance, perhaps based on Iraq's vast oil reserves. But those who assert that the Babylon of the end times must be the literal ancient city of Babylon, simply because it is called "Babylon," run into a number of significant textual problems.

Firstly, in order to be consistently literal, the literalist approach must take all symbolic references in Revelation 17 and 18 to be literally fulfilled. A literal view therefore has to believe that the statement "in her was found the blood of prophets and of saints and of all who have been slain on the earth [this includes all slain unbelievers who were killed throughout history]" (18:24) must also be literally true. Secondly, ancient Babylon was located on the plain of Shinar and therefore cannot be associated with literally being seated on "seven mountains."

But as we had seen before, the description of "Babylon" is a highly complex combination of symbolic and literal language. Babylon herself is called a "mystery," and John says that understanding her requires a "mind which has wisdom" (17:9). There is therefore no need to insist that Revelation's "Babylon" *must* inevitably be the ancient Babylon. Likewise, Old Testament prophecies about ancient Babylon do not necessitate a resurrection of the city from obscurity to world prominence (see the text box).

Old Testament Prophecies About Babylon

A common argument that ancient Babylon must be rebuilt in order to represent the harlot city of Babylon bases itself on Old Testament prophecy. Several passages in Isaiah and Jeremiah are said to have had no historic fulfillment and therefore must come about through a literal reconstruction of the historic city:

> For behold, I am going to arouse and bring up against
> Babylon
> A horde of great nations from the land of the north,
> And they will draw up their battle lines against her;
> From there she will be taken captive.
>
> Jeremiah 50:9

> The broad wall of Babylon will be completely razed
> And her high gates will be set on fire.
>
> Jeremiah 51:58a

> "Therefore the desert creatures will live there along with
> the jackals;
> The ostriches also will live in it,
> And it will never again be inhabited
> Or dwelt in from generation to generation.
> As when God overthrew Sodom
> And Gomorrah with its neighbors," declares the LORD,
> "No man will live there,
> Nor will any son of man reside in it."
>
> (Jeremiah 50:39–40)

> Flee from the midst of Babylon,
> And each of you save his life!
> Do not be destroyed in her punishment,
> For this is the LORD'S time of vengeance.
>
> (Jeremiah 51:6)

The arguments derived from these passages are as follows:

1. Historically, Babylon was not attacked from the north but from the west—and not by several nations but by the Persians under Cyrus.

2. Cyrus did not actually destroy Babylon but left it completely intact. Babylon was not razed to the ground, its wall was still standing, and there was no sudden, sweeping destruction as compared to the fate of Sodom and Gomorrah.

3. People did not flee Babylon or become evicted from the city but remained there. Babylon continued to be populated for centuries after its fall to the Persians. Therefore, the prophecy still awaits its complete fulfillment.

The first of these arguments is the weakest. Cyrus led a coalition of Medes and Persians. In Jeremiah 50:3 the attackers are simply called "a nation," indicating that verse 9 likewise does not imply a coalition of many nations, although the Medes and Persians may well have had foreign mercenaries in their midst. Additionally, their empire was in fact located both north and west of Babylon (they had previously taken the northern Assyrian city of Nineveh together with the surrounding regions), and it is therefore accurate to describe their attack as coming from the north.

In order to examine the other points, we should take a step back and analyze how a similar prophecy regarding Israel came to be fulfilled. In Deuteronomy, God makes the following threats to His people should they be unfaithful to His covenant with them:

> Now the generation to come, your sons who rise up after you and the foreigner who comes from a distant land, when they see the plagues of the land and the diseases with which the LORD has afflicted it, will say, "All its land is brimstone and salt, a burning waste, unsown and unproductive, and no

> grass grows in it, like the overthrow of Sodom and Gomorrah,
> Admah and Zeboiim, which the LORD overthrew in His
> anger and in His wrath."
>
> (Deuteronomy 29:22–23)

Here, as with Babylon, the destructive punishment is compared to the fate of Sodom and Gomorrah. But did that mean that Israel or Jerusalem would be destroyed in such a sudden and drastic way, with nothing left? No. Instead, God's punishment was gradual. The Israelites were exiled in several stages by different Assyrian and Babylonian kings. When Nebuchadnezzar took the city in 586 BC, he burned the temple and razed the walls, but he did not burn the entire city to the ground. Some people were left in the city, giving Nehemiah a foundation for rebuilding it over a century later. God's "Sodom-and-Gomorrah" punishment for Israel was not an instant and total annihilation, as was the case with these two cities. Rather, it was a symbolic picture of the vast (although not complete) destruction that Israel would be subjected to.

Likewise, the "Sodom-and-Gomorrah" judgment over Babylon also took place in stages. Its first phase occurred under the Assyrians. Soon after his ascension to power, Sennacherib crushed a Babylonian rebellion against him and deported 208,000 captives to the Assyrian regions.[8] In 689 BC, after Babylon's rebelliousness had continued to threaten his throne, Sennacherib leveled and burned the city to the ground, exiling its population and causing the city to be completely deserted for several years. Several years after King Cyrus took the city in 539 BC without a major battle, Babylon rebelled against Medo-Persian rule (approx. 522–516 BC). Under Darius, Cyrus' successor, Babylon was eventually captured a second time. This time, severe punishment was inflicted on the city. The Greek historian Herodotus wrote:

> Dareios [Darius] when he had overcome the Babylonians, first took away the wall from round their city and pulled down all the gates; for when Cyrus took Babylon before him, he did neither of these things: and secondly Dareios [Darius] impaled the leading men to the number of about three thousand....[9]

Now, Babylon's wall was razed and the gates destroyed, just as prophesied by Jeremiah. In subsequent centuries, the city was conquered by numerous other rulers and experienced varying degrees of destruction and desolation as its importance continued to decline. In 275 BC, the Seleucid ruler Antiochus I forcibly removed most of Babylon's inhabitants in order to populate his new capital Seleucia. In 130 BC, the Parthians invaded the city. They treated its residents with "extreme cruelty," selling many of those who had remained into slavery and burning its main parts (all in further fulfillment of Jeremiah 50–51).[10] When the city became deserted, the Parthian kings used it as a "park for wild beasts," just as stated in Jeremiah 50:39.[11] By the first century AD, nothing was left of Babylon but sand-covered ruins. Since then, as Jeremiah foretold, it was "never again ... inhabited" (50:39). From that perspective, one could even argue that Babylon must in fact never ever be rebuilt, so that God's Word through Jeremiah is not contradicted.

Secondly, the literal Babylon proposition runs into the problem that there are several literal aspects that *must indeed be literally fulfilled in order for John's vision to make sense. But for those,* a rebuilt ancient Babylon cannot fit the bill. Most importantly, the end times Babylon must have a deep-water seaport for it to be a major hub of trade and commerce. The problem here is that ancient Babylon was only located at the Euphrates River, which has by now shifted away from its original location. At present, the ruins of Babylon are about 400 miles away from the Persian Gulf. Furthermore, nowhere in Iraq can we find a deep-water port because nearly the entire Persian Gulf is very shallow (incidentally, Rome suffers from the same problem, being landlocked and 50 miles away from the nearest seaport.[12])

Additionally, the Persian Gulf is tucked away between the Arabian peninsula and Iran, which entirely rules out that it will ever become a global trade hub—not because of politics, which can always change, but because it is not located on the way to anywhere. The only use for the gulf is oil export. Any tradesmen would consider it absurd, for example, to route goods shipments from Asia to Europe through the gulf, then via the Euphrates and perhaps additional canals into Babylon, then re-load them and ship them right back the same way.

Moreover, Babylon's description in Revelation speaks of an incredibly international and culturally-diverse trade hub that buys and sells all kinds of goods and which houses craftsmen, artisans, musicians, and culturally-sophisticated people of all walks. Even if the Antichrist were capable of forcibly removing the world's financial and cultural institutions and artificially transplanting them into such an awkward corner of the world, it would just make no sense at all. It is even more absurd to think that he would rebuild Babylon at a vast expense and then soon after totally destroy it.

All arguments for ancient Babylon seem so completely contrived that its proponents really only have one single rationale: that their perspective is the most "literal" and therefore by implication the best. But this is precisely what we want to argue against. In our view, biblical literalism is essential and important, but there are contexts in which literalism itself necessitates figurative interpretation, as we have just shown. There are parts of Revelation that are explicitly intended to be symbolic. "Babylon" as harlot and city belongs in the symbolic category, because she is said to be a "mystery" that requires "wisdom," as her interpretation is not immediately obvious (the hint of it being a "mystery" also speaks against Rome, which would have been the by far most obvious understanding of John's contemporaries). Moreover, Babylon's description as both woman (not a literal woman!) and city (with literal aspects but also many symbolic implications) are closely intertwined: John writes that "the woman whom you saw is the great city" (17:18). This is not literally but spiritually true. Here, it is significant that the Old Testament referred to several cities as "harlots" (Tyre, Nineveh, Jerusalem) but never called ancient Babylon by this name! In the case of the end times Babylon, therefore, an overly literal approach obscures the complex spiritual message that God is trying to convey to us.

When it comes to the end times, people invariably switch into "instant coffee" mode. Suddenly, because the topic is the "end times," everything is believed to be possible, regardless of how unrealistic or contrived it may sound. Logical thinking is turned off, and even the wildest speculations will find open ears. Even though the end times are of course a very special and highly supernatural time in human history, we believe this "instant coffee" understanding of the end times to be inherently flawed. Babylon's rise will almost certainly not be a supernatural "rush job" of the Antichrist, aided by massive geographical shifts so that the city might somehow come to be located by a river or sea (such events are not implied by any of the first five seals, during which the reconstruction of the city would have to occur at the very latest). Rather, it is far more likely that the growth of "Babylon" has been occurring for quite a while!

We believe that Satan has been nurturing Babylon the "great city" for some time. After all, the city is said to totally embody the harlot in the minds of the world. This must mean that its very name will immediately evoke connotation of power, materialism, and wealth. Such strong associations do not develop in a few months or years, through an "instant coffee" town stamped out of the ground. Besides, the ancient Babylon was, above all, a symbol of ancient religion and cultural achievement, whereas commerce, trade, and economic power were associated with major harbor cities such as the Phoenician Tyre, Egyptian Alexandria, or medieval Venice. Likewise, the world's great lament and grief over Babylon's fall is a certain indication that the city has been developing a long-standing reputation.

Babylon "the great" has almost certainly played a hegemonic role at least since the second great historic convergence of World War II and perhaps since the advent of capitalist mass production, mass consumerism, and global finance. Throughout the advance of modernity, it has been actively shaping world history as we are nearing the end, placing itself in a position to be the "Babylon" of the final days. Babylon the "great city" is not a sudden revelation of the end times. Instead, it is a city that has all along been groomed for its role at the end of the age, a city that has developed into the hub of global capitalism since the dawn of modernity in the early 20th century. Which city will first come to people's minds when you ask them about the financial center of the world, about the heart of the globe's economic "spider web," where all threads converge? In all likelihood, that city is "Babylon the Great."

Identifying "Babylon the Great City" of the End Times

Identifying a literal modern "Babylon" is difficult. Both Babylon and Rome were not only capitals of empires but also major religious and economic centers. In today's multi-polar world, which is no longer dominated by one single superpower or empire, there is no straightforward equivalent to all that Rome or Babylon all represented. But interestingly, during Sennacherib's time, Babylon was not actually the capital or primary city. It did not exert direct political control and probably did not have as large a population as the empire's capital, Nineveh. However, Babylon was nevertheless of great spiritual, economic, and symbolic importance. The city's very name was full of meaning and inspiration for people throughout the Assyrian empire.

The same may well be the case with the "Babylon" of the end times: it does not have to be a literal world capital that dominates every facet of the global world system. The Antichrist may not necessarily have his primary headquarters there (especially since he ends up destroying it). But it must be a place of great spiritual, economic, and global significance, capable of symbolizing the deceptive power of the satanic harlot. From Scripture, it is evident that the Babylon of the end times must be a truly vast and powerful megacity just like ancient Rome and Babylon were. Even the literal Greek points to the fact that it must be a "megacity": the Greek words for "great city" in Revelation 17:18 are *polis megale*, from which we get the English term megapolis or megacity!

Even though Scripture does not permit a certain identification and our assessment might change as we get closer to the time, there are several factors that can help point us towards a particular major modern metropolitan area. We feel that the time has now indeed come to identify who "Babylon the Great" really is.

Global Cities 2008/2025 by GMP and Population

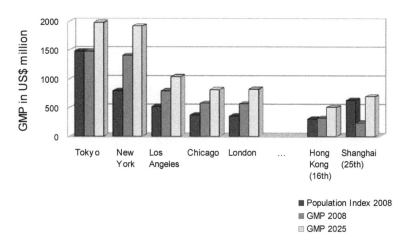

Figure 17. Global Cities 2008/2025 by GMP and population

When we look at the world's largest metropolitan areas in terms of economy (Gross Metropolitan Product or GMP) and population, both now and projected into the future (2025), the only obvious choices are Tokyo and New York, both with a current GMP around US$1.4 trillion, almost twice as that of the third-placed city. Los Angeles, London, and Shanghai deserve some additional consideration because of their significance in media (Hollywood), finance (London) and future growth potential (Shanghai has the highest growth rate, although it is still not projected to catch up to the top by 2025). The other places cannot really be considered mega-cities by either criterion.

However, besides economy and population, we must also examine other factors. The harlot Babylon is not just an economic powerhouse of considerable size. She also plays a pivotal role in commerce, finance, and trade, a financial world capital so to speak; she is incredibly rich and a major consumer of luxury goods; she is a status symbol, a brand name that stands for the deceptive value system of the harlot; she is a center of the spirit of the age that draws people to itself and deceives them with its appeal; and finally, she is an incredibly international city, sitting "on many waters," which represent "peoples and multitudes and nations and tongues" (Revelation 17:1, 15). This does not literally refer to multiple streams or rivers. Rather, it casts the megacity of Babylon as a vast multi-ethnic melting pot that combines many different cultures and value systems.

Interestingly, several research institutions have been developing indexes that attempt to measure what a "global city" is. These indexes measure world cities based on a wide range of criteria, including economic importance, political power, and influence over global policy, as well as decision-making processes, cultural and media activities (including publishing, news, and movie production), and how international a city is—as measured by the share of its foreign residents, the number of international visitors, and the amount of international organizations that it headquarters or whose meetings it hosts. Knight Frank also calculated a projection of their index 10 years into the future (for the year 2021). For the table below, we have added several other factors, especially markers of financial influence such as hedge funds volume and stock market size. Finally, we included the size of cities' homosexual populations as a relevant factor, since the destruction of Babylon is not just an act of the Antichrist's hate but also of God's judgment on her for her sorcery and immorality (Revelation 16:19; 17:17; 18:9).

Table 26. Comparison of influential factors of major global cities

Rank	Knight Frank Global Cities Index (2011)[13]	K.F. World's Leading Cities for 2021	Global Power City Index (2011)[14]	Global Cities Index (2010)[15]	No. of billionaires (2011)[16]	Hedge funds volume (2009)[17]	Largest stock exchanges[18] (2011)	Homosexual population (US only)[19]
1	New York	New York	New York	New York	Moscow (78)	New York (47%)	New York (NYSE, $20.2tn)	New York (272,000)
2	London	London	London	London	New York (57)	London (21%)	New York (NASDAQ, $13.6tn)	Los Angeles (154,000)
3	Paris	Beijing	Paris	Tokyo	London (39)	Boston (7%)	Tokyo ($3.3tn)	Chicago (114,000)
4	Tokyo	Shanghai	Tokyo	Paris	Hong-Kong (38)	Greenwich (7%)	London ($3.2tn)	San Francisco (94,000)
5	Brussels	Hong-Kong	Singapore	Hong-Kong	Istanbul (30)	Westport (4%)	Shanghai ($2.4tn)	Phoenix (63,000)

When we combine all of these factors, only one clear winner remains, even when we look 10 years into the future: **New York City**, home of Wall Street and the United Nations. In the 1930s, New York surpassed the population of London and became the world's first megacity (defined as a city whose population exceeds 10 million).[20] Together with London, another key global financial city but much smaller in terms of population and economy, it is effectively the financial headquarter of the world. The combined trade value of its multiple stock exchanges is over four times larger than that of second-placed London ($45.2 versus $10.3 trillion) and more than the rest of the top 10 global stock markets combined. The city's hedge funds manage about half of the world's entire hedge funds' assets, implying incredible financial leverage and control over world economic affairs.

Not many are aware that New York's Federal Reserve Bank holds the world's largest gold repository in its underground vault, valued at $415 billion,[21] which is 70 percent more than at Fort Knox and mostly owned by the central banks of other nations. The aggregated annual personal income of its population (that is, the amount of money earned by all people who live there) stands at just under $1 trillion, almost twice as high as that of Los Angeles.[22] Overall, New York City is the undisputed figurehead of global capitalism. Among the rich and influential people around the globe, it has become popular to own a second apartment in Manhattan. Therefore, even if Moscow recently surpassed New York in the number of billionaires who live there as their primary residence, the financial decision-making influence of New York is far greater than that of Moscow

Figure 18. The New York Stock Exchange, Wall Street, New York City. Source: Wikimedia Commons.

or any other city in the world. Even by 2021, this is not projected to change.

Besides financial dominance, there are other factors of spiritual significance to consider. The combined media power of New York City represents a major force through which the enemy can broadcast the values and messages of the postmodern spirit of the age around the world. The city houses seven of the world's top eight global advertising agency networks, three of the world's four largest record labels, four of the United States' top 10 newspapers, all four major American broadcast networks, and the United States' largest (the world's second largest[23]) theater district, which attracts over 12 million tourists annually to its stages. This has earned it the title of being the "media capital of the world," ahead of Los Angeles.[24]

But New York's influence extends beyond finance and media. Knight Frank ranked New York as the second most politically powerful city in the world after Washington D.C. (with Brussels, the seat of the European Union, only coming third).[25] It headquarters the United Nations, which will play a significant role in end times dynamics. Being home to the UN opens up the important possibility that the destruction of "Babylon"/New York will be linked to a growing competition between the Antichrist and the UN, even though initially the UN will probably pave the way for the Antichrist's rise to global power.

The financial and commercial power of New York places it right at the heart of "Babylon" as a global financial and economic system, the visible side of the satanic harlot. But the city is also an essential part of the underlying spiritual system. New York epitomizes the American dream of individual happiness through wealth, a false aspiration that has been shaping the aspirations and desires of the whole world. This dream is essentially about the individualistic pursuit of pleasure and happiness through entertainment and materialism—precisely what the harlot Babylon stands for. In that way, the harlot has played a crucial role in the creation of lukewarm Christianity. Many foolish virgin believers are the direct result of Babylon's hold over the church. This is especially rampant in churches that have fallen prey to the deceptions of the prosperity gospel.

Another important aspect is that the city headquarters many large, non-profit organizations such as the Ford Foundation, the Mellon Foundation, the Rockefeller Foundation, the Carnegie Corporation, and the Soros Open Society Foundations. Every year, these foundations disburse millions of dollars into education, research, charitable, and political causes. As a consequence, they exercise vast control over the future direction of scientific advances. In contrast to the Bill Gates Foundation, for example, New York's foundations are mostly focused on the social sciences (humanities), putting them at the forefront of promoting postmodernity's humanist, liberal, and relativistic views and values.

New York City even has a prominent symbol of humanist enlightenment right in its midst. The Statue of Liberty was given to the United States by France in 1886 as a token of friendship that had grown between the two nations during the American Revolution and the subsequent French Revolution. The statue's official name is "Liberty Enlightening the World," and its design was inspired by Libertas, the Roman goddess of liberty. Libertas is also depicted on the New York state flag. Even though the statue was intended to symbolize freedom from human oppression and tyranny, its true spiritual meaning is humanity's

Figure 19. The Statue of Liberty. Source: Wikimedia Commons.

independence from God. It is this kind of "freedom" from their creator that is enshrined right in the center of New York, symbolized by the very icon that the city most identifies itself with.

New York, world capital of money and pleasure, truly epitomizes what the harlot represents because of this individualistic, humanistic, and utilitarian worldview that it has been broadcasting to the world. The worship of individual "freedom" also forms the basic attitude behind postmodern relativism and New Age religions: feel free to assemble your belief system based on what suits you best, reflecting Satan's core lie of "do what you want." New York's influence therefore stems not just from its record-setting economic and other figures, but from the magic pull that its value system has exerted over all nations. Just as the serpent deceived Eve into eating the apple in the Garden of Eden, at the end of the age, Satan is using the "big apple" to mislead the entire world.

New York City may perhaps be overtaken in terms of sheer economic size by ascending rivals such as Shanghai within the next 20-40 years, and other cities trump it in selected individual disciplines—for example, London for the total value of annual financial transactions, San Francisco for the percentage of the homosexual population, Washington D.C. or Beijing for political power, or Shanghai for cargo shipping volume. But its combined significance and symbolic status as the global figurehead of capitalist materialism and humanistic freedom from God will remain until the end. Even though it may not necessarily become a political world capital that exerts literal political power, New York will likely be the "Rome" and the "Babylon" of the end times—a city that "rules" the world through the combined impact of its ideological and financial influence. When it goes up in flames, the world's loss will be great indeed. Its kings and merchants will truly lament and weep, exclaiming "What city is like the great city?" (Revelation 18:18). The destruction of New York will rob the world of all it wanted and craved for. It will be like a drunk who watches in disbelief as his vast liquor reserves go up in flames, even while he is taking the last sip out of his bottle.

Chapter 12 Notes

1. See http://en.wikipedia.org/wiki/Hail.
2. Richard A. Gabriel, *Great Captains of Antiquity* (Westport, CT: Greenwood Press, 2001), 59.
3. Alexander the Great died in Babylon in 323 BC.
4. Many considered his removal of the statue of the chief Babylonian god Marduk to be an infamous act of heresy.
5. Incidentally, these "ten" kings are not the same as the "ten" horns/kings of Daniel 7, because the Antichrist subdues three of the kings mentioned in Daniel 7, and they arise before him. In contrast, the "ten" kings of Revelation 17 are said to arise together with the Antichrist for "one hour," and they will willingly yield their power to him. Like the "ten" kings of Daniel 7, their number is most likely symbolic rather than literal.
6. *Strong's Concordance*, G3404.
7. "Gottesdienstteilnehmer Katholisches Deutschland," http://fowid. de/fileadmin/datenarchiv/Kirchliches_Leben/Gottesdienstbesucher_ Katholiken_1950_2009.pdf. "Where now for weekly Mass attendance," The Irish Catholic, http://www.irishcatholic.ie/site/content/where- now-weekly-mass-attendance-michael-kelly.
8. From both city and surrounding region. See D. D. Luckenbill, *The Annals of Sennacherib,* Oriental Institute Publications, vol. 2 (Chicago: University of Chicago Press, 1927), 10, http://oi.uchicago.edu/pdf/oip2.pdf.
9. Herodotus, *The Histories of Herodotus. Volumes I and II (complete),* 3.159 trans. G.C. Macaulay (MobileReference, 2009).
10. George Rawlinson, *Parthia* (1893; repr., New York: Cosimo Books, 2007), 119, Google Books e-book. Peter Christensen, *The Decline of Iranshahr: Irrigation and Environments in the History of the Middle East, 500 B.C. to A.D. 1500* (Copenhagen: Museum Tusculanum Press, University of Copenhagen, 1993), 61.
11. Johann Jahn, Jacques Basnage (sieur de Beauval), *Jahn's History of the Hebrew Commonwealth* (New York: G. & C. Carvill, 1828), 224, Google Books e-book.
12. Rome's nearest seaport is the relatively small town of Civitavecchia. This port is of no particular international significance and certainly does not feature in the list of the world's 50 busiest ports. See http://en.wikipedia. org/wiki/World%27s_busiest_container_port.
13. The Knight Frank Global Cities Index is published by the London-based estate agent Knight Frank LLP together with Citibank. See http://www. knightfrank.com/wealthreport/2011/global-cities-survey.
14. The Global Power City Index is produced by the Institute for Urban Strategies at The Mori Memorial Foundation in Tokyo.

15. The Global Cities Index represents a collaboration between the journal *Foreign Policy*, A. T. Kearney, and the Chicago Council on Global Affairs.
16. See http://www.forbes.com/sites/calebmelby/2012/03/16/moscow-beats-new-york-london-in-list-of-billionaire-cities/.
17. Based on the world's top 100 hedge funds, by assets under management. See http://hedgefundblogman.blogspot.de/2009/08/top-hedge-fund-cities-based-on-aum.html.
18. Measured by the value of stocks trade. When measured by the market capitalization of their listed companies, the NSE ranks 1st, NASDAQ 2nd, and Tokyo's TSE 3rd. See http://en.wikipedia.org/wiki/Stock_exchange.
19. The New York metropolitan area's total gay, lesbian, transsexual, and bisexual (LBGT) population was estimated to be three times as high as San Francisco's, although in San Francisco the share of this group of the total population is higher (15.4 percent compared to New York's 4.5 percent). Data based on the American Community Survey, 2006, http://en.wikipedia.org/wiki/Gay_village#LGBT_populations. Exact figures for the LBGT population of other world cities are difficult to find. In Tokyo, LGBTs are not widely accepted, and Tokyo remains one of the few major world cities that does not hold gay parades. Moreover, in Japan same-sex marriages are not legal, whereas New York State legalized such marriages in June 2011.
20. NYC remained the world's only megacity until 1962, when Tokyo's population surpassed 10 million. See "Tokyo's History, Geography and Population," http://www.metro.tokyo.jp/ENGLISH/PROFILE/overview01.htm.
21. In 2011, see http://en.wikipedia.org/wiki/Federal_Reserve_Bank_of_New_York.
22. In 2006, the total annual personal income of the New York City metropolitan area stood at 935 billion, compared to Los Angeles's 513 billion and Chicago's 393 billion. See *State and Metropolitan Area Data Book*, U.S. Census Bureau, April 2009, http://www.census.gov/compendia/smadb/TableB-08.pdf.
23. The world's largest theater district is the West End in London.
24. New York has the U.S.'s second largest film industry after Los Angeles.
25. In this category, Beijing ranked fourth, London fifth, Paris sixth, and Tokyo seventh.

Chapter 13

The Final Battle and Entrance Into the Millennial Kingdom

These [the Antichrist and his kings] will wage war against the
Lamb, and the Lamb will overcome them, because He is Lord of
lords and King of kings, and those who are with Him are the called
and chosen and faithful.
Revelation 17:14

The Defeat of the Antichrist at Armageddon

The fall of Babylon the Great City will quite closely coincide with the destruction of the Antichrist's world empire. His move against Babylon is probably one of his last acts before gathering the world's armies for the final battle at Armageddon. This process is described in Revelation 16:

> And I saw coming out of the mouth of the dragon and out of the mouth of the beast and out of the mouth of the false prophet, three unclean spirits like frogs; for they are spirits of demons, performing signs, which go out to the kings of the whole world [lit. the whole inhabited earth, Gr. *oikoumenon holos*], to gather them together for the war of the great day of God, the Almighty.... And they gathered them together to the place which in Hebrew is called Har-Magedon.
>
> (Revelation 16:13–14, 16)

The evil trinity—dragon, Antichrist, and false prophet—engages in their final and ultimate act of deception, causing the nations to assemble in battle against God Himself. This indicates that the final army will be greater than the Antichrist's "ten" king alliance, as those kings are already his willing subjects and do not need to be deceived into doing something for him.

The place of this great final battle is popularly known as Armageddon, but the Greek word Har-Megiddon is in fact a composite of the Hebrew words *har* for hill or mountain;[1] and *Megiddon* or Megiddo,[2] a city mentioned in Joshua 17:12 as one of the places of the Canaanites that the Israelites failed to conquer after entering the promised land. No such mountain is mentioned in any biblical record, nor does it exist in the present time. Megiddo was in fact a plain, the scene of several Old Testament battles (Judges 4–5; 2 Kings 9:27), as well as the place where the British general Lord Allenby decisively defeated the Ottoman Turks in 1918, freeing today's Israel from Muslim hands and making it part of the British Empire (he had previously taken Jerusalem in late 1917).

Mountains, however, carry a strong symbolic meaning in the Old Testament, symbolizing strength and power. The designation "Mountain of Megiddo" may therefore refer to a specific geographical location, but it certainly is an affirmation that the battle of Armageddon is all about God's decisive victory over the forces of evil. Moreover, the designation "mountain" links Armageddon with the great battle prophesied by Ezekiel (ch. 38–39), where Gog's armies are said to be destroyed on "all My [God's] mountains" (38:21). In Joel 3, God says that He will destroy the nations in the "valley of Jehoshaphat," which clearly cannot refer to a mountain. Therefore, it is likely that Har-Megiddon does not actually refer to a mountain, but to the plain of Megiddo, with the valley of Jehoshaphat possibly being nearby.[3]

Ezekiel's final battle prophecy is remarkably similar to the description of Armageddon in Revelation 19, a confirmation that both passages are talking about the same event, which is also described in Zechariah 12 and 14. These passages depict a great massacre of enemy forces.

Table 27. Comparison of final battle passages in Ezekiel, Revelation, and Zechariah

Ezekiel 39:17–20	Revelation 19:17–21	Zechariah 14:2–5,12
As for you, son of man, thus says the Lord GOD, "Speak to every kind of bird and to every beast of the field, 'Assemble and come, gather from every side to My sacrifice which I am going to sacrifice for you, as a great sacrifice on the mountains of Israel, that you may eat flesh and drink blood. You will eat the flesh of mighty men and drink the blood of the princes of the earth, as though they were rams, lambs, goats and bulls, all of them fatlings of Bashan. So you will eat fat until you are glutted, and drink blood until you are drunk, from My sacrifice which I have sacrificed for you. You will be glutted at My table with horses and charioteers, with mighty men and all the men of war,' declares the Lord GOD."	Then I saw an angel standing in the sun, and he cried out with a loud voice, saying to all the birds which fly in midheaven, "Come, assemble for the great supper of God, so that you may eat the flesh of kings and the flesh of commanders and the flesh of mighty men and the flesh of horses and of those who sit on them and the flesh of all men, both free men and slaves, and small and great." And I saw the beast and the kings of the earth and their armies assembled to make war against Him who sat on the horse and against His army. And the beast was seized, and with him the false prophet ... these two were thrown alive into the lake of fire which burns with brimstone. And the rest were killed with the sword which came from the mouth of Him who sat on the horse, and all the birds were filled with their flesh.	For I will gather all the nations against Jerusalem to battle, and the city will be captured, the houses plundered, the women ravished and half of the city exiled, but the rest of the people will not be cut off from the city. Then the LORD will go forth and fight against those nations, as when He fights on a day of battle. In that day His feet will stand on the Mount of Olives, which is in front of Jerusalem on the east.... Then the LORD, my God, will come, and all the holy ones with Him! ... ... Now this will be the plague with which the LORD will strike all the peoples who have gone to war against Jerusalem: their flesh will rot while they stand on their feet, and their eyes will rot in their sockets, and their tongue will rot in their mouth.

Ezekiel also gives us the wider context in which these events will take place. In chapter 37, he is shown a valley of dry bones, a mass grave of a vast army. God then tells Ezekiel to prophesy to the bones, and flesh, skin, and sinews come on them. However, they are not yet alive and breathing. This is an image of the physical restoration of Israel as a nation since 1948: God regathered the nation, but Israel remains in unbelief and is therefore still spiritually dead, like the restored bodies who are yet without life (vv. 11–13). Then God commands Ezekiel to prophesy the breath of the Spirit into these bodies. Ezekiel obeys, and immediately the bodies come to life, symbolizing the spiritual restoration of the Jewish people at Christ's return (v. 14).

However, Zechariah 14 and Ezekiel 39 indicate that there will be a yet another, third, exile for the Jewish people. In Zechariah 14:2, cited above, we read that "the city will be captured … and half of the city [will be] exiled" before the Lord comes and destroys the enemy. Likewise, Ezekiel 39:28 states, "Then they will know that I am the LORD their God because I made them go into exile among the nations, and then gathered them again to their own land." This refers neither to the Babylonian exile from 586 BC nor to the Roman exile after 70 AD, because this regathering occurs after the end times battle, and results in them truly knowing God as "the LORD their God." This sequence is confirmed by verse 26, which describes Israel moving on after having transgressed against God and again dwelling securely in their own land: "They will forget their disgrace and all their treachery which they perpetrated against Me, when they live securely on their own land with no one to make them afraid."

This statement seems puzzling at first, because Gog's attack on Israel occurs when they have been "gathered from the nations" (v. 12) and "live securely" (v. 11). So, after they are brought back to their land beginning in 1948, and are then attacked by Gog and his army when they feel secure because of the peace covenant that they made with him at the beginning of the 70th week (Daniel 9:27), they are again exiled. The "treachery" in Ezekiel 39:26 therefore refers to Israel's evil pact with the Antichrist, which will seem to promise peace, but will end in national disaster: a third exile, followed by a final restoration. When God therefore assures the Jews in this verse that they will dwell securely, He means a genuine peace and security that only God can give, as opposed to the false security afforded by their treacherous pact with the Antichrist.

Table 28. Israel's Exiles

Israel's Exiles		
First exile	586/7 BC–537 BC	Babylonian exile–Jews exiled by Nebuchadnezzar, officially ended with King Cyrus' decree recorded in Ezra
Second exile	70 AD–1948 AD	Time of the Gentiles exile–exile began after Roman destruction of Jerusalem, effectively ended with the establishment of modern Israel
Third exile	2nd half of the 70th week of Daniel	Half of Jerusalem exiled when the Antichrist turns his back on his peace treaty with Israel in the middle of the 70th week of Daniel

The third exile of the Jews and the capture of Jerusalem by the Antichrist are also prophesied in Revelation 11:2, which affirms that "the nations ... will tread under foot the holy city for forty-two months." It is probably during this time that two-thirds of the Jews will "be cut off and perish," and God will refine the surviving third part in the "fire" until they will finally "call on My name" (Zechariah 13:8–9). Then, rescue is underway as "the Lord, my God, will come, and all the holy ones with Him!" (Zechariah 14:5), and the survivors will call on "the name of the Lord" and be "delivered" (Joel 2:32).

Whereas Revelation 16 calls the place of the final battle Armageddon or Mount Megiddo, in Joel God gives it the symbolic names "valley of Jehoshaphat" or "valley of decision." Jehoshaphat means "the Lord judges"; therefore, the name of this valley is basically "judgment valley":

> Hasten and come, all you surrounding nations, and gather yourselves there. Bring down, O LORD, Your mighty ones. Let the nations be aroused and come up to the valley of Jehoshaphat, for there I will sit to judge all the surrounding nations. Put in the sickle, for the harvest is ripe [grape harvest of God's wrath, as in Revelation 14:17–20]. Come, tread, for the wine press is full; the vats overflow, for their wickedness is great. Multitudes, multitudes in the valley of decision! For the day of the LORD is near in the valley of decision. The sun and moon grow dark and the stars lose their brightness.

(Joel 3:11–15)

All of these passages refer to a great and decisive battle that forms the climax of God's wrath against mankind. As a result of this battle, the Antichrist's forces are slaughtered, and he and his false prophet are "thrown alive into the lake of fire" (Revelation 19:20). This momentous historic event will effectively end the history of mankind as we know it. Representing a terrifying judgment, it will also prepare the millennial reign of Christ. Humanity will come to realize the enormity of its rebellion against the true God. Isaiah wrote:

> "All mankind will come to bow down before Me," says the Lord. "Then they will go forth and look on the corpses of the men who have transgressed against Me....and they will be an abhorrence to all mankind."
>
> (Isaiah 66:23b–24)

Then, God will send some of the survivors of the wrath and of Armageddon "to the nations" to "declare My glory among the nations" (Isaiah 66:19):

> Then they [the nations] shall bring all your brethren from all the nations as a grain offering to the Lord, on horses, in chariots, in litters, on mules and on camels, to My holy mountain Jerusalem....
>
> (Isaiah 66:20)

Finally, all the Jews who are scattered around the globe will be gathered by those who had persecuted them, and brought before God:

> Behold, I will lift up My hand to the nations
> And set up My standard to the peoples;

340

And they will bring your sons in their bosom,

And your daughters will be carried on their shoulders.

Kings will be your guardians,

And their princesses your nurses.

They will bow down to you with their faces to the earth

And lick the dust of your feet;

And you will know that I am the Lord....

(Isaiah 49:22–23)

Entrance Into Jesus' Millennial Kingdom

Before we examine the nature of Jesus' millennial reign on the earth in the next chapter, we first need to look at what happens between Armageddon and the beginning of this reign. Many Bible students consider the sheep and goat judgment of Matthew 25 to be the next event. This passage is commonly interpreted as being about the judgment of the Gentile (non-Jewish) survivors of God's wrath and of Armageddon. The sheep are those who helped the Jews during these difficult times. Their reward is either seen to be salvation or at least entrance into the millennial kingdom. In contrast, the goats are assumed to have neglected the Jews and are consequently banned from this kingdom. But let us examine the passage ourselves:

> But when the Son of Man comes in His glory, and all the angels with Him, then He will sit on His glorious throne. All the nations will be gathered before Him; and He will separate them from one another, as the shepherd separates the sheep from the goats; and He will put the sheep on His right, and the goats on the left.
>
> Then the King will say to those on His right, "Come, you who are blessed of My Father, inherit the kingdom prepared for you from the foundation of the world. For I was hungry,

341

and you gave Me something to eat; I was thirsty, and you gave Me something to drink; I was a stranger, and you invited Me in; naked, and you clothed Me; I was sick, and you visited Me; I was in prison, and you came to Me." Then the righteous will answer Him, "Lord, when did we see You hungry, and feed You, or thirsty, and give You something to drink? And when did we see You a stranger, and invite You in, or naked, and clothe You? When did we see You sick, or in prison, and come to You?" The King will answer and say to them, "Truly I say to you, to the extent that you did it to one of these brothers of Mine, even the least of them, you did it to Me."

Then He will also say to those on His left, "Depart from Me, accursed ones, into the eternal fire which has been prepared for the devil and his angels; for I was hungry, and you gave Me nothing to eat; I was thirsty, and you gave Me nothing to drink; I was a stranger, and you did not invite Me in; naked, and you did not clothe Me; sick, and in prison, and you did not visit Me." Then they themselves also will answer, "Lord, when did we see You hungry, or thirsty, or a stranger, or naked, or sick, or in prison, and did not take care of You?" Then He will answer them, "Truly I say to you, to the extent that you did not do it to one of the least of these, you did not do it to Me."

These will go away into eternal punishment, but the righteous into eternal life.

(Matthew 24:31–46)

We will analyze this passage by asking four basic questions about it:

1. Who is being judged?
2. What are the criteria for the judgment?
3. What is the final outcome of the judgment?
4. When will this judgment take place?

1. Who is Being Judged?

The key for answering this question lies in the word "nations." Christ will gather "all the nations" before Him. We had seen before that the Greek word for "nations," *ethnos*,[4] means ethnic group or people group. In the Bible, this term is also used to refer to the Gentiles, to those who are not Jews. In the book of Revelation, however, *ethnos* always means people group and emphasizes the diversity of all humanity before God. Since the sheep and goat judgment is an event of the end times, it seems reasonable to consider it a judgment of all nations, including the Jews.

This is all the more the case because by "brothers," Jesus is referring to spiritual brothers, meaning the church saints and not merely the Jews as His ethnic brothers. In Mark 3, Jesus astonished His disciples with these words about His biological family:

> Then His mother and His brothers arrived, and standing outside they sent word to Him and called Him. A crowd was sitting around Him, and they said to Him, "Behold, Your mother and Your brothers are outside looking for You." Answering them, He said, "Who are My mother and My brothers?" Looking about at those who were sitting around Him, He said, "Behold My mother and My brothers! For whoever does the will of God, he is My brother and sister and mother."
>
> (Mark 3:31–35)

In other words, Jesus considers not so much those who are literally His brothers to be His "brothers" but those who have become His spiritual "brothers" by obeying God. Likewise, in Matthew 28:10 He told the women who came to the grave to "go and tell my brothers to go to Galilee" (ESV). Here, "brothers" refers to His disciples, and therefore by implication to all of His followers regardless of ethnicity. In the same vein, Paul wrote in Romans:

> For those whom he foreknew he also predestined to be conformed to the image of his Son, in order that *he might be the firstborn among many brothers.*
>
> (Romans 8:29 ESV, emphasis added)[5]

In Romans 8:15, Paul had already affirmed the fact that we have been adopted into God's family. From this, it logically follows that God is our heavenly Father, and Jesus, God's Son, is not just our divine King but also like an older brother to us. Therefore, the sheep and goat judgment is not restricted to certain nations or ethnic groups. Rather, by saying that "all the nations" will be gathered before Him, Jesus is emphasizing that this judgment will universally apply to all of humanity. This will become more obvious as we look into the next questions.

2. What Is the Final Outcome of the Judgment?

Some of those who hold to the classical pretribulational interpretation of the sheep and goat judgment believe that the sheep receive salvation as they enter Jesus' millennial kingdom. Others simply assert that the sheep are not yet saved but get to be part of the kingdom and therefore obtain the opportunity to come to Christ.

But this latter perspective contradicts the wording of the passage. Jesus calls the sheep "the righteous" (*dikaios*[6]). When we compare this with numerous other passages such as Matthew 13:43, "the righteous [*dikaios*] will shine forth as the sun," and the fact that the Word of God only ever calls God's own people "righteous," it becomes clear that this must necessarily refer to born-again believers. Anything else would be contradictory, because the righteousness of the saints is none other than the righteousness of God Himself, since no one but God is righteous.

Likewise, Jesus refers to the sheep as "blessed," again a term that in all of Scripture exclusively describes those who have become God's own children. In contrast, the goats are called the "accursed." This contrast, the "righteous" versus the "accursed," cannot refer to anything else than the difference between believers and unbelievers.

The final and decisive argument about the eternal outcome of the sheep and goat judgment comes from the last verse of the passage: "These will go away into eternal punishment, but the righteous into eternal life" (v. 46). There can be no doubt whatsoever as to what "eternal life" versus "eternal punishment" refer to: heaven versus hell. John 3:16 famously proclaims, "For God so loved the world, that He gave His only begotten Son, that whoever believes in Him shall not perish, but have *eternal life*." This is precisely what the sheep and goat judgment is all about.

3. What are the Criteria for the Judgment?

Jesus' criteria for the judgment are given to us in great detail: the works (assistance, provision, practical love) that people did or did not do for "one of these brothers of Mine, even the least of them" (v. 40). The common argument here is that the sheep are not actually born-again believers. Rather, they are those of the unrepentant world who helped the Jews in their distress. Because of these "good works," they are given a favorable judgment. They are therefore not saved by faith in Jesus, but somehow, their deeds for the Jews are credited them as a kind of retrospective "salvation." Van Kampen, who holds this view, tries to explain this contradiction by asserting that the sheep are retrospectively given a "salvation by faith" based on their works.[7] However, this means that works precede faith, with saving faith being attributed through works. Though this theory makes works the foundation on which salvation is awarded, the idea is presented as being a salvation not based on works.

This astonishing kind of reasoning about salvation merits a closer look at what the Bible actually says about saving faith. Romans 10 illuminates the biblical process of salvation:

> "THE WORD IS NEAR YOU, in your mouth and in your heart"—that is, the word of faith which we are preaching, that if you confess with your mouth Jesus as Lord, and believe in your heart that God raised Him from the dead, you will be saved; for with the heart a person believes, resulting in righteousness, and with the mouth he confesses, resulting in salvation.
>
> (Romans 10:8–10)

Paul's words clarify that the scriptural sequence of salvation is as follows:

1. Firstly, one must hear the Word, the gospel, in order to know what one should believe.
2. Secondly, the Word of God must come "near," meaning that it must be believed in one's "heart" and confessed with one's "mouth."

A few verses later, this sequence is again affirmed:

> How then will they call on Him in whom they have not believed? How will they believe in Him whom they have not heard? And how will they hear without a preacher? How will they preach unless they are sent? Just as it is written, "How beautiful are the feet of those who bring good news of good things!"...So faith comes from hearing, and hearing by the word of Christ.
>
> (Romans 10:14–15, 17)

Again, people must first hear the Word preached to them. Only then can they believe that which they hear and call on God's name: "faith comes from hearing, and hearing by the word." This sequence of hearing, believing, salvation is also reflected in the case of Abraham. Romans 4:3 states, "Abraham believed God, and it was credited to him as righteousness." First, God *spoke* His Word to Abraham, giving Him a promise. After hearing the Word, Abraham *believed* what he heard. This act of believing God was then credited to him as *righteousness*, meaning salvation by faith. Likewise, Ephesians 2:9 tells us that salvation comes "through faith; and that not of yourselves, it is the gift of God; not as a result of works, so that no one may boast."

Consequently, the sequence of salvation taught in Scripture turns out to be the complete opposite of that proposed by Van Kampen and other interpreters. Rather than receiving salvation retrospectively at the time of judgment based on works, God's people *are first saved* by faith *without any works whatsoever*, and then they are called to go and perform "good works, which God prepared beforehand so that we would walk in them" (Ephesians 2:10). Any other teaching would be a distortion of clear biblical truths. This means that the sheep in Matthew 25 cannot be unsuspecting unbelievers who showed kindness to God's people but otherwise had not experienced spiritual rebirth through personal faith in Jesus! Rather, the sheep are the "righteous"—the saints, the truly born-again people of God who are headed for "eternal life."

But if salvation is only by faith, then why are the only criteria cited in Matthew 25 good deeds performed for others? Why is faith not even mentioned in the passage? How can this judgment be solely based on works? The reason for this puzzling absence is simple. All judgment passages in Scripture make extensive references to works as the necessary evidence for true salvation. As we had already highlighted in chapter 1, true faith must bear fruit. Fruit (works) is not the basis for salvation but its necessary outcome. It is like a broken down car with a dead engine. If you put a new engine into that car, it will not be the same—when you turn the key, that car will start up and drive you around. If it doesn't, then the new engine was obviously never put in. Likewise, when we receive our new spirit nature, it will certainly make a difference!

Let us examine a number of final judgment passages and see what they say:

Do not marvel at this; for an hour is coming, in which all who are in the tombs will hear His voice, and will come forth; *those who did the good deeds to a resurrection of life, those who committed the evil deeds to a resurrection of judgment.*

(John 5:28–29, emphasis added)

Behold, the Lord came with many thousands of His holy ones, to execute judgment upon all, and to convict all the ungodly of all their ungodly deeds which they have done.

(Jude 14–15)

But because of your stubbornness and unrepentant heart you are storing up wrath for yourself in the day of wrath and revelation of the righteous judgment of God, who WILL RENDER TO EACH PERSON ACCORDING TO HIS DEEDS: *to those who by perseverance in doing good seek for glory and honor and immortality, eternal life; but to those who are selfishly ambitious and do not obey the truth, but obey unrighteousness, wrath and indignation.*

(Romans 2:5–8, emphasis added)

For the Son of Man is going to come in the glory of His Father with His angels, and WILL THEN REPAY EVERY MAN ACCORDING TO HIS DEEDS.

(Matthew 16:27)

Not everyone who says to Me, "Lord, Lord," will enter the
kingdom of heaven, *but he who does the will of My Father who
is in heaven will enter.*"

(Matthew 7:21, emphasis added)

Therefore I say to you, the kingdom of God will be taken
away from you and *given to a people, [who will be] producing the
fruit of it.*

(Matthew 21:43, emphasis added)

And I saw the dead, the great and the small, standing before
the [Great White] throne, and books were opened; and another
book was opened, which is the book of life; *and the dead were
judged from the things which were written in the books, according to
their deeds.* And the sea gave up the dead which were in it, and
death and Hades gave up the dead which were in them; *and
they were judged, every one of them according to their deeds.*

(Revelation 20:12–13, emphases added)

The principle of fruit-bearing as the necessary evidence of genuine
spiritual rebirth is also affirmed by James:

What use is it, my brethren, if someone says he has faith but
he has no works? Can that faith save him? If a brother or sister
is without clothing and in need of daily food, and one of you
says to them, "Go in peace, be warmed and be filled," and yet
you do not give them what is necessary for their body, what
use is that? *Even so faith, if it has no works, is dead.*

(James 2:14–17, emphasis added)

The reason for this is quite simple: deeds reveal the true heart. Likewise,
the sheep and goat judgment affirms that Jesus evaluates genuine saving

faith based on people's deeds. As John MacArthur observes, they are the *effects* of salvation, not its *cause*.[8] The fact that the sheep in the story react somewhat surprised to Jesus' judgment show both how many believers are not clearly aware of this teaching (or even deny it), and that they may have forgotten about their good deeds precisely because they were done naturally, out of habit, and not in order to earn merit.

More specifically, it seems that Jesus used the sheep and goat judgment to make a strong statement about separating *true believers* (sheep) from *pretenders* (goats). In ancient times, sheep and goats would mix and mingle during the day, but they were separated each night. The goats needed to be brought into stables as they were more susceptible to the cold. Likewise, in this age, true believers and pretenders mix and mingle freely and are often difficult to distinguish, but at the judgment, they will be separated into two very distinct groups.

The parable of the dragnet reveals a very similar slant: while the fish are in the net, they all look alike, just like church-goers may seem similar on the surface. It is only once the fish are taken out and carefully examined that the difference between the good and the bad fish becomes evident. Likewise, the final judgment will be a time when the full truth about every person will be revealed. This appears to be the primary message of Jesus' illustration and explains why the bulk of the story centers around the works-oriented criteria for the judgment. It also explains the surprised reaction of the goats to the reasons for their condemnation: they were either not aware of the fact that true faith must result in genuine fruit or they performed what they thought were "good deeds" but now realize that these deeds were not done for Jesus.

4. When Will This Judgment Take Place?

After examining the first three questions, we have arrived at interpretations that may differ from those that some of us have been taught in the past. However, they are in harmony with other scriptural truths. Based on this foundation, we are now able to assess when the sheep and goat judgment will actually take place and what it has to do with entrance into the millennium.

When Jesus tells the sheep to "[c]ome ... inherit the kingdom prepared for you from the foundation of the world," the classical pretribulationist view interprets "kingdom" as the millennial kingdom—the reign of Christ on earth—which takes place before the advent of the eternal kingdom. In order to ascertain whether "kingdom" should be understood as the millennium as opposed to the eternal kingdom of heaven, we need to look at the word "inheritance." The Greek word, *kleronomeo*,[9] means to obtain by right of inheritance, to receive an allotted portion as the rightful heir. This term is found in Luke 18:18, when the young ruler asks Jesus: "what shall I do to inherit [*kleronomeo*] eternal life?" Likewise, it occurs in Revelation 21:7, which says about the eternal New Jerusalem, "He who overcomes will inherit [*kleronomeo*] these things." Similarly, Hebrews 1:14 talks about "those who will inherit [*kleronomeo*] salvation."

From these passages, it becomes evident that the concept of inheritance used in Scripture is always applied to the *eternal* kingdom in heaven and not to the *temporary* millennial kingdom of Christ on earth. After all, the promised inheritance of the saints is *permanent* and *eternal*, and not *temporary* or *perishable*. Another insight about the nature of the "kingdom" comes from Jesus' assertion that it has been "prepared for you [the righteous] from the foundation of the world" (v. 34). This again clearly points to the eternal and not the temporary millennial kingdom.[10]

Ephesians 5:5 asserts that "no immoral or impure person or covetous man ... has an inheritance [*kleronomeo*] in the kingdom of Christ and God." Here, it is important to add that entrance into Christ's millennial reign on earth does by no means equate to salvation. We know from the description of this reign that there will be both glorified saints and unsaved populations—otherwise this era would hardly be described as ruling the nations "with a rod of iron" (Revelation 19:15; see the next chapter for a comprehensive discussion). Since there is still sin in the millennium, its non-glorified inhabitants still need to decide whether to believe in Jesus and be saved (Micah 4:1–2), and many of them end up rebelling against God after the millennium (Revelation 20:7–9). Ephesians 5:5 clearly implies that the concept of inheritance applies to the *eternal* kingdom. There, only born-again believers can enter and all possibilities of sinning are fully removed. Conversely, the millennium is mankind's final chance to repent and return to their true Maker.

Finally, passages such as Jude 1:15 and Revelation 19:11 that depict Jesus as coming to the earth (to Armageddon) in order to "execute judgment" do not imply that the sheep and goat judgment will then follow. Rather, Armageddon itself is a time of judgment, the moment when the final judgment begins. Christ's judging then continues throughout the millennium, when He will "judge between nations" (Isaiah 2:4) and punish those who transgress His laws, when judgment will fall on those who do not send representatives to Jerusalem (Zechariah 14:17–19). Then, the judgment of sin and unbelief will climax at the Great White Throne judgment. All of these are phases of the final judgment process that will ultimately usher in the sinless state of eternity.

Will Only Believers Enter the Millennium?

A common pretribulational view is that only believers will enter Jesus' millennial kingdom. Several passages are cited in support of this view, for example:

> While they are saying, "Peace and safety!" then destruction will come upon them suddenly like labor pains upon a woman with child, and they will not escape.
>
> (1 Thessalonians 5:3)

> But the same day that Lot went out of Sodom it rained fire and brimstone from heaven, and destroyed them all.
>
> (Luke 17:29)

However, there are several arguments against such an interpretation. Firstly, it is clear that enough unbelievers and unbelieving nations survive to assemble a vast army against Jesus at Armageddon. Since this occurs at the very end of the wrath, it is clear that the wrath does not kill all those who remain on the earth. None of the descriptions of the different phases of God's wrath indicate that there will be no survivors. To the contrary, most of them clearly state that their scope only affects part of the globe. Moreover, the battle of Armageddon describes a slaughter of armies, not of the remaining populations such as women, children, or the elderly who will not participate in the actual battle. Likewise, in Haggai 2:22 God announces that He will "overthrow the thrones of kingdoms and destroy the power of the kingdoms of the nations." Their "power" will be destroyed at Armageddon, but again this does not imply a complete annihilation of the entire populations of these nations.

The two passages cited above do not contradict this. The statement that "they will not escape" refers to the fact that no unbeliever will escape the time of God's wrath. They will all have to go through it, but it does not mean that they will all be annihilated! Likewise, Luke 17:29 affirms that all unregenerate people will have to go through the judgment of God's wrath. But will they all be destroyed, just like all of Sodom was destroyed?

Such an interpretation is contradicted by a number of other scriptures, which clearly state that there will be surviving unbelievers that enter the millennium:

> [T]he time is coming to gather all nations and tongues. And they shall come and see My glory. I will set a sign among them and *will send survivors from them* [from the nations] to the nations.... And they will declare My glory among the nations.
>
> (Isaiah 66:18–19, emphasis added)

This passage tells us that at the time when God gathers all nations for the judgment of His wrath (we had looked at this context in the previous section), He will send survivors from all nations back to their nations to proclaim His glory. These "survivors" are those who lived both through God's wrath and through the battle of Armageddon.

> Then it will come about that *any who are left of all the nations that went against Jerusalem* will go up from year to year to worship the King, the Lord of hosts, and to celebrate the Feast of Booths. And it will be that whichever of the families of the earth does not go up to Jerusalem to worship the King, the Lord of hosts, there will be no rain on them.
>
> (Zechariah 14:16–17, emphasis added)

Here, we are again very clearly told that there will be those who are "left of all the nations that went against Jerusalem" to fight against God's people and against Jesus. These survivors are obviously not believers. Neither will they get saved right when they enter the millennium, because once that new era starts, those of them who refuse to worship Jesus will be punished.

> Indeed, My decision is to gather nations,
> To assemble kingdoms,
> To pour out on them My indignation,
> All My burning anger;
> For all the earth will be devoured
> By the fire of My zeal.
> For then I will give to the peoples purified lips,
> That all of them may call on the name of the Lord.
> (Zephaniah 3:8–9)

Here in Zephaniah, God proclaims that He will pour out His "indignation" on the nations (wrath/Armageddon), judging them so that these "peoples" (Hebrew: *am*,[11] peoples or nations) will call on His name with "purified lips." Clearly, God's wrath has a redemptive purpose for these unbelievers which comes out as they enter the millennium and witness the glorious reign of Christ. This passage also shows that sweeping statements of destruction ("all the earth will be devoured") do not actually mean that there will not be survivors. No, it is "then," after God's devastating judgment and wrath, that those who are left will call on His name as the millennial reign begins. This is confirmed by the next passage:

> Thus says the Lord of hosts, "It will yet be that peoples will come, even the inhabitants of many cities. The inhabitants of one will go to another, saying, 'Let us go at once to entreat the favor of the Lord, and to seek the Lord of hosts; I will also go.' So *many peoples and mighty nations will come to seek the Lord of hosts in Jerusalem* and to entreat the favor of the Lord." Thus says the Lord of hosts, "In those days *ten men from all the nations will grasp the garment of a Jew*, saying, 'Let us go with you, for we have heard that God is with you.'"
> (Zechariah 8:20–23, emphases added)

These verses again describe the beginning of Christ's millennial reign from Jerusalem. The nations will at that point realize that they have entered a new historic era. Drawn by the very presence of Jesus on His throne, they will embark on pilgrimages to Jerusalem in order to "seek the Lord." But they are not yet saved; otherwise, they would not so desperately cling to the "garment of a Jew." These people's salvation will occur as they continue to seek the Lord, so that "He may teach us about His ways and that we may walk in His paths" (Micah 4:2). These are not the words of born-again, glorified saints, but of unsaved seekers who are attracted to the powerful presence of Christ. Moreover, this worldwide pilgrimage certainly does not seem to occur later in the millennium, but right at its beginning, when the nations first realize in what a marvelous time they now live. In contrast, those nations who enter the millennium and refuse to serve Jesus will be punished:

> For the nation and the kingdom which will not serve you
> will perish, and the nations will be utterly ruined.
>
> (Isaiah 60:12)

This obviously cannot refer to believers or nations that only consist of born-again saints. Rather, it refers to nations that are yet to believe in Christ.

From this brief study, we can conclude that passages such as 1 Thessalonians 5:3 or Luke 17:29 cannot be taken to depict the complete annihilation of all unbelieving populations. Not even all of those who come to battle at Armageddon will be killed. The Lord will spare a remnant of people from all nations so that they can populate the millennium. There, He will give them an opportunity to enter His glorious presence, while those who refuse to obey will be ruled with a "rod of iron" (Revelation 19:15).

When we combine all of these scriptural insights about the sheep and goat judgment, only one conclusion is possible: this judgment represents a symbolic depiction of all the final judgments that every human being will have to go through. However, these judgments will not take place at the same time, but will be separate events. John 5:29 speaks of the righteous experiencing a "resurrection of life," whereas the unregenerate will go through a "resurrection of judgment." Likewise, Luke 14:4 speaks of the "resurrection of the righteous" and Hebrews 11:35 of those who "obtain a better resurrection." This resurrection of the saints is described in Revelation 20 as the "first resurrection": "Blessed and holy is the one who has a part in the first resurrection; over these the second death has no power" (v. 6a). In contrast, the "resurrection to judgment" leads to the "second death," which is eternal damnation in the lake of fire (v. 14). Both resurrections not only differ in their final outcome but also in their timing. The "first resurrection" takes place *before* the millennial reign, and those who are resurrected then "will be priests of God and of Christ and will reign with Him for a thousand years" (v. 6b). Conversely, the resurrection of all unbelievers takes place *after* the millennium and after the final rebellion of mankind against God.

In summary, we have these facts about the two judgments for all those who experienced physical death (meaning who were not raptured):

1. Firstly, the judgment of the saints before the judgment seat of Christ or of God (*bema* in Greek),[12] which occurs after each saint is resurrected or raptured (Romans 14:10; 2 Corinthians 5:10). This is called the "first resurrection" or "resurrection to life."

2. Secondly, the Great White Throne judgment of all unbelievers, which will come to pass after the millennium and before the advent of eternity in heaven (Revelation 20:11–15). This is the "resurrection to judgment," which results in the "second death" in the eternal lake of fire.

The sheep and goats judgment represents *both* of these judgments. It will therefore take place both *before* and *after* the millennium. This explains why this judgment passage is different from the Great White Throne judgment but also reflects a number of similarities. In His account, Jesus combines these two judgments in order to create an understandable and powerfully intuitive mental picture of the final judgments in the minds of His disciples. As in so many other places in Scripture (such as the comings of Christ), *two distinct events are conflated into a single one*. But how can this be?

The answer is simple. Jesus had a very precise mission to achieve—to reach and prepare the "lost sheep of the house of Israel" for the coming salvation (Matthew 15:24), and He was careful not to go beyond this aim. His primary focus in Matthew 25 was to teach His Jewish disciples about His future coming and the fact of the final judgment. Consequently, Jesus' account of the sheep and goat judgment preserves the correct sequence of the two judgments, but—for the sake of His listeners—*portrays them as if they occurred at the same time*. Here, He simply wanted to communicate these main points:

1. All will stand before Christ to be judged.
2. There will only be two kinds of people: the righteous (God's born-again people, both Jews and Gentiles) and the accursed (all others).
3. The judgments will be based on the presence or absence of manifest evidence of having truly been born again (in the form of fruit/works).
4. The judgments will only have two outcomes, both of which are final (and eternal).

The sheep and goat judgment is deliberately set up as a dichotomy—a division of two mutually-exclusive, totally opposite parts. Jesus achieves this by conflating two separate events into one. Only in that way can He build up such a wonderfully sharp contrast between the two groups.

But does this method of narration not represent a deception of Jesus' hearers? Not at all. Firstly, a close look reveals that the passage does not actually state that both events must take place simultaneously! Jesus simply says that He will first deal with the sheep on His right, and then with the goats on His left. This does not deny the possibility of a time gap in-between! Secondly, Jesus' approach follows the common Old Testament practice of not sharply distinguishing between two types of events, be it the two appearances of Christ or the two future kingdoms (millennial and eternal). Isaiah 65, for example, first gives us a description of the new heavens and the new earth and then suddenly talks about how long people will live before they die, about child-bearing, etc. These are all things that clearly belong into the millennium, as they will no longer exist in eternity (see the next chapter for details). In that and many other passages, these two realms are not clearly distinguished, simply because God preferred to conceal the fullness of this teaching until the appointed time, reserving it to the book of Revelation. As a result, there were two factions of Jews at Jesus' time—those who expected a literal national restoration of Israel as a millennial reign of Jesus on earth and those who only believed in the eternal state.

Rather than clearly differentiating these two kingdoms, Jesus made matters even more complex by introducing a third type of "kingdom": "behold, the kingdom of God is in your midst" (Luke 17:21, compare Matthew 10:7). There are therefore three kinds of "kingdoms." Firstly, the present church age, the kingdom in our midst, which represents the initial phase of the kingdom. Colossians 1:13 tells us that God has already now "rescued us from the domain of darkness, and transferred us to the kingdom of His beloved Son." Secondly, there will be the millennial kingdom of Christ on earth. Thirdly, we will inherit the kingdom of heaven in eternity.

In His words, Jesus often did not clearly differentiate between these various "kingdoms." For example, in Luke 22:30 He speaks about the apostles reigning with Him in "My kingdom"—clearly the millennial reign—while in John 18:36, He uses this exact same phrase to state that "My kingdom [eternity] is not of this world" and that therefore the angelic hosts would not be fighting for Him. Likewise, the "kingdom of heaven" parables in Matthew 13 do not make a clear distinction between millennium and eternity or between the timings of different judgments: the fact that the wheat/good fish are judged first and then get to be part of the millennial reign, whereas the judgment of the tares/bad fish occurs after the millennium, is not salient to Jesus' main focus here. What matters is that both groups will be judged and will face two very different eternal destinies. That is the point that Jesus wanted to drive home. Just as He left the most important accounts about salvation by grace to Paul's letters, Jesus hinted at the distinction of millennial and eternal kingdoms but reserved the primary account of it for the Book of Revelation. Whatever He said and whichever illustration He used for which audience was always perfectly in line with His earthly mission.

Who Will Enter the Millennial Kingdom?

If the sheep and goat judgment does not determine entrance into the millennium, then the immediate question is *who* will enter and on *what* basis. The answer is that everyone who survives God's wrath and the battle of Armageddon will enter the millennium. Scripture does not give us any criteria by which this entrance is determined. Since the millennial kingdom represents the "iron rule" of Christ with the believers over the "nations," and a large-scale rebellion against Him will take place immediately afterward, it is evident that many of those who will enter will be unbelievers. All in all, the following three groups will enter the millennial kingdom:

1. The glorified church-age saints, who were raptured or resurrected and then judged at the judgment seat of Christ, will enter in their resurrection bodies (Romans 14:10; 2 Corinthians 5:10).

2. The surviving Jews, who were brought into a true covenant with God (Ezekiel 20:35–37; Zechariah 13:8–9), will enter in their human bodies. All of them are born-again believers, but they have not yet received a final judgment.

3. The surviving unbelievers, who made it through God's wrath and receive another opportunity to believe in Christ during the millennium. (Micah 4:1–2; Isaiah 2:3, 62:23–24; Jeremiah 3:17; Zechariah 8:22). Some of them will come to Jesus during that time, while others will not and will end up joining mankind's final rebellion, which will take place afterwards.

Chapter 13 Notes

---

1. *Strong's Concordance,* H2022.
2. Ibid., H4023.
3. Craig Keener's *IVP Bible Background Commentary, New Testament* (Downer's Grove, IL: IVP Academic, 2000), suggests that it may be another name for the valley of Jezreel, which lies near the plain of Megiddo (entry under Revelation 16:16).
4. *Strong's Concordance,* G1484.
5. The Greek word for "brothers," *adelphos* (*Strong's Concordance,* G80), can also be translated as brethren, but the original Greek term makes no such distinction.
6. *Strong's Concordance,* G1349.
7. Van Kampen, 390.
8. John MacArthur, *New Testament Commentary* (Chicago: Moody Press), John 5:25-30, Olive Tree Bible Software, Inc.
9. *Strong's Concordance,* G2816.

10. Throughout the Gospels, Jesus uses the expressions "kingdom of heaven" or "kingdom of God" to refer to the eternal kingdom; for example see Matthew 18:3, where He emphasizes that "unless you are converted and become like children, you will not enter the kingdom of heaven." Compare also Matthew 7:21.

11. *Strong's Concordance,* H5971.

12. The *bema* (*Strong's Concordance,* G968) referred to the raised platform, tribune, or special throne-like seat occupied by rulers who had the authority to pass judgment.

Chapter 14

Reigning With Christ: What That Means and How We Can Prepare for it

*For He must reign until He has put all His enemies under His
feet.... When all things are subjected to Him, then the Son Himself
also will be subjected to the One who subjected all things to Him,
so that God may be all in all.*
1 Corinthians 15:25, 28

If we endure [or: persevere], we will also reign with Him.
2 Timothy 2:12

Introduction: The Millennium and the Forces of Evil

One day, all born-again believers will reign together with Jesus in His earthly Kingdom. It is a fact. But it is quite rare to meet believers who are truly aware of this fact, passionate about its coming, or are actively preparing for it. Why is that so? Probably because the prospect of reigning with Christ seems like a remote and abstract thing, something that may happen in the distant future but has little relevance for our daily living. Additionally, there is confusion as to who will get to be part of it: will only the martyrs of the tribulation participate? Or perhaps only those Christians who have been overcomers? Also, some believe that the millennial Kingdom is the same as the eternal state in heaven. Others maintain that it is merely symbolic of the present church age, meaning that we are—in a symbolic sense—already reigning with Christ right now. What is the truth?

In order to help us understand the truth about the millennial reign, we will address the following questions in this chapter:

- Will there be a literal reign of Christ on this earth, which is different from eternity in heaven, or is it just "symbolic"?
- Who will get to be part of this reign?
- What is the purpose of this reign?
- What are the unique characteristics of this reign? What conditions will prevail on the earth during it?

Let us begin by examining the key passage in the book of Revelation that describes the millennium:

> Then I saw an angel coming down from heaven, holding the key of the abyss and a great chain in his hand. And he laid hold of the dragon, the serpent of old, who is the devil and Satan, and bound him for a thousand years; and he threw him into the abyss, and shut it and sealed it over him, so that he would not deceive the nations any longer, until the thousand years were completed; after these things he must be released for a short time.
>
> Then I saw thrones, and they sat on them, and judgment was given to them. And I saw the souls of those who had been beheaded because of their testimony of Jesus and because of the word of God, and those who had not worshiped the beast or his image, and had not received the mark on their forehead and on their hand; and they came to life and reigned with Christ for a thousand years....
>
> ... When the thousand years are completed, Satan will be released from his prison, and will come out to deceive the nations which are in the four corners of the earth, Gog and Magog, to gather them together for the war; the number of them is like the sand of the seashore. And they came up on the broad plain of the earth and surrounded the camp of the saints and the beloved city, and fire came down from heaven

and devoured them. And the devil who deceived them was thrown into the lake of fire and brimstone, where the beast and the false prophet are also; and they will be tormented day and night forever and ever.

(Revelation 20:1–4, 7–10)

This passage comes right after Jesus rides with His armies to battle at Armageddon and decisively defeats the Antichrist and the armies of the world. The Antichrist and his false prophet are both thrown into the lake of fire. Interestingly, Satan himself will not meet that fate until after the millennium (Revelation 20:10). Rather than being destroyed along with his evil minions, he is neutralized, shut away, and therefore unable to "deceive the nations" during the millennial age. Likewise, the Great White Throne judgment, where all unbelievers are judged and condemned to the lake of fire, does not take place until later that chapter. Finally, the eternal state, where the believers live forever with Jesus and His Father, does not occur until the following chapter. It is only then that sin, death, suffering, war, and the deceptive workings of Satan are forever destroyed. Prior to this, the final battle of the universe, the last time when there will be death and destruction, is yet to occur. The devil's last attempt to harm God's people is not at Armageddon. No, it is right after the millennial reign that he deceives and mobilizes the nations to march one last time against the "beloved city." This sequence of events is affirmed by Daniel:

Then I kept looking because of the sound of the boastful words which the horn [Antichrist] was speaking; I kept looking until the beast [the dreadful fourth beast from which the Antichrist arises] was slain, and its body was destroyed and given to the burning fire. As for the rest of the beasts [symbolizing other empires], *their dominion was taken away, but*

> *an extension of life was granted to them for an appointed period of*
> *time* [the millennium].
>
> (Daniel 7:11–12, emphasis added)

As prophesied, Hitler's empire was torn away from him, and he was killed and his body burned by his guards. But what about the other "beasts" and their empires? It says that their "dominion was taken away." What does that mean? Further along in the same chapter, we find the explanation:

> Then the sovereignty, the dominion and the greatness of all
> the kingdoms under the whole heaven will be given to the
> people of the saints of the Highest One; His kingdom will
> be an everlasting kingdom, and *all the dominions will serve and*
> *obey Him.*
>
> (v. 27, emphasis added)

Daniel 7 teaches us that the empires of the world will have to surrender their dominion to the saints, meaning us believers. However, they will not cease to exist. Instead, they will continue for "an appointed period" of time, which is none other than the millennial reign of Christ, a reign that lasts not for eternity but for a specific length. This agrees with the Revelation 20 passage, which clearly implies that the nations of the earth will continue to exist during Jesus' reign. Otherwise, it would hardly be possible for Satan to mobilize them for war after the millennial age, or for Jesus and His people to "rule them with a rod of iron" (Revelation 2:26–27; 19:15; Psalm 2:7–8).

A key oversight of the amillennial position, which views Revelation 20 as an allegorical account that will not literally come about, is to interpret the binding of Satan as having occurred 2,000 years ago through Christ's death on the cross. Now, it is true that Jesus' sacrificial death gained us victory over the evil one. Hebrews 2:14–15 says, "…

that through death He [Jesus] might render powerless him who had the power of death, that is, the devil, and might free those who through fear of death were subject to slavery all their lives [the believers]." Similarly, John wrote in 1 John 3:18 that "[t]he Son of God appeared ... to destroy the works of the devil." In chapter 8, we had already seen that Jesus bought us freedom from our slavery to the father of lies. In chapter 9, we learned that we have been given an overcomer nature and are able to overcome the strongholds and devices of the devil in our lives.

However, there is a crucial difference when comparing the present age to the millennium: even though Satan's power has been broken for those who have been spiritually born again, the enemy still "prowls around like a roaring lion, seeking someone to devour." (1 Peter 5:8). Likewise, in Matthew 6:13 Jesus exhorts us to pray regularly that we would be kept from "temptation" and delivered "from evil [or: from the evil one, meaning Satan]."[1] Despite the fact that we have been given the power to overcome, we must closely watch ourselves lest we be deceived.

In contrast, during the millennial era not even the unbelieving nations can fall prey to the devil's ploys! He is completely and literally shut away and (symbolically) put in "chains," utterly incapacitated and powerless to deceive even the most gullible and imprudent soul. Revelation 20:3 puts a particular emphasis on Satan's full removal from *any* sphere of influence over humanity by describing how the angel "shut it [the abyss] and sealed it over him." The picture here is one of total confinement, a condition that is entirely different from the present church age! Christ's victory over Satan and sin has already occurred, but the final realization of this victory will not take place until after His earthly reign. On the other hand, the millennium is also very distinct from the eternal state because in the latter, Satan has been thrown into the lake of fire, and even the very possibility to sin no longer exists. Eternity will be a totally sinless realm where unbelief and deception will be forever past.

Our Role in the Millennium

The fact that the millennium is a unique intermediate phase between the current church age and the eternal state also follows from the role that we believers will play during this period. Revelation 20 mentions two types of saints that will be part of the millennial reign. Firstly, there are those on "thrones" who receive the authority to execute "judgment" (v. 4). The Greek word for judgment, *krima*, is the noun form of the verb *krino*, which means to judge, rule or govern. *Krino* occurs in the very passages that promise that God's people will one day reign with Him:

> And Jesus said to them [the apostles], "Truly I say to you, that you who have followed Me, in the regeneration when the Son of Man will sit on His glorious throne, *you also shall sit upon twelve thrones, judging [krino] the twelve tribes of Israel.*"
>
> (Matthew 19:28, emphasis added)

> You [the apostles] are those who have stood by Me in My trials; and just as My Father has granted Me a kingdom, I grant you that you may eat and drink at My table in My kingdom, and *you will sit on thrones judging [krino] the twelve tribes of Israel.*
>
> (Luke 22:28–30, emphasis added)

> Or do you not know that *the saints will judge [krino] the world*?
>
> (1 Corinthians 6:2, emphasis added)

We had already seen that the 24 elders who reside on thrones around the throne of God represent the overcoming saints throughout history. Since they are on thrones and it is prophesied that in the millennium believers will sit on "thrones" and "judge" the world, it is not difficult to establish that Revelation 20:4 talks about the first fruits (Jesus' promise to the twelve apostles to judge the "twelve tribes of Israel" symbolizes our reign over all nations). Then, the passage mentions those who had "not worshiped the beast or his image, and had not received the mark on their forehead and on their hand" and were consequently martyred. These are the foolish virgins, the non-overcoming saints who had to go through the tribulation but ultimately also overcome, and therefore equally get to share in the overcomer promise of reigning with Christ.

What exactly is the purpose of our reign with Christ? How does it differ from the current church age on the one hand and the eternal state in the New Jerusalem on the other? Firstly, it is extremely important to establish that nowhere in Scripture are we believers promised to be co-regents with Christ *during this present age.* All of these promises refer to a period *after* Jesus' return. The crucial mistake of Augustine and the Catholic church was to alter these future references so as to interpret them as being about the present. Even though we have been given spiritual authority and the power to overcome the evil one, we have not yet received authority to "judge [*krino*] the world." As part of church government, we believers are called to judge and punish those within the church who refuse to repent from sinful behaviors. But this does not give us the right to govern the affairs of those outside the church. As Paul notes, "For what have I to do with judging outsiders? Do you not judge those who are within the church? *But those who are outside, God judges*" (1 Corinthians 5:12–13, emphasis added). It is true that we have already been adopted into God's royal family and been made a "royal priesthood" (1 Peter 2:9). But this current age is still a preparation time until we are made ready to take up our thrones, until our priesthood role will find its ultimate fulfillment.

Therefore, if we consider ourselves as reigning with Christ in the present age, we are seriously overstepping the boundaries of authority that God has given us! This is why amillennialism ended up paving the way for the crusades, and Dominion Theology is making a similar mistake by promoting the postmillennial view that it is our present duty to gradually bring about God's Kingdom during this church age.[2] According to God's Word, it is only *after* we ourselves have been judged at the judgment seat of Christ that we are in turn given positions of judgment ourselves, and we can only take up these positions once we are under the direct supervision of Jesus Himself. Scripture is clear that all those who reign with Christ are either resurrected or raptured saints, which means that we will have received our brand-new immortal bodies (remember that both the first fruits symbolized by the 24 elders and the great multitude from Revelation 7 are depicted as standing glorified in white robes before the throne of God *prior* to the beginning of the millennium). By the start of the millennium, we will be perfect and literally spotless followers of Christ (1 Corinthians 15:51–54; Philippians 3:21). Only at that point will we be walking in the fullness of His knowledge, His love, and the priestly and kingly power and authority that He bestows on us based on our faithfulness to Him during our previous lives. It is this glorified state that will qualify and enable us to truly reign with Christ. Consequently, the view that we are already reigning with Christ right now is either the epitome of conceitedness or a reduction of this amazingly glorious reign to nothing more than our present Christian experience.

On the other hand, the believers' reigning with Christ is not something that can or will happen in the eternal era. Scripture clearly implies that we will judge and reign over the "nations" (Revelation 2:26), ruling them with a "rod of iron." This can only refer to a governmental rule over entities and populations who are not (yet) in full subjection to Christ. It does not mean that some saints will exercise disciplinary authority over other saints; in sinless eternity, such an authority relationship would neither be necessary nor possible. Therefore, this promise, which will surely be fulfilled, can only refer to the special intermediary period of the millennium.

Ruling the Nations With a "Rod of Iron"

What will it be like to reign with Christ, and what is the purpose of such a government? In order to answer this question, we need to examine God's rationale for ordaining the millennium in the first place. A major reason why many scholars, especially the more liberal ones, question a literal millennial reign is that they do not see what such an earthly rule would achieve. However, the Bible gives us several important objectives for its existence.

The first reason is given in 1 Corinthians 15, where Paul states that "He [Jesus] must reign until He has put all His enemies under His feet. ... When all things are subjected to Him, then the Son Himself also will be subjected to the One who subjected all things to Him, so that God may be all in all." (vv. 25, 28). This verse describes a gradual process of subjugation. Firstly, Jesus will reign on earth until He has step-by-step subjected all opposing powers and principalities of this world to His authority. Psalm 110:1 states the same truth: "The LORD [God the Father] says to my Lord [Jesus]: Sit at My right hand until I make your enemies a footstool for Your feet." In a sense, this represents the fulfillment and completion of our spiritual struggles against "principalities, against powers, against the rulers of the darkness of this age, against spiritual hosts of wickedness in the heavenly places" (Ephesians 6:12 NKJV).

Both 1 Corinthians 15 and Psalm 110 indicate that this subjugation will not be instantaneous but will be a *process*; both use the word "until," indicating that Jesus' millennial rule *is not completed until* this objective has been achieved. Afterward, Jesus concludes his reign by handing the Kingdom over to the Father, so that in the end God will supremely be "all in all." The millennium therefore represents an intermediate stage during which Jesus will increasingly achieve divine dominance over all earthly powers and authorities, until, in the end, the eternal state starts with God being in a position of ultimate supremacy. This is also the reason why the believers' "rod of iron" reign with Christ cannot refer to the eternal state, because after the Great White Throne judgment, all opposing forces that have not willingly submitted to God will have been overthrown.

This progressive dominion of Christ begins with a thundering start at the onset of the Day of the Lord, the wrath of God described in the seventh seal and the seven trumpets, culminating in the battle of Armageddon in Revelation 19. But the Day of the Lord does not finish there; 2 Peter 3:10 states that this Day will not be completed until the "heavens will pass away with a roar," which refers to Revelation 20:11 and 21:1, after the millennium is over. The millennium is therefore part of the Day of the Lord, which is God's wrath. Consequently, Christ's millennial reign is also an expression of God's judgment of the earth, but it differs from the wrath: rather than being primarily destructive and wrathful as the latter, it represents a powerful and authoritative rule of righteousness over a formerly unregenerate and God-rejecting world.

This progression is reflected in the passages that describe the "rod of iron" rule of Christ. In Psalm 2, the text where this rule is first directly mentioned in the Bible, it says that Jesus will "*break* them [the kingdoms of the world] with a rod of iron ... [and] *shatter* them like earthenware" (v. 9). Here, the emphasis is on a literal breaking and destroying, which literally takes place during the outpouring of God's wrath in the seventh seal.[3] In contrast, the New Testament passages on this subject all state that Christ and the believers will "*rule* all the nations with a rod of iron." The Greek term for "rule," *poimaino*,[4] literally means to "tend as a shepherd" and is used, for example, in the verse that talks about "a ruler who will shepherd [*poimaino*] my people Israel" (Matthew 2:6). The Greek for "rod," *rhabdos*[5] can either mean a disciplinary rod, a shepherd's staff, or a royal scepter. Shepherding involves both a rod and a staff, and the term used in Revelation can indeed refer to both.[6] What is in view here, then, is not the same "rod of iron" rule as during the first phase of the Day of the Lord, but a shepherding reign, yet still one that employs punitive discipline and is enforced with absolute royal authority. Jesus seeks to guide the nations towards His righteousness, and for this, He uses both rod and staff—loving guidance as well as punitive enforcement.

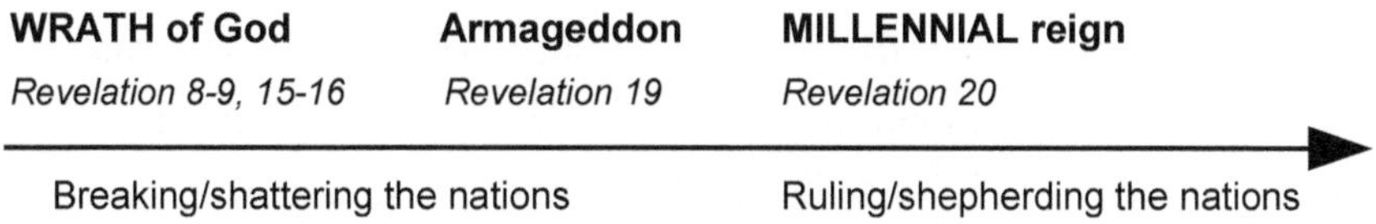

WRATH of God	**Armageddon**	**MILLENNIAL reign**
Revelation 8-9, 15-16	Revelation 19	Revelation 20

Breaking/shattering the nations   Ruling/shepherding the nations

Figure 20. Christ's "rod of iron" rule during the Day of the Lord

Isaiah 60 and Psalm 72 provide us with more details as to what Christ's shepherding "rod of iron" rule will look like:

> Your [millennial Jerusalem's] gates will be open continually; they will not be closed day or night, so that men may bring to you the wealth of the nations, with their kings led in procession. For the nation and the kingdom which will not serve you will perish, and the nations will be utterly ruined.
>
> (Isaiah 60:11–12)

> May he also rule from sea to sea and from the river to the ends of the earth. Let the nomads of the desert bow before him, and his enemies lick the dust. Let the kings of Tarshish and of the islands bring presents; the kings of Sheba and Seba offer gifts. And let all kings bow down before him, all nations serve him.
>
> (Psalm 72:8–11)

The result of Christ's authoritative rule is that the nations will humbly come and bow before Him, offering Him presents in recognition of His glory. In ancient times, it was customary to honor an important ruler with lavish gifts. An important outcome of the millennial reign is that all nations will acknowledge Jesus as supreme King, in fulfillment of

Philippians 2:10–11, which says that "at the name of Jesus every knee will bow ... and that every tongue will confess that Jesus Christ is Lord, to the glory of God the Father." During the millennium, a certain level of recognition and worship of the King of kings will be mandatory, and those of the "families of the earth" who fail to observe the commanded feasts will face punishment such as a lack of rainfall (Zechariah 14:17–19). Again, this is something we can neither see in the present age nor in the eternal age where Jesus will only receive the freely-offered worship of His own people.

Many Christians question not only the purpose but also the morality of such a "rod of iron" rule. They feel that this is somehow not compatible with a loving God. But the very fact that we doubt God's right to subjugate His creation under Himself only shows how completely we have lost the plot. Not a few church-goers have a perception of God as a harmless old man who would not squash a fly. But while humility and gentleness are indeed important aspects of God, so are righteousness, justice, and a holy wrath for that which refuses to submit itself to Him. Those who question a strict millennial rule over the nations must also doubt the extensive and terrible wrath that God clearly says He will pour out on the unbelieving world, as well as the eternal damnation of all unbelievers in the lake of fire! We modern 21st century humans apparently have no idea what it means to be humbled under the mighty hands of an all-powerful king, nor do we realize that the King of the universe has every right in the world to expect, demand, and enforce the full submission of His entire creation.

It seems that we have clearly forgotten that while Jesus possesses deep love and compassion even for His enemies, he is also like a strict Master who will have unfaithful servants severely punished: "cut ... in pieces" and thrown into a place of "weeping and gnashing of teeth" (Matthew 24:51), or ordered to "receive many lashes" based on their degree of disobedience (Luke 12:47). From millennial passages, we can ascertain that there will likely be capital punishment for serious offenders (Isaiah 11:5, cited below). This points to the truth that those who reject Christ will ultimately suffer a much worse fate than death by execution. At the same time, however, we know that the rule of Christ will not be a repetition of the gruesome medieval crusades which He never authorized, nor will He torture anybody into believing in Him. Rather, the authoritative reign of Christ will combine love and compassion with strictness and an iron-fist approach against sin, evil, and injustice. It will establish Jesus as a both righteous and loving King, demonstrating all of His personal qualities to an awestruck world. At present, we may struggle to picture how this earthly reign will unfold in reality. But when it happens, everything about it will feel perfectly "right."

Establishing Justice and True Peace

Apart from bringing glory to Himself and to the Father, there will be another essential outcome of Christ's "rod of iron" reign. Both of the two passages cited above show that Jesus' strict and uncompromising governance of the entire earth bring about justice for the "poor and needy" and freedom from "oppression and violence":

> And He will not judge by what His eyes see, nor make a decision by what His ears hear; But with righteousness He will judge the poor, and decide with fairness for the afflicted of the earth; and He will strike the earth with the rod of His mouth, and with the breath of His lips He will slay the wicked.
>
> (Isaiah 11:3–5)

> For he will deliver the needy when he cries for help, the afflicted also, and him who has no helper. He will have compassion on the poor and needy, and the lives of the needy

he will save. He will rescue their life from oppression and violence, and their blood will be precious in his sight.

(Psalm 72:12–14)

Indeed, many Old Testament passages testify that Jesus' "rod of iron" rule will lead to an unprecedented era of peace and righteousness:

> And He will judge between many peoples and render decisions for mighty, distant nations. Then they will hammer their swords into plowshares and their spears into pruning hooks; nation will not lift up sword against nation, and never again will they train for war. Each of them will sit under his vine and under his fig tree, with no one to make them afraid.

(Micah 4:3–4; see also Isaiah 2:4)

Jesus' millennial reign will therefore benefit *all* people: those who have been at the very bottom of human society, but also everyone else, who can, for the first time in human history, enjoy a period of true peace.

Amongst amillennial scholars, it is common to interpret passages such as these as referring to the eternal state and not to a special millennial era. But the scriptures cited above can only refer to the unique in-between state that the millennium represents. On the one hand, they speak of a much greater peace than could ever be imagined in this present fallen world. But on the other hand, they cannot refer to sinless eternity, because there clearly still is the potential for sin, war, and oppression. Christ and His people have to actively and continually enforce peace, justice, and righteousness throughout the world. Otherwise, even with Satan's deceptive presence being removed, people's fallen natures will still tend to engage in such sinful behaviors. The millennium is a state where the pervasive power and reach of sin is more restricted than at present, but it is not the totally sin-free environment that only eternity will offer.

Additionally, millennial passages indicate that the millennium represents an exclusive opportunity for unsaved people from all nations to freely come and "go up to the mountain of the Lord" so that they can learn God's ways and be saved:

> And it will come about in the last days that the mountain of the house of the LORD will be established as the chief of the mountains. It will be raised above the hills, and the peoples will stream to it. Many nations will come and say, "Come and let us go up to the mountain of the LORD and to the house of the God of Jacob, that He may teach us about His ways and that we may walk in His paths. For from Zion will go forth the law, even the word of the LORD from Jerusalem.
>
> (Micah 4:1–2[7])

The millennium is therefore still a period when people can decide for or against Jesus, although this time without the deceitful interference of Satan. In fact, the unhindered revelation of Jesus to the entire world is a key feature of the millennial age. Jesus will force the unbelieving populations of the world to adhere to certain standards of righteousness and justice and to offer homage to Him. But the decision to truly submit to and believe in Him will still be up to each individual. Satan's final release after this period will then prove to be the ultimate test of people's true allegiance, showing that many will unfortunately end up rejecting the Savior that they were able to behold with their own eyes. This is the very reason why the Great White Throne judgment does not take place until *after* the millennium.

Again, amillennial scholars use the final rebellion of the nations against Christ after the millennium to argue that His rule would then seemingly have failed to achieve its objective; consequently, the millennial reign cannot be understood to occur literally. But we forget that during His first coming 2,000 years ago, Jesus did not use all means to convince every person to believe in Him. Quite the contrary, He encrypted His teachings in parables and deliberately employed hard sayings, such as "My flesh is true food, and My blood is true drink," fully aware that as a result "many of His disciples withdrew and were not walking with Him anymore" (John 6:55, 66). Even with Satan being bound, humanity during the millennium will still have to make a conscious choice against their fallen sin nature in order to experience true spiritual rebirth. The fact that vast numbers of people ultimately follow Satan rather than Jesus is not a testimony to Jesus' inabilities but to the utter depravity and wickedness of fallen mankind.

But despite this final rebellious act, the millennium will not have failed its purposes of glorifying Jesus and the Father, of subjugating all powers to Him and to God, of giving the world a unique chance to share in the blessings of a Jesus-led government of the earth, and of providing people with an unprecedented opportunity to witness the life of Jesus and His glorified saints first-hand. In fact, the millennium's success has been prophesied a long time ago: "Many nations will join themselves to the LORD in that day and will become My people" (Zechariah 2:10).

Palingenesia: The Millennium as Progressive Regeneration

Finally, an important purpose of the millennial age is a progressive reversal of the curse that God placed on Adam and Eve in Genesis 3. After they ate from the forbidden tree, God pronounced the following curse over humanity:

> To the woman He said, "I will greatly multiply your pain in childbirth, in pain you will bring forth children; yet your desire will be for your husband, and he will rule over you."

> Then to Adam He said, ".... Cursed is the ground because
> of you; in toil you will eat of it all the days of your life. Both
> thorns and thistles it shall grow for you; and you will eat the
> plants of the field; by the sweat of your face you will eat bread,
> till you return to the ground, because from it you were taken;
> for you are dust, and to dust you shall return."
>
> (Genesis 3:16–19)

God's curse was fourfold. Firstly, He cursed the process of child-bearing, making it painful and potentially dangerous. Secondly, He cursed the relationship between husband and wife, making them live in strife, caught up in the desire to dominate and manipulate each other, a condition that also poisoned all other types of relationships.[8] Thirdly, He cursed the ground, so that its produce would come forth unreliably and through much toil. Fourthly, God had told Adam and Eve that if they ate from the tree they would "die" (v. 3). With their disobedience followed both spiritual and physical death, as well as psychological and physical illness.

It is wonderful to see how the millennium is poised to partially reverse the negative effects of all four aspects of the Genesis 3 curse. Jesus' reign will change the biological, physical, social, and spiritual conditions of our planet. Through His sovereign intervention, we will not only see greater peace in human relations, but also increased human and agricultural fruitfulness, lengthened lifespans, as well as a reduction of suffering and pain through sickness.

The first curse reversal will restore longevity, health, and blessings in child-bearing:

> No longer will there be in it an infant who lives but a few days,
> or an old man who does not live out his days; for the youth
> will die at the age of one hundred and the one who does not
> reach the age of one hundred will be thought accursed.

> They will build houses and inhabit them; they will also
> plant vineyards and eat their fruit. They will not build and
> another inhabit, they will not plant and another eat; for as the
> lifetime of a tree, so will be the days of My people, and My
> chosen ones will wear out the work of their hands. They will
> not labor in vain, or bear children for calamity; for they are
> the offspring of those blessed by the LORD.
>
> (Isaiah 65:19–23; compare also Zechariah 8:4)

The second curse reversal will restore a fruit-bearing environment, abundant agricultural production, and the restoration of deserts to blooming lands:

> Do not fear, beasts of the field, for the pastures of the wilderness
> have turned green, for the tree has borne its fruit, the fig
> tree and the vine have yielded in full…. And He has poured
> down for you the rain, the early and latter rain as before. The
> threshing floors will be full of grain, and the vats will overflow
> with the new wine and oil.
>
> (Joel 2:22–26)

> Then the lame will leap like a deer, and the tongue of the
> mute will shout for joy. For waters will break forth in the
> wilderness and streams in the Arabah. The scorched land will
> become a pool and the thirsty ground springs of water.
>
> (Isaiah 35:6–7)

The third curse reversal will restore harmony and peace in relations between animals and between animals and humans:

> And the wolf will dwell with the lamb, and the leopard will
> lie down with the young goat, and the calf and the young lion

and the fatling together; and a little boy will lead them. Also
the cow and the bear will graze, their young will lie down
together, and the lion will eat straw like the ox. The nursing
child will play by the hole of the cobra, and the weaned child
will put his hand on the viper's den. They will not hurt or
destroy in all My holy mountain.

(Isaiah 11:6–9)

Here, we need to add that our literal interpretation of millennial
passages such as these does not mean that we should blindly ignore the
wealth of symbolisms they contain. The images depicted especially in
the last citation from Isaiah 11 symbolize a restored harmony within
God's creation. However, there is no need to assert that lions will
literally "eat straw like the ox." Although God could certainly conduct
supernatural digestive systems surgery on these animals if He wanted
to, the deeper meaning expressed here is a picture of profound peace
amongst all of God's creation. It is important to understand and discern
the rich symbolisms that are embedded in these prophecies. But such
symbolic interpretation does not imply that all millennial passages can
be allegorized.

During the millennial era, the reversal of the curse will not yet be
complete. There will still be physical death, and the on-going presence
of sin will still be felt in human relationships—although not as strongly
as in the present age. Creation will only be completely "set free from
its slavery to corruption" (Romans 8:21) when the eternal era has
been ushered in. Only then will there "no longer ... be any curse"
(Revelation 22:3).

The millennium is therefore an intermediary period of partial
regeneration. In Matthew 19:28, Jesus used that very term to describe
this age: "you who have followed Me, in the regeneration [*palingenesia*]
when the Son of Man will sit on His glorious throne, you also shall sit
upon twelve thrones...." The Greek term *palingenesia* is derived from

the words *palin*, to repeat or do again, and *genesis*, which means birth or origin (as in "Genesis," the first book of the Bible). *Genesis* stems from the same root as *gennao*, the term Jesus employed in John 3:7 where he said that we must be "born [*gennao*] again." Consequently, when Jesus tells us that the millennium is an era of *palingenesia*, he confirms all of the Old Testament prophecies cited above which demonstrate that this era represents a spiritual rebirth of our current world. This time, not just individual human beings but the entire globe will be regenerated by being born [*genesis*] again [*palin*]. This also shows us what the millennium is *not*: it does *not* represent a complete and total destruction of the old in order to replace it with something entirely new. Instead, it is a partial regeneration of the old, ultimately leading to Christ "making all things new" (Revelation 21:5)—which is the establishment of "a new heaven and a new earth" (Revelation 21:1) in the eternal age. Again, Scripture testifies that the millennial age is a unique time, distinct from both the present age and the eternal state.

Table 29. Comparing the current church age, the millennial age, and the eternal age

	Church age	Millennial age	Eternal age
Satan's power and sin's power	Satan was defeated at the cross, but he can still deceive and incapacitate God's people. Sin still "easily entangles us" (Hebrews 12:1). Satan and sin still have full power over the unsaved, having "blinded the minds of the unbelieving" (2 Corinthians 4:4).	Satan is banished into the abyss, so that for the first time since the fall "he would not deceive the nations any longer" (Revelation 20:3). However, the power of sin is still present, meaning that humans are still capable of sinning through their fallen natures. People can choose to call on the name of the Lord, learn His ways, and get saved (Micah 4:2; Isaiah 2:3). But they can also reject God and be destroyed (Revelation 20:9, 15).	Satan is thrown into the lake of fire (Revelation 20:10). All unbelievers are eternally condemned (Revelation 20:15). The power of sin is forever removed—eternity is a completely sin-free environment. All decisions for or against Christ are now final.
Effects of the Genesis 3 curse	All four aspects of the curse on child-bearing, nature, relationships, and spiritual/physical/emotional illness are in full effect. Believers can in many ways counter them through Christ (although not perfectly). Jesus achieved victory over spiritual death (1 Corinthians 15:56), but mortality continues. Believers who die before Christ's return only die physically, not spiritually.	The impact of the curse is diminished but still present. There is no more death at childbirth, human lifespans are prolonged, deserts turn green, fertility and agricultural production increase; human relations and relations between humans and the natural environment are dominated by peace. But people can still sin, oppress others, and there is still death (physical and spiritual). Only those who were saved before the millennium already walk in immortal glorified bodies (1 Corinthians 15:52–55).	Sin and death are no more (Revelation 21:4), and there will no longer "be any curse" (Revelation 22:3). Death is now finally defeated and thrown into the lake of fire (Revelation 20:14). The impact of the curse is fully removed as all those in eternity now possess glorified bodies and there is no more corruption or suffering. There is no more marriage or childbirth (Matthew 22:30).
Christ's authority on earth	Christ does not yet exercise the full authority over the earth that He has been given by the Father. He can be opposed, marginalized, and misrepresented in both society and church. Satan is still the "god of this world" (2 Corinthians 4:4). Presently, God withholds His judgment, sending "rain on the unjust and the unrighteous" (Matthew 5:45).	Christ reigns "to the ends of the earth" (Ps. 72:8). He progressively subjects all earthly dominions and powers to Himself through His "rod of iron" rule, together with the believers (1 Corinthians 15). Now, "all rulers will worship and obey him" (Daniel 7:27). There is punishment for people and nations who do not submit (Zechariah 14), oppress others, or act wickedly (Psalm 72:4; Isaiah 11:4). But after the millennium, the nations will rise against Him in a final act of rebellion (Revelation 20:8–9).	Christ is enthroned amongst His people and there is no longer any opposition to Him (Revelation 22:1).

Our authority and position	We have been given the power to overcome Satan and His works, including sickness (Mark 16:15–20; 1 John 3:8, 5:4). We are adopted into the royal family and exercise priestly authority in our ministries (1 Peter 2:9; Revelation 1:6). We have authority to judge those in the church but not outsiders (1 Corinthians 5:12–13). While we are in this world, we will face tribulation (John 16:33).	We will fully participate in Christ's millennial reign and will "rule them [the nations] with a rod of iron" (Revelation 2:27), just as He does. We will sit on thrones and execute judgment over the whole world and not just over fellow believers (Matthew 19:28; 1 Corinthians 6:2; Revelation 20:4). Our "royal priesthood" will be raised to a new level as we exercise both spiritual and governmental authority under Christ. Believers with greater spiritual fruitfulness during the church age will now enjoy greater authority (Luke 19:17–18)	We will spend eternity with God and Christ, worshiping before their throne (Revelation 7:9–10; 19:1–6; 21–22). Believers who lived more spiritually fruitful lives will enjoy greater rewards in eternity (1 Corinthians 3:11–15; Revelation 22:12).

The Relationship Between the Millennial World and the New Jerusalem

A common argument against a literal millennial reign of Christ is that many prophetic texts do not neatly distinguish between descriptions of millennial and eternal conditions. Amillennial scholars often point to Isaiah 65:

> For behold, *I create new heavens and a new earth*; and the *former things will not be remembered or come to mind*. But be glad and rejoice forever in what I create; for behold, I create Jerusalem for rejoicing and her people for gladness. I will also rejoice in Jerusalem and be glad in My people; and *there will no longer be heard in her the voice of weeping and the sound of crying.*
>
> (Isaiah 65:17–19, emphases added)

The difficulty with this passage is that it combines scenes from the eternal state with depictions of the millennium. In fact, it closely corresponds to John's vision of the New Jerusalem in Revelation 21, which outlines eternity with God:

Then I saw *a new heaven and a new earth*; for *the first heaven and the first earth passed away*, and there is no longer any sea. And I saw the holy city, New Jerusalem, coming down out of heaven from God, made ready as a bride adorned for her husband.... He will *wipe away every tear from their eyes*; and there will *no longer be any death*; there will *no longer be any mourning, or crying, or pain; the first things have passed away.*

(Revelation 21:1–2, 4, emphases added)

In both passages we see characteristics of the eternal state: no more pain, no more tears, and no more death. John is told that the overcomers will inherit the New Jerusalem, but that those who reject God will instead be in the lake of fire. The glorious city descending from heaven can only be referring to eternity with God.

But when we look at the subsequent verses in the Isaiah 65 passage, we observe that the section from verse 20 is a description of millennial conditions:

No longer will there be in it an infant who lives but a few days, or an old man who does not live out his days; for the youth will die at the age of one hundred and the one who does not reach the age of one hundred will be thought accursed.

(Isaiah 65:20)

We know that in eternity there will be no childbirth or marriage, nor will there be aging, decay, frailty, or death. The possibilities of infant death or of someone dying after having reached old age only exist in the millennial age. Moreover, John's glorious vision of the New Jerusalem in Revelation 21 also shows a mixing in of elements that can only pertain to the millennial state:

The nations [*ethnos*] will walk by its light, and the kings of the earth will bring their glory into it. In the daytime (for there will be no night there) its gates will never be closed; and they will bring the glory and the honor of the nations [*ethnos*] into it; and nothing unclean, and no one who practices abomination and lying, shall ever come into it, but only those whose names are written in the Lamb's Book of life.

(Revelation 21:24–27)

In Revelation 21:1, it says that "there is no longer any sea." This somewhat perplexing statement becomes clearer when we interpret this "sea" not as a literal body of water but as symbolic of a "sea of nations"—a source of evil and wickedness. Ancient peoples often viewed the sea as dangerous and threatening. In Isaiah 57:20 the wicked are compared to "the tossing sea," and it is no coincidence that the beast, the Antichrist, is depicted as arising "out of the sea" (Revelation 13:1). At the final judgment, it is the "sea," and not the land, that is described to give up "the dead which were in it," even though the vast majority of humans are buried on land. Finally, in Revelation 17:15 the angel tells John that "[t]he waters [*seas*] which you saw where the harlot sits, are peoples and multitudes and nations and tongues." The eternal state no longer having a "sea" therefore tells us that there will no longer be evil powers, nor will the eternal state feature any political nations or ethnic or racial divisions (the Greek word *ethnos*, translated as "nations" in Revelation 21:24–27 can refer to either of these). People will retain their personal ethnic diversity and display it before God's throne (Revelation 7:9), but these identities no longer form structures of power or divisiveness. (This interpretation of "sea" does not preclude that there may not literally be any large water bodies, but that is almost certainly not the point that Revelation 21:1 is trying to make.)

Now, if there are no "nations" or ethnic groups in eternity, then the "kings of the earth" cannot be bringing the "glory and the honor of the nations" into the eternal New Jerusalem. This is further confirmed by the fact that "nothing unclean" is said to enter this place, but only "those whose names are written in the Lamb's book of life." But if all unclean and evil things have been banished to the lake of fire, how can there even be the possibility of them entering the New Jerusalem? If God's people reside *inside* the New Jerusalem, how can there be anyone else whose permanent residence is obviously *outside* of it? The answer is that these verses simply do not fit to the conditions of the eternal age.

Another puzzling passage is John's vision of the "river of the water of life" (22:1–2). It says that the tree's leaves are "for the healing of the nations [*ethnos*]" (v. 2). Will there still be ethnic or political structures in the New Jerusalem? Would this verse likely use the term "nations [*ethnos*]" if it would only refer to resurrected and raptured saints? Also, will glorified believers need on-going healing after all their tears have been wiped away, the former things are forgotten ("passed by"), and they have all received immortal resurrection bodies? Certainly not. But if this is not just about eternity, then what is John trying to tell us?

The fact that Old Testament prophecy blends both millennial and eternal elements does not mean that both can be equated. After all, the Old Testament writers also did not clearly distinguish between the first and the second comings of Christ. But why would we find such blending in the New Testament? While the precise relationship between the millennial and the New Jerusalem is a hotly debated topic, the most logical explanation is that Revelation 21–22 is simply a description of the New Jerusalem *during* the millennium. Since this eternal city obviously interacts with the millennial Kingdom—"kings of the earth" and "nations" which require "healing" enter it—it must already be in existence during the millennial era. In fact, John purposely mixed descriptions of both millennial and eternal conditions in order to tell us that the millennial earth and the New Jerusalem as the eternal abode of the glorified saints will exist alongside. Especially the river of life passage lends itself to such a conclusion: it is intended for the "healing of the nations," but it flows from the "throne of God" through the center of the New Jerusalem into the millennial earthly Jerusalem, and from there to both East and West (Zechariah 14:8). These waters of spiritual, emotional, and physical healing are for the populations of the earth who have been severely bruised by the pre-wrath birth pangs, the tribulations, and by God's terrible wrath.

Therefore, the description of the eternal city in Revelation 21–22 envisions the operation of this city during the millennium, prior to the final eternal state. Once the millennial earth has "passed away," the New Jerusalem will go on to exist forever. Its presence during the millennium will not contaminate its perfect and sinless condition, because it clearly says that "nothing unclean ... shall ever come into it" (Revelation 21:27). For the millennial earth, the New Jerusalem will be like a sanctuary of healing and blessing. From its description, it is clear that only saved persons can enter it, meaning that the "kings of the nations" mentioned in Revelation 21 will all be converts of the millennial phase. This is not surprising, since Christ's authority structures during this time will certainly rely on a government that consists of His people, at least for those in important leadership positions. A mixing and mingling of the saints in their glorified bodies with mortal humans poses no particular scriptural problem, in contrast to what some believe. After all, Jesus Himself walked on the earth in His resurrection body before He ascended to heaven.

This relationship between millennial earth and eternal city is further illuminated by the way the New Jerusalem is depicted. It says that this glorious city has "no temple" but that God and the Lamb "are its temple" (21:22). What does that mean? It means that the entire New Jerusalem is itself like a giant temple. Its perfect cubic shape described in Revelation 21:15 exactly corresponds to the shape of the Holy of Holies (or "inner sanctuary") of Solomon's temple (1 Kings 6:20). Similarly, the overcoming believer is promised to be a symbolic "pillar in the temple of My God, and he will not go out from it anymore" (Revelation 3:12). In the next verse, it says that overcomers will have the name of the New

Jerusalem written on them, indicating that the New Jerusalem is this "temple" that the saints will never leave. In contrast to the temples in the Old Testament, this eternal "temple" is not so much a physical structure as it is about the persons that inhabit it: God, the Lamb, and God's people together constitute "the temple." After all, the 12 tribes symbolically represent its gates, and the 12 apostles its foundations, meaning that the city and God's people are one unit.

Viewing the eternal Jerusalem as being like a "temple" of the millennial age also corresponds to Ezekiel's millennial prophecy that God will "set My sanctuary in their midst forever" (Ezekiel 37:26). Moreover, it explains why the kings of the earth will bring their glory into it (see also Isaiah 60:7, 13; Haggai 2:7). By having both millennial earth and eternal city coexist alongside, God will give the world a glimpse of His full glory and of the eternity that awaits those who accept Him as King.

Will the Millennium feature a literal earthly temple and animal sacrifices?

A particular point of contention is the question of whether the millennium will have its own temple and whether both Jews and Gentiles will be required to worship Jesus exclusively in a temple-based priesthood and sacrificial system. Many conservative scholars interpret the prophecy of Ezekiel 40–48 to indicate that there will be a so-called millennial temple, complete with a Levitical priesthood and animal sacrifices. Their argument is that the temple prophecy contained in this passage has never been fulfilled and consequently awaits its realization in the millennial age.

Attempts at non-literal interpretation have, for example, suggested that this temple was meant to be symbolic of the future establishment of the church. But such spiritualizing interpretations do indeed seem inappropriate in light of the meticulous level of detail contained in Ezekiel's prophecy. The most important argument against interpreting these passages as prescribing a millennial temple and priesthood is that the New Testament so clearly teaches us that the sacrificial system of the Old Covenant has been fully replaced by the New Covenant, established through Jesus' ultimate sacrifice on the cross. Against this injunction, the millennial temple advocates argue that the temple worship outlined in Ezekiel is not simply a re-institution of the Aaronic system given to Moses, but contains significant changes.[9] Moreover, they suggest that the book of Hebrews, which argues that Christ completely replaced the old sacrificial system, was written for Christians and not for the Jews. In their view, we cannot insist that Jews become like Christians even once they are truly saved. The resurrection of a literal system of feasts and animal sacrifices would therefore be a legitimate way for Jews to worship their millennial Messiah. It would not constitute a revival of the old Mosaic system.

The issue of whether there will be a millennial temple and Old Testament-style priesthood or not is not a secondary question. It profoundly affects our understanding of the millennial era and how we and the non-glorified populations of the world can relate to Jesus.

A careful examination of Ezekiel 40–48 shows that the offerings prescribed in this passage are by no means merely ceremonial or just commemorating the death of Christ, as scholars like Thomas Ice or John Walvoord suggest. To the contrary, everything in this temple prophecy indicates that these sacrifices are meant as atonement for sin, just as under Mosaic Law. To cite several examples:

1. Sin offering to cleanse the altar:

> "You shall give to the Levitical priests who are from the offspring of Zadok, who draw near to Me to minister to Me," declares the Lord GOD, "a young bull for a *sin offering*. You shall take some of its blood and put it on its four horns and on the four corners of the ledge and on the border round about; thus *you shall cleanse it and make atonement for it*."
>
> (Ezekiel 43:19–20, emphases added)

2. Sin offering to cleanse the priests:

> "They [the priests] shall not go to a dead person to defile themselves; however, for father, for mother, for son, for daughter, for brother, or for a sister who has not had a husband, they may defile themselves. After he is cleansed, seven days shall elapse for him. On the day that he goes into the sanctuary, into the inner court to minister in the sanctuary, *he shall offer his sin offering*," declares the Lord GOD.
>
> (Ezekiel 44:25–26, emphases added)

3. Sin offerings for the leader (the "prince") and the people:

> On that day the prince shall provide *for himself and all the people of the land a bull for a sin offering.*
>
> (Ezekiel 45:22, emphasis added)

> The priest shall take some of the blood from the *sin offering* and put it on the door posts of the house, on the four corners of the ledge of the altar and on the posts of the gate of the inner court. Thus you shall do on the seventh day of the month *for everyone who goes astray or is naive; so you shall make atonement for the house.*
>
> (Ezekiel 45:19–20, emphases added)

Ice argues that "animal sacrifices during the millennium will serve primarily to remove ceremonial uncleanness and prevent defilement from polluting the temple envisioned by Ezekiel."[10] But what the text actually outlines is much more than a removal of "ceremonial uncleanness"! It prescribes a removal of sin, the very "atonement" that Jesus' death on the cross achieved for us (2 Corinthians 5:18–19). Yet Christ's sacrifice not only atoned for our sin, it also provided the very cleansing and purification that is required in Ezekiel's vision and was formerly done under Mosaic Law:

> [H]ow much more will *the blood of Christ,* who through the eternal Spirit offered Himself without blemish to God, *cleanse your conscience from dead works* to serve the living God?...
>
> ... Therefore it was necessary for the copies of the things in the heavens to be *cleansed with these,* but the heavenly things themselves *with better sacrifices than these.*
>
> (Hebrews 9:14, 23, emphases added)

> [B]ut if we walk in the Light as He Himself is in the Light,
> we have fellowship with one another, and *the blood of Jesus*
> *His Son cleanses us from all sin.*
>
> (1 John 1:7, emphasis added)

Under the New Covenant, we believers are washed and cleansed by the blood of Christ and the Word of God (John 15:2), not by the blood of sacrifices—even if they are meant to be purely symbolic. But the rituals contained in Ezekiel's vision are not described as merely symbolic; rather, they seek to *literally* achieve that which Christ did on the cross. They also do not appear to be backward-looking, so as to commemorate what Christ did in the past. Not once in the vision do words such as "remember," "memorial," or "commemoration" occur and neither is such a meaning implied. Rather, the prescribed sacrifices are literally taken from the Levitical system and applied for the same reason of removing sin (Ezekiel 40:39; 42:13; 43:27; 45:17; 46:20). Therefore, these sacrifices are not backward-looking so as to commemorate what Christ did in the past. Instead, they are forward-looking like in the Mosaic system, requiring the use of blood to atone for sin as if Christ had not yet died. Consequently, the sacrificial system envisioned by Ezekiel is essentially a modified version of that given to Moses, which was rendered obsolete once Christ had come to be our ultimate sacrifice, once and for all.

Even though Ezekiel's temple contains no veil or partitioning wall to exclude the Gentiles, there are a number of other factors that closely link it with the Aaronic priesthood. The priesthood that Ezekiel saw as administering the temple sacrifices must only consist of literal descendants of the sons of Zadok (40:46; 43:19; 48:11). The other Levitical descendants of Aaron who had committed spiritual compromise by offering to idols can only serve in the house (44:10–14). Moreover, priests can only marry virgins from Israel, thus keeping the entire priesthood strictly Jewish (44:22). Even more problematic is the clear commandment that all worshipers, including non-Jews, must be "circumcised in heart and circumcised in flesh," meaning that literal, physical circumcision is mandatory for all who would participate in the temple worship (44:9). These prescriptions all imply that Israel will be the exclusive mediating nation for worshiping God and Jesus. To this, Ice comments, "The millennium will return history to a time when Israel will be God's mediatory people."[11]

By now, the millennial temple advocates are utterly at odds with the entirety of New Testament teaching. Paul expressly condemned the practice of forcing Gentile believers to be literally circumcised, because circumcision was only a symbolic act whose sole purpose was to point to Christ (Galatians 5:2–6). He even went as far as saying that "if you receive circumcision [for spiritual reasons], Christ will be of no benefit to you" (5:2). Moreover, we who have Jesus *no longer need any mediator* to come to God: "For there is one God and one Mediator between God and men, the Man Christ Jesus" (1 Timothy 2:5 NKJV). Also, an exclusive priesthood restricted to the descendants of Zadok directly contradicts the priesthood of all believers taught in 1 Peter 2:9 and Revelation 1:6. Revelation 20 clearly states that all those who reign with Christ will be "priests of God and of Christ" (v. 6).

Finally, any reference to the Messiah Jesus is absent from Ezekiel's prophecy, even though Jesus is obviously meant to be the prime focus of the millennial reign. Since He freely mixed and mingled with all people at His first coming 2,000 years ago, do we suppose that for His millennial reign He will remain aloof and remote, only to be worshiped from a distance and through a complex system of ritual sacrifices administered by a Jewish priesthood? Will He prescribe worship through a sacrificial system that was expressly abolished by His atoning death, not only for non-Jews but also for the Jews? Those who assert that the book of Hebrews was not written for the Jews might as well say that the Jews don't need to come under the New Covenant established by Jesus' death but can just keep offering the blood of bulls to atone for their sin. Without the New Covenant made through the blood of Christ, there is no spiritual rebirth and no salvation.

Also, can it be expected that animal sacrifices, which were very familiar and meaningful for ancient peoples such as the Jews in Moses' times, will communicate and reveal the nature of Jesus to a modern people, most of whom have never even witnessed the butchering of an animal and who were not raised in a ritualistic society? Any assertion that a quasi-Mosaic sacrificial system will meaningfully commemorate the death of Him who is said to personally rule all nations completely misunderstands how culturally and historically specific this system was. Moreover, it is inconceivable that Jesus, the Messiah, will seek to relate to His special people, the Jews, through what is called "a mere shadow of things to come; but the substance belongs to Christ" (Colossians 2:17). Will Jesus withhold Himself, the "substance," until the eternal state? Is that compatible with the purposes and aims of the millennium, when "the earth will be filled with the knowledge of the glory of the LORD" (Habakkuk 2:14)? Certainly not!

The final fatal problem of the millennial temple theory is the description of the "prince" of the people, who is given a prominent place in Ezekiel's vision. This prince seems to be their main ruler, and many temple advocates see in Him a resurrected David (based on Ezekiel 37:24–25), who is prophesied to "be their prince forever" (v. 25, compare Jeremiah 30:9). Some believe that the saints will serve under this Prince David. But the very text of the prophecy itself precludes such a possibility. The prince is required to provide a sin offering not only for his people but also for himself. Moreover, he is exhorted to deal justly with the people and "not take from the people's inheritance," unlike the previous princes of Israel (46:18). Finally, he is told to give an inheritance to his sons. All three stipulations mean that this can only refer to a non-resurrected mortal human being. We had already seen that every single resurrected believer will receive an immortal, glorified body after having passed by the judgment seat of Christ; from then on, they walk in a sinless, eternal state of being, and they will no longer marry or have children. A resurrected David would have to undergo the same procedure. God does not resurrect His saints in a mortal condition with a fallen nature that is capable of sinning. No, "this perishable must put on the imperishable, and this mortal must put on immortality" (1 Corinthians 15:53). This applies to all saints from both Old and New Covenants (which includes David), and there are no exceptions. Moreover, how could it be that glorified, sinless saints, who now live in perfect union with Christ, would be put under the leadership of a mortal, imperfect human being? Revelation says that the saints will "reign with Christ" and be priests to Him. Both promises are directly at odds with Ezekiel's vision of prince and priesthood!

Other problems with trying to fit Ezekiel's temple into the millennium are that the river of healing that springs from it is said to flow to the east into the Dead Sea, while Zechariah's vision has the millennial river also flowing westward into the Mediterranean Sea (14:8). Moreover, the area of land assigned to Israel in Ezekiel's description is significantly smaller than the region that God promised to Abraham's descendants (Genesis 15:18), meaning that Ezekiel's vision fits much better into the era before Christ.

But if Ezekiel's temple is not a millennial temple, what are we to make of it? Will the millennium even have a temple? The answer is both yes and no. There will be a "temple" but not as a literal temple building, for the New Jerusalem will be like a "temple" to the millennial earth. God's promise that "the Levitical priests shall never lack a man before Me to offer burnt offerings" (Jeremiah 33:18) can only be meant symbolically, because Revelation clearly teaches that the New Jerusalem will not have a temple. The meaning of this passage is simply that there will always be spiritual descendants of the Levitical priesthood, us the believers, who are a "royal priesthood" which ministers before God. In that sense, the New Jerusalem is the ultimate physical, as well as spiritual "temple," both a building and a worshiping assembly of God's people around His throne. If God's temple and priesthood promises in regards to the eternal state are symbolic and spiritual, then the same can certainly apply to the millennium. After all, Revelation 20 does not speak about a millennial temple but only about the priesthood of the believers, in constrast to Ezekiel's vision of an exclusively Zadokian priesthood.

If the millennium is indeed an intermediate state leading humanity *towards* eternity, then it makes no sense whatsoever that this period would return to a temple-based sacrificial system, which, even if understood symbolically, would be widely associated with the Old Covenant. Instead, God promised that He "will shake all the nations; and they will come with the wealth of all nations, and I will fill this house with glory" (Haggai 2:7). Where does Revelation 21:24 say the kings of the earth will bring their glory into? They will bring it into the New Jerusalem. Therefore, "this house" and the New Jerusalem are one and the same thing: God's "temple" into all eternity.

How then are we to understand Ezekiel's vision? From our discussion above, it seems evident that this temple can only have been meant to be built in Ezekiel's time or at a time before the first coming of Christ. Its construction would have required God's supernatural intervention, both to occupy all of the promised regions and to construct such a massive structure. Chapter 43 clearly states that Ezekiel was to personally present the plan to the exiled Jews, and he himself was called to cast the lot in order to establish the new prophesied land divisions (48:29). Therefore, this temple may well have been a conditional promise to the Jewish exiles from Babylon who had returned to their land under the leadership of Ezra. Ezekiel was commanded to show them his prophecy so that *they and their generation* should carry it out:

> As for you, son of man, describe the temple to the house of Israel, that they may be ashamed of their iniquities; and let them measure the plan. *If they are ashamed of all that they have done, make known to them the design* of the house, its structure, its exits, its entrances, all its designs, all its statutes, and all its laws. And write it in their sight, so that they may observe its whole design and all its statutes and do them.
>
> (Ezekiel 43:10–11, emphasis added)

From this passage, it appears that Ezekiel's vision was *conditional* on the obedience and faithfulness of His people. God wanted them to be "ashamed of their iniquities," using Ezekiel's glorious vision to provide a stark contrast with their own low spiritual condition. All of the exhortations contained in the prophecy directly corresponded to contemporary malpractices of the priesthood, the leaders, and the people. The whole vision was therefore specific to the culture and society of Ezekiel's time. As Jory Steven Brooks wrote,

> Scholars believe that Ezekiel's temple and sacrifices will never actually be realized; it was an offer from heaven during the captivities of Israel and Judah (6th century, B.C.) of what God WOULD HAVE DONE for His people at that time if they had immediately repented and turned back to Him. God WOULD HAVE cut short their captivity, brought all of dispersed Israel and Judah back to Canaan, allowed the building of a wonderful and truly unique post-exile temple (unlike anything before or since), and all 12 tribes WOULD HAVE been re-established in Canaan in newly redesignated tribal lands. But God's people DID NOT REPENT AND

> ACCEPT THE OFFER. It was refused! We read these wondrous chapters of Ezekiel today and ponder what COULD HAVE BEEN...."[12]
>
> Regardless of which stance one ultimately adopts towards Ezekiel's temple vision, its description clearly does not fit with the conditions of the millennial era.

Chapter 14 Notes

1. The Greek term for evil, *poneros*, can refer both to evil in general and to the "evil one," meaning the devil.
2. Dominion Theology argues that the church must take increasing control over governmental and social institutions, until politics, economy, and society are all dominated by Christian principles and values. The foundation for such a dominion is seen in the teachings of the Old Testament law. See for example Thomas Ice and H. Wayne House, Dominion Theology: Blessing or Curse? (Sisters, OR: Multnomah, 1988).
3. For the meaning of the Hebrew word for "break," *ra`a`* (*Strong's Concordance*, H7489), compare also Job 34:24 or Jeremiah 31:28.
4. *Strong's Concordance,* G4165.
5. Ibid., G4464, compare also Hebrew: *shebet*, H7626.
6. The New Testament term for rod, *rhabdos*, can be equally translated as rod or staff. The Old Testament word, *shebet*, also carries both of these meanings, but in Psalm 23:4 where it talks about "your rod and staff," *shebet* is used to refer to the rod. Compare also the well-known passage: "A scepter [*shebet*] of righteousness is the scepter of Your kingdom" (Psalm 45:6 NKJV).
7. Compare Isaiah 2:3 and 62:23–24; Jeremiah 3:17; Zechariah 8:22.
8. The passage "yet your desire will be for your husband, and he will rule over you" (3:16b) is here interpreted in light of Genesis 4:7: "sin is crouching at the door; and its desire is for you, but you must master it." Genesis 4:7 uses the same Hebrew word for "desire" as 3:16b. The implication has been aptly summarized by John Piper: "When it says, 'Your desire shall be for your husband,' it means that when sin has the upper hand in woman she will desire to overpower or subdue or exploit man. And when sin has the upper hand in man he will respond in like manner and with his strength subdue her, or rule over her. So what is really described in the curse of 3:16 is the ugly conflict between the male and female that has marked so

much of human history." From John Piper, "Manhood and Womanhood: Conflict and Confusion After the Fall," Desiring God, 1989, http://www. desiringgod.org/resource-library/sermons/manhood-and-womanhood-conflict-and-confusion-after-the-fall.

9. Thomas Ice, "Why Literal Sacrifices In The Millennium," 2009, Tom's Perspectives, http://www.pre-trib.org/data/pdf/ Ice-WhySacrificesinTheMi.pdf.

10. Ice, ibid.

11. Ice, "Why Literal Sacrifices In The Millennium."

12. Joy Steven Brooks, "Ezekiel's Temple and Sacrifices: When???" quoted in "Ezekiel's Temple and Sacrifices: Will Temple Sacrifices Resume in the Millennium?" an adapted version of the original article written by Thomas H. Whitehouse, "Ezekiel's Temple and Sacrifices. Pre-Christian? Zionist? Or Millennial? A Prophetican Enigma and Its Solution," (London: Thynne & Co., 1935), http://hope-of-israel.org.nz/ezekielstemple.html

Chapter 15
Conclusion

Behold, I am coming like a thief. Blessed is the one who stays
awake and keeps his clothes,
so that he will not walk about naked and
men will not see his shame.
Revelation 16:15

"Therefore Be Careful How You Walk"

After examining all these truths about the dangerous and eventful times we live in, let us again turn to this key passage in Revelation 14, which so aptly describes the first fruits of the church:

> These are the ones who have not been [spiritually] defiled … for they have kept themselves chaste [pure]. These are the ones who follow the Lamb wherever He goes. These have been purchased from among men as first fruits to God and to the Lamb. And no lie was found in their mouth; they are blameless.
>
> (Revelation 14:4–5)

These first fruits qualities remarkably correspond to Paul's exhortation to the Ephesians, which fits perfectly into our current end times context:

> Therefore be careful how you walk, not as unwise men but as wise, making the most of your time, because the days are evil. So then do not be foolish, but understand what the will of the Lord is. And do not get drunk with wine, for that

is dissipation, but be filled with the Spirit, speaking to one
another in psalms and hymns and spiritual songs, singing and
making melody with your heart to the Lord; always giving
thanks for all things in the name of our Lord Jesus Christ to
God, even the Father; and be subject to one another in the
fear of Christ.

(Ephesians 5:15–21)

With these simple yet concise words, Paul is making the following
points:

- Walk carefully: in God's wisdom, not your own understanding.
- Make the most of time by focusing on the right priorities.
- Do not dilute or dissipate (waste) your spiritual life with empty
  worldly pursuits.
- Cultivate an attitude of continual worship.
- Walk in continual thankfulness for all things that God allows to
  touch your life, both good and suffering.
- Be humble, submitting to others, and remaining under your
  God-given authorities.

Paul's exhortations distinguish "foolish virgin" believers from the
"wise virgins" of the church. Those who actively pursue these first-fruits
qualities in God's grace (His strength) will surely end up being amongst
the wise. However, those who fail to heed Paul's warnings or are not
proactive about them are already in danger of becoming like the foolish
virgins. God does not seek to instill an unhealthy fear in us, but He gives
us clear warnings and expects us to respect the fact that He is a God who
justly rewards His servants according to their deeds: "For he who does
wrong will receive the consequences of the wrong which he has done,
and that without partiality" (Colossians 3:25). There are no exemptions
from this principle. If our understanding of salvation by grace causes us

to deny the fact that God's evaluation of our lives will be based on our "walk" (what we actually are) and not merely on the "talk" (what we profess to be), then we have missed the point. If we minimize the truth that our God is a God of consequences, who is "not mocked" by our excuses but will see to it that "whatever a man sows, this he will also reap" (Galatians 6:7), then we have not understood the biblical principle of stewardship.

"Well Done, Good and Faithful Servant"

Once we are saved by faith through grace alone, our Christian life is all about stewardship. Stewardship is a theme that runs through almost every one of Jesus' teachings. We have seen that God has mightily empowered us with a perfectly-created new spirit nature and entrusted us with abundant spiritual resources. He has given us spiritual authority over the schemes of the enemy. Every day, He is ready to work with us to crucify our old nature and to breathe life and growth into our new self so that we can be fruitful. This is His eternal promise to us:

> If you abide in Me, and My words abide in you, ask whatever you wish, and it will be done for you. My Father is glorified by this, that you bear much fruit, and so prove to be My disciples. Just as the Father has loved Me, I have also loved you; abide in My love. If you keep My commandments, you will abide in My love; just as I have kept My Father's commandments and abide in His love. These things I have spoken to you so that My joy may be in you, and that your joy may be made full.
>
> (John 15:7–11)

As we abide in Christ, we allow Him to transform our lives, making us more fruitful every day. But fruitfulness requires pruning—the death of the old nature—so that the new spirit life in us can mature to perfection.

The Greek word for maturity or perfection, *teleos*,[1] literally means that which is brought to the end, or that which has reached its intended end. God, the loving Vinedresser, is daily at work in His vineyard to ensure that we remain on the narrow path of discipleship until the very end. His careful, personal attention to each one of us gives us everything we need to master the spiritual challenges of each day. His guidance helps us to stay clear of dangerous places, and prevents us from getting lost in unproductive or dangerous dead-end streets.

Therefore, the choice for or against faithful stewardship is ours, and it is a choice that we must make every single day. We can:

- Be wise virgins, filled with the Spirit and ready to meet the Bridegroom; or foolish virgins, who run out of the Spirit before the Bridegroom comes (Matthew 25:1–13).
- Yield ourselves to righteousness, and be slaves to God; or yield ourselves to sin, and become slaves of sin (Romans 6:11–23).
- Walk in our new nature, and please God; or walk in our old nature, and grieve His Spirit (Romans 8; Ephesians 4:30).
- Regularly abide in Christ and bear much spiritual fruit; or rarely abide in Christ and bear little fruit (John 15).
- Build on God's foundation in us with gold, silver, and precious stones, and receive a rich reward; or build with wood, hay, or straw, and have it all burned up before the judgment seat of Christ (1 Corinthians 3:12–15).
- Be alert and sober, watching carefully how we walk; or be asleep and drunk along with a godless world (1 Thessalonians 5:6).
- Be good and faithful stewards, and use the material and spiritual resources that God entrusted us for His Kingdom and for the benefit of others; or be unreliable, self-centered stewards, who waste God's resources on ourselves or on other, seemingly "good" endeavors that God never authorized (Luke 16).

- Be diligent, focused, and ready for when the Master returns and hear His "well done"; or be lazy, distracted, and unprepared for His return and face His rebuke over our poor stewardship (Matthew 25:14–28).
- Be overcomers and reap eternal rewards; or fail to overcome, and face the consequences both now and later (Revelation 2–3).

The letters to the seven churches of Revelation provide us with key information about how to navigate through this challenging end times phase. Within these letters, we can identify the core temptations that our contemporary end times church is facing: legalism, spiritual lukewarmness, superficial spirituality, compromise with the world, and negligent leadership.

In contrast, the first fruits of the church draw on the power of their new natures to stay clear of all of them:

1. They choose to walk closely with Jesus, going "wherever He goes."
2. They choose to keep themselves blameless and "unstained by the world" (James 1:27).
3. They choose not to lie by excusing their sins, which would "make [God] a liar" (1 John 1:10), but to walk in the light and in the power of "the blood of Jesus … [which] cleanses us from all sin" (1 John 1:7).

None of this comes automatically or easily. It requires a daily choice, a regular tapping into the power (grace) of God that is available to all of us: "For the Kingdom of God is not just a lot of talk; it is living by God's power" (1 Corinthians 4:20 NLT). Perhaps you feel spiritually weak and emotionally wounded, unable to rise up to the first fruits challenge in your own strength, unable to walk with Jesus and be a "good Christian." But there is good news for you: 1 Peter 2:24 promises us that "by His wounds you were healed." The Kingdom of God truly is more than words: it is the very power of God available to us, often provided through others whom God has specially called to minister His healing power to us if we are willing and humble to receive it. Nobody can follow Jesus in their own strength—our responsibility is to remain in the Vine. The Vine is the very place where God put us when He gave us our new natures, and where He will keep us every day: "by His doing [not on your own strength] you are [remaining, abiding] in Christ Jesus" (1 Corinthians 1:30).

Under the New Covenant, God has given us ample provisions to guard against the enemy's schemes and temptations. But if we do not actively make use of them and fail to walk in our new nature through God's power and grace, we are certain to be fooled and get off track. Therefore, the choice is ours. We know that by God's grace, we all can be wise virgins, first fruit believers in Jesus. Let us stop making excuses. Let us refrain from pursuing material things and preoccupations that are of no eternal value, instead storing up "treasures in heaven" (Matthew 6:20). Let us proactively stay away from the deceptive pleasures of sin, which "which so easily entangles us" (Hebrews 12:1). Let us "press on toward the goal for the prize of the upward call of God" (Philippians 3:14). Then, when Jesus comes, we will be blessed by these weighty words of our faithful Master:

> **"Well done, good and faithful servant. You have been faithful over a little; I will set you over much. Enter into the joy of your master."**
>
> (Matthew 25:21)

A Call to Salvation

If you have been inspired by this book to walk with Jesus and experience the transformational promises that He gives to those who submit to Him as their Lord and Savior, then we invite you to become born-again by confessing Jesus as the Lord of your life. God's Word tells us that "all have sinned and fall short of the glory of God" (Romans 3:23). Nobody is acceptable to God on the basis of being a "good person" or of "trying to be good." Our rightful destiny is eternal punishment in hell.

Only Jesus can bridge the gap between us and God that was created when Adam and Eve first sinned. That is why God sent His Son to receive the death penalty that we had deserved, so that by His death, we can receive eternal life:

> For God so loved the world, that He gave His only begotten
> Son, that whoever believes in Him shall not perish, but
> have eternal life.
>
> (John 3:16)

This invitation is freely available to all. However, before you would believe in Jesus, first make up your mind about the cost of this calling. Jesus warned those who would follow Him to first be serious about the commitment that this involves:

> For which one of you, when he wants to build a tower,
> does not first sit down and calculate the cost to see if he
> has enough to complete it?
>
> (Luke 14:28)

Following Jesus will cost you everything you have been building your life on. It means to renounce worldly pleasures, worldly success mindsets, and the many things that have been giving you meaning and identity—such as career, income, lifestyle, or society's approval. God may choose to take these things away from you, or He may choose to let you keep them (or return them to you later). But what He does with your life and your priorities will now be entirely up to Him.

However, faith in Jesus means that you will gain that which is truly of eternal worth. Now, your identity will be based on what God made you to be. The meaning of your life will center on your relationship with your Maker. Following Jesus will bring you the most incredible inner freedom beyond all imagination. It gives you adoption into God's very own family. Finally and most importantly, acknowledging Jesus as your King will give you a true hope for the future: eternal life in the heavenly New Jerusalem!

Chapter 15 Notes

1.   *Strong's Concordance,* G5046.

Ingram Content Group UK Ltd.
Milton Keynes UK
UKHW040743120423
420010UK00012B/69/J

9 781449 769086